Leaving
Other
People
Alone

Leaving Other People Alone

Diaspora, Zionism, and Palestine in Contemporary Jewish Fiction

Aaron Kreuter

UNIVERSITY *of* **ALBERTA** PRESS

Published by

University of Alberta Press
1-16 Rutherford Library South
11204 89 Avenue NW
Edmonton, Alberta, Canada T6G 2J4
amiskwaciwâskahikan | Treaty 6 |
Métis Territory
uap.ualberta.ca | uapress@ualberta.ca

Library and Archives Canada
Cataloguing in Publication

Title: Leaving other people alone :
    diaspora, Zionism, and Palestine in
    contemporary Jewish fiction / Aaron
    Kreuter.
Names: Kreuter, Aaron, author.
Description: Includes bibliographical
    references and index.
Identifiers: Canadiana (print)
    20220424179 | Canadiana (ebook)
    20220424241 | ISBN 9781772126570
    (softcover) | ISBN 9781772126945
    (EPUB) | ISBN 9781772126952 (PDF)
Subjects: LCSH: American fiction—
    Jewish authors—History and criticism.
    | LCSH: Canadian fiction—Jewish
    authors—History and criticism. |
    LCSH: Jewish diaspora in literature. |
    LCSH: Zionism in literature. | LCSH:
    Zionism and literature. | LCSH:
    Palestine—In literature.
Classification: LCC PS153.J4 K74 2023 |
    DDC 813/.54098924—dc23

First edition, first printing, 2023.
First printed and bound in Canada by
Houghton Boston Printers, Saskatoon,
Saskatchewan.
Copyediting and proofreading by
Angela Pietrobon.
Index by Adrian Mather.

This book has been published with
the help of a grant from the Canadian
Federation for the Humanities and
Social Sciences, through the Awards to
Scholarly Publications Program, using
funds provided by the Social Sciences and
Humanities Research Council of Canada.

University of Alberta Press gratefully
acknowledges the support received for its
publishing program from the Government
of Canada, the Canada Council for the
Arts, and the Government of Alberta
through the Alberta Media Fund.

Canada   Canada Council   Conseil des Arts
          for the Arts   du Canada

 Alberta
Government

This book is dedicated to Steph Korn

And to my great-grandparents

Contents

Acknowledgements

FIRST, I MUST THANK EVERYBODY at University
of Alberta Press, especially Michelle Lobkowicz and Duncan Turner.
Thanks to Alan Brownoff for designing an amazing cover. And a special
thank you to Angela Pietrobon, copy editor extraordinaire. My deepest
thanks and gratitude as well to the two anonymous peer reviewers, who
gave this monograph their time and expertise.

I also must thank the English department at York University, where
this monograph began. Without the support, guidance, and feedback from
Julia Creet, Art Redding, and Marie-Christine Leps (who was a major part
of my graduate studies and who left us far too soon), the earliest drafts of
this book would never have been written. Deborah Britzman and Ranen
Omer-Sherman also offered invaluable feedback. Thanks as well to Sarah
Philips Casteel, my postdoc supervisor, at Carleton University.

A lot of the work in this book has been presented at conferences
in Canada, the United States, and Europe. I would like to thank the

organizers, panel moderators, and chairs of these conferences, for allowing me to share and shape the readings and analyses that find their final form here. Thanks to the Philip Roth Society for choosing my essay—excerpted from chapter 1 in this book—as the winner of the 2018 Siegel McDaniel Award for Graduate Student Writing. And thanks to Aimee Pozorski and Maren Scheurer, who edited an extended version of the paper for publication in *Philip Roth Studies*. Thank you to Marie Carrière, Ursula Mathis-Moser, and Kit Dobson for including my essay on Ayelet Tsabari's short story "Tikkun" in the collection *All the Feels / Tous les sens: Affect and Writing in Canada / Affect et écriture au Canada*.

I wouldn't be the writer and scholar I am if it weren't for my friends, my colleagues, and my friend/colleagues: Kristina Getz, Eric Schmaltz, Tyler Scott Ball, MLA Chernoff, Myra Bloom, David Huebert, Dan Sadowski, and Alex Smith. To Steph, my partner, who heard many of these readings and ideas first, often in jumbled form. To Piper, silent partner of long writing days. To my parents, Cath and David, who instilled in me a love of Jewishness, of political struggle, of literature, and of music. I couldn't have written this book without them. To Steph's parents, Mark and Susan. To my siblings and their partners: Ben, Rachel, Jenn, Daniel, Rebecca, Sam, Jon, and Dana.

Finally, I want to acknowledge Noa, my daughter, who was born during the writing of this book. I hope we are able to imagine a better world for you to grow up in.

Introduction

Playing Jewish Geography

IN THEODOR HERZL'S 1902 NOVEL *Altneuland*,
the protagonist, Friedrich, finds himself in the New Society, the Jewish
commonwealth established in Ottoman-era Palestine. The fictional
Jewish state reignites his belief in humanity, and Friedrich decides he
wants nothing more than to join it: "To remain was his most ardent
wish. To become a member of the New Society, to join hands with its
valiant men" (269). In Philip Roth's 1993 novel *Operation Shylock*, a young
Israeli soldier recounts an argument he had with his father about the
morality of the Israeli nation-state: "A state does not act out of moral
ideology, a state acts out of self-interest. A state acts to preserve its existence," his father said, to which the young soldier exclaimed, "Then
maybe I prefer to be stateless" (169). In Ayelet Tsabari's 2016 short story
"A Sign of Harmony," Maya, an Arab Jewish Israeli who lives in India,
is asked by a fellow Israeli traveller what she's running from. "Isn't it
what we're all doing?" she responds, "Running away from everything

back home?" (171). In the final pages of David Bezmozgis's 2014 novel *The Betrayers*, Soviet Jewish refusenik and Israeli politician Baruch Kotler remembers his triumphant arrival in Israel after thirteen years spent in the gulag as being "filled with joy" and "the high point of his life" (224). "He still retained his wonderment at the thought of Israel," readers are told: "that after a millennia of exile, this country existed; that he'd had the good fortune to be born into this time; and that he had prevailed against an awesome foe to gain his place there" (224).

All four of the above moments take place in fiction written by Jewish authors living in diaspora, and span more than a century, from when a Jewish sovereign state was a distant possibility to the current reality of Israel's existence both as the self-proclaimed national home of the Jewish people, with more than six million Jewish inhabitants gathered from all corners of the globe, and as a nation-state with nuclear capabilities and an army and government that acts as military occupier and oppressor of millions of stateless Palestinians. All four of these moments interact with the themes of national belonging, diaspora, home, and Zionism in highly divergent ways. All four also raise a number of tangled questions. What does it mean to write fiction about a place like Israel/Palestine and from a place like the United States or Canada (or, in Herzl's case, Austria)? What is at stake? What does fiction written about Israel/Palestine tell us about the Jewish diaspora's relationship with Israel, with the political ideology of Zionism, with the idea of home and the ethical potential of diaspora? Do the novels and short stories I investigate in this book attempt to alter how the Jewish diaspora imagines Israel, through critique or through celebration? And, perhaps most importantly, what does it mean if they do?

In attempting to answer these questions, *Leaving Other People Alone: Diaspora, Zionism, and Palestine in Contemporary Jewish Fiction* explores Jewish fiction from Canada and the United States that takes the nation-state of Israel as its setting and subject matter. Informed by thinkers of diaspora such as Daniel and Jonathan Boyarin, I argue that an ethics of diasporic belonging—while not perfect—has the potential to act as a strong counterweight to the hegemonic power structures of the Israeli nation-state. Moreover, the diasporic consciousness that manifests—or fails to manifest—in a number of striking ways in the texts under study opens up possibilities for group belonging that resist a global nation-state system that is predicated on borders, internal and external others, late capitalist modes of production, and essentialisms ethnic, cultural, and linguistic. Bringing together canonical authors (Philip Roth, Leon Uris, Theodor Herzl) with early-career contemporary writers (Ayelet Tsabari, David Bezmozgis), this book charts how the tensions between nation-state and diaspora play out in the crucible of Jewish fiction. A secondary objective of *Leaving Other People Alone*, therefore, is to make a case for the unique ability of fiction—whether novels or short story collections—to challenge dominant narratives, such as that of the Zionist narrative of the creation, maintenance, necessity, and teleological nature of Israel, imagine alternative possibilities, and map out alternative modes of Jewish belonging not predicated on what Daniel and Jonathan Boyarin term the "myth of autochthony" (699), or a myth of natural belonging to a piece of land—a myth upon which nation-states are always based. As such, the historically informed and politically nuanced readings that form the bedrock of this book take special notice of how the books under study present Israel/Palestine, Zionism, and diaspora.[1]

Central to the readings in this book is my concept of diasporic heteroglossia. Not meant to be an ironclad theory of diaspora and/or literature, diasporic heteroglossia, as we will see, is about reading openly and ethically, with a constant eye to power dynamics and borders literary and societal. To define it briefly, diasporic heteroglossia occurs when an author takes the natural heteroglossic structure of the novel form—as theorized by Mikhail Bakhtin—and uses that multivocal, non-centralized structure to challenge national centres, through multiple voices, narratives, viewpoints, and other elements of a diasporic consciousness. Because of this, diasporic heteroglossia is anti-colonial, anti-racist, and against borders and dominant narratives based on othering and exclusion. Since I discovered and developed diasporic heteroglossia while grappling with Roth's *Operation Shylock*—and since *Shylock* remains the best example of the phenomenon—the bulk of my theorizing of the concept will unfold in this book's first chapter, which is on Roth. For now, let me just say that read through the lens of diasporic heteroglossia, novels such as *Operation Shylock* and short story collections like Ayelet Tsabari's *The Best Place on Earth* not only refute the claims of ethnic nationalism and Jewish superiority inherent in Zionism, but demolish the Zionist claim of Israel's centrality in the Jewish world. Likewise, deploying diasporic heteroglossia as an interpretive model reveals how Zionist texts like Leon Uris's *Exodus* and David Bezmozgis's *The Betrayers*, in refusing to take the potential of diasporic consciousness seriously—either through disavowal of diaspora as a whole or through masking their nationalist rhetoric with the veneer of pluralism and multiplicity, respectively—do serious damage to the possibility of an ethical relationship to the land and to one's fellow humans. Overall, I claim that *what* these fictional texts say about the terrain of Jewish geography *affects* that terrain, and requires critical and careful unpacking in order to understand these effects, and, in some cases, to counteract them. In the following chapters, I use diasporic heteroglossia as a tool for this necessary unpacking.

If "Jewish geography" is a game that one can play, as this introduction's title wryly suggests, it is a game, to borrow a phrase of Philip Roth's, of deadly seriousness.[2] By using the phrase Jewish geography, I have more in mind than just geography's primary meaning of land, though land is of the utmost importance when discussing Zionism and diaspora; I wish for Jewish geography to connote the layered geographies of diaspora, of the nation-state, and of who and what gets included in the fictional terrain of novels and short stories that take place in Israel/ Palestine. A relatively new player to this Jewish game of deadly seriousness is the Palestinian people, who have borne the brunt of the Zionist settler-colonial project. Regardless of the outcome of the Middle East conflict—one binational state, unending apartheid, genocidal war— one thing will remain true: that the Palestinians were forced into the Jewish narrative, and will remain there for the foreseeable future. As Palestinian poet Mahmoud Darwish succinctly put it, "The Israelis changed the Palestinians and vice versa. The Israelis are not the same as they were when they came, and the Palestinians are not the same people that once were. In the one, there is the other" (qtd. in Yeshurun 68–69). This undeniable truth, I suggest throughout this book, comes with weighty ethical responsibilities, and must be a significant part of any sustained engagement with contemporary Jewish literature, especially texts that focus on Israel/Palestine. Because of this, in the following chapters I pay close attention to how the texts feature—or, just as importantly, fail to feature—the Palestinian narrative. In other words, it's not just about how these texts fictionalize Zionism and Israel, but how they represent/fictionalize the diaspora's relationship with the Palestinian. This is yet another necessary element in the swirl of voices that is diasporic heteroglossia.

There are a small number of scholarly works that examine diasporic Jewish literature about Israel/Palestine, the two most significant being Andrew Furman's 1997 *Israel Through the Jewish-American Imagination: A Survey of Jewish-American Literature on Israel, 1928–1995*, and Ranen Omer-Sherman's 2002 *Diaspora and Zionism in Jewish American Literature: Lazarus, Syrkin, Reznikoff, and Roth*.[3] Omer-Sherman's monograph is an eclectic exploration of what he calls the "creative tension between personal and collective myth that has proved so rewarding for the development of Jewish American literature" (3) in fiction and poetry. Furman's book is a series of close readings of Jewish American fictional texts from 1928 to 1995, tempered with Furman's clearly stated liberal Zionism. There is significant overlap in primary texts: both Furman and I look at *Operation Shylock* and *Exodus*, and as we shall see, our differing political outlooks deeply impact our readings of these two novels. The questions that guide Furman's study are just as pertinent for this book, even if the answers look entirely different: "How have Jewish-American writers imagined Israel? What does this imaginative writing reveal about the relationship between the Israeli and the Diaspora Jew over the years? How has the literature gauged the impact of the Jewish state on the American Jewish community?" (1). Both Furman and Omer-Sherman are interested in how Jewish American literature on Israel/Palestine is contingent on the shifting historical, cultural, and political contexts of the author's times, what Omer-Sherman presents as "the staggering variety of literary riffs on Zionism's and Diaspora's intrinsic roles in the formation of Jewish subjectivity—a struggle of competing representations renewed and intensified in each generation" (4). Together, they show how important and productive the work of placing this literature into historical and political frameworks can be.

While I am indebted to both Furman and Omer-Sherman for leading the way on book-length investigations into Jewish fiction on Israel/Palestine, *Leaving Other People Alone* moves radically beyond them. This is for a number of important reasons. One of them is simply the fact that the scholarship has yet to catch up with the recent proliferation of Jewish North American novels responding to Israel, of which there has been a veritable boom in the past decade (I consider the reasons/ implications of this boom in the book's conclusion). Moreover, in placing texts written by both Canadian and American authors in conversation with each other (as well as Herzl in the second chapter), I am significantly expanding the geographical scope of prior studies. The United States and Canada represent the height of contemporary Jewish diasporic success, a diasporic success nonetheless rooted in a wider, violent settler colonialism, an aspect of the North American Jewish story that requires deep attention. How Jewish authors respond to Zionism and Israel from these two national locales is incredibly instructive in how different diasporic communities operate.

Besides differences in temporal and national range—since this book is being produced two decades after Furman's and Omer-Sherman's, the canon of available texts has, of course, changed—the biggest distinction between their work and mine is my placing of the texts in an anti-Zionist, diasporic context. From this vantage point, then, the ways in which Jewish authors respond/react to a nation-state that claims it is the natural home for all Jewish people—the teleological claim inherent in the Zionist narrative—are extremely instructive, revealing not only Zionism's success but possible chinks in its ideological armour. In rejecting Furman's liberal Zionism and going further than Omer-Sherman in his critiques of the use and abuse of Jewish power, and in affirming the necessity of including the Palestinian narrative in any literary endeavour situated in Israel/Palestine, this book hopes to further the study of Jewish literature on Israel/Palestine, to assert the ethical potential of the diasporic existence, and to argue for the role of fiction in both upholding dominant narratives and subverting them.

As mentioned, I approach the fiction under study in this book from an anti-Zionist perspective, which entails being critical of Zionist narratives and rejecting subsequent worldviews, especially the central Zionist claim that the Jewish people are safe only in a nation-state of their own.[4] Let me state clearly here my thoughts on Israel/Palestine: I see Israel as a settler-colonial project that is predicated on ethnic superiority and the removal of the Indigenous Palestinian population from their land. I see, along with Steven Salaita, the Law of Return as "the most egregious marker of Israel's ethnonationalism" (Israel's Dead Soul 26), especially in light of the state's adamant refusal to allow Palestinian refugees back (refugees that have been living in Gaza, in camps in Lebanon and Jordan, or elsewhere in the diaspora since 1948). I see the occupation of the West Bank, the Gaza Strip, the Golan Heights, and East Jerusalem as highly immoral, violent, and destructive, and as a continuation of the ethnic cleansing of 1948. Unlike liberal and some post Zionists, I also see the events of 1948—the ethnic cleansing by the nascent Israeli army, the four hundred destroyed Palestinian villages, the refusal to allow refugees back in, the confiscation of property, the military rule inflicted upon Palestinians within Israel until 1966—what the Palestinians refer to as the Nakba, or catastrophe, as a historical, ongoing violence that is at the root of the problem.[5] Salaita is exactly right when he writes: "Now that Israel has been a nation-state for over sixty-years, it is easy to observe that the original goals of Zionism were a failure. Jews do not appear to be any safer now than they ever were. Anti-Semitism has not been cured. Jews are no more liberated than any other ethnic group whose cultural identity has been articulated through the nation-state" (Israel's Dead Soul 24). While the situation is desperate, I believe there is hope for a just solution, where all Israeli Jews and Palestinians can live in a demilitarized society as equals before the law, and where the injustices of the past seventy-plus years can be addressed, rectified, and, given enough time, healed.

My arguments and historical contextualizations regarding Israel/ Palestine and the Zionist project—which are threaded throughout the book—are based on a vast, and ever-growing, literature that historicizes, critiques, places into comparative frameworks, and offers alternatives to Zionism (a few of the scholars and writers I look at include: Judith Butler, Yehouda Shenhav, Ali Abuminah, Nur Masalha, and the Boyarins). My readings of the primary texts are thoroughly grounded in historical, theoretical, and political scholarship. In addition to purely scholarly discourses, I develop a wide-ranging archive of fiction, drama, film, essays, tweets, film reviews, and soldier testimonies. Moreover, in tying the texts to contemporary debates and issues (for example, how Herzl's Altneuland has recently come up in discussions on Marvel Studio's Black Panther film), I show how fiction is alive and a productive part of the wider cultural and social world. Finally, including non-Jewish voices in Leaving Other People Alone is an important part of my commitment to working toward a just solution in Israel/Palestine. Palestinian scholars such as Edward Said, Ali Abuminah, Nur Masalha, and Rashid Khalidi provide this book with a contextual framework that attempts to make space for voices of the historically voiceless victims of the Israeli national project. I strongly believe in the importance of citational practices.[6] As such, I have endeavoured to include and cite Palestinians (and other Arabs), Mizrahi Jews, and other positionalities not central to Zionism or the Ashkenazi Jewish world, which can be seen as my own attempt at diasporic heteroglossia. After all, I agree wholeheartedly with Judith Butler that the critique of Zionism cannot be conceptualized as a uniquely Jewish critique: "Equality, justice, cohabitation, and the critique of state violence can only remain Jewish values," Butler explains, "if they are not exclusively Jewish values" (*Parting Ways* 5).

The overarching goal of this book is to perform deep, historically nuanced, politically engaged readings of the five primary texts. The works of fiction I explore here—Philip Roth's *Operation Shylock* in chapter 1; Theodor Herzl's *Altneuland* and Leon Uris's *Exodus* in chapter 2; Ayelet Tsabari's short story collection *The Best Place on Earth* in chapter 3; and David Bezmozgis's *The Betrayers* in the fourth and final chapter—were chosen according to several different criteria. First, the text had to engage with Israel or Zionism in some way, either through being partly or wholly set in Israel/Palestine or in focusing on Israeli characters and Zionist narratives. Second, the text's fictional world had to refract, rework, or reinterpret some aspect of the relationship between the Jewish diaspora and the nation-state of Israel, in particular, fictionalizations of the political, social, and cultural underpinnings of the Israeli nation-state, its guiding Zionist ideology, and its claims of Jewish teleology. Finally, I am interested in texts that, in featuring—or not featuring—the political victims of Zionism (the Palestinians, but also Arab Jews, those in the diaspora whose livelihoods are affected by the state of Israel, and others), begin to challenge the narrative of Zionism and its concomitant national state as a purely redemptive, necessary, and ethical one. It is my hope that the texts, and my sometimes contrapuntal readings of them—borrowed from Edward Said, reading contrapuntally is to read a text against its rhetorical or ideological grain (*Culture and Imperialism* 66)—reveal the power of fiction to elicit real political, social, and cultural change, through its ability to allow the narratives of the powerless to contend with the dominant, hegemonic forces that would rather their voice was the only one with bandwidth, the only one within range.

Roth's complex challenging of Zionism, as one of the preeminent Jewish fiction writers of the twentieth century, shows us what is possible in creative critiques of Jewish ethnic nationalism. The utopic imaginings of Herzl yoked to the celebratory, racist narrative of Jewish national success in *Exodus* reveal how fiction written about Israel/Palestine from the vantage point of diaspora has real power in determining how the diaspora views Israel, and its subsequent actions. In the short stories of Ayelet Tsabari, the fluid, non-static identities of her Arab Jewish characters deflate any Zionist claim of Jewish purity, and in so doing they enact their own border demolishment. Finally, in Bezmozgis's *The Betrayers*, we see what happens when a careful study of a dying diasporic community—the Soviet Jewish world, as represented by the Crimea—is joined with a liberal Zionist, politically problematic representation of Israel/ Palestine. Overall, I want my readings of this fiction to begin to push us out of what Judith Butler calls the "narrative lockdown," where Israel is seen as a "historical and ethical necessity" after the Nazi genocide (*Parting Ways* 24, 25).[7] The fiction I explore in this book does not just reflect the world of Jewish geography back to us, it is a part of the very terrain of that world, and is imbued with the ability to affect the diaspora's relationship with Israel. What these texts imagine, therefore, and what they don't imagine, what they see and don't see (or pretend not to see), what they challenge and leave unchallenged, what they celebrate or lament, and what they allow into their heteroglossia, have deep political, cultural, and ethical ramifications.

We are entering a momentous period in Jewish history. The Zionist consensus in the Jewish world—a hundred years after the Balfour Declaration, seventy years after the creation of the state of Israel and the devastation of the Nakba, and fifty years since the occupation of Gaza, the West Bank, the Golan Heights, and East Jerusalem—is beginning to fray. The ethnocentrism always contained in the Zionist ideology continues reaping disastrous results, and a growing number of writers, scholars, and activists, Jewish and not Jewish, have begun to push back. I hope that this book can play a part, however small, in this sea change. If, as Slavoj Žižek has it, Israel/Palestine is the "symptomal knot" of the Middle East (126), what will happen if this knot is untied? One possible answer is that we could move beyond the nation-state, beyond ethnic absolutism, and beyond the myth of autochthony and its need for borders and displacement, and move toward what Arab Jewish sociologist Yehouda Shenhav calls "post-Westphalian sovereignty," where self-determination is not predicated on private or state ownership of land (*Beyond the Two State Solution* 140). Whatever the solution, whether a binational state with protections for both Palestinians and Jews embedded in law or Shenhav's post-Westphalian sovereignty, I believe that a just solution to the century-old conflict can be found for both the Jewish and Palestinian populations of Israel/Palestine (as well as their various diasporic communities), and I believe that literature, and the necessary, concomitant serious consideration of literature, can—and should—be a part of this solution. The Jewish fiction I read in *Leaving Other People Alone* has a role to play in the future of Israel/Palestine, and I therefore insist on the necessity of holding these texts to a high ethical standard.

"Particularism Plus Power": Diaspora Studies, the Boyarins, and Diasporic Futures

The main theoretical lens through which I read the novels and short stories in this book is diaspora theory; it is also the discursive field wherein I make this book's major critical intervention: diasporic heteroglossia, conceptualized in the first chapter and refined throughout the book. As such, it is worth spending significant time here, in the introduction, defining diaspora, contextualizing the field of diaspora studies, and discussing the radical potential of diaspora, best evinced—for me—in the work of Daniel and Jonathan Boyarin. The term "diaspora" comes to us from the Greek, and translates literally as "spreading of seeds" (diaspora is, therefore, among everything else it is, an ecological metaphor)("Diaspora"). The term was first used in the *Septuagint*, the Greek translation of the Hebrew Bible in the third century BCE, and until quite recently, was almost exclusively related to the Jewish experience of living outside of the kingdom of Judea, which Jewish people have done for almost two thousand years.[8] A telling example of this originary usage is the four-page definition of "diaspora" in the 1937 edition of *Encyclopaedia of the Social Sciences*; written by Simon Dubnow (an early proponent of the ethical nature of the Jewish diaspora), the entry names both the Greek and Armenian diasporas in the first paragraph, but then spends the rest of the long entry discussing the Jewish diaspora in heavy historical detail.[9]

In recent decades, however, diaspora has come to encompass a wide range of peoples, relationships, and modes of being. Taken together, the study of this varied conglomeration is what has become known as diaspora studies, or diaspora theory, with Jana Evans Braziel and Anita Mannur's definition of diaspora as a "dislocation from the nation-state or geographical location of origin and a relocation in one or more nation-states, territories, or countries" (1) being the new, primary meaning of the term. Besides the plethora of Jewish diasporas at play in this book (the North American, the Arab Jewish, the Israeli, the Soviet), and as a reflection of the (relatively new) capaciousness of the term, other, non-Jewish diasporas—such as the Filipino foreign workers diaspora, the Crimean Tatar diaspora, and the Palestinian diaspora, all of which appear in the primary texts—will be touched upon throughout the book.

Situated in diverse fields and modes of inquiry, theorists of diaspora are interested in how group belonging is fused with/in tension with home countries, host countries, and networks of communication and movement (whether violent or voluntary) among them. I follow André Levy and Alex Weingrod who, in their introduction to *Homelands and Diasporas: Holy Lands and Other Places*, divide diaspora theory into two main discursive camps: diaspora-as-typology, whose practitioners are "primarily interested in better understanding why and how different kinds of diasporas have emerged, and...in the on-going dynamics of diaspora-homeland relationships"; and diaspora-as-metaphor, whose adherents are "more concerned with showing how the phenomenon of 'diaspora' may contradict and ultimately subvert the internal exclusivity of modern nation-states" (7–8). Diaspora-as-typology is concentrated in sociology departments, and includes scholars such as William Safran, Robin Cohen, and Khachig Tölölyan; diaspora-as-metaphor is often housed in anthropology, cultural studies, and literary studies departments, and includes practitioners such as Paul Gilroy, Stuart Hall, Rey Chow, Daniel and Jonathan Boyarin, and others. As David Chariandy, one of the more astute critics of the field, explains: "For Gilroy, Chow and Hall, the term diaspora is not whimsical or ineffective because it is understood as figurative; on the contrary, its very status as figurative enables these critics to make inventive demands on existing political, institutional, and epistemological constraints" (np). Chariandy agrees broadly with the bisecting of diaspora theory into typology and metaphor, but cautions us to bring more nuanced considerations to bear on both sections of the discipline.[10] While I fall squarely in the diaspora-as-metaphor camp, believing as I do that diaspora can be an ethical, achievable way to organize human collectives, I also engage with the scholarship of the first camp. Striking a balance between diaspora-as-typology and diaspora-as-metaphor seems to me the best way forward for the important work this book is focused on; the Jewish diasporas have a relationship with Palestine, and with the nation-state of Israel, that is material, political, and cultural, and at the same time the Jewish diaspora can be used to develop a mode of belonging that rejects violent ownership of land. Overall, as we will see, diaspora, as a mode of living that, as the Boyarins put it, "leave[s] other people alone" (707)—an axoim which lends itself to this book's title—can act as a powerful antidote to ethnic nationalism.

How exactly, then, does diaspora-as-typology organize its formulations? William Safran, one of the first scholars to codify contemporary diasporic thinking (and a staunch diaspora-as-typologist), lays out a framework for locating and authenticating diasporas. For Safran, a diaspora should meet a substantial number of the following six conditions: the diaspora community, or their ancestors, "have been dispersed from a specific original 'center' to two or more 'peripheral,' or foreign, regions"; the diaspora community retains "a collective memory, vision, or myth" of this original centre; the diaspora community feels that they are not fully accepted by the host country, and feel alienated from it; the diaspora community regards "their ancestral homeland as their true, ideal home" and wishes to eventually return; the diaspora community believes "that they should, collectively, be committed to the maintenance or restoration of their original homeland"; and finally, the diaspora community continues "to relate, personally or vicariously, to that homeland in one way or another" and feels that "their ethnocommunal consciousness and solidarity are importantly defined by the existence of such a relationship" (83–84). Notice how the last three conditions are concerned with the relationship to the homeland, which Safran says a diasporic community should be committed to returning to, and rebuilding.[11] This is the conservative approach to diaspora, and one which this book rejects; diaspora could, and perhaps should, exist without a relationship to a homeland, especially when that homeland is an ethnic nation-state. It also reveals one of the major differences between the two diaspora studies camps: for Safran and other typologists, a diasporic relationship to a homeland is often taken as a given; the approach I take here, conversely, is that living in the diaspora, diasporic consciousness, and diaspora ethics are not predicated on an extant homeland, especially a militarized, nationalist one that claims all of the diaspora as its purview.

One scholar of diaspora-as-typology I rely on heavily in this book is the French theorist Stéphane Dufoix (though he would reject this label). Dufoix's four-pronged schema of the relationship between a diaspora and its "home," whether real or imagined—what Dufoix calls the "referent-origin"—lends me a productive framework for my analysis of the complex relationship between the Jewish North American diasporas and Israel/ Palestine. It is also useful in spelling out how, in real, political, and geographical terms, diasporas relate to their home or their idea of home, without Safran's insistence on the need or desire to *return* home. Dufoix is wary of all encompassing categories, and wishes to get down to what diasporas actually *do*: "Rather than assigning migrant populations a place in a palette of preexisting terms (exile, diaspora, or refugee community), why don't we first try to identify the phenomena and processes linked to collective existence outside of a land—real or mythical—constructed as a place of origin, a point of departure or of reference?" (57). Dufoix locates four modes of connection between a diaspora and its referent-origin, and spatializes these connections, appropriately enough, as different kinds of landmass. In the centroperipheral mode (spatialized as a penin- sula), the referent-origin is the controlling force on the diaspora; in the enclaved mode (spatialized as an island), there is no connection with the referent-origin, and there are no flows or exchanges between different communities; in the atopic mode (spatialized as an archipelago), there is no connection with the referent-origin, but there are networks of commu- nication between various communities; and, finally, in the antagonistic mode (also an archipelago), the connected collectivities use their common origin to work against the referent-origin, whether to enact political or social change or to challenge its hold over them.

To take the Jewish example as a case study, for centuries— for millenia—the Jewish diaspora was atopic, existing without any connection to a nation-state or national territory (and with the desired return to Israel functioning as a religious and spiritual desire, not a political or national one). Dufoix calls the atopic mode a "transtate mode" that "does not seek to acquire a physical territory" (63). The Boyarins concur when they discuss the centuries where no substantial Jewish community existed in the homeland: "the Jewish diasporic relation to the homeland (rather than the relation of its various branches to each other) is primarily commemorative" (Powers of Diaspora 11). However, with the advent of Zionism in the late nineteenth century, the mass Jewish deaths of the Shoah, and the creation of the nation-state of Israel in 1948, the diaspora-referent-origin relationship transformed, nearly overnight, into a centroperipheral one, with the Israeli government and Zionist narrative exerting tremendous and, at its recent height, hegemonic power over the entirety of the Jewish diaspora.[12] In recent years, one could begin to chart a shift from the centroperipheral to the antagonistic mode, with certain segments of the Jewish diaspora challenging the notion that Israel speaks/acts for them, and critiquing the basic tenets of Zionism. The goal of anti-Zionism and what could be called the recently resurgent Jewish left, therefore, is to move through the antagonistic mode back toward the atopic. The texts I am investigating fall on numerous points on this spectrum, though regardless of where they land, they all, collectively, challenge the binary of diaspora/home, where home is the transcendent goal of diaspora.[13]

Chariandy's interventions into the theoretical and ethical contours of diaspora, which revolve around definitions of the terms diaspora, nation-state, globalization, and capitalism, are extremely useful in furthering our understanding of the possibilities inherent in the Jewish diaspora. Chariandy rightly challenges what seems like a given—in the work of Paul Gilroy, for example—that diasporas automatically challenge the nation-state system. He writes that "it is, in fact, not altogether clear that these two terms are necessarily oppositional, or at times easily distinguishable," and goes on to trouble the dichotomy further: "just as there is no guarantee that nations are inclined towards fascism, there is also no guarantee that diasporas are socially pluralist, devoid of 'ethnic absolutism,' and brimming with postcolonial liberation" (np). He mentions Hindu, Sikh, and Jewish "diasporic individuals" as examples. There is definitely truth here—yes, there are fierce Jewish Zionists with nothing but disdain for Palestinians in the diaspora, but there are also plenty of Jewish diasporic individuals who fight against Israel and its hold on the Jewish world. Moreover, Chariandy draws our attention to the sobering fact that, in many ways, the movements and relocations that diaspora encompasses are paralleled by the networks of late capitalism. We should ask ourselves, Chariandy insists, "if there is more than mere coincidence that the flourishing of diasporic theory comes in an era of free trade and globalization, an era where the virtues of fluid and border-crossing identities are endorsed not only by radical scholars, but, sometimes, ever more earnestly, by the powers-that-be" (np). In other words, diaspora seems to call for the same borderless world that late-stage capitalism desires, raising the question of whether nation-states even hold hegemonic power anymore. I would like to suggest that the nation-state is still the prime holder of power in our contemporary world. With the resurgence of fascism and xenophobia, combined with the coming (and already here) environmental disasters and refugee crises, I think it is beyond debate that the violent power of the nation-state is going to get worse before it gets better. The resource extraction, flows of capital, and bottomless need for ever-expanding markets of consumers that mark late capitalism may very well cover the world in a boundary-less chokehold, but they do so in tandem with the nation-state and its ever-growing violent maintenance of those who belong and those who do not.

Chariandy's concept of postcolonial diasporas, which focuses on racialized peoples in the West, raises an important aspect of diaspora studies: the place of the Jewish diaspora in our thinking on diaspora. Though virtually all theorists of diaspora locate the Jewish example as the originary, classic case,[14] it appears that, due to both the recent success of the Jewish diaspora communities in the United States, Canada, and elsewhere, and, more so, the reality of the state of Israel, the Jewish diaspora is no longer seen as central or even pertinent in the articles and monographs of diaspora studies. I want to push back against this. If anything, the political and geographic reality of Israel shows the all-too-present dangers of what happens when a diaspora community desires to return home, or in this case, desires to create a home and claim it as original. I concur, therefore, with the Boyarins when they argue in *Powers of Diaspora* that "It is important to insist not on the *centrality* of Jewish diaspora nor on its *logical priority* within comparative diaspora studies, but on the need to refer to, and better understand, Jewish diaspora history within the contemporary diasporic rubric" (10).

Practitioners of diaspora studies seem to shy away from stating the obvious when discussing the Jewish case: that Israel is not the home of the Jewish diaspora.[15] The Jews did not originate in the modern nation-state of Israel, they were not exiled or expelled from there, they do not have cultural or religious traditions that can be traced back to there. The original home of the Jewish diaspora—if there is one—is a land, place, and time that no longer exists (particular Jewish diasporas have all kinds of more recent homes, of course, including Eastern Europe, Spain, North Africa, and Iraq). Building a state on top of religious and biblical sites does not a homeland make, no matter the historical validity or ethnic connection to those sites; the very idea of Israel as the home to the Jewish diaspora is an egregious error in chronology. That the modern nation-state of Israel has been able to centre itself as the one true home of a diasporic people who existed for thousands of years before the nation-state did, creating new homes wherever they landed, speaks to the power of the Zionist mythos, a mythos that Jewish fiction had a part in establishing, and that it can have a hand in dismantling as well. The case of Israel can, and should, push the theories and goals of diaspora theory further, showing, as it does, the dangers of a diaspora that decides it wants to go home, a going home that entails dispossessing an Indigenous population that is rooted on land that the returning diaspora considers its sole belonging.

One thing the *contemporary* Jewish diaspora can bring to diaspora studies, then—as opposed to the example of the *originary, exemplary* Jewish diaspora—is to reveal how a diaspora can be made complicit in settler colonialism through its desire to return home, and how it can, at the same time, challenge this complicity. The historical fact that the longest-surviving diaspora has resulted in an ethnic nationalist state that continuously abuses its newfound military and political power is not something to be lightly swept aside. This is especially the case when Jewish thinkers locate diaspora as the polar opposite of nationalism and Zionism, a locating central to the readings in *Leaving Other People Alone*.

Most significant to my thinking on diaspora is, undoubtedly, the work of Daniel and Jonathan Boyarin. The Boyarins' importance to this book cannot be overstated: throughout their large corpus, but partic-ularly in "Diaspora: Generation and the Ground of Jewish Identity" and *The Powers of Diaspora*, the Boyarin brothers present a vision of diaspora that is not predicated on the myth of (Jewish) authochthony, on borders, on xenophobia, or on cultural hegemony of any kind, but that is fluid, accepting of cultural differences, and not dependent on centralized power—whether military, political, cultural, or otherwise—for survival. It is in their field-defining article "Diaspora: Generation and the Ground of Jewish Identity"—first published in the summer 1993 issue of *Critical Inquiry* before appearing in the 2003 *Theorizing Diaspora: A Reader*—that their ethical vision of diaspora is most clearly articulated. This article is fundamental to my thinking on diaspora, nationalism, and Jewishness, and is worth spending significant time unpacking, mulling over, and, at times, disagreeing with. The ethical power of (most of) their claims is worth rehashing, again and again. When this article is cited in the literature—which it often is—the same three or four pull quotes are usually used, leaving behind the vitally important work being done in the entirety of the text. By paying closer attention to the work that brings the Boyarins to make their famous pronouncements regarding diaspora, Zionism, Israel, and Christianity, I hope to show the depth of their thinking and the basis of their arguments in their immense archive of Jewish religious, historical, and political knowledge. The following pages, then, form the ground from which, in the following chapters, I build diasporic heteroglossia.

In "Generation and the Ground" the Boyarins argue that diaspora, "and not monotheism, may be the most important contribution that Judaism has to make to the world" (723). Part of this contribution is that the diasporic existence of the Jewish people reveals the fact that "peoples and lands are not naturally and organically connected" (723). Diaspora, as cogitated by the Rabbis of the Talmud period—which, for the Boyarins, is a highly important and foundational period of Jewish history—is a form of survival for a people without land, nation, or power, a form of survival that can be dangerous when transferred into positions of hegemonic power. The Boyarins explain: "The Rabbis produced their cultural formation within conditions of Diaspora, and we would argue that their particular discourse of ethnocentricity is ethically appropriate only when the cultural identity is an embattled (or, at any rate, nonhegemonic) minority" (718). The Rabbis' genius in creating a system of survival that did not need a national home or a rebuilt Temple is a messianic genius: "The point is not that the Land was devalued by the Rabbis but that they renounced it until the final redemption; in an unredeemed world, temporal dominion and ethnic particularity are impossibly compromised" (718). The always-deferred arrival of the Jewish messianic age means that the world will remain unredeemed, with temporal dominion and ethnic particularity always already a violent, oppressive combination. The truth of this is gleaned not only in Israel/Palestine, but throughout the world.

Throughout "Generation and the Ground," the Boyarins lay the foundations of diaspora as an ethical mode of being. First, what the cultural identity of diasporas reveals is "that cultures are not preserved by being protected from 'mixing' but probably can only continue to exist as a product of such mixing. Cultures, as well as identities, are constantly being remade" (721). Already we can see the Boyarins' insistence on variety, fluidity, and mixing. While all cultures are constantly forming and reforming, "diasporic Jewish culture lays it bare because of the impossibility of a natural association between this people and a particular land—thus the impossibility of seeing Jewish culture as a self-enclosed, bounded phenomenon" (721). The Jewish diaspora, for the Boyarins, is a cultural mechanism that allows for survival without hegemony. Second, the Boyarins point out that the Jewish diaspora was already very much in existence at the time of the destruction of the Second Temple, with more Jews already living outside of Judea than within it, in hundreds of towns and cities scattered throughout the Mediterranean world. This puts a massive hole in the Zionist narrative, since it follows that the Jewish diaspora "is not the forced product of war and destruction—taking place after the downfall of Judea—but that already in the centuries before this downfall, the majority of Jews lived voluntarily outside of the Land" (722). Finally, the Boyarins argue that a diasporic identity is a "disaggregated identity," disrupting national, genealogical, and religious identities because it insists on the connections, the bleed, between all of these (721). Therefore, the Zionist belief in a "pure Jewish cultural essence that has been debased by Diaspora seems neither historically nor ethically correct" (721).

Throughout the article, the Boyarins hammer against the Zionist claim of the primacy of the land. They write that diaspora allowed Jews to create "forms of community that do not rely on one of the most potent and dangerous myths—the myth of autochthony" (699). By autochthony, they mean a form of belonging to the land that is natural, pure, and God-given, which they place in contrast to Indigenous forms of belonging, which are historical and political. For the Boyarins, Indigenous claims of belonging—whether Palestinian or Native American—are morally correct, while any and all claims of autochthony are not, a position I push back against below.[16] The Boyarins put into a simple equation what happens when myths of autochthony are fulfilled: "Particularism plus power yields tribal warfare or fascism" (706). A diasporic society would be one based on the "dissociation of ethnicities and political hegemonies," and is "the only social structure that even begins to make possible a main-tenance of cultural identity in a world grown thoroughly and inextrica-bly interdependent" (723). Their call for the "renunciation" of temporal power (723) is the rallying cry of a radical diasporic ethics, and is at the heart of diasporic heteroglossia.

Overall, the Boyarins wish to use a diasporic cultural formation to rework the human world into a more just society. "What we wish to struggle for, theoretically," they write, "is a notion of identity in which there are only slaves but no masters, that is, an alternative to the model of self-determination, which is, after all, in itself a Western, imperialist imposition on the rest of the world" (711). They therefore propose diaspora "as a theoretical and historical model to replace national self-determina-tion" (711). Through diaspora, temporal power is renounced, and other people are left alone. Diasporic existence "would, ideally, simultaneously respect the irreducibility and the positive value of cultural differences, address the harmfulness, not of abolishing frontiers but of dissolution of uniqueness, and encourage the mutual fructification of different life-styles and traditions" (711). They hasten to add that this version of ideal diaspora would be "generalized from those situations in Jewish history when Jews were both relatively free from persecution and yet constituted by strong identity" (711). What the Boyarins have—perhaps, too easily—glossed over here is the Shoah and other historical moments of Jewish persecution; the dangers of diaspora must be included in any discussion of its ethical potential, and these will come up repeatedly in this book.

As can already be seen, their celebration of the diasporic leads the Boyarins to reject Zionism. Except as "an emergency and temporary rescue operation" in the wake of the Shoah, the Boyarins see Zionism as a "subversion of Jewish culture and not its culmination" (712). "Capturing Judaism in a state transforms entirely the meanings of its social practices" (713), they warn. Zionism is a political ideology that "in fundamental ways merely reproduces the exclusivist syndromes of European nationalism" (701). An alternative, and diasporic, story of the Jewish people that hews closer "to the readings of the Judaism lived for two thousand years, begins with a people forever unconnected with a particular land, a people that calls into question the idea that a people must have a land in order to be a people" (718). Diaspora is preferable to Zionism and ethnic nationalism because it reveals that "it is possible for a people to maintain its distinctive culture, its difference, without controlling land, a fortiori without controlling other people or developing a need to dispossess them of their lands" (723). A diasporic consciousness is one that is well aware that the Jewish people do not have an autochthonous claim to any land—this is what led to the birth of diaspora in the first place.[17] The Israeli state must either "entirely divest itself of the language of race and become truly a state that is equally for all of its citizens and collectives or the Jews must divest themselves of their claim to space. Race and space together form a deadly discourse" (714). "[T]he only moral path," the Boyarins conclude, "would be the renunciation of Jewish hegemony qua Jewish hegemony" (713).

Importantly, it is not just Zionism and Jewish ethnic particularity that the Boyarins dismantle, but Christian universalism as well (if not more so). They write:

> If particularism plus power tends toward fascism, then universalism plus power produces imperialism and cultural annihilation as well as, all too often, actual genocide of those who refuse to conform. Our thesis is that Judaism and Christianity, as two different hermeneutic systems for reading the Bible, generate two diametrically opposed and mirror-image forms of racism—and also two dialectical possibilities of antiracism. (707)

In other words, what is distinctive to both Judaism and Christianity—particularism and universalism, respectively—when imbued with political power, quickly veers into violence. Diaspora, as a form of temporal and geographical powerlessness, holds such ethical potential exactly because it does not have power over other people. The Boyarins continue: "The genius of Christianity is its concern for all the peoples of the world; the genius of Judaism is its ability to leave other people alone. And the evils of the two systems are the precise obverse of these genii. The genies all too easily become demons" (707). If leaving other people alone is the ethical imperative of diaspora, then, in Zionism and the state of Israel, we see what happens when Jewish particularism does not leave other people alone, but turns them into Others.[18]

The Boyarins take umbrage with those who blame the Bible itself for the ills of the modern world, calling this confusion between Jewish and Christian biblical hermeneutics a flattening of history, and an "exoneration of European Christian society that has been, after all, the religious hegemonic system for virtually all of the imperialist, racist, and even genocidal societies of the West" (709–710). As they emphatically state, "There were no Jewish missionaries in the remote islands and jungle enclaves" (710). While the role of Christianity in colonialism and the global European empires is undeniable, the Boyarins are probably too black and white here: there were Jewish individuals involved in the slave trade and all aspects of the colonial endeavour. Still, in terms of state power, until the success of the Zionist movement in creating a state, the argument stands. The Boyarins admit as much when they write that "Jews and Jewish culture will have to answer for the evil that we do (especially to the Palestinians), but it is absurd for 'the Jews' to be implicated in practices in which they had no part and indeed have had no part even until now: forced conversion, deculturation, genocide" (710).[19] "Generation and the Ground" thus becomes a critique of both Christian universalism and Jewish particularism, especially when infused—when polluted—with power.

There are two aspects of the Boyarins' theorization of diaspora that I would like to reconsider. The first is simply that while it is significant that diaspora correlates to the Jewish religious experience of the past two thousand years, it by no means had to in order to be a legitimate mode of being. Even if the Rabbis themselves had not codified diaspora, it would still be an ethical alternative to nationalism and military power. Second, and more complexly, is the Boyarins' total excoriation of autochthony. Just because autochthony is a myth for the Jewish people, it does not mean it is a myth for other peoples; there is more than one way for a people to connect with a land. The Boyarins repeatedly compare the Jewish claim of autochthonous belonging to what they see as the similar claims of Indigenous Peoples. They write that the "Jewish conception of the Land of Israel is similar to the discourse of the Land of many (if not nearly all) 'indigenous' peoples of the world" (714). They go on to state that

> It is profoundly disturbing to hear Jewish attachment to the Land decried as regressive in the same discursive situations in which the attachment of native Americans or Australians to their particular rocks, trees, and deserts is celebrated as an organic connection to the Earth that "we" have lost. The uncritical valorization of indigenousness (and partic- ularly the confusion between political indigenousness and mystified autochthony) must come under critique, without wishing, however, to deny the rights of native Americans, Australians, and Palestinians to their Lands, precisely on the basis of real, unmysterious political claims. (714–715)

The Boyarins' favouring of Indigenous claims of belonging over autoch- thonous claims is crystal clear here. However, while I agree with the Boyarins that the Jewish people do not have the right to make autoch- thonous claims of belonging—due to their two thousand years of living in the diaspora—I nonetheless believe that Indigenous Peoples do have, and can make, legitimate autochthonous claims. Autochthony is not ipso facto violent or unethical; autochthony coupled with hegemonic power is. Those Indigenous Americans and Australians the Boyarins mention— it is hard to read the sentence mentioning "their particular rocks, trees, and deserts" without sensing sarcasm or primitivism—do not have the same relationship to land that Europeans and the Western world (includ- ing the Zionists) have, and that the latter have spread across the globe through empire, colony, and resource extraction. Part of a diasporic consciousness must be the insistence that other (non-violent) forms of relationship to the land can, do, and must exist side by side.

The Jewish people have diaspora. Indigenous Peoples have their sacred relationship to the land. As Okanagan writer Jeanette Armstrong explains: "All my elders say that it is land that holds all knowledge of life and death and is a constant teacher. It is said in Okanagan that the land constantly speaks. It is constantly communicating. Not to learn its language is to die. We survived and thrived by listening intently to its teachings—to its language—and then inventing human words to retell its stories to our succeeding generations" (146). This relationship to land—the Okanagan taken as one example of hundreds—is of an entirely different epistemological valence than Western ones, including the Jewish. The Second Temple period is not the same thing as First Nations' attachment to the land; the systems of living are totally different, existing in distinctive epistemological worldviews. When autochthony leads to ethnic particularity, borders, xenophobia, othering, ethnic cleansing, and nation-states, it is indeed a violent ideology, but when it leads to ethical and ecological relations to the land (relations that are not based on private property, extraction, or materialism), it is as positive a force as diaspora, if not more so. The bald fact is that Jewish people do not have access to autochthonous claims, whereas Indigenous Peoples most certainly do.[20] What Jewish people do have is diaspora.

Chapter Overview

As will be seen in the following chapter overview, this book proceeds from rigorous, often against-the-grain readings of the texts under scrutiny. The parameters for my analysis, though engendered from the themes, motifs, and narrative strategies of the individual texts themselves, are grounded in historical, political, and theoretical contexts. The book is arranged along a number of different axes. The first half of the book focuses on canonical, established texts, whereas the last two chapters examine newer, contemporary fiction. As such, the first two chapters dig deep into the scholarly discourses orbiting their texts, whereas the last two chapters rely more on historical and political contextualization, as well as interviews and reviews. Some of the chapters break the geographical boundaries I have set as the parameters of this study; I do this purposefully, to enact in my work my belief in the need to break borders. The second chapter, most significantly, includes a novel that was not written in an American or Canadian context.

The book's opening chapter is a close reading of Philip Roth's 1993 *Operation Shylock*, a novel that challenges Jewish belonging/identity in any national framework, whether Israeli, American, or European. In order to perform my reading of the novel, I first expound on my theory of diasporic heteroglossia. *Shylock* is an excellent example of the diasporic heteroglossic novel: not only are there three Philip Roths—the author, the narrator, and the imposter—in dialogue with each other, but characters from a wide range of political, ethnic, and cultural spaces are given room to speak. The chapter will focus on four different thematic nodes of the novel in order to attempt to unpack its swirling heteroglossia. The first section looks closely at how ideas of Jewish justice, especially when represented in a courtroom, operate in the novel. The second section unpacks Pipik's Diasporism, his belief that Israeli Jews should reverse migrate back to Eastern Europe. The third section focuses on the novel's Palestinian characters, especially George Ziad. The fourth and final section presents a new reading of the end of the novel, where there is a "missing" chapter, which supposedly details Roth's adventures as a spy for the Mossad against Ziad and his friends. Unlike the majority of critics, who accept that the missing chapter unambiguously signifies that Philip Roth does in fact become a spy, I suggest that Roth the character's (as opposed to Roth the author) decision to excise the last chapter can be read in multiple ways, including as a wrongheaded capitulation to Zionist pressure, and does not negate the novel's acceptance of the Palestinian narrative of displacement, victimization, and violent occupation.

In the second chapter, I perform a novel comparison of Theodor Herzl's *Altneuland*, a utopic novel of 1903 that imagines a future Jewish state thriving in Ottoman Palestine, and Leon Uris's 1958 *Exodus*, a hagiographic, deeply problematic, deeply racist genre novel of the state's founding. These two early novels of Israel—one imagining a place that does not yet exist, the other fictionalizing the very recent founding of the country (and a runaway bestseller that had, and continues to have, a deep impact on North American Jewish views on Israel)—allow me to raise some of the issues at stake when it comes to representing Israel/Palestine through fiction. Though I locate *Altneuland* as what I call settler-colonial utopic fiction and *Exodus* as a cowboys and Indians melodrama, both novels are committed to justifying the necessity of the Zionist state, though Herzl's was written before the creation of the state and Uris's afterwards; because of this, both novels work *against* diasporic hetero-glossia. I will compare the two novels' different conceptions of Jewish time—in *Altneuland*, it is the Zionist belief in what Eyal Chowers calls "sundered history" (654) that allows the Jews to break into historical time and create a state for themselves, whereas in *Exodus*, the founding of the state is the result of the entire Jewish history of suffering; explore how language and translation operate in both texts; and compare each novel's inclusion of Arab and Palestinian characters. Overall, I argue that as diasporic fiction, *Altneuland* is a powerful example of imagining non-diasporic futures, where *Exodus* is a powerful and damaging example of how the Zionist rejection of diaspora leads to the celebration of violent ethnic nationalism.

The book's third chapter performs a reading of Ayelet Tsabari's short story collection *The Best Place on Earth*, using the book's disman-tling of pure ethnic or national identities to present alternatives to Zionist ethnic nationalism. This is also the juncture in the book where I move from readings of canonical American texts (as well as *Altneuland*) into readings of contemporary Canadian texts. In Tsabari's collection, the stories' Israeli characters—Arab Jews from Yemen, Egypt, Tunisia, and Jerusalem—allow a vantage point into Israeli life that has remained mostly hidden in English literature, where the Ashkenazi viewpoint remains dominant. I present *The Best Place on Earth* as an example of the diasporic heteroglossic potential of the short story collection form, where the stories in a collection are in dialogue with each other and reject national ideologies. In story after story, Tsabari dismantles any essential-ist claim for national, ethnic, or racial identity. Deploying Ella Shohat's concept of diasporic polycentric perspectives ("Introduction" 14), I argue that diasporic heteroglossia operates even within Israel itself, revealing the violent paradox at the heart of the Zionist settler-colonial project.

The book's final chapter looks at David Bezmozgis's *The Betrayers*. This short novel pits two divergent Jewish trends in direct conflict: the Zionist/national, embodied in the character of Baruch Kotler, and the diasporic, embodied in the character of Chaim Tankilevich. I suggest that any work of diasporic fiction that engages with the political situ-ation of Israel/Palestine, as *The Betrayers* does, but does not give space to the Palestinian narrative is a moral failure; in this way, the text is an example of a diasporic Jewish novel that does *not* make use of diasporic heteroglossia, even though on first glance it might appear that it does. Overall, I read the text as a Zionist novel written from the diaspora that reveals the major impact that the recent immigration of a million Soviet Jews to Israel has had on the country.

Throughout the book, I will look closely at the decisions the five authors have made in their diasporic fictional imaginings of Israel/Palestine. How do Tsabari and Bezmozgis explore their chosen diasporic groups—Arab Jews and Soviet Jews, respectively—and their massive immigrations into Israel, especially in light of the fact of the Zionist need to maintain a Jewish majority by whatever means necessary? What does it mean that in Tsabari's stories diasporic time continues (through her characters' connections to their Arabness), while in Bezmozgis's novel the diasporic time of the former Soviet Union is described as coming to an end? What can be made of the fact that Roth is the only author in this book to make generous space for the Palestinian narrative and characters, even though he was writing twenty-plus years before Tsabari or Bezmozgis? Does the fact that *Exodus* and *Altneuland* are still used as Zionist justifications say something about their literary quality, or about their use and abuse? In answering these questions, this book shows how vital these fictional texts are in the ongoing push and pull between the Jewish diaspora and the Zionist state.

The issues raised by the fictional texts in this book are incredibly pressing: immigration, borders, minority rights, ethnic nationalism, ethnic cleansing, judicial mechanisms, xenophobia, militarism, and the role of fiction, to name a few. It is my hope that in putting these Jewish texts together and performing a rigorous, historically-inflected reading of them, I will show how fiction—and what fiction allows writers and readers alike to imagine—has an important role in fighting for a just world. I believe that fiction, here North American Jewish fiction, must be a part of what Udi Aloni calls writing binationalism (108). Only through changing the story, adjusting the narrative, can an ethical, pluralistic solution be found. This goes some way toward explaining why I am so hard on a number of these texts. Fiction on Israel/Palestine has tremendous bearing on the real world, and therefore has tremendous responsibility.

Philip Goes to Israel

Jewish Justice, Diasporism,
Palestinian Voices, and
Zionist Self-Censorship
in *Operation Shylock*

PHILIP ROTH IS RIGHTLY ACKNOWLEDGED as one
of the first Jewish American authors to write serious, nuanced, probing
literary fiction about Israel/Palestine that does not just resort to Zionist
platitudes. As Andrew Furman notes, Roth's Israel novels "show just how
far Jewish-American fiction on Israel has come since Leon Uris's *Exodus*"
and Roth, "the preeminent craftsman of Jewish mischief, refuses to look
toward Israel with a myopic eye, bedazzled by Masada, the Western Wall,
and all other things Jewish" (151, 130). In this opening chapter, I set out
to examine why this is so—what makes Roth's fictional forays into the
Middle East so noteworthy, even explosive? What I find in my analysis
of *Operation Shylock*, the second of Roth's two major Israel novels—or,
as Ranen Omer-Sherman calls them, Roth's "Israel-situated" novels
(203)—published in 1993, will not be surprising when considered in the
context of Roth's writing career as a whole. As he had been since he first
started publishing fiction—in the short stories of *Goodbye, Columbus*,

in Portnoy's Complaint, and in The Ghost Writer and the other early Zuckerman books—Roth was unafraid to satirize the Jewish world, to challenge dominant ideas and narratives, to break boundaries, and to say the unsayable. Is it any wonder, then, that once Roth turned his fictional eye to Israel/Palestine, the results would be as challenging and as fecund, as infuriating (to some) and liberating (to others) as they indeed turned out to be? Unlike the majority of North American Jewish fiction writers whose works came before Shylock and Roth's earlier Israel-situated novel, The Counterlife (1988), and a good number of those that came after, Roth used his fiction to severely trouble Zionism and its claim on modern Jewish identity.

As such, I will read Operation Shylock through the lens of a diaspora-centred Jewish geography. In Shylock, Roth thoroughly and energetically dismantles the Zionist narrative of Israel as the redemption of the Jewish diaspora, as the end of Jewish history, and as an innocent, unimpeachable state that now has the power to speak for—and act on behalf of—the entirety of the Jewish people. The difficult realities of Jewish justice, the theory of Diasporism that Philip encounters in Pipik, his double, the novel's strong Palestinian voices, and the shocking moment of self-censorship that ends the novel all come together to reveal Roth's commitment in Operation Shylock to exposing the distorted worldview that is required in order for Jewish Americans to continue supporting the self-proclaimed Jewish state. This is not to say that Shylock is not without its problems or its detractors, but it is to strongly suggest that Roth gives us an example of the destabilizing power that diasporic fiction on Israel/Palestine can attain.

Central to my reading of Shylock is my concept of diasporic heteroglossia, which is a conjoining of Mikhail Bakhtin's theory of heteroglossia with the more radical currents of diaspora theory, in particular the work of Daniel and Jonathan Boyarin. There are a number of striking similarities between these two modes of thought: both are predicated on multiplicity, open-endedness, and dialogue; both are dynamic, fluid, and non-static; and both have deep political, ethical, and cultural ramifications. Bakhtin's theory of heteroglossia states that the novel is a genre based on bringing together a multiplicity of voices. The novel, he writes, "can be defined as a diversity of social speech types (sometimes even diversity of languages) and a diversity of individual voices, artistically organized" (262). He continues: "The novel orchestrates all its themes, the totality of the world of objects and ideas depicted and expressed in it, by means of the social diversity of speech types...and by the differing individual voices that flourish under such conditions. Authorial speech, the speeches of narrators, inserted genres, the speech of characters are merely those fundamental compositional unities with whose help heteroglossia...can enter the novel" (263). Each one of these speeches allows for different voices, and for the connections between the voices to come into focus: "These distinctive links and interrelationships between utterances and languages, this movement of the theme through different languages and speech types, its dispersion into the rivulets and droplets of social heteroglossia, its dialogization—this is the basic distinguishing feature of the stylistics of the novel" (263). Overall, according to Bakhtin, language is an unending dynamic process: "stratification and heteroglossia widen and deepen as long as language is alive and developing" (272).

Likewise, for the Boyarins, as we saw in the introduction, a diasporic consciousness is one that is open to change (from without and within), and that exists comfortably in a world of proliferating others, unlike the strict border policing of nation-states. Their hope that diaspora, would, as they put it, "simultaneously respect the irreducibility and the positive value of cultural differences, address the harmfulness, not of abolishing frontiers but of dissolution of uniqueness, and encourage the mutual fructification of different life-styles and traditions" ("Generation and the Ground," 711) squares remarkably well with Bakhtin's insistence on the open-endedness of language. With diasporic heteroglossia, then, I suggest that in bringing together Bakhtin and the Boyarins (as representatives of a radical diasporic consciousness), we are presented with a new critical vocabulary to help us understand what is at stake in novels that are both not beholden to nationalist rhetoric and that contain multiple, multiplying voices/narratives often at odds with such rhetoric.

Language, to return to Bakhtin, is always a site of tension—between marginal and authoritative voices, between centre and periphery, between multivocality and univocality. The place where this tension manifests is at the level of the utterance; every piece of uttered language exists in the matrix of this push and pull, which Bakhtin conceptualizes as centripetal and centrifugal forces. Bakhtin writes: "Alongside the centripetal forces, the centrifugal forces of language carry on their uninterrupted work; alongside verbal-ideological centralization and unification, the uninterrupted processes of decentralization and disunification go forward" (272). Language, though it is always being pressured into conforming to a centralized system, nonetheless is continuously expanding, breaking off, reforming, and taking on different registers, syntaxes, ideologies, and positionalities. This is what Bakhtin means by the dialogism of language, or heteroglossia, which, as Michael Holquist points out, is at the root of all of Bakhtin's thought (xix). As Michael Bernard-Donals explains in his historiography of Bakhtin studies in English literature, this is the "difficult problem" at the heart of "Bakhtinian language theory": "that working against whatever liberatory or revolutionary tendencies language might have as it operates dialogically (or polyvalently, or prosaically), is an opposite tendency that drives language back to monologism (or authoritarianism, or theoretism), thereby potentially squelching any positively valorized linguistic or social change" (430). While I am not going to get into the various attempts to solve this problem here—which Bernard-Donals suggests is basically unsolvable—and while I am interested in Bakhtin more as a conceptual springboard than as an airtight theory of literature, I do want to stress how compatible this dynamic theory of language is with diaspora theory. It is here, at the ongoing contestation between heteroglossia and univocality, between diaspora and nation, that diasporic heteroglossia comes into being.

As we saw in the introduction, Stéphane Dufoix gives us the language to show how, in the twentieth century, Jewish geography moved from an atopic schema—a series of connected diasporas without connection to a "referent-origin," or nation-state—which it had been for millenia, to a centroperipheral schema, with the creation of Israel and the victory and subsequent dominance of the Zionist narrative in the Jewish world. Now, as portions of the Jewish diaspora start the shift to an antagonistic relationship to Israel, Jewish geography is in a remarkably similar situation to Bakhtin's theory of language. The centripetal—with Israel as the univocal centre of the Jewish world— comes into contention with the centrifugality of diaspora. Diaspora, in its fluid myriad manifestations not reliant on ownership of land or political power, is the true ethical mode of Jewish belonging, whether in the Boyarins' sense of generation over ground, George Steiner's text as home, the Rabbinic tradition as codified in the Talmud, or the Yiddish cultural formation, which, in the newer diasporas of the Americas, Australia, and so on, has become a secular-cultural diasporic belonging. Zionist univocality, in its desire to subsume and pacify diasporic heteroglossia, results in the violent ethnic nationalism that is on daily display in Israel, Gaza, and the occupied territories. To borrow from Bakhtin, when disparaging scholars for not taking the heteroglossic nature of the novel into account, but instead focusing on only one element or the other, Zionism "transposes a symphonic (orchestrated) theme on to the piano keyboard" (263). Instead of multiple instruments playing variations of the Jewish theme, we have the pale singularity of the Zionist keyboard.

What, then, does this have to do with Roth, with the novel, and with Jewish fiction? Much like Bakhtin locates the novel as the genre of heteroglossia,[1] I see the Jewish diasporic heteroglossic novel as one that uses the novel's innate ability to house differentiated voices, competing ideologies, and counter-narratives in order to help diaspora reclaim its hold on the Jewish imagination. Diasporic heteroglossia is the multi-voiced novelistic manifestation of the diasporic ethos, where the novel form houses the multivocality of a group outlook that is fluid, open to others, and not predicated on ownership of land or rigid forms of cultural hoarding. Diasporic heteroglossia is anti-colonial, anti-racist, and against dominant narratives that negate other voices, flows, and modes of being. Diasporic heteroglossia works against what Bakhtin calls the "victory of one reigning language (dialect) over the others, the supplanting of languages, their enslavement" (271). The "decentralizing, centrifugal forces" (273) that shaped the novel as Bakhtin theorizes it can also be harnessed to decentre Zionism's hold on the Jewish world, to insist that diasporic consciousness is preferable to autochthonous claims over land that lead to ethnic superiority and the forced removal of the land's Indigenous Peoples (the Palestinians, the Bedouin, and the Druze). Roth's Israel-situated novels, perhaps more so than any other text under study in this book, reveal the promise of diasporic heteroglossia. The cacophony of voices found in *Operation Shylock*, in all their diasporic heteroglossic splendour, act to dedoxify (to use Linda Hutcheon's phrase), to destabilize, and to reconfigure, re-energize, and reset Jewish geography—and show what could happen when heteroglossia is discarded for the damaging univocality of ethnonationalism.

Reading *Operation Shylock* through the lens of diasporic hetero-glossia, I argue that Roth mounts a complicated defense of diaspora at the same time he shrewdly dismantles the most sacred tenets of Zionism. I disagree with Omer-Sherman's evaluation that Roth's narratives "presuppose that there is no longer a truly Jewish exilic experience relevant to the circumstances of American Jewry, a loss he construes as a form of blurring of identities or a fatal closure that revokes a certain Jewish literary privilege" (271). Instead, I see Roth's Israel novels as exploding the hold Zionism has had on the American Jewish imaginary since 1948, and which further calcified in 1967. Furthermore, if Debra Shostak is right that "Israel poses an identity crisis for the Diaspora Jew largely because of its symbolic power as the Jewish 'home'" (742), then Roth wields this identity crisis to smash Israel's symbolic power. That *Operation Shylock* came out in 1993 is telling: well before other Jewish North American authors even turned their attention to the Middle East, Roth was furiously, rigorously, and satirically demolishing the dangerous national myths of Zionism and of Israel's role as the sacred homeland of the Jewish people.

Before turning to *Shylock*, it is instructive to look at how Roth deals with similar material in his earlier Israel-situated novel, 1986's *The Counterlife*. The fifth novel to feature Roth's alter ego, author Nathan Zuckerman, *The Counterlife* is rightly considered to be among Roth's most structurally ambitious novels, broken as it is into a series of alternate narratives following Nathan and his brother Henry as they contend with heart disease, impotence, and differing manifestations of Jewish belonging. Through these disjointed narratives Roth pits the "family Zionism" (60) of Nathan Zuckerman's grandparents, who left Eastern Europe to find a better life for themselves in America (family Zionism being really just a Rothian euphemism for diaspora), against the Zionism of settler-philosopher Mordecai Lippmann, whose right-wing West Bank settlement is joined by Zuckerman's brother Henry in one of the novel's four alternate timelines. As such, *The Counterlife* presents diaspora, in particular the Jewish American diaspora, as an ethical alternative to the ethnic nationalism of the Israeli state.

However, *The Counterlife*, at times, still inadvertently conforms to some of the more dangerous aspects of Zionism. As Furman insightfully points out, the lack of Arab or Palestinian voices in *The Counterlife* means that "Roth represents the Arab not only as a senseless murderer of children but as downright sadistic as well…unequivocally stripping the Arab of any moral high ground" (644).² Overall, the structure of this complex novel—four alternate timelines, two where Henry has heart disease, two where Zuckerman has heart disease, with both brothers having an opportunity to survive their impotence-eradicating surgeries, but also to never leave the operating table—is itself one that adheres to the chronotopes of diaspora, since in only one of the timelines does Henry become a Zionist and forgo his diasporic existence for one of strict ethnic and ideological purity, and because the struggles Zuckerman faces when he moves to (antisemitic) Britain seem more truly Jewish to him than anything he encountered in Israel or the West Bank.

If, then, in *The Counterlife*, Roth mounts a vigorous defense of diaspora in the face of damaging ethnic nationalism, in *Operation Shylock*, Roth, through a more fully-realized diasporic heteroglossia, lays siege to the Zionist narrative so long hegemonic in the Jewish world.³ *Operation Shylock* follows its first-person protagonist, a writer named Philip Roth (who in all biographical and literary respects maps near-perfectly onto the author himself) recently recovered from a mental breakdown due to the sleeping pill Halcion, as he travels to Israel and confronts an imposter pretending to be Philip. This imposter, who Philip eventually nicknames Pipik,⁴ is publicly promoting a political program he calls "Diasporism," which, in a reversal of classic Zionism, calls for the Ashkenazi inhabitants of Israel to resettle in Eastern Europe in order to avoid certain destruction. While in Israel dealing (or failing to deal) with Pipik, Philip attends the trial of accused Nazi war criminal John Demjanjuk; interviews Israeli author Aharon Appelfeld on his books and being a fiction writer after the Shoah (these interviews are real, and further muddle Roth's ironic insistence that the events of the novel are themselves factual); gets involved with an old college friend, the Palestinian George Ziad, who is now a radical intellectual and anti-Zionist activist; and undertakes espionage work for the Israeli Mossad and its elderly representative, Mr. Smilesburger. The novel plays out over a short period of sleepless days, with Philip—who gets loopier with every missed meal and each new encounter—questioning not only his decisions and actions, but the reliability of his mind, his own sanity, and the identity of all those he encounters. The novel shares a tone and narrative propulsion that is reminiscent of Hunter S. Thompson's *Fear and Loathing in Las Vegas*, an earlier example of the American paranoid nonfiction/fiction genre.[5]

The novel includes moments of high satire and serious contemplation, and is through and through a novel of voices. Brett Ashley Kaplan calls it "a mad, comic, manic novel filled with the ranting of fanatics and the rich imaginings of paranoid characters" (64). Sidra DeKoven Ezrahi, in the *Tikkun* round-table on the novel published shortly after *Shylock's* release—and which is a great source of initial reactions to the novel in the Jewish world—writes that "Operation Shylock is, in fact, a very noisy novel. Words are flung like stones, done and undone like refugee bundles on an endless highway" (np). Mark Shechner calls the novel an "explainer's paradise" (140). Accepting the Palestinian narrative of displacement, victimization, and violent occupation through the vehicle of the explainer's paradise, the novel deeply troubles Israel's mythic origins.

My reading of *Operation Shylock* centres on four aspects of the novel: the ethics of Jewish judgment and Jewish justice; Diasporism, or Pipik's program of reverse migration, with the Ashkenazi Jews of Israel returning to their European countries; the Palestinian characters in the novel, most significantly George Ziad, but also Anna Ziad; and, finally, Philip's decision to excise the novel's final chapter, which details his experiences spying for the Mossad in Athens and elsewhere. I argue that this excision is a direct affront to the diasporic heteroglossia the novel has thus far been aligned with, and that it reveals the power of Zionism to silence even its most intelligent critics.

Overall, what becomes apparent in unpacking the novel in the way I have laid out above—judgment, Diasporism, Ziad/Anna, and the excised chapter—what rises above the cacophonic din that is enough to almost drown the hapless Philip, leading him to distrust everything including his own intellect and to think he is once again under the throes of a Halcion breakdown, is *Shylock's* adamant refusal to accept the bedrock claim of Zionism that Israel is the final, necessary, unavoidable stage in Jewish history. In Philip, Roth creates a character—a double of himself as different as Pipik is from Philip—who is bamboozled into discarding his own sense of morality, his own deeply held beliefs on the power of fiction, in order to appease the Israeli state. Philip's shocking act of self-censorship that closes the novel, playing out against the backdrop of the Demjanjuk trial, the absurdities of Diasporism, and the troubling narratives of George and Anna, must be read as a horrible mutation of the Jewish commitment to dialogue, argument, multiplicity, and heteroglossia that has thrived in the diaspora, perhaps reaching its most full flowering in the fictional genre of the novel.

Determining Justice: Demjanjuk, Ramallah, and a Tribunal from The Future

During Philip's adventures in Israel and the West Bank, Roth's fictional counterpart encounters an array of manifestations of Jewish justice, most significantly the (real-life) trial of John Demjanjuk, a Ukrainian American accused of being Ivan the Terrible, a sadistic, torturous Treblinka gas-chamber guard personally responsible for hundreds of thousands of deaths during the Shoah. Philip's observations from his two visits to the trial have been interpreted in a number of ways: as a Rothian deconstruction of the "juridical legitimacy of the witness" that leads to a "Holocaust testimonial that speaks of unspeakability, that maintains silence and history" (Dobozy 38); that the unsolvable paradox of Demjanjuk, as Ivan the Terrible, who was supposedly killed at the end of the war, is both alive and dead informs the novel's "governing aesthetic philosophy" (McLoughlin 117); and as a springboard to dive into issues of identity (porous versus closed), witnessing (to have semantic authority or to not), and Jewish senses of self (based on pre-Shoah existence or on the Israeli reality) (Alphandary). Surprisingly, none of these readings— regardless of the validity of their arguments—bring into their discussion the novel's two other instances of what I am calling "Jewish justice" in Israel/Palestine: Philip's visit with George Ziad to an Israeli military court in Ramallah, where Palestinian teenagers are being tried for resisting the occupation, and Smilesburger's ruminations on his and Philip's trial in a future Palestinian courtroom.[6] In unpacking these three trials—one very real, one representative of the daily realities of the occupation, and one part of an imagined future—I make the following connected arguments. One, that Jewish justice in the Zionist mode—as represented by the Jerusalem and Ramallah courtroom—in its belief that it pursues justice for all of the Jewish world through the mechanism of the state, must fall disastrously short of its mark. Two, the Israeli state trying Demjanjuk as having committed horrendous crimes against the Jewish people on an almost unimaginable scale, in another country before the state of Israel even existed, and at the same time that, across the Green Line, the state is trying Palestinian teenagers for crimes against the Jewish people of a highly divergent magnitude (throwing molotov cocktails at Israeli soldiers), reveals a number of troubling characteristics of the Israeli state. And finally, I argue that true justice cannot be meted out by a state whose loyalties lie plainly with a privileged group, in this case Jewish Israelis, to the unimaginable detriment of the state's others, here the Palestinians. Seen through the eyes of Philip, who is visiting Israel as a diaspora outsider, these three moments of (failed) Jewish justice showcase what's possible in a diaspora fiction that makes no excuses for what it encounters in the self-declared national home.

The Demjanjuk trial acts as setting, backdrop, and thematic reflecting/refracting pool for Philip's adventures in Israel/Palestine. Readers get alerted to the importance of the trial in the novel's first sentence: "I learned about the other Philip Roth in January 1988, a few days after the New Year, when my cousin Apter telephoned me in New York to say that Israeli radio had reported that I was in Jerusalem attending the trial of John Demjanjuk, the man alleged to be Ivan the Terrible of Treblinka" (17).[7] This is a remarkable opening sentence, introducing the main conflict—Pipik—and underlining the theme of imposters, others, and fictional identities (Demjanjuk is "alleged" to be Ivan; Apter calls about the "other" Philip Roth). It also foregrounds the importance of the Demjanjuk trial itself. Philip himself attends two different sessions of the trial (on January 26th and 27th, 1988), reads through a packet of newspaper clippings on the trial, discusses Demjanjuk at length with Appelfeld, Pipik, and Smilesburger, and even stays at the same hotel as Demjanjuk's (fictional) twenty-two-year-old son, John Junior, and his legal team. It is Pipik's plot to kidnap John Junior with the help of the fascist Meir Kahane that brings Philip to the trial the second time. Moreover, during the climactic showdown between Philip and Smilesburger in an abandoned Israeli classroom—where Smilesburger convinces Philip to spy for the Mossad— the trial is playing on the classroom's television.

Some of the most affecting and disturbing writing in the novel occurs when Philip first sees Demjanjuk, during the afternoon session of the trial on January 26th. Philip imagines himself into Demjanjuk from an array of perspectives: he dwells for a long paragraph on Demjanjuk's power and joy as the violent, abusive, murderous gas chamber guard in Treblinka, a "Vigorous, healthy boy" doing "good, hard work" that elicited "wild, wild, untainted joy" (60); as an old man remade as a Ukrainian American who would "Rather tend tomatoes now and raise string beans than bore a hole in somebody's ass with a drill" (61); and as an unrepentant antisemite on the docket blaming the Jews for his current predicament. This entire section is punctuated with Philip's exclamations of "there he was," sometimes in italics, the last two times with a further "or wasn't" (62, 64), hammering home Demjamjuk's startling embodiment of the horror of the Shoah. Philip also attempts to think through the problem of squaring Demjanjuk's life as Ivan the Terrible with the elderly, benign, seemingly imperturbable Demjanjuk accused of thousands of horrendous murders: "you are" both, he writes, "your appearance proves only that to be both a loving grandfather and a mass murderer is not all that difficult" (63), an insight that could have come directly from Hannah Arendt's reporting on the Eichmann trial. In a passage that speaks right to the novel's interest in doubles, split identities, and insoluble differences, Philip, addressing Demjanjuk directly, writes:

> You've really only lived sequentially the two seemingly antipodal, mutually excluding lives that the Nazis, with no strain to speak of, managed to enjoy simultaneously—so what, in the end, is the big deal? The Germans have proved definitively to all the world that to maintain two radically

divergent personalities, one very nice and one not so nice, is
no longer the prerogative of psychopaths only. (63)

Throughout this whole section, Philip more or less buys into Demjanjuk's
guilt, to his identity as Ivan the Terrible, a charge Demjanjuk vehemently
denies.

Philip's first visit to the trial is mostly taken up with these
thoughts, flights of fancy, and fictionalizations of Demjanjuk's time
as a murderer, American autoworker, and captive of the Israeli justice
system; the second visit, in the fourth quarter of the novel, is taken up
with the witness for the prosecution, Eliahu Rosenberg, and the issues
of testimony, memory, and narrating trauma in light of the unspeakable
atrocities of the Shoah. For this visit, Philip is out of his head, exhausted,
starving, and worried that John Junior is going to be kidnapped at any
moment. Rosenberg—who was also a witness at the Eichmann trial—is on
the stand, and is being hammered for the veracity of his testimony identifying Demjanjuk as Ivan the Terrible. This is because of a new piece of
evidence the defense has: a memoir written by Rosenberg shortly after
the war that states Ivan the Terrible was killed the night of the Treblinka
revolt. As Kate McLoughlin points out, in order to up the drama and have
the scene make chronological sense, Roth makes some crucial fictional
changes to Rosenberg's testimony, making the knowledge of the memoir
a surprise, where in actuality the court was well aware of Rosenberg's
writing about Ivan the Terrible's death (123). Roth, even when writing
about actual trials he actually attended, is more than willing to fictionalize details. The defense attempts to use this new information to discredit
Rosenberg's testimony: "So how can you possibly come to this court and
point your finger at this gentleman when you wrote in 1945 that Ivan was
killed?" (299). Rosenberg's answer boils down to a mixture of wish fulfillment and the exigencies of storytelling. For McLoughlin, "The testimony
of Treblinka survivor Eliahu Rosenberg—namely, that Ivan the Terrible
is both dead and alive—is the crucial conundrum" (117) of the novel, and
is central to McLoughlin's understanding of the juridical "tenor of the
novel" (117), which acts to "establish competing truth systems, to spot-
light the process of determining identity, and to make the book's central
point about plausibility that truth is stranger than fiction" (117–118). In
regard to Rosenberg, Dobozy writes that "the lapses and contradictions

in Rosenberg's testimony raise the specter of testimony as narrative, pitting the consistency required for juridical credibility against the illogic evident in the elisions of storytelling" (39). The pivotal moment in the cross-examination of Rosenberg is when Demjanjuk himself calls Rosenberg, in Hebrew, a liar. Thematic valences aside, Dobozy uses this dramatic moment to further his claim that, in the novel, Demjanjuk, in a deeply ironic twist, becomes "the moral conscience of twentieth-century Jewish history" (39), because in calling Rosenberg a liar, Demjanjuk accidentally hits on a truth about the impossibility of properly telling the Shoah, since the Shoah exists outside of one person's singularity. What Dobozy's paradox of "the necessity of maintaining the unspeakability of the Holocaust" while at the same time "not permitting the Holocaust to lapse into silence" (38) means is that to speak the Shoah is to speak the unspeakable, a paradox that it is nonetheless incumbent on us to continue performing endlessly.

Both Dobozy and McLoughlin's readings of the trial in Shylock are strong and incisive, making a provocative argument for Roth's commitment to non-closure, fluidity, and the diasporic heteroglossia required to never allow narratives of such monumental trauma to be foreclosed: the Shoah, infinitely unspeakable, must constantly be spoken, in as many voices as possible. As Dobozy eloquently puts it, "What is determinate is oppressive, arbitrary, and false; what is indefinable, ambiguous, and formless is, more often than not for Roth, the theater of life" (41). Moreover, if, as Roth suggests, and McLoughlin and Dobozy tease out, the courtroom is not the proper place to speak the Shoah, then, I would add, nor is it possible to speak on behalf of the Jewish people—all Jewish people, alive or dead—within the walls of the court. Building on Dobozy's reading, it is not just Rosenberg who lies, it is also Zionism, when its practitioners claim it can adjudicate on behalf of the Jewish people.

In hindsight, of course, Rosenberg was both wrong and right: he was right that the man known as Ivan the Terrible was dead (as he recorded in his memoir), but he was wrong that that man was also John Demjanjuk (as he identified him at the Israeli trial). And though Demjanjuk was convicted, when the decision was appealed at the Israeli Supreme Court, he was acquitted; once the Soviet Union collapsed and access to the archives opened up, it was proved without a doubt that a man named Ivan Marchenko was Ivan the Terrible. Demjanjuk would eventually be convicted for working at the death camp of Sobibor, though not by an Israeli court, but by a German one. As Lawrence Douglas neatly sums up—in words that resonate with the closing lines of Hannah Arendt's Eichmann in Jerusalem—"Demjanjuk was rightly convicted not because he committed wanton murders, but because he worked in a factory of death. He was convicted of having been an accessory to murder for a simple and irresistible reason—because that had been his job" (16). Douglas's 2016 book The Right Wrong Man: John Demjanjuk and the Last Great Nazi War Crimes Trial is the fullest, most up-to-date treatment of the Demjanjuk saga, and allows us to further tease out the paradoxes and implications of state-sanctioned Jewish justice.[8] The book is a fascinating narrative of how the legal world attempted/attempts to deal with perpe- trators of the Shoah, following Demjanjuk from when he was first accused of being a collaborator, through his first denaturalization and extradition trials, to the Israeli trial, which Operation Shylock fictionalizes, to his eventual acquittal, return to the United States, second denaturalization and extradition,[9] and final trial in Germany. For Douglas, the Demjanjuk case "asks us to think critically about the justice of trying old men for superannuated crimes. It invites us to reflect on the nature of individual responsibility in the orchestration of state-sponsored crimes. It demands that we think carefully about the nature, causes, and possible justifica- tions of collaboration in the perpetration of atrocities" (3). Finally, "it provides a crucible in which three distinct national legal systems—the American, the Israeli, and the German—sought to create legal alloys potent enough to master the legal challenges posed by the destruction of Europe's Jews" (3).

According to Douglas, the Demjanjuk trial in Israel failed for several reasons. These include: mistakes the Israeli authorities made in their identification of Demjanjuk as Ivan the Terrible, including the original advertisement looking for survivors to positively identify Demjanjuk, which called him Ivan Demjanjuk, already implying his guilt, what Douglas calls "a colossal mistake" (102); the prosecution's over-reliance on survivor testimony, "to treat [it] with dignity and to confer public recognition upon it—pushed the court badly in the wrong direction" (82), showing how survivor-centred didactic trials like the Eichmann trial do not always work; the actions of the Office of Special Investigations in America, which hid evidence that Demjanjuk was not

Ivan (evidence that came to light after the trial was concluded); and, finally, the prosecution's insistence in placing Demjanjuk at Treblinka, though all the evidence placed him at Sobibor (this major mistake allowed Demjanjuk to truthfully deny the charges: he never *was* at Treblinka). Douglas also unpacks Israel's "Nazis and Nazi Collaborators (Punishment) Law" (NNCL). This law, passed in the Knesset in 1950, adopts the language of the atrocity model "pioneered at Nuremberg," except with a major change: instead of "crimes against humanity" the law refers specifically to "crimes against the Jewish people." "Once codified," Douglas writes, "'crimes against the Jewish people' would extend the juridical reach of the Jewish state to include Jewish people wherever they might reside and crimes of an earlier moment. It was a creative gesture, designed to address the reality that the state of Israel did not exist at the time of the Nazis' exterminatory acts" (65–66). In other words, true to its Zionist understanding of the Jewish world, the Israeli government codified into law its belief that it had the right to act on behalf of all Jews. Again, we see the univocal Zionism doing battle with the pluralism of a diasporic world of multiple voices.

Legal scholars Michael J. Bazyler and Julia Y. Scheppach, in their article "The Strange and Curious History of the Law Used to Prosecute Adolf Eichmann," detail the history of the NNCL from its murky beginnings in the Knesset to the last time it was used, which was to prosecute Demjanjuk. Bazyler and Scheppach's title is not an exaggeration; the law has definitely had a "strange and curious history." Apparently, the law's original, primary intention was to "prosecute Jews accused of collaboration with the Nazis and persecution of their Jewish brethren" (418). Bazyler and Scheppach deftly show how these early trials were not so much held to bring these Jewish Kapos (concentration camp prisoners who were given special privileges to supervise their fellow Jews) to justice, but to attempt to expunge the shame Israelis felt toward the growing population of Shoah survivors arriving in Israel. This can be read as another form of Zionist discounting of the diaspora. As such, in the 1950s and early 1960s, somewhere between thirty and forty Jewish Israelis were tried as Nazi collaborators (421) (the exact number is unknown because the trial records, as of this writing, still remain sealed, even though Israel's state archivist believes they should be made public; see Lozowick np). One of those tried, Yehezkel Enigster, seems to have been a real monster, beating and abusing the Jews under his charge at the labour camps of Graeditz and Fauelbruch (432). After the NNCL was used to prosecute Adolf Eichmann, what Bazyler and Scheppach call the law's "crowning glory" (418), the law was never used to try Jewish collaborators again, and was only used one more time, to prosecute Demjanjuk, which, as we have seen, proved to be a disaster. Overall, Bazyler and Scheppach make it clear how "unique" the NNCL is, due to the fact that it was designed to apply "retroactively and extra-territorially" (441). This one-of-a-kind law, which can be applied to Jewish collaborators and non-Jewish, non-Israeli citizen collaborators at one and the same time, is a telling example of the dangers inherent in any ethnic-centred manifestation of state-sponsored justice that disregards both temporal and spatial boundaries.[10]

Overall, then, the two major takeaways from Douglas's book are that most of the perpetrators of the Shoah were never held accountable—if being held accountable was ever really a possibility—and that justice, being always contained in a national or ideological framework, will always be fundamentally imperfect. As Roth shows us in *Operation Shylock*, a justice system that is chained to an ethnonationalist nation-state is inherently flawed, and puts the possibility of true Jewish justice at an even farther remove than before the Zionists started laying the groundwork for a state. To take just one more pertinent example—and one that shows without a doubt the connections between literature, nation-states, and systems of law—some thirty years after the Demjanjuk trial that Philip witnesses, the Israeli Supreme Court was tasked with deciding whether a portion of author Franz Kafka's archives, in the possession of Eva and Ruth Hoffe (the daughters of Max Brod's secretary, to whom he originally left the documents), could be sold on the open market, or if they would become the property of the Israeli National Library. Judith Butler explored the implications of this trial in a 2011 article in the *London Review of Books*. "So it seems we are to understand Kafka's work as an 'asset' of the Jewish people," she writes, "though not a restrictively financial one" (np). If Kafka is a Jewish writer, he and his work therefore belong to the Jewish people. "This claim," Butler writes, "already controversial (since it effaces other modes of belonging or, rather, non-belonging), becomes all the more so when we realize that the legal case rests on the presumption that it is the state of Israel that represents the Jewish people." This same presumption was at the heart of the Demjanjuk trial, not to mention the earlier Nazi war crimes trial of Adolf Eichmann.[11] Who, exactly, do the Israeli courts act on behalf of? The citizens of the country, or the entirety of a people spread across the globe it considers itself the steward of? The Kafka trial (as read by Butler) and the Demjanjuk trial (as fictionalized by Roth) both reveal the extent to which the Israeli state is willing to utilize its claim to be the representative of the Jewish people, while at the same time allowing the contradictions of such a claim to come into the light.

The Demjanjuk trial is far from the only representation of Jewish justice Roth gives us in Shylock. Most significantly, Philip visits what is in many ways the dark inverse of the Demjanjuk trial, when George Ziad takes him to an Israeli military court in the West Bank city of Ramallah, where a number of Palestinian youth are on trial. With all the time spent describing and interrogating the Demjanjuk trial, this juxtaposition can be no accident. Philip himself makes the connection between the two trials: "My second Jewish courtroom in two days. Jewish judges. Jewish laws. Jewish flags. And non-Jewish defendants. Courtrooms such as Jews had envisioned in their fantasies for many hundreds of years, answering longings even more unimaginable than those for an army or a state. One day we will determine justice!" (140). The two trials, at least in the geography of the novel, could not be more clearly linked. Still speaking of the fantasy of Jewish justice, Philip notes with warranted skepticism: "Well, the day had arrived, amazingly enough, and here we were, determining it. The unidealized realization of another hope-filled human dream" (141). The novel unmistakably sets up these two courtrooms as conjoined manifestations of the same longing for Jewish justice, and, taken together, the two trials—both trying non-Jewish defendants who are not Israeli citizens, Demjanjuk because he never lived in Israel, and the Palestinian youth because they are under the apartheid of military occupation—show just how "unidealistic" the "hope-filled dream" has indeed become.

Though it is much less of a national event than the Demjanjuk trial, Philip encounters the flip side of Zionism's ethnic nationalism at the

Ramallah courthouse. Chapter 5 opens with a description of the court-house: "The Ramallah military court lay within the walls of a jail built by the British during the Mandate" (138). This unequivocally places the Israeli courthouse in the context of British colonialism, the Zionist insti-tutions merely picking up from where the British left off. Philip sees the face of a young Palestinian boy awaiting his trial, the "terror on his face" discernible "even from thirty feet away" (139). This is unlike Demjanjuk, whose face showed no fear. The trial that Ziad and Philip witness is for Ziad's friend Kamil's younger brother, who is accused of throwing molotov cocktails. Philip meets a variety of people involved in the over-seeing of Israeli military justice. There is Kamil, the "poet-lawyer" (140), who believes his brother is not only innocent but has been drugged with an "injection" to "weaken his constitution" (141). Kamil believes that the Israelis use torture that does not "leave marks" in order to "suppress the revolt of the nationalist core" (141), and he gives Philip an earful about the similarities between the Israeli system and South African apartheid. There is the judge, who Philip describes as listening "to the proceedings with the perspicacious air of a mild, judicious person—one of 'us'" (139), and who later, when Philip attempts to leave the court-room to get away from Kamil, who has infuriated Philip by expanding his analogy of Israeli colonialism from South African apartheid to Nazi racial destruction, "ringingly announces to the courtroom, 'Mr. Roth is morally appalled by our neocolonialism'" (143). There is the lawyer for the defense, Shmuel, who to Philip's surprise, "wasn't an Arab but an Orthodox Jew, an imposingly bearded bear of a man, probably in his fifties, wearing a skullcap along with his black legal gown" (140), who outside the courtroom gives Philip a lecture on Muslim taqiya, or dissimulation, which reeks of Orientalism (145–146).[12] On the drive to Ramallah, George Ziad insists that Kamil's brother's charge is "unsup-ported by a single shred of evidence, unsubstantiated, another filthy lie" (127), and that his only crime was being at a demonstration, where he was arrested, and then interrogated with methods that blur into torture (leaving aside entirely the question of whether fighting back against military occupation can be considered a "crime" in the first place). This courtroom, where Israeli military justice is dispensed to its occupied population, is just one node of the daily reality of the Palestinians living in the West Bank in the late 1980s.

These two diametrically opposed courtrooms, where those "Jewish longings" for justice are answered, raise a question of the utmost urgency and importance: does a state have the right—or even the ability—to mete out "Jewish" justice? The first thing to point out is that the military courts in the West Bank are illegal under international law. Emily Schaeffer Omer-Man offers an excellent exegesis of the unequal application of justice in the Occupied West Bank. "For nearly half a century," Omer-Man writes,

> Israel has managed to normalize a situation in which crimi-
> nal law is applied separately and unequally in the West Bank
> based on nationality alone (Israeli versus Palestinian), inven-
> tively weaving its way around the contours of international
> law in order to preserve and develop its "settlement enter-
> prise." What is more, while the law is enforced vigorously and
> aggressively upon Palestinians suspected of crimes against
> Israelis, Israeli settlers enjoy virtualimpunity for acts against
> Palestinians. (np)

The main way the Israeli state does this is by trying Palestinians in a military court, such as the one Philip and Ziad visit in Ramallah, but trying
Israeli citizens who commit crimes in the West Bank under domestic law,
which is illegal because it entails defacto annexation. What this means in
practice, of course, is that "Israeli and Palestinian neighbors accused of
committing the very same crimes in the very same territory are arrested,
prosecuted and sentenced in drastically different systems—each featuring staggeringly disparate levels of due process protections" (Omer-Man
np). What Ziad reveals to Philip is the inequality inherent in the Israeli
system of law, where Palestinians are tried under different, illegal courts. It
appears that Philip is right to be skeptical of the efficacy of Jewish justice.

Second, besides the legality of the military court trials, is the question of the ethics of them. While Demjanjuk—regardless of his identity
as Ivan the Terrible or not—is being accused of crimes against the Jewish
people that include murdering tens of thousands of innocent Jewish men,
women, and children, Palestinian teenagers such as Kamil's brother are
being charged with crimes against the Jewish people of an unimaginably
different magnitude: that of resisting military occupation and ethnic

cleansing. These two courtrooms, therefore, speak to the ethical bind
the Israeli state and the Zionist narrative have created for themselves,
prosecuting war criminals who committed their crimes before Israel
even existed as a state—raising the related question of Israel's right to
try Nazi criminals at all—and at the same time prosecuting Palestinian
youths for fighting against their own toxic dehumanization, removal from
their land, and other forms of ethnic cleansing. The novel, then, answers
Jacqueline Rose's question, "Can you even talk about the suffering of the
Jewish people and the violence of the Israeli state in the same breath?"
(xiv) with a definitive yes. Ziad speaks directly, and brutally, to this when
he tells Philip:

> while this court for Demjanjuk is carefully weighing
> evidence for the benefit of the world press, scrutinizing
> meticulously, with all kinds of experts, the handwriting and
> the photograph and the imprint of the paper clip and the age
> of the ink and the paper stock, while this charade of Israeli
> justice is being played out on the radio and the television and
> in the world press, the death penalty is being enacted all over
> the West Bank. Without experts. Without trials. Without
> justice. With live bullets. Against innocent people. (272)

Ziad goes further than comparing the courtrooms of Jerusalem and
Ramallah, making the uncomfortable connection between the highly
publicized pursuit of Jewish justice and the unequivocally unjust state
that privileges one ethnic group. Moreover, Roth pushes the questioning
of Jewish justice in the Jewish state by having Philip glance at a newspaper headline about "three judges who were to be put on trial and three
others who were facing disciplinary action on charges of corruption"
(265). Jewish justice not only fails to materialize because of the ethnic
nationalism of the state, but because of the unavoidable human corruption that exists in any justice system. Ultimately, Philip's experiences at
the two trials reveal a striking truth about the Zionist state: the hyper-
bolic claim of the state as protector and avenger of the Jews, overlaid
with the quotidian reality of the occupation.

Roth continues the interrogation of the possibility of Jewish
justice into the political future as well, but now it is the Jewish actors of

the Zionist state who are being tried, answering Palestinian dreams of justice no less fecund than the Jewish desire Philip waxes poetic about. While a captive of Smilesburger, who has just revealed himself as a Mossad agent, the elderly spy brings up the possibility of a future trial held by a Palestinian state after a Palestinian victory. Before he does so, Smilesburger forcefully admits to Israel's unethical nature:

> What we have done to the Palestinians is wicked. We have displaced them and we have oppressed them. We have expelled them, beaten them, tortured them, and murdered them. The Jewish state, from the day of its inception, has been dedicated to eliminating a Palestinian presence in historical Palestine and expropriating the land of an indigenous people. The Palestinians have been driven out, dispersed, and conquered by the Jews. To make a Jewish state we have betrayed our history—we have done unto the Palestinian state what the Christians have done unto us: systemically transformed them into the despised and subju-gated Other, thereby depriving them of their human status. (349–350)

Though everything Smilesburger says has to be taken with a grain of salt, his comments ring all too true, and are not without their historical prec-edents: some of the most reactionary Zionists, including the Revisionist Zionist Menachem Begin, have at times, in public speeches and private letters, admitted to the truth of the situation, much like Smilesburger does here.

Having given a reading of the Israel/Palestine crisis not clouded by ideology, Smilesburger goes on to imagine how he will act if he is ever held to account for his misdeeds. "Will I invoke as my justification the millen-nial history of degrading, humiliating, terrifying, savage, murderous anti-Semitism?" Smilesburger asks Philip (350). "Will I repeat the story of our claim on this land, the millennial history of Jewish settlement here? Will I invoke the horrors of the Holocaust?" (350–351). Surprisingly (at first reading), Smilesburger answers his own questions in the negative: "Absolutely not," he declares. He continues:

I don't justify myself in this way now and I will not stoop to
doing it then. I will not plead the simple truth: "I am a tribes-
man who stood with his tribe," nor will I plead the complex
truth: "Born as a Jew where and when I was, I am, I always
have been, whichever way I turn, condemned." I will offer no
stirring rhetoric when I am asked by the court to speak my
last words but will tell my judges only this: "I did what I did
to you because I did what I did to you." And if that is not the
truth, it's as close as I know how to come to it. (351)

What first reads as a startling admittance of guilt, and as a pragmatic
approach to the conflict, somewhat loses its power when we realize that
Smilesburger's imagined future war crimes trial is an imagined future
that Smilesburger believes will never actually materialize, and that he
works tirelessly to keep from becoming a historical possibility. What
seems to be a declaration of criminality becomes a rhetorical move
wedded to a rigorous delaying of true justice.

According to Smilesburger's version of the future Palestinian trial,
Philip himself would not be spared. Regardless of his liberal credentials,
if Philip answers in the affirmative to the question "But did you approve
of Israel and the existence of Israel, did you approve of the imperialist,
colonialist theft that was the state of Israel?" (351), which Smilesburger
believes he would, using Appelfeld and the Shoah as justification, Philip
would be sentenced to death as well, just like Smilesburger, "as indeed"
he should be (351). This is where Smilesburger's rhetorical game starts
to become clear. Smilesburger tells Philip that his only way out of being
found guilty by the future imaginary Palestinian tribunal is to continue
pretending to be Pipik, and to undertake the spy mission for Smilesburger
and the Mossad. "And your last words to the judges?" he asks Philip, and,
besides the neat slippage between future Palestinian judges and actual
current readers of the novel, the goal of Smilesburger's verbal tactic here
reveals itself: to push Philip a little further toward his decision to spy
on Ziad for the Israeli state. Nonetheless, the trial Smilesburger invents
for the purpose of persuasion reveals how very different Jewish justice
would look if the roles of judge and defendant were reversed, and gives
extra weight to early Zionist Ahad Ha'am's statement that "they who
judge today will not escape scot free from the tribunal of tomorrow"

(qtd. in Rose 102). Additionally, Smilesburger's vision of a Palestinian court is filtered through his own ideological perspective, one where Palestinians would want, and would pursue, total revenge against any and all Jewish people who considered themselves Zionist.

The Demjanjuk trial, the West Bank military court, a future Palestinian war crimes trial: why would Roth include all of these elements in his novel if not to get readers to think critically about ideas of Jewish justice, Jewish vengeance, Jewish violence, Jewish oppression, and Jewish horror? And while the question of what exactly the novel has to say about these pressing moral and political issues is perhaps ultimately an unanswerable one, dependant as it is on one's own ideological perspective—not to mention that day's feelings toward a notoriously difficult text—Roth asks us, through his inclusion of all of these iterations of justice, to not take the claims of the Israeli state at face value. In the context of the tensions between diaspora and nationalism central to my reading here, I believe that the novel has to be read as coming down clearly on the side of a diasporic world outlook, one that does not consider the arms of justice as both a retributive tool and a means of violent occupation and oppression. The geography of Jewish justice mapped out in *Operation Shylock* (a mapping out that is only possible in the physics lab of fiction) is one that, when grouped together, juxtaposed, and unpacked, acts to dedoxify the Zionist narrative of Israel as the final moral arbiter of the Jewish people.

There is one more conclusion I would like to draw out of this discussion of the impossibilities of Jewish justice, and that looks back to the discussion of Kafka and Demjanjuk. Is it possible that not only Kafka's version of justice, as espoused in texts like *The Trial*—a justice never arrived, always postponed, and therefore messianic—but also his writings on departure and arrival more generally, constitute a more Jewish version of justice than the one promulgated by Israel and Zionism? In her reading of Kafka's fables, Butler suggests that

> in Kafka's parable and other writings we find brief
> meditations on the question of going somewhere, of going
> over, of the impossibility of arrival and the unrealisabil-
> ity of a goal. I want to suggest that many of these parables
> seem to allegorise a way of checking the desire to emigrate
> to Palestine, opening instead an infinite distance between

the one place and the other—and so constitute a non-Zionist
theological gesture. (np)

In fact, the Boyarins locate a form of this Kafkaesque eternal deferment in
the Bible itself, writing that "the biblical story is not one of autochthony
but one of always already coming from somewhere else" ("Generation and
the Ground" 715) and that "Any notion, then, of redemption through Land
must either be infinitely deferred...or become a moral monster" (714).
The moral monster the Boyarins warn against is on full display in Roth's
representation of Jewish justice in the Jewish state. Finally, Dobozy
and McLoughlin's reading of the Demjanjuk trial in Shylock also fits this
paradigm of infinite deferral: the Shoah can never be properly spoken
or witnessed, which paradoxically calls for its ceaseless speaking and
witnessing; though closure will never come, it is our ethical obligation to
never stop speaking, to continuously maintain diasporic heteroglossia in
the face of state violence and genocidal horror.

"No More Suitcases, No More Jews":
Diasporism and Zionism

When Philip discovers that somebody pretending to be him is travelling
around Israel and Europe espousing the tenets of the political ideology
that he calls Diasporism, it is the act of impersonation more than anything
else that rankles him. Philip is not necessarily wrong about this: much of
the novel's action, comedy, and absurdity spring from the act of Pipik's
doubling, and this has been one of the more salient aspects of the text for
Roth's critics. While my reading of the novel will not dwell on the relationship between Philip and his double,[13] it will unpack Diasporism, which
is, after all, Pipik's invention. Even with all of the theory's ahistoricality,
obvious hyperbole, satiric intent, and problematic implications,[14] the
ideology that Pipik frames as the solution to Zionism—with Pipik himself
as the nascent movement's Herzl—has a lot to show us about Zionism,
diaspora, Jewish geography, and Jewish history. With Diasporism, Roth
has created a fictional mechanism that talks back to the essentialist,
monomaniacal, messianic attributes of Zionism.

    The ins and outs of Pipik's Diasporism are worth summarizing.[15]
Diasporism is structured as the mirror image of Zionism: where Zionism

locates its central problem as the everlasting antisemitism of Europe and the solution to this problem as the establishment of a Jewish state in the biblical homeland of the Jewish people, Diasporism locates its central problem as the very *existence* of a Jewish state, with the solution entailing Israel's Ashkenazi Jewish inhabitants' return to their European countries of origin. The reason Israel is Diasporism's central problem is simple: "Israel," in Pipik's formulation, "has become the gravest threat to Jewish survival since World War II" (41). This is due mainly to the threat of Arab destruction: "The destruction of Israel in a nuclear exchange is a possibility much less farfetched today than was the Holocaust itself fifty years ago" (43). Furthermore, Europe, not Israel, is "the most authentic Jewish homeland there has ever been, the birthplace of rabbinic Judaism, Hasidic Judaism, Jewish secularism, socialism—on and on" (32). Europe is also, of course, the birthplace of Zionism, a fact that Pipik does not shy away from pointing out. But Zionism "has outlived its historical function. The time has come to renew in the European Diaspora our preeminent spiritual and cultural role" (32). (By claiming that Zionism had a historical function at all, Pipik is dabbling in post-Zionism here.) Diasporism sees the garrison mentality of the Israeli state as horribly damaging, at the same time it sees the destruction of the Israeli Jewish population at the hands of the "Arabs" as a very real possibility, and as the tragic continuation of Hitler's exterminatory project. As the creator, main (sole) polemicist, and ambassador of Diasporism, Pipik models himself on Theodor Herzl, the father of political Zionism. Pipik claims to have studied Herzl's life and diaries (46), and is planning on using Herzl's negotiations with the Ottoman sultan as the model for his upcoming meetings with the president of Romania (46) (this meeting is a telling moment of Rothian satire). Even Philip makes the connection, writing that Pipik is a "stentorian Diasporist Herzl" (72). Roth's comparison of Pipik with Herzl is a brilliant satirical move, somewhat dampening the critique of Diasporism being impossible; as Pipik points out numerous times, Diasporism is as impossible seeming as Zionism was in Herzl's time.[16] Overall, the thrust of Diasporism can perhaps best be summed up in Pipik's own pithy equation: "Zionism has tragically ruined its own health and must now accede to vigorous Diasporism" (44). Daniel Lazare elaborates on the health of diaspora Jews and Israelis, writing that "The 'neuroticism' of the Diaspora Jew is actually the result of political and ethical engagement with an imperfect, conflict-ridden world, whereas Zionist 'health' is the result of the opposite: ethical disengagement and surrender to the amoral realpolitik that governs relations between and among nation-states" (Tikkun np). Lazare believes that "In a moral sense, it's healthier to be neurotic" (np). This neuroticism is yet another facet of the diaspora existence, the need to be aware of the political violence of the world, while not being/becoming a part of it.

When Philip puts on his Pipik impression, he does not stray too far from the original tenets of Diasporism, though he does add to it, and in some cases further satirizes it. He tells the Ziads that after his successful meeting with Lech Walesa he is setting up an audience with the pope. His talk of a "World Diasporist Congress" (156) furthers the comparison to early Zionism, at the same time it mercilessly satirizes it. Philip goes on a long tangent about how Irving Berlin is the "greatest Diasporist of all" (157), and fleshes out Pipik's fear of nuclear war, except he flips it on its head: it is no longer nuclear destruction at the hands of the Arabs that Diasporism fears, but the moral toll on the Jewish soul itself if Israel is forced to drop the bomb.[17] The state might survive, Philip intones, but with the loss of morality that comes from deploying nuclear weapons, there would no longer be Jews as such to populate the state. "The Israelis will have saved their state by destroying their people," Philip-as-Pipik laments: "They will never survive morally after that; and if they don't why survive as Jews at all?" (158). This equation of being Jewish as being moral is one that simmers just under the textual surface of the novel. Moreover, when Philip mentions this fear of the Jewish nuclear bomb in his summary of Diasporism in chapter 8's rundown on the novel's plot thus far, Pipik's Diasporism and Philip's Diasporism have melted together. When Philip continues the Pipik masquerade to Gal, the Israeli soldier who has stopped Philip's taxi on the way back from Ziad's house in Ramallah, Philip declares that "Diaspora is the normal condition and Zionism is the abnormality" (170). A wide range of Jewish thinkers, including the Boyarins, George Steiner, and Judith Butler, would concur. Even Gal, who as disillusioned with the Israeli state and army as he is still holds fast to liberal Zionist precepts, sees the danger of a state based on ethnic superiority. When Gal's father says, "Take the British, put them here, face them with what we are facing—they would act out of morality? The Canadians would act out of morality? The French? A state does not act out of moral ideology, a state acts out of self-interest. A state acts to preserve its existence," Gal responds by stating, "maybe I prefer to be stateless" (169). (Of course, the British, Canadian, and French states *already* act immorally, which somewhat furthers Roth's point.) If the choice is between acting moral or being a state, Gal suggests, he would pick being moral, even if, as his father believes, "We tried it...It didn't work out" (169). Diasporism is Pipik's attempt to try it again.

From an anti-Zionist perspective, the most troubling aspect of Diasporism is Pipik's antipathy toward the Arabs. Anti-Islamism appears to be a core feature of Diasporism. Pipik is quoted in the newspaper interview as saying: "The so-called normalization of the Jew was a tragic illusion from the start. But when this normalization is expected to flourish in the very heart of Islam, it is even worse than tragic—it is suicidal" (32). This sentiment is totally ahistorical, ignoring those long periods when Judaism and Islam did "flourish" together, most significantly in Muslim Iberia, but also in Iraq, Iran, and other Muslim countries until the 1950s (see chapter 3). Moreover, it elides the very real reasons for Palestinian antipathy toward Israeli Jews, acting as if their feelings exist in a vacuum. The reason this so-called Jewish normalization is suicidal, for Pipik, is because "Exterminating a Jewish nation would cause Islam to lose not a single night's sleep, except for the great night of celebration" (45). Zionism is dangerous specifically because it locates its state in the heartland of the West's deepest Orientalist fantasies: "Diasporism plans to rebuild *everything*, not in an alien and menacing Middle East but in those very lands where everything once flourished, while, at the same time, it seeks to avert the catastrophe of a second Holocaust brought about by the exhaustion of Zionism as a political and ideological force" (44). This "second Holocaust" would be at the hands of the Arabs, specifically the Muslim Arabs (Pipik makes no distinction between Christian and Muslim Arabs, though, as we will see below, he does make room for Jewish Arabs in his calculations). As already quoted above, "The destruction of Israel in a nuclear exchange is a possibility much less farfetched today than was the Holocaust itself fifty years ago" (43). The problems with this are manifold: 1) Pipik makes no distinction between Arab states, Arab individuals, Arab governments, or the Palestinians; and 2) Pipik implicitly believes that Arab hatred of Israel and of Jews is a historical given that has nothing to do with Israel's actions, policies, laws, or cultural assumptions. Pipik is not the only character in the novel to feel this way. Gal, though fed up with the current government and his own role in the occupation, still tows the Zionist line: "It is Israel's fate to live in an Arab sea. Jews accepted this fate rather than have nothing and no fate. Jews accepted partition and the Arabs did not" (169–170). This is one of the central elements of the Zionist creation myth. Gal continues: if the Arabs "said yes, my father reminds me, they would be celebrating forty years of statehood too. But every political decision with which they have been confronted, invariably they have made the wrong choice... Nine tenths of their misery they owe to the idiocy of their own political leaders" (170). While there might be some truth to this, the case is greatly overstated.[18] Philip mildly calls Pipik out on this, "So what Diasporism comes down to is fearful Jews in flight, terrified Jews once again running away" (45). Pipik answers: "To flee an imminent cataclysm is 'running' away only from extinction. It is running *toward* life" (45). Pipik goes on to state that more Jews should have fled Germany in the 1930s, to which Philip (pretending to be the French journalist Pierre Roget) replies that they would have if they had had somewhere to go. Both of these statements have historical validity, and neither excuse Pipik's Orientalism nor Israel's violent, ongoing displacement of the Palestinians.

In other ways, too, the narrative itself works against Pipik's anti-Arab sentiments. "I think you would agree," he tells Pierre/Philip, "that a Jew is safer today walking aimlessly around Berlin than going unarmed into the streets of Ramallah" (45). This—going unarmed into the streets of Ramallah—is exactly what Philip does later in the novel, coming to no harm. Moreover, Philip's life is more at risk at the hands of Israeli Jews than of Arabs or Palestinians, deflating Pipik's fears further through humanizing the so successfully othered Palestinians. Finally, it is necessary to point out that Pipik's plans for the resettlement of Ashkenazi Jews in Europe exclude the Arab Jews who also emigrated to Israel. Pipik states: "The Jews of Islam have their own, very different destiny. I am not proposing that Israeli Jews whose origins are in Islamic countries return to Europe, since for them this would constitute not a home-coming but a radical uprooting" (42). In Pipik's plan, the Arab Jews will remain in a de-militarized Israel, among their Arab brethren, in peace. The Mizrahi or Arab Jews have always been an integral but often overlooked part of the Israeli/Zionist story; I will explore the figure of the Arab Jew in chapter 3.

For now, suffice it to say that Pipik's anti-Arab racism appears to extend to the Jewish Arab citizens of Israel as well.[19]

True to its nature as a heteroglossic novel, we are treated to a wide array of responses to Diasporism. As already mentioned, Lech Walesa—in a stroke of satiric genius—is on board with the resettlement program, declaring that "Poland needs Jews" (31). The idea of Poland excitedly accepting thousands of Jewish settlers, Poles literally crowding the train stations to "welcome them," "jubilant" and "in tears" (45), is one of the more far-fetched aspects of Diasporism—one that, nonetheless, speaks to a very real problem with the idealization of diaspora: its dependence on the magnanimity of the host country.[20] Walesa goes on to proclaim that we should be talking about "a thousand years of [Jewish/Yiddish] glory rather than four years of war" (31), a sentiment Pipik corroborates when he tells Pierre to "not confuse our long European history with the twelve years of Hitler's reign" (42). While the Jewish experience in Europe should not be forgotten or discarded, neither should what happened during Hitler's reign: both need to be held in the head together, the promise of diaspora and its hideous, disastrous pitfalls. Besides Walesa, we get Wanda "Jinx" Posseski, Pipik's girlfriend and a recovering antisemite, who, to no surprise, fully supports Pipik's program. There is also Smilesburger, disguised as an elderly Jewish American retiree who wants to donate a million dollars to the Diasporism cause, who has this to say: "Before it's too late, Mr. Roth, before God sends to massacre the Jews without souls a hundred million Arabs screaming to Allah, I wish to make a contribution" (110). Note that Smilesburger (who is playing a role here) fully agrees with Pipik's anti-Arab feelings. Smilesburger's interruption of Philip and Aharon Appelfeld's lunch leads to an amazing exchange. Smilesburger asks Aharon if he owns a suitcase. "Threw it away," Aharon responds (111). Smilesburger: "Mistake...No more suitcases, no more Jews" (111). Smilesburger, a ruthless Mossad agent who in many ways orchestrates the events of the novel (not least with the one-million-dollar check he hands Philip, pretending to mistake him for Pipik), masquerading as an elderly American Jew painfully disillusioned with Zionism and with Israel, gives voice to a central belief of the diasporic existence. Ziad takes to Diasporism with activist zeal: "Old friend, we need you, we all need you, the occupiers as much as the occupied need your Diaspora boldness and your Diaspora brains...You come with a vision, a fresh and brilliant vision to resolve it—not a lunatic utopian Palestinian dream or a terrible Zionist final solution but a profoundly conceived historical arrangement that is workable, that is *just*" (137). We also hear from Philip. At first, he acts as if he is totally uninterested, focused entirely on Pipik as double. "I am not even against his so-called Diasporism," he tells Jinx, "I have no interest in those ideas either way" (98). Later, he admits to Pipik: "the vehemence and intelligence of your criticism of Israel makes you into something more than just a crackpot…The argument for Diasporism isn't always as farcical as you make it sound. There's a mad plausibility about it. There's more than a grain of truth in recognizing and acknowledging the Eurocentrism of Judaism, of the Judaism that gave birth to Zionism, and so forth. Yet it also strikes me, I'm afraid, like the voice of puerile wishful thinking" (191).

So: what *are* we supposed to make of Diasporism? Diasporism is highly problematic with its already-discussed Arab racism, but also in its discarding of Israeli culture and identity, and its impossible wish for Jewish rebirth and renewal through mass immigration—what Philip rightly calls "antihistorically harebrained" (287). Nonetheless, I would argue that besides its obvious flaws—and even *in light* of them— Diasporism acts as a mechanism that dismantles the Zionist narrative, and ends up coming down hard on the side of diaspora over ethnic nationalism. Morris Dickstein concurs, writing that Diasporism "is not only a rebuttal to Zionism but a mischievous parody of it, with its own Law of Return, casting Israel itself as the vulnerable and suffocating Jewish ghetto" (*Tikkun* np).[21] What Diasporism surfaces is the always-present possibility for radical change. While the Ashkenazi Jews leaving Israel for their ancestral European homes seems impossible, even thinking about it opens up other possibilities. For one, the Ashkenazi Jewish population leaving Israel will not alleviate the problems with Israel, because the problems stem not from the Jewish population, but from ideology, ethnic nationalism, and their manifestation in the government, army, and institutions of the state. If, instead, we followed the Boyarins' suggestion that Israel "reimports diasporic consciousness—a consciousness of a Jewish collective as one sharing space with others, devoid of exclusivist and dominating power" (*Powers of Diaspora* 103), Zionism could be reworked from within. Pipik's Diasporism, given full voice in Shylock's diasporic heteroglossia, opens up such possibilities for what the Boyarins call "a specieswide care" that does not eradicate "cultural difference" (103). Regardless of how Roth intended Diasporism—whether as straight-up satire or nuanced conceptualization—Pipik's theories, once let loose in the heteroglossic stew of the novel, help bring Zionism down a notch or two, and reinvigorate the ethical possibilities of a non-exclusionary, non-autochthonous, and non-militarized diaspora, within or without Israel.

"Palestine is a lie! Zionism is a lie! Diasporism is a lie!": *Shylock*'s Palestinians

In *The Counterlife*, Zuckerman does not encounter any Palestinians, nor does he engage with any Palestinian narrative. Roth self-corrects that error in *Shylock*, not only through the creation of nuanced Palestinian characters, but by opening a narrative space in the novel to allow a range of Palestinian perspectives, outlooks, and worldviews to exist on a somewhat level playing field with the novel's other voices. George Ziad, his wife Anna, and his friend Kamil—it is Kamil's brother who is on the docket in the Ramallah military court—are some of the most fully-realized, complex, voluble, heart-breaking Palestinian characters in Jewish North American fiction. It is here, through these Palestinian characters, though mostly through Ziad, that the diasporic heteroglossia of the novel is on its fullest display. Roth, in giving Ziad room to speak his mind, make his case, and reveal his foibles and blindspots, commits to the diasporic heteroglossic call to counter any and all hegemonic voices with those of the Other, the dispersed, and the dispossessed.

I agree with Karen Grumberg that Ziad is "One of Roth's most fascinating characters" (36); a good part of the reason for this comes from Ziad's total, destabilizing transformation from the dapper literary student Philip knew in graduate school to the obsessed, paranoid (though not delusional), depleted political activist with whom Philip becomes entangled when Ziad purposefully runs into him in the Jerusalem market. The differences between the two men at their reunion are striking. Unlike Philip, Ziad has become consumed by the Israeli/Palestinian conflict. Returning to Ramallah after a lifetime in the Palestinian diaspora, Ziad has given himself—and his wife and teenage son, somewhat against their wills—to the Palestinian cause. Roth brilliantly bases Ziad's internal conflict on one between father and son, placing him in the same company of many of Roth's characters and alter egos. Ziad's father was a successful middle-class Christian Palestinian living in Jerusalem, who fled for Egypt with his young family after the creation of the Israeli state. When Ziad was young, he had attempted to distance himself from his father's devotion to his lost home, to the house that was "still exactly where it was" (120). Ziad tells Philip that since his father "couldn't forget...I would" (120). Ziad's father was constantly "Weeping and ranting all day long about everything he had lost to the Jews: his house, his practice, his patients, his books, his art, his garden, his almond trees—every day he screamed, he wept, he ranted, and I was a wonderful son, Philip. I couldn't forgive him his despair for the almond trees" (120). It was not until his father passed away that Ziad's own longing awoke in him: "And now the trees and the house and the garden are all I can think about. My father and his ranting are all I can think about. I think about his tears every day. And that, to my surprise, is who I am" (121). Roth shows how the success of the Israeli state created the Palestinian refugee problem, along with Palestinian shame, Palestinian anger, and Palestinian resistance.[22]

Philip is astounded at Ziad's transformation: "he'd been living under an ice cap, a son trying in vain to stanch the bleeding of a wronged and ruined father, with his wonderful manners and his refined virility not only masking the pain of dispossession and exile but concealing even from himself how scorched he was by shame, perhaps even more so than the father" (123). Philip sees Ziad's struggles as inter-generational to their core: "The shaming nationalism that the fathers throw on the backs of their sons, each generation, I thought, imposing its struggle on the next. Yet that was their family's big drama and the one that weighed on George Ziad like a stone" (151). As we will see in the next chapter, unlike *Altneuland*'s Reschid Bey, who is a one-dimensional representative of the Arabs, speaking German to his fellow Jewish citizens, grateful for the Jewish settlement of Palestine, which was a blessing for all Arabs (and whose wife is not allowed to speak in front of men), and unlike the Arabs in *Exodus*, either bloodthirsty murderers and rapists or apologists for the murderers and rapists, George Ziad is a character within and beyond his Arabness.

This is not to imply that Ziad does not represent the Palestinian narrative as well. Roth gives Ziad all the space he needs to explicate the Palestinian position, and Ziad voraciously takes it. "Alas, I am not a stone-throwing Arab," he admits, "I am a word-throwing Arab, soft, sentimental, and ineffective, altogether like my father" (121). Philip concurs: "George never stopped talking; he couldn't stop. An unbridled talker. An inexhaustible talker. A frightening talker" (128). Grumberg goes so far as to call Ziad a "frenzied hysteric" (49). All this goes to show how important Ziad is to the novel's diasporic heteroglossia. Ziad mercilessly critiques the occupation, the Israeli government, the Israeli army, Israeli culture, Israeli identity, Israeli accomplishments, and Israeli arrogance. Ziad hammers particularly hard at Zionism's use of the Shoah as justification for the crimes of Israel: "The state of Israel has drawn the last of its moral credit out of the bank of the dead six million—this is what they have done by breaking the hands of Arab children on the orders of their illustrious minister of defence. Even to world Jewry it will be clear: this is a state founded on force and maintained by force" (135). As Andrew Furman rightly points out, Ziad's claim "cuts to the heart of the real life concerns of several Jews on the political left" (146) (though at least one of the two examples Furman gives of these left-wing Jews, Thomas Friedman, has not aged so well). Ziad, like the sleep-and-food-deprived Philip, is paranoid, suspicious of everybody, and prone to conspiracy. There is an obvious resonance here with Lazare's belief that to be neurotic in an "imperfect, conflict-ridden world" is a deeply ethical response (Tikkun np). Importantly, Ziad does not give his fellow Palestinians a free pass. "Because I," he tells Philip, "who will not capitulate, am a patriot too, who loves and hates his defeated, cringing Palestinians probably in the same proportion that you, Philip, love and hate your smug, self-satisfied Jews" (136). Ziad is yet another shadow of Philip, one whose main differences are where he was born, to whom, and on what side of the Semitic divide.

One of Ziad's main rhetorical moves is to compare the Israeli Jew—which he sees as corrupt, bankrupt, and over-militarized— with the diaspora Jew, in particular his rather idealistic vision of the American Jew. In a much-quoted line, Ziad tells Philip: "There is more Jewish spirit and Jewish laughter and Jewish intelligence on the Upper West Side of Manhattan than in this entire country—and as for Jewish conscience, as for a Jewish sense of justice, as for Jewish heart...there's more Jewish heart at the knish counter at Zabar's than in the whole of the Knesset!" (122).[23] Ziad teaches Portnoy's Complaint to his students, trying to "convince them that there are Jews in the world who are not in any way like these Jews we have here. But to them the Israeli Jew is so evil they find it hard to believe" (122). Ziad's elevation of the diaspora Jew at the expense of the Israeli Jew has some striking resemblances to the Boyarins' own thinking on diaspora: Ziad laments that "people with the Jewish sense of survival that was all human, elastic, adaptable, humorous, creative, and all this they have replaced here with a stick! The Golden Calf was more Jewish than Ariel Sharon, God of Samaria and Judea and the Holy Gaza Strip!" (126). Ziad intuitively grasps that the Boyarins' Jewish particularism plus political power, what Marc Ellis brilliantly terms "Constantinian Judaism" (qtd. in Landy 57), is a violent aberration from Jewish diasporic survival.

Moreover, Ziad is not just a walking critique of Israel; Roth is careful to humanize Ziad's outpourings. For starters, not everything he says is factually correct. He offhandedly claims, for example, that Meryl Streep played a Jew in the NBC Holocaust miniseries, which is not true: she played a Christian German who married a Jew, an intermarriage that supplies pivotal dramatic tension to the television narrative. As well, Ziad is tragically aware of the toll his passion is taking on his family, and is wracked with guilt. "My stupidity...My fucking stupidity!" he laments in a moment where his ideological ire is lowered (163). Philip responds skeptically to his transformed friend: "at the core of everything was hatred and the great disabling fantasy of revenge" (129). Ziad is aware of how he comes across: "You think, He is crazy, hysterical, reckless, wild. And what if I am—wouldn't you be? Jews! Jews! Jews! How can I not think continually about Jews! Jews are my jailers, I am their prisoner. And, as my wife will tell you, there is nothing I have less talent for than being a prisoner" (136). These moments of doubt humanize Ziad, while not letting go of the fact that it was Israeli settler colonialism that created the situation Ziad finds himself in.

Philip seems unable to make his mind up about Ziad. At times, he wonders if he is a double agent, working for the Mossad. At times, he thinks his mind is gone. At other times, Ziad very clearly has a better handle on the situation than Philip does. When Ziad states that Israel is a military state, "established by force, maintained by force, committed to force and repression," Philip responds by saying, "Please, I don't see it that way" (271). In this case, Ziad's statement has more truth than Philip wants to admit. Overall, Ziad, far less ideological or radical than he has been read, is Roth's deepest mining of what oppression and dehumanization can do to one's identity and sense of self. The fact that Ziad is the only major character in the novel to die (the death of Pipik is also reported, but in a letter Philip imagines Jinx writing him) further shows how precarious Ziad's position as a voluble Palestinian is.

Though critics have taken offense at Ziad's accusations, with Dobozy calling him "rabidly anti-Zionist" (41), for example (with the term anti-Zionist loaded with negative connotations here), Andrew Furman is correct to note that "Roth's depiction of the contemporary Middle East scene goes a long way toward salvaging George Ziad's credibility" (147). Omer-Sherman disagrees with Furman, writing in regard to Shylock that "at the heart of the novel lies an essential conservatism. For as much as the Palestinian Ziad (who loves Diaspora Jews but hates Israelis) and Moishe Pipik's diasporism [sic] may speak to a reader's heart, Roth forces the rhetoric of both characters to such absurd extremes that the moral validity of their arguments collapses" (233). We have already looked in the prior section at how Pipik's Diasporism is not so much about the *valid-ity* of its argument—though it does have some validity, nonetheless—but how it acts as a mechanism to trouble Zionism. Likewise, I question to what "absurd extremes" Ziad's rhetoric really goes. At times, yes, Ziad slips into over-generalization and stereotypes the Israeli Jewish character, but Roth carefully tempers these moments by filtering them through Ziad's own paranoia, neuroticism, and impending mental collapse; nevertheless, the core of Ziad's critique of Israeli nationalism, Israeli ethnic cleansing of Palestinians, and the loss of the Jewish diasporic consciousness endemic to the Israeli character all carry substantial weight. Though I (surprisingly) have not encountered any critic who wonders where Roth got the content for Ziad's speeches, one likely source is Edward Said, who was, when Roth was writing, the most visible Palestinian critic of Israel (also note the similarity of their last names, and the fact that both men are Christian Arabs). In his book *The Question of Palestine*—first published in 1979—for example, Said's stated goal is to try to place the Palestinian question into the minds of the West, to dispose of the dominant perception of the Palestinian merely as a terrorist.

Said makes an extremely convincing case that Zionism—built on European imperialism and colonialism—through a wide range of institutions, narratives, and hegemonic practices, has managed to successfully render the Arab inhabitants of Palestine invisible. Said is an extremely careful thinker, paying heed to the power of Zionism and the need for relief after the Jewish catastrophes of Europe, as well as constantly stating his horror at the violence perpetrated by both sides. Said writes that "whereas Israel and its history have been celebrated without interruption, the actuality of Palestinians, with lives being led, small histories endured, aspirations felt, has only recently been conceded an existence" (xxxix). Similar to Ziad, Said wonders if "our dispossession and our effacement, by which almost a million of us were made to leave Palestine and our society made nonexistent, [were] justified even to save the remnant of European Jews that had survived Nazism?" (xlii–xliii). Furthermore, he admits that "Such as it is, the Palestinian actuality is today, was yesterday, and most likely tomorrow will be built upon an act of resistance to this new foreign colonialism" (8), words that still hold true today. Said makes a compelling case for how Zionism and "its Western ideological parents" used Orientalism: "it is a perfect instance of how propaganda, politicized scholarship, and ideological information have power, implement policy, and, at the same time, can appear to be 'objective truth'" (26). Showing his compassion toward all peoples in the region, Jewish and Arab, Said writes:

> Much of the despair and pessimism that one feels at the whole Palestinian–Zionist conflict is each side's failure in a sense to reckon with the existential power and presence of *another* people with its land, its unfortunate history of suffering, its emotional and political investment in that land, and worse, to pretend that the Other is a temporary nuisance that, given time and effort (and punitive violence from time to time), will finally go away. (49)

In a statement with which I wholeheartedly agree, Said concludes: "The actuality is that Palestinian and Israeli Jews are now fully implicated in each others' [sic] lives and political destinies, perhaps not in any ultimate way—which is a subject not easily bracketed in rational discussion— but certainly now and in the forseeable future" (49). With this brief foray into Said's thinking on Israel/Palestine, it becomes abundantly clear that Roth's Ziad did not come out of nowhere, and that Ziad, as Furman suggests, has plenty of historical and political reality behind his sometimes-overblown lamentations. Shylock's diasporic heteroglossia, which makes abundant room for Palestinians to speak, is firmly grounded in real-world Palestinian thought and language.

Roth goes farther than giving us only one Palestinian character; most significantly, there is Anna Ziad, George's wife, who, unlike Reschid Bey's wife in *Altneuland*, gets the chance to speak her mind (if minimally, compared to Ziad), and in mixed company. In Anna, we see yet another Palestinian position: that of the tired realist. Anna is a humanist, as skeptical of Palestinian nationalism as she is of Zionism. Her overriding concern is the well-being of her son, Michael, who has not taken to the new conditions of their life and is about to be sent back to America. Anna sees the Israeli/Palestinian conflict as one between victims, and rightly sees that that particular formulation cannot work, or lead to a solution: "how many victims can possibly stand on this tiny bit of soil?" (160), she asks Philip. Anna does not have high hopes for the future of the region: "There is nothing in the future for these Jews and these Arabs but more tragedy, suffering, and blood. The hatred on both sides is too enormous, it envelops everything. There is no trust and there will not be for another thousand years" (161). Anna manifests a certain diasporic cosmopolitanism in her critique of Ziad's and Philip's—though here, remember, she is mistaking Philip for Pipik—re-entry into ethnic strife. "You were right to run," she says, "both of you, as far as you could from the provincialism and the egocentricity and the xenophobia and the lamentations, you were not poisoned by the sentimentality of these childish, stupid ethnic mythologies, you plunged into a big, new, free world with all your intellect and all your energy, truly free young men, devoted to art, books, reason, scholarship, to *seriousness*" (161). Though she is a minor character whose time on the page is infinitesimal compared to Ziad, Roth allows Anna's pointed anger to give her an enlarged presence in the text.

In direct contrast to her husband, Anna does not see a Palestinian state as a solution to the conflict. "Now there can be a Palestinian flag flying from every building and everybody can stand up and salute it twenty times a day," Anna says with unmistakable sarcasm, when Ziad shows her Smilesburger's million-dollar cheque. She goes on, "Now we can have our own money, with Father Arafat's portrait on our very own bills...Palestinian Paradise is at hand" (160). Anna rightly shows here that entrenched Palestinian nationalism, once wedded to power (again: particularism plus power), would not be an outcome any more ethical or just than that of the Israeli state. Would Anna have agreed, then, with Ali Abunimah, who, in both One Country: A Bold Proposal to End the Israeli-Palestinian Impasse and The Battle for Justice in Palestine, makes the case for a single, binational (but not nationalistic) state in all of historic Palestine?[24] Though we can never know the answer to this question, in her best lines, Anna nonetheless tears apart any ideological conviction as fabricated, as arbitrary. "Palestine is a lie!" she declares, to an exasperated Ziad and Philip—the latter of whom is himself astounded at his Diasporist scree, thinking all the while, "My sympathies were entirely with George's wife" (158)—"Zionism is a lie! Diasporism is a lie! The biggest lie yet! I will not sacrifice Michael to more lies!" (162). In an important way, Anna is right that all of these things are lies, because the very container of nationness is a lie. What is not a lie, however, is the reality of Palestinian oppression at the hands of the Israelis.

Andrew Furman rightly critiques the moments where Arab voices and narratives are missing, stereotyped, or oversimplified (more so in The Counterlife than in Operation Shylock). "The critics' refusal," he concludes, "to acknowledge the absent 'other' [i.e., Palestinians] in The Counterlife raises interesting questions concerning their unconscious complicity in the anti-Arab strategies that Roth employs (also unconsciously, I believe) through his narrative" (142). However, immediately after saying this, he somewhat backtracks: "That said, let me note that I do not presume to prescribe a short list of mandatory voices the Jewish-American writer must create when thoughts of Israel bestir the imagination (e.g., one Arab voice/one American voice/one Israeli voice)" (142). He then further qualifies that statement by writing that The Counterlife's "absence of Arab voices contributes to the anti-Arab elements of the text" (142). I would like to consider further Furman's idea of "mandatory voices." While I might agree that the characters or voices in any given novel should not be "mandatory," that does not mean that they are not necessary. What I mean by this is that a Jewish novel that attempts to say something about Israel/ Palestine cannot do so without making space for Palestinian narratives (as we will see in the chapter on *The Betrayers*). Politics and ideology play a major role here, of course. In the next chapter's reading of *Altneuland* and *Exodus*, it becomes apparent that having speaking Arab or Palestinian characters does not mean that space for Palestinian narratives has been made; Palestinian characters can exist in an exclusively Zionist fictional frame. Another way of putting this is that a list of "mandatory voices" utterly misses the mark: it is not the voices that are vital here, but what they are allowed to say; in *Shylock*, it is diasporic heteroglossia that gives Ziad and Anna room to present their own narratives.

Ziad, of course, is not just there to give the Palestinian side of things; he plays a major role in the "operation" of the title. It is Ziad who organizes Philip's meeting with the supposedly Jewish backers of the PLO in Athens. Unfortunately, however, we do not get to meet these characters, as Philip deletes the chapter detailing his experiences with them. This deletion, I argue below, is an affront to the novel's otherwise robust diasporic heteroglossia, and proves that even somebody like Philip— even after what he saw in Ramallah and heard from Ziad and from his own diasporic sense of self—is still susceptible to the pull of the Zionist metanarrative.

Against "Jewish Totalism":
Operation Shylock's Missing Chapter

So far, this chapter has looked at how *Operation Shylock* is a novel of what I call diasporic heteroglossia, or fiction that is not beholden to national ideologies and that allows divergent voices into its textual architecture. I elaborated on the problematics of Jewish justice that act as a backdrop to the events of the novel. I suggested that Pipik's Diasporism can be read as a mechanism for challenging Zionism. I showed how the novel's Palestinian characters—especially George and Anna Ziad—not only represent the Palestinian narrative but are fully-realized fictional characters in their own right. In the final section of this chapter, where I turn to the novel's (missing) ending, we will see all of these various threads converge.

The novel's epilogue opens with Philip making the startling confession that he has excised the novel's last chapter, which supposedly details his experiences spying for the Mossad on Ziad and his radical Palestinian—and possibly Jewish—compatriots in Athens, gathering information on the "Jewish anti-Zionist elements threatening the security of Israel," as Philip's handlers put it (358). My reading of this excision—and Philip's justification for it—rests on two assertions: that there is a crucial distinction between Philip the narrator and Roth the author; and that Philip's decision to "suppress those forty-odd pages" (357) goes against the nature of the diasporic heteroglossia to which the novel has otherwise been so loyal. Though critics have read the excised chapter in a number of ways—as a metaphor for the elusive nature of Jewishness (Shostak 747–750), as revealing "a common Jewish element which transcends national allegiances and differences" (Lehmann 92–93), and as a refusal to practice loshon hora, Hebrew for gossip, which Smilesburger gives a multi-page lecture on as the downfall of the Jewish people (Parrish 590)—I am most interested in the ethical implications of the excision itself. The fact that Philip gives in to the demands of the Israeli state as embodied by Smilesburger—not just by removing the chapter, but by agreeing to become a spy in the first place—does not mean that Roth the author condones this behaviour; no robust understanding of fiction should allow for this slippage between author and narrator. In reading Philip the narrator *against* Roth the author, I suggest that Philip's self-censorship is *meant* to be read as unethical, and as against the heteroglossic dialogism of the novel, showing, in the words of Omer-Sherman, "how easily Jewish Americans are duped, for the sake of 'identity,' into supporting Israel's breaches of Jewish ethics" (233).[25]

The epilogue, which is long enough to stand as its own chapter, is almost entirely concerned with Philip's decision to remove the final chapter.[26] It opens with the confession of the excision itself:

> I have elected to delete my final chapter, twelve thousand
> words describing the people I convened with in Athens,
> the circumstances that brought us together, and the subse-
> quent expedition, to a second European capital, that devel-
> oped out of that educational Athens weekend. Of this entire
> book, whose completed manuscript Smilesburger had

asked to inspect, only the contents of chapter 11, "Operation Shylock," were deemed by him to contain information too seriously detrimental to his agency's interests and to the Israeli government to be published in English, let alone in some fifteen other languages. (357)

Several things stand out immediately in this blunt opening paragraph. Most telling, perhaps, is that the title of the removed chapter is "Operation Shylock," the code name of Philip's spy mission and the title of the novel itself, clearly signifying the thematic importance of the deleted chapter to the book as a whole. Timothy Parrish writes that the fact that "the missing episode depicting his spy mission, his chosen silence, becomes the title for the book suggests that *Operation Shylock* is not so much about the stories that Roth has told, as critics have always complained, but the story he has not told" (592) (notice the slippage between Philip and Roth here).[27] Second, Philip gives us a tantalizing hint of what is in the missing chapter: apparently, not only was his mission to Athens a success, but he continued on to a "second European capital." What did he see there, what voices was he exposed to, what *happened*? We will never know. Finally, Philip insists, as he does throughout the epilogue, that the decision to excise the final chapter was his and his alone—he "elected" to have it removed. Elect is an interesting word choice. According to the *Oxford English Dictionary*, it could mean "To pick out, choose," which is the primary meaning here. However, it could also mean "To choose (a person) by vote for appointment to an office or position of any kind," which resonates with voting processes, citizenship, and the ethnic democracy of Israel. It could also mean "Of God: to choose (certain of his creatures) in preference to others, as the recipients of temporal or spiritual blessings" ("Elect"), which here could refer to the Jewish people as God's "chosen people," or, in other words, the special group of people in whose name Philip took on the spy mission and for whose benefit he lopped off the eleventh chapter, revealing the ethnocentric character of the Israeli state. For the above reasons, it would not be a stretch to claim that the missing chapter is the most significant element of *Shylock*. Philip's decision to elect to suppress the eleventh chapter, which he claims to have come to on his own, is the most drastic thing Philip does in a novel of drastic decisions.

As we find out later in the epilogue, however, the decision was not entirely Philip's to make; Smilesburger has deployed intense pressure on Philip to remove the chapter. Though Philip realizes "how specious were my reasons for getting myself to do as he'd asked" (376), Philip still seems unable to not conform to Smilesburger's demands. The fact that Philip sent Smilesburger the manuscript for inspection in the first place should give us pause. "Never in my life had I submitted a manuscript to any inspector anywhere for this sort of scrutiny," Philip writes (377). Once Smilesburger makes his demand to remove the chapter known (though at first he only suggests Philip change it or fictionalize it), Philip goes through a series of arguments for keeping the chapter in. He defends the chapter's verisimilitude: "I went where I went, I did what I did, met whom I met, saw what I saw, learned what I learned—and nothing that occurred in Athens, absolutely nothing, is interchangeable with something else" (383). A little later, Smilesburger attacks even this claim of verisimilitude: "This is not a report of what happened, because, very simply, you haven't the slightest idea of what happened. You grasp almost nothing of the objective reality. Its meaning evades you completely" (390). Philip states that he is no longer recovering from Halcion but is his old self again, back in America, writing books. In response, Smilesburger puts it bluntly: "Publish the book without its ending" (387). Smilesburger appeals to Philip as a Jew: "As a Jew you went to Athens and as a Jew you will suppress this chapter...Can you not cede to the Jews, who have given you *everything*, one eleventh of this book?" (388). In the novel's final scene, Smilesburger tries to bribe Philip, handing him a suitcase filled with money, "To cover the costs you incurred spying at the fountainhead of Western civilization" (396). Until the very end of the epilogue, Philip resists Smilesburger. Smilesburger even gets the last line in the novel: standing on the streets of New York City, outside of the restaurant where they have had lunch, with Philip asking what he should do in return for keeping the money, Smilesburger simply says, "Let your Jewish conscience be your guide" (398). Are we to believe, then, that Philip's removal of the chapter was what his "Jewish conscience" told him to do? A better reading, I suggest, is that Philip gives in not to his conscience, but to Smilesburger.

Smilesburger, as the novel's clearest representative of the Israeli state, is the one who convinces Philip to take on "Operation Shylock" in the first place. It is not insignificant that out of everybody that Philip or Ziad worries is a spy or is not who they say they are, only Smilesburger is definitively outed to not be who he originally claimed to be: the elderly American Jewish retiree who moved to Israel and who is now an ardent supporter of Diasporism. In the last extant chapter of the novel—chapter 10—we find out that Smilesburger, if not having outright orchestrated all of the events of the past two days, is at least marginally responsible for Philip's tussles with Pipik and his experiences with Ziad, corroborating Parrish's reading of Smilesburger as a "trickster figure" (598) and even Philip's own label of him as a "Borscht Belt deus ex machina" (245). "It is with intelligence agencies as it is with novelists," Smilesburger explains to Philip, "the God of Chance creates in us. First the fake one came along. Then the real one came along. Last the enterprising Ziad came along. From this we improvise" (344). It is here, with Philip kidnapped in the Hebrew school classroom, the Demjanjuk trial on the television behind them, that Smilesburger tells Philip that he wants him to spy on Ziad. The goal of the spy mission is to find out if the PLO is really backed by "two-faced fifth-column Jews" (343), as Ziad claims, a claim that Smilesburger, against his better judgment, cannot stop obsessing over.[28] Philip adamantly refuses to take on the job: "But I was not taking the job. I had not been extricated from an implausible plot of someone else's devising"—he means Pipik's—"to be intimidated into being an actor in yet another" (345). Philip (rightly) feels "cruelly misused" by "these phenomenally high-handed Israelis" (345). "They had been running me like a rat through a maze," he realizes (345). Philip's resolve holds until the end of the chapter, which is also the end of the novel proper.

And yet, Philip takes on the spy mission. In this way the ending of the tenth chapter and the ending of the epilogue mirror each other: Philip says he will not spy for the Mossad, but then he does; Philip says he will not remove the final chapter, but then he does. Philip becomes a spy for the Jewish state; Philip caves to Smilesburger's demands to hide Philip's actions during the mission, which Philip apparently performed "expertly" (381). So why, then, does Philip give in to Smilesburger's demands? "But why," in Philip's own words, "did I do it"? (358). Why does Roth have Philip turn off the novel's heteroglossic tap, which has otherwise been levered to maximum pressure for the preceding four hundred pages?

My answer to this question, pivotal to one's understanding of the novel, begins with the understanding that Philip turns his back on diasporic heteroglossia the moment he decides to become an agent of the Israeli state. In fact, this idea, that spying for Israel is actually bad for the Jewish people, is presented much earlier in the novel, when Philip encounters Pipik in the flesh for the first time. Pipik tells Philip that, "Once again the Jewish people are at a terrible crossroad. Because of Israel. Because of Israel and the way that Israel endangers all of us" (81). As an example of this endangering, Pipik starts talking about Jonathan Pollard, the US citizen who was arrested and convicted for giving military secrets to the Israeli government in 1987,[29] saying, "I am haunted by Jonathan Pollard" (81). Pipik goes so far as to say, "What the Dreyfus case was to Herzl, the Pollard case is to me" (193).

It is not just Pipik who is haunted by Pollard, it is *Operation Shylock* itself. Pollard, who according to *The New York Times* is "The only American ever sentenced to life in prison for spying for an ally" (Baker and Rudoren np), is a constant touchstone in the novel, being discussed or mentioned at least eleven times. Pipik explains his obsession with Pollard with a speech that is worth quoting nearly in full:

> I'm frightened because if I'd been in his job with U.S. naval intelligence, I *would have done exactly the same thing* [become a spy]. I daresay, Philip Roth, that *you* would have done the same thing...Pollard had fantasies about saving Jewish lives. I understand that, *you* understand that: Jewish lives must be saved, and at absolutely any cost. But the cost is not betraying your country, it's *greater* than that: it's defusing the country that most endangers Jewish lives today—and that is the country called Israel! ...Pollard is just another Jewish victim of the existence of Israel—because Pollard enacted no more, really, than the Israelis demand of Diaspora Jews *all the time.* I don't hold Pollard responsible, I hold Israel responsible—Israel, which with its all-embracing Jewish totalism has replaced the goyim as the greatest intimidator of Jews in the world; Israel, which today, with its hunger for Jews, is, in many, many terrible ways, deforming and disfiguring Jews as only our anti-Semitic enemies once had the

power to do. Pollard loves Jews. I love Jews. You love Jews. But no more Pollards, please. (81–82)

Philip, in spying for Smilesburger and then excising the chapter detailing the spying, ends up becoming a Pollard-like character, succumbing to the "Jewish totalism" that Israel has forced onto the Jewish world through its centroperipheral relationship to the diaspora. This is doubly ironic considering how throughout the novel Philip, in his paranoid state, thinks literally everybody he meets is a spy, but then he ends up being the spy himself.[30] Even Smilesburger is aware of the comparison. In the epilogue, Smilesburger mentions numerous times how he will not treat Philip like the Mossad treated Pollard, "abandoning him in his hour of need" (386). Overall, the novel clearly wants readers to associate Philip's spy work with the Pollard case. If we accept Pipik's belief that Pollard's case shows how ideologically swayed diaspora Jews are by Israel, and how this is damaging to the diaspora (and to Israel, in the long run), why then does Philip do it? Here is where the crucial distinction between Philip the protagonist/narrator and Roth the author comes in. Philip's joint decisions to spy and self-censor on behalf of Smilesburger and Israel are far from outlying bad decisions; Philip makes bad choices throughout the novel.

The tendency seems to be to read Philip as more or less Roth: intelligent, confident, and in control, if not authorially, at least rationally. But this does not square with the Philip of the novel. What Roth is doing here is showing us how even somebody like him—because again, as similar as Roth and Philip are, Philip is not Roth—somebody who never acquiesced to outside pressures, especially Jewish pressures, can succumb to the powerful magnetism of Zionism as represented by Smilesburger. The Philip of *Operation Shylock* is unlike any other Philip in any other Roth novel.[31] When trying to figure out why he allowed Ziad to think Philip was Pipik and to take him to Ramallah, Philip says, "And this, the very best reason for my not doing what he told me I had to do, was exactly why I knew I had to do it" and calls his decision "bad judgment" (128). Other examples of Philip's bad judgment include: taking the cheque from Smilesburger, instead of telling him that "he had the wrong Mr. Roth" (110); letting Jinx into his hotel room and sleeping with her, which he calls "the stupidest thing I'd yet done in Jerusalem and perhaps in my entire life" (237); running with it each time he gets mistaken for Pipik: with Smilesburger, with Ziad, and with Shmuel, the Orthodox lawyer.

Philip constantly remarks on all of the mistakes he has been making. Riding back from Ramallah with an older Arab taxi driver, he thinks that it "had to be a mistake but so was coming out with George, so, surely, was everything I had just said and done" (163). Later on, he admits that he had "mismanaged just about everything having to do with Pipik and was probably mismanaging still" (287). It is this Philip, who has already made so many bad decisions when it comes to Pipik, Diasporism, and Ziad, who excises the eleventh chapter; it is not Roth the author— the excision does not have his seal of authorial approval.

It is important to correct this slippage between Philip and Roth because Roth does not condone Philip's caving in to Smilesburger.[32] I would argue that the opposite is true: Roth disapproved of Philip's actions, and, as it turns out, a goal of the novel as a whole was to show how dangerous it is to give in to the demands of Zionism. Not giving in to Jewish demands is something Roth knew intimately. Emily Miller Budick begins to address this when she points out that Smilesburger's request for Philip to do what is best for the Jewish state mimics in fascinating ways how the Jewish American community responded to Roth's early work: "Making Roth into a PR man is clearly what Smilesburger... intends for Roth to become for him and the Jewish state at the end of the novel, producing a new Israeli version of the American-Jewish community's expectations of Roth earlier in his career" (71). I agree with Grumberg when she writes that, "The amputation of the eleventh chapter, then, confirms the aims of the mission itself and illuminates Philip's position as a loyal Diaspora servant who fulfills his 'Jewish duty' by aiding Israel. By cutting the chapter, he actively chooses to sacrifice his nationless Diaspora individuality to the virile Israeli-Jewish collective" (53), which, as we see from Diasporism's inversions and Ziad's heady critiques, is a sacrifice that carries with it dire consequences, not the least of which is collaborating with a violent ethnocratic state.

However, I disagree with Budick's claim that Philip does not actually give in to Smilesburger, but short-circuits his demands by writing the epilogue itself, which is "as close to a chapter 11 as this book will ever get" (75). Budick writes that the epilogue

is, as it were, chapter 11 under erasure, surgically operated on, and yet still there, in so many words. In so doing
and undoing chapter 11, Roth concedes the need to avoid
wantonly publishing materials detrimental to the Jewish
state. At the same time, however, he also avoids fashioning
the novel according to the demands of his ever-censoring
Jewish public, now represented by Israel rather than
America. (75)

This reading requires quite a stretch of interpretative moxy; significantly,
Budick not only unquestioningly accepts that Philip's decision to remove
the last chapter is approved of by Roth, but that Roth believes chapter
11 would have been "detrimental to the Jewish state." Budick forces this
reading onto the ending of Operation Shylock to make it conform to her
own Zionist worldview.[33] My reading, that Roth has Philip remove the
chapter to show how easy it is to give in to the Zionist current, is one that
snugly fits the heteroglossic contours of the novel.

Fascinatingly, there is a clear connection between the excised
chapter 11 and another moment of shocking textual censorship found
in The Counterlife: Henry Zuckerman's destruction of "Draft #2," his
recently deceased brother's manuscript of a book that seems to resemble
The Counterlife itself, and that details Henry's various affairs. These two
moments of textual erasure solidify my claim that for Roth, censorship of
any kind is anathema to the goals of fiction writing, and to the demands
of diasporic heteroglossia. Of course, the two acts of textual mutilation
come from very different places and have very different outcomes. In The
Counterlife, Henry's decision to steal from Zuckerman's study all of "Draft
#2" except for "Christendom," the only chapter that does not mention him
or his infidelities directly, is entirely self-motivated. Henry is terrified of
his affairs coming out; his act of textual terrorism is Roth's way of showing
how the creation of one's identity and public persona is intimately related
to the telling of stories integral to fictional pursuits. Conversely, Philip
censors the eleventh chapter because of his capitulation to Smilesburger
and the Jewish totalism of Zionism—he allows his own writerly independence to be compromised by his misguided allegiance to the Zionist centre.
Henry's absconding with the manuscript reads with comic, satiric joy,
whereas Philip's explanation of his decision reads in a more confessional

mode.[34] The biggest difference between the two moments of textual sacrifice—one to Henry's vanity, the other to Philip's Zionism—is that in *The Counterlife*, the pages Henry destroys are still extant, comprising as they do the book we have just read, whereas in *Shylock* the chapter is actually missing, from the fictive world of the novel as well as in the real world of text and reader. In other words, Henry's textual violence is unsuccessful, but Philip's is entirely too successful.[35] While readers have what Henry did not want made public—which gives the novel an extra surge of scandalous energy—readers of *Shylock* will forever be left wondering what was so damning that Smilesburger felt Philip had to suppress it.

Though we will never know, it is still worth considering what was actually contained in those forty-odd pages.[36] For some reason, the possible content of the eleventh chapter has usually been brushed off. For example, Parrish writes that "the key to the mission is not in what Roth chooses to keep from the reader but in what he keeps from the Mossad" (590), and if he is loyal to Israel or not, which is a strange argument to make—and, besides, does Philip's censoring of the chapter not conclusively confirm his allegiance to Israel? What is not a stretch is the intriguing fact that Smilesburger, out of everything else in Philip's manuscript, wants only the contents of chapter 11 suppressed. As he tells Philip, "I can only tell you that this last chapter will not go unnoticed" (383). If Smilesburger is acting out of self-interest, which he has been proven to do at all times, saying whatever needs to be said, doing what needs to be done, that means that what Philip discovers in Athens must be far more damning of Israel and Zionism than the already-lusty critiques we have gotten from Ziad, from Pipik, from Gal, from Philip, and even from Smilesburger himself.

Philip ends up building himself a self-destructive text, in that the act of the excision itself acts as a stronger troubling of Zionism than it might have if it was still extant, if Smilesburger had let it remain. *Shylock* is so open to other voices, to the centrifugal languages of Diasporism, of the Palestinian narrative, of all the cacophonous talking and arguing that constitutes the novel, that Philip's centripetal move of censoring the eleventh chapter plugs up the whole system. If read from the anti-Zionist perspective of diasporic heteroglossia, once the chapter that will not go unnoticed is noticed, Smilesburger's plans may indeed one day backfire.

Roth seems to be suggesting, then, that in order to get diaspora out from the mighty weight of Israeli Jewish totalism, to begin the work of breaking free from the centroperipheral hold, one must be constantly attuned to all the voices of Jewish geography, including—especially—the Palestinian ones. Against ethnocentrism, against the ideological silencing of Smilesburger's *Loshon Hora*, against the closing of identity to ownership of land, but *for* the infinite speaking of the unspeakable, for the deferment of Jewish justice, for the making of narrative space for the disenfranchised and the oppressed, we must commit to the fictional possibilities of diasporic heteroglossia. Philip, under intense pressure from Smilesburger and the Zionist mythology he embodies, makes the wrong choice. But readers of *Shylock* do not have to make the same choice.

Letting Our Jewish Conscience Be Our Guide: Conclusion

In *Operation Shylock* Philip Roth allows North American readers—Jewish and non-Jewish alike—to come into contact with Israel through a fictional perspective that is not beholden to Zionism. The novel, making use of diasporic heteroglossia, showcases a wide range of voices: from the decolonial neuroticism of Ziad to the ruthless word-spinning of Smilesburger, from realist Anna Ziad to Orientalist Orthodox lawyers. Through its dismantling of various Zionist conventions and narratives—and through Philip's final *capitulation* to the Jewish totalism of Zionism—*Operation Shylock* thoroughly challenges the Israeli claim that the state is a functioning democracy devoid of moral responsibility for the occupation. If, as readers, we take Smilesburger's advice and let our Jewish conscience be our guide, this novel, if read in a certain light, can act as our Jewish guidebook. The way *Shylock* acts and reacts with the Zionist narrative makes it abundantly clear that the recently born centroperipheral relationship between the Jewish diaspora and the state of Israel is deeply unethical and destructive to both Jewish and Palestinian geography.

In a recent book-length reconsideration of Roth's oeuvre, Brett Ashley Kaplan makes the compelling argument that "Philip Roth's novels teach us that Jewish anxiety stems not only from fear of victimization but also from fear of perpetration" (1). Kaplan believes that "Roth's texts probe Israel-Palestine and the Holocaust with varying degrees of intensity but all his novels scrutinize perpetration and victimization through

examining racism and sexism in America" (1).[37] Kaplan's matrix of victim/
perpetrator is the perfect place to end this chapter. For Kaplan, there is
a constant Jewish fear not only of being a victim, but of being a perpetrator; this manifests in Roth's work as "a dual anxiety about the scant
historical happenstance that prevented one from being a Holocaust
victim and also the acute and opposing anxiety that one has the potential
to become a perpetrator" (11). Kaplan, referring to *Shylock*, writes that
"The presence of Demjanjuk in the text mirrors the always present question of the victim or survivor that Roth's Jewish-American characters
could have been because Demjanjuk's 'normal' life veils his perpetrator's
life" (71). The dual nature of Demjanjuk is homologous to the dual nature
of Israel's stated goal of being the saviour of the Jewish people, but at
the same time being the oppressor of the Palestinians. Kaplan asks: "If
Demjanjuk can switch between genocide and the American dream, who
is to say that any of us 'ordinary' people could not perpetrate hate crimes,
whether racist, Islamophobic, or anti-Semitic?" (71). What Roth begins
to unveil in his two Israel-situated novels is that Zionism has enacted
this exact transformation, from victim to perpetrator, and has brought
the Jewish diaspora along for the ride. As Kaplan puts it, this "terror of
becoming the other who perpetrates anti-Arab violence that one could
have become had one made *aliyah*" (54) is the terror of giving in to Israel's
centripetal vortex. Since 1948, Zionism has successfully rerouted Jewish
geography to flow solely toward Israel; it is incumbent upon us to begin
to reverse the current, or even to break it wide open. One way to do this
is through rigorous, sustained fictional explorations of Israel/Palestine.
Roth's two entries into this genre are excellent starting points.

We should not forget, however, that Roth's two Israel-situated
novels were conceived, written, and published within the first thirty
years of the occupation—before Oslo, before the second Intifada, before
the unilateral pull out from Gaza, before the total ascendancy of the
Israeli right. We are now entering the second half of a century of occupation. While certain things have not changed, others have changed. As the
Jewish diaspora moves toward a more fraught relationship with Israel/
Palestine, the lessons of Roth's novels, of the possibilities of diasporic
heteroglossia, but also of the ease with which even well-intentioned
Jews can be sucked into the Zionist current, should not be forgotten.

Herzl
Meets
Uris

Altneuland and *Exodus*
in Diasporic Comparison

IN 1899 AND THEN AGAIN IN 1958, two very differ-
ent men living in very different times set out to write fictional accounts
of a viable Jewish collective living in Palestine. The former of these men
had only his political aspirations, techno-utopic fantasies, and literary
imagination to guide him; the latter had the actuality of a Jewish state,
complicated feelings toward Jews living in the diaspora, and a recently
undertaken crash course in Jewish history. Neither wrote their novels
in Hebrew (one wrote in German, which he assumed would be the lingua
franca of any future Jewish state, the other in English, the language of his
main target audience: Americans, both Jewish and non-Jewish). Both saw
the creation of a sovereign Jewish collective in Palestine as an unalloyed
ethical good, both for the Jews and the wider, non-Jewish world. Neither
gave much thought to the good of the Palestinians.

The two novels I am referring to are, of course, Theodor Herzl's
Altneuland, an idealist utopic imagining of a future technocratic Jewish

commonwealth, and Leon Uris's *Exodus*, a hagiographic genre novel of the founding of the Israeli state that has sold millions of copies.[1] In the interstice between these two fictional imaginings, a Jewish state was, in fact, established in Palestine. In this chapter, I will discover what happens when these two novels of Jewish national fulfillment are brought into contact with each other. Since it is more than fifty years—and two world wars and a raft of technological, social, and geopolitical earthquakes— that gap these two texts, my comparison will utilize several conceptualizations of time, history, and narrative. Using the creation of the Israeli state as the fulcrum, what happens when we bend *Altneuland* and *Exodus* through space-time and bring them face to face? What do they have to say to each other? Will they even recognize each other? This time-folding comparison is part and parcel of this book's heteroglossic methodology.

In this chapter, I argue that reading these two novels in comparison reveals the power fiction can have in not only shaping a diaspora's relationship to a national centre, but in helping to lay the groundwork for bringing that centre into existence in the first place. Where Herzl's imagining into the future a Jewish national entity fictionalized the Zionist desire for a state while embedding the problems and hopes of this desire, Uris's novelization of the Zionist success in Palestine helped obscure the realities of Israel's settler-colonial and genocidal emergence and ethnic nationalist, militarized policies. And as we will see, while Herzl and Uris, living in very different national and cultural times, differ in certain respects, in others—including their negative feelings toward diaspora Jews, their internalization of antisemitic tropes, and their indifference to the Arab Indigenous inhabitants of Palestine—they also align in shocking harmony, not least of which is both novels' belief in the redemptive power of a Jewish reinsertion into national time. Nonetheless, in unpacking how both texts use anachrony, deploying Eyal Chowers's (1998) concept of sundered history and Michael André Bernstein's (1994) theorizations of back- and sideshowing, I show how these two Zionist novels, when read contrapuntally, can disrupt the centroperipheral relationship between Israel and the Jewish diaspora.

Both *Altneuland* and *Exodus* help further conceptualize diasporic heteroglossia in telling ways. Herzl's and Uris's novels, in their shared rhetorical project of entrenching Zionism in the Jewish collective imagination, reject the heteroglossic functions of fiction—if we take Bakhtin

(1982) as the ultimate arbiter of literary success, this means that as novels, they both fail. These are two deeply univocal texts, even though both purport to be filled with voices, especially (as we will see) *Exodus*. Diasporic heteroglossia only exists when the voices of a fictional text push back against the centralizing narrative of ethnic nationalism, not when these voices are simply subsumed by the narrative, or play act at difference; in this way, both *Altneuland* and *Exodus* are telling counterexamples of the diasporic heteroglossic novel, with subtle, yet important distinctions. Herzl's novel, as a settler-colonial utopia, imagines a national, though utopic, future, and sidesteps some of the more damaging effects of the nationalist univocal novel; Uris, on the other hand, writes what we can consider to be the ultimate example of the nationalist univocal novel. Furthermore, these two novels were written before diasporic heteroglossia was a possible organizing function of Jewish literary texts (with *Exodus* written just on the cusp); without a nation-state to write against, without Zionism as the dominant mythos of the Jewish world, there was no need for diasporic heteroglossia. Taken together, then, *Altneuland* and *Exodus* are both major landmarks on the journey from the atopic Jewish world of linked diasporas freefloating from any national centre to the centroperipheral world, with Zionism and its heavily armed state inventing itself as the home referent.

In this chapter, I tease out how these two novels from the Jewish diaspora helped to engender the hegemonic rise of Zionism in the Jewish world. In the rest of this introduction, I briefly introduce both texts, discussing their similarities and differences. I then move on to a temporality-based reading of the novels that relies heavily on the work of Eyal Chowers and Michael André Bernstein. In comparatively exploring the publication history and critical reception of the two novels, I show how Zionism was never a given in the Jewish world: its power had to be manufactured, created, and held. As such, in this chapter, I am interested in how these two books actually move through the world, and how they are seen, read, and utilized today. The chapter ends with a comparison of how both texts represent Arabs and Palestinians: even though *Altneuland* has one speaking Palestinian character and *Exodus* has many, they do not act as heteroglossic interlocutors, but as mouthpieces for the books' Zionist ideologies. Throughout the chapter, and in keeping with the temporal methodology of my reading of these two novels, I am interested in what it means to read these texts *now*, in the first decades of the twenty-first century.

Surprisingly, considering the striking similarities outlined below, there has yet to be any critical comparison between the two novels. Perhaps this is because both texts, for very different reasons, have been given short shrift in the past: *Altneuland* as a minor, forgettable text of Herzl's, *Exodus* as schlocky genre fiction. This, of course, does not mean that these texts have not been scrutinized—as we will see, they have been read in a number of interesting, divergent ways—but their place in the canon of Jewish world literature has been somewhat downplayed. In any case, comparing Herzl's utopic novel with Uris's redemptive narrative of Jews claiming their national mantle lets some fundamental aspects of fiction's power in shaping a diaspora's relationship to a nation-state come to light, aspects that will be carried forward into the rest of this book. While *Altneuland* shows us how diasporic fiction can imagine non-diasporic futures, *Exodus* reveals how diaspora fiction can rewrite an entire people's narrative in the justification of violent ethnic nationalism.

In many ways, *Altneuland* is the ultimate pre-1948 Jewish novel that imagines a national homeland, and not only because it was written by the man known as the father of political Zionism. The novel takes the progressive hopes of European utopic thought, yokes it to the Zionist program of national rehabilitation, and jumps twenty years into the future, all to make the argument that with a state of their own, the Jews of Europe can escape antisemitism, create a thriving new economic, technological, and social order, save the Arabs from themselves, and improve the well-being of the entirety of mankind (though, in particular, European mankind). For Herzl, these objectives are imminently realizable, as long as European Jews are allowed to conduct their national experiment in Palestine. As Friedrich—the young, disillusioned Viennese Jew—and Kingscourt—the curmudgeonly, rich, misanthropic Christian with whom Friedrich retires to a private island for twenty years— discover the wonders of what the Jewish colonists of Palestine call the New Society, led around the country by David Littwack, one of its leading men, they learn about the rebirth of the Jewish people; by the end of the novel, they have discarded their former pessimism about humankind, and have decided to become members of the New Society. They too are reborn in the cauldron of Jewish national freedom.

Altneuland has somewhat of a debated place in the Jewish literary canon. As Michael Gluzman puts it, "If Altneuland is a foundational fiction, it is because it has come to be perceived as a text that foreshadowed the birth of the State of Israel" (110). According to Jeremy Stolow, the novel "has received remarkably little attention in the literature" (56). Muhummad Ali Khalidi concurs, claiming that Altneuland is "scarcely mentioned and seldom remembered," going so far as to call it "widely ignored" (55). Even though the overall critical opinion of Altneuland is that, as literature, it fails, and therefore its novelistic qualities are not worthy of study, I want to start my reading of the novel from a different position: that it is, in fact, the fictional elements of the novel that make it worthwhile for literary study. Herzl's fictional engagement with themes of time, dreams, broken love, suicide, and, even with its major insurmountable problems, the utopic belief that a better world is possible, add a fecund element to Herzl's politics. Unlike most of its critics, I remain committed to reading Altneuland as fiction, as a novel about the immense human potential of Zionism—potential that was either illusory or did not pan out, but that, if nothing else, exists as fiction in Herzl's last major text. Or, as Herzl himself wrote in his diary: "Perhaps these ideas are not practical ones at all and I am only making myself the laughingstock of the people to whom I talk about it seriously. Could I be merely walking within my novel?" (qtd. in Chowers 678).

Unlike Herzl during the composition of Altneuland, Uris had the historical realities of mass Jewish immigration to Palestine, of Jewish institution building, of Jewish colonization, and of the establishment of the Jewish nation-state of Israel to use as fodder for his fictionalization of Jewish redemption and revitalization that became Exodus. (Uris also had the life and writings of Herzl himself, who appears as a minor character in the text.) Also unlike Altneuland, whose place in the canon is unsettled at best, Exodus was a runaway bestseller, selling in the millions—in February 1959 the book was selling "approximately 2,500 copies a day"; by November of that year, there had been 399,384 hardcover and 1,675,000 paperback copies sold (Nadel 109)—and solidifying American Jewish perspectives on Israel. Though often critically dismissed as mere genre fiction, the novel still deserves rigorous attention. This is mainly because its monumental role as a fictional text that forever altered how Israel and Zionism are viewed by both Jewish communities—in North America mostly, but also in Soviet Russia and elsewhere—and the non-Jewish world is hard to overstate. According to M.M. Silver—whose book *Our Exodus: Leon Uris and the Americanization of Israel's Founding Story* is the only monograph-length scholarly exploration of *Exodus*—Uris's novel, "more than any other single artifact, set the narrative frames for a sympathetic worldwide understanding of modern Israel's genesis" (5). Or, as Uris's biographer Ira B. Nadel puts it, Uris "was a mythmaker who redefined the cultural status of the Jew for North Americans" (5).

Exodus's main narrative starts just after World War II and ends in 1957, but during that decade-long period, goes deep into Jewish historical time, as well as into the death pits of the Shoah. The novel, which opens at the British-run Jewish refugee camp on the island of Cyprus and ends in the triumphant-yet-sorrowful aftermath of the Israeli War of Independence, is a sustained, relentless argument for the justice and righteousness of the Jewish state—and, as we will see, Uris's monomaniacal lifting up of the Jewish heroes of Israel has its counterpart in the novel's ruthless disparaging of Palestinians and Arabs. Every single sentence in the novel is bent toward one purpose: the affirmation of Israel as the one proper home of the Jewish people, unassailable, unimpeachable, and beyond normal moral considerations. And hidden within every sentence is the people at whose cost the Jewish state will be founded: the Palestinians.

Typical to its genre fiction pot-boiler structure and aesthetic, the novel is overrun with plot, subplot, characters, and settings. As Amy Kaplan puts it, "The epic sweep of the plot is not easily summarized" (874). Divided into five books to purposefully mirror the five books of the Torah (*Altneuland* is also five books), the novel covers the entire history of Zionism in Palestine up to the writing of the book. The hero of the novel is Ari Ben Canaan, the "crack agent of the Mossad Aliyah Bet" (13), with his tireless exploits to bring the Jewish state into reality, as well as his torturous romance with Kitty Fremont, a Christian American nurse who starts off the novel benignly antisemitic and wanting nothing to do with Jews or their national pretensions, but by the end has overcome her prejudices and has fallen in love with both Ari and the Zionist state. Ari is perhaps Uris's most enigmatic creation, a New Jew taken to its logical extreme: "Ari Ben Canaan was a machine. He was an efficient, daring operator. Sometimes he won, sometimes he lost. But once in a while Ari Ben Canaan looked at it all with realism and it nearly crushed him" (320). Ari's eventual emotional release when he declares his love for Kitty does nothing to dampen his outsized heroic, masculinized efficiency. Narrative arcs of the other major characters also further represent the power of Israel to turn weak Jews from the diaspora into strong self-sufficient ethnic nationalists. Dov Landau goes from a destroyed, bitter Shoah survivor to an expert forger, fierce fighter, and passionate lover of Karen. Barak and Akiva Ben Canaan—Ari's father and uncle, respectively—start off as Jossi and Yakov, two powerless Jews from the Pale of Settlement, who literally walk to the Promised Land and become a part of the growing Jewish Yishuv, with Barak embodying the tireless diplomatic and pioneering spirit of Zionism, and Akiva, through his founding of the Maccabees—an underground militia and terrorist organization, loosely based on the Irgun and Stern Gang—representing the violent retributive justice and terrorist flipside of Zionism. Kitty, as already mentioned, sheds her antisemitism. Even a minor character like the antisemitic British general Caldwell feels the power of the Jewish state when he is murdered by the Maccabees for purposefully leaving a Jewish teenager in a "hostile" Arab village where they brutally kill him. Elsewhere in the novel, Uris is committed to confirming Israel as the natural endpoint in the Jewish historical narrative of oppression, dehumanization, and state-sponsored genocide. There are two long sections that detail entire eras of Jewish history: the first follows Dov Landau's Polish family's destruction in the Shoah; the second narrates Barak and Akiva Ben Canaan's transformation from young shtetl Jews in the Russian Pale of Settlement to leading figures of the Yishuv, a transformation that includes many pages of Jewish and world history. Uris clearly celebrates Ari and his fellow Israelis' creation of a state as the crowning glory of the Jewish people since the Bible, to which the characters constantly compare themselves or from which they often quote.

I want to state clearly here that I feel that deeply scrutinizing a text like *Exodus*—a scrutiny that includes sustained attention to the actual content of the novel, which is rarely the case in scholarship on the book—is important exactly because of its ideological power. Moreover, reading *Exodus* through an anti-Zionist, diasporic lens uncovers the ethical problems built both into the political program of Zionism and Uris's narrative of said program as the glorious final destination of Jewish history. Silver's Zionist reading of *Exodus*, while often insightful, downplays Uris's racism and the novel's role in cementing anti-Arab views in the Jewish diasporic imaginary, and consistently endorses Uris's project of ethnic uplift. On both of these points, I will take the opposite position, performing a contrapuntal reading of the novel. The historical distortions and vilification of the Palestinians in *Exodus*, regardless of the novel's role in rejuvenating a downtrodden post-Shoah American Jewry, deserve rigorous, sustained critique.

For two novels that at first glance could not appear farther apart, there are a striking number of thematic, narratological, and histori-cal connections between *Altneuland* and *Exodus*. Both novels centre on immensely compelling New Jews who act symbolically as founder and defender of the state: in *Exodus*, the iron-willed Ari, in *Altneuland*, the thoughtful, committed David. Both protagonists are resourceful, intelli-gent, ruthless, committed Zionists (they are both also male). Both novels have a major subplot where a non-Zionist, non-Jewish (read: Christian) character ends up, against their better judgment, falling in love with the Jewish state and its people, in both cases through their infatuation for a Jewish child or baby. In *Altneuland*, it is Kingscourt who is seduced by David and his wife Sarah's baby, Fritzchen; in *Exodus*, it is Kitty's love for the orphan Karen Hansen that convinces Kitty to stay in Palestine after the Exodus successfully runs the British blockade and lands in Palestine. Both novels include scenes set at a Passover Seder, connecting Zionism's triumph directly to Jewish history; except, where Herzl celebrates the multicultural acceptance of the New Society by having members of different faiths and Christian denominations (but no imams) at the cele-brations, Uris ends his novel with a Seder in the newly established state tinged with sadness due to Karen's recent murder at her kibbutz on the Gaza border. Both of these texts sit uneasily in history: *Exodus*, for its blatant racism and skewed, asymmetrical narrative; *Altneuland*, for its transformation from a fictional utopic novel that imagined a glorious Jewish/world future into a historical document of a time and place still suffused with the wildly meliorist attitudes of the European nineteenth century, and one where two world wars, the dissolution of the Ottoman and Habsburg empires, the rise of America and Russia as global super-powers, and even the Shoah are not historical inevitabilities.

The novels' differences are just as telling. For one thing, Herzl's imagined Jewish commonwealth does not have borders, an army, politicians, or a state apparatus of any kind, and did not rely on violence or coercion during its creation (the feasibility of this will be looked at later in the chapter). Conversely, Uris's novel is obsessed with the establishment and heroic deeds of Jewish soldiers and army units in their struggle to create a state apparatus so they can proudly join the family of state apparatuses. Moreover, while Altneuland is written as high literature—light on plot, heavy on Platonic-like dialogue, with pages and pages on the minute workings of the ideal newspaper system and on economic policy—Exodus is melodramatic genre fiction, chock-full of plot, action, casual sexism, and exclamation marks, but containing nonetheless a surprising amount of Jewish history and forceful ideological argument. Perhaps, however, the most significant connection between the two novels is their respective author's internalized negativity about the Jewish diaspora, which they both saw as weak, feminized, and in need of saving. To look at it through Dufoix's schema, Altneuland is a text from the atopic mode period, where various Jewish diasporic communities have contact with each other, but there is no connection with the referent-origin (because there is no "referent-origin"); Altneuland, however, is part of the process to create a referent-origin and therefore move to the centroperipheral model. Exodus, conversely, is a product of the new centroperipheral relationship that Herzl attempted to make a reality, and it helped cement Israel's new hold over the Jewish diaspora. Both novels can be seen as precursors to the birth of diasporic heteroglossia, with Exodus being one of the first post-state Zionist texts to refuse it in favour of univocal Zionist time.

Temporality, History, and Jewish Time

From the co-optation of biblical time to justify the colonization of Palestine, to the temporal framing of the 1967 occupation of the West Bank, Gaza Strip, and Golan Heights (which effectively erases the temporal ramifications of the 1948 War), time is a potent force in Zionist

narratives.[2] The diaspora experience is also a deeply temporal one, span-
ning from the diasporic openness of Jewish history to the delayed action
of Jewish messianic time. To begin my temporal-frame-bending analysis
of Altneuland and Exodus, then, I will look at several different conceptualizations of narrative and historical time, placing the two novels and their
use of Jewish time side by side. As such, I will also unpack how Herzl's
and Uris's differing sense of Jewish temporality functions in their respective texts. Where Herzl believes that the natural unfolding of human
time can be bent (or broken) to the benefit of Europe's Jewish population,
Uris employs the Jewish past—which he reads as a horrific stumbling
from one deadly catastrophe to another—to justify the use of Jewish
force to bring about the paradoxically inevitable, teleological end of the
Jewish diaspora: the Jewish state. As we will see, both Altneuland and
Exodus deploy non-chronological narrative time—the former jumping
twenty years into the future, the latter deploying long flashback digres-
sions during various periods of (Uris's particular Zionist version of)
Jewish history— to further their respective rhetorical and ideological
projects. In both cases, the project is to force a Zionist intervention into
Jewish time and history, either through imagining a Jewish presence in
Palestine, or by attempting to legitimize the violent founding of the state.

One way into the different configurations of time at play in the
two novels is through the question of genre. Herzl's novel, as a utopic
imagining of an entirely fictitious thriving Jewish presence in
Palestine, is entirely geared toward the future; the novel, which can
be classified as a utopia—in spite of Herzl's admonishments against
such a classification—places all of its hope of Jewish renewal in the
after now.[3] Altneuland conforms to Miriam Eliav-Feldon's definition
of a utopia as "a literary work describing an ideal imaginary society
created on this earth by human powers alone" (85). Taking the definition further, Ulrich E. Bach writes that even though utopian fiction
"dramatizes the need for social change," it is "neither literature presenting fictional experiences nor social theory presenting totalities" (76).
Instead, these works "achieve their greatest influence" through their
mediation between what Phillip E. Wegner calls "the world that is and
that which is coming into being" (qtd. in Bach 76). In "The Utopia of
Theodor Herzl," Uri Zilbersheid attempts to turn the entirety of Herzl's
political writing—as culled from The Jewish State, his diaries, and

Altneuland—into a unified political program, a program that Zilbersheid locates as thoroughly utopian. Zilbersheid shows how Herzl's thinking evolved from a belief in the welfare state to a belief in the abolishment of the state, and how that progression can be marked out both in *The Jewish State* (where there is a socialized state apparatus that sets the stage for utopia) and in *Altneuland*, where the state falls away and we are left with non-coercive collective co-operatives. In *Altneuland*, Zilbersheid writes, "Herzl openly presented himself as a socialist belonging to the great utopian tradition" (89). Though Zilbersheid makes a convincing case for a unified theory of Herzl's political ideology, a glaring omission in his exegesis is the colonial reality of Herzl's political program. Can a utopia really exist on a bedrock of settler colonialism? Because of this, I think it is more accurate to call *Altneuland* a Jewish *settler-colonial* utopia, with all the paradox such a phrase denotes.

Exodus, conversely, narrates the past, both the recent past—the founding of the state—and the distant Jewish past. However, it does so through a particular genre lens, and that is the genre of a melodramatic western. As Rachel Weissbrod cogently argues, Uris fits his ideological project into the melodrama form, with uncomplicated, archetypal characters, the battle between clearly delineated good (the Jews) and evil (the Nazis, the British, and the Arabs), and a "visibly stylized outlook" that has "no pretense to realism" (130). As Weissbrod explains, "Because melodrama neatly divides the world into diametric opposites, it provides the ideal vehicle for transmitting clear ideological messages" (133). Silver, while disagreeing that *Exodus* is a melodrama, does agree with Weissbrod on the clear good/evil dichotomy of the novel, calling it Uris's "cowboys and Indians" worldview, or, in other words, the worldview of the western (the settler-colonial paradigm captured in "cowboys and Indians" is also significant) (see Silver 194–195). Nadel concurs, writing that Uris "relied extensively on the conventions of the western" for his screenplays and fiction writing, drawn to "the traditional opposition between law and violence, the conflict between social and legal borders" (86). Nadel also points out that the western has always had "an undisputed moral clarity. Good and bad were self-evident" (88). In forcing the story of Jewish colonization into the mould of a western, Uris takes a narrative of settler colonialism and Palestinian dispossession and dehumanization and mutates it into a story of unassailable Jewish cowboys

defeating evil Indians. As Uris himself said in a Publishers Weekly interview in 1976: "You can write westerns in any part of the world" (qtd. in
Nadel 87). We will see how this ideological worldview plays out on the
bodies of Arabs and Palestinians in Uris's narrative. In any case, both
novels believe in the redemptive power of a Jewish reinsertion into
national time.

In his article, "Time in Zionism: The Life and Afterlife of a
Temporal Revolution," the Israeli philosopher Eyal Chowers argues that
the end of the nineteenth century in Europe saw the advent of what he
calls "sundered history." Chowers defines sundered history as "an inter-
lude during which human existence in time is seen as open and without
clear course: devoid of any guidance, whether in the form of divinity,
natural order, an invisible-hand-like mechanism, or unfolding reason"
(654). Chowers argues that it was during this period of sundered history
that Zionist thinkers were able to imagine the creation of a Jewish state,
to wrest control over their destiny, away from the broken metanarratives
of prior centuries; this type of thinking was only possible "after teleological conceptions of history began to lose their allure" (654). Chowers
investigates how the Zionist belief that "human affairs" can "succumb
to the will and imagination, to the longings of the heart" functions in
both what he calls the Nietzschean and Marxist strands of Zionism (655).[4]
Significantly, Chowers shows how the Jewish European population until
that moment, by eschewing national time (of both the Herderian and
Hegelian modalities), was firmly entrenched in a diasporic temporality
that showcased a number of fluid, ethical parameters. "Rather than valo-
rizing [national] self-assertion," Chowers writes, "this tradition valued
messianic expectation; rather than preaching exclusivity and enclosure,
it aspired to strengthen moral consciousness and cosmopolitanism; and
rather than mooring identity to a particular space, it grounded identity
in a temporal continuity sustained by the study of the Book" (663). The
tradition that Chowers characterizes here is one that the Boyarins would
recognize as diasporic, and that I would argue is thoroughly heteroglossic.[5] However, once the teleological metanarratives ceased to hold sway
in European political thought, sundered history emerged, and with it,
"Zionism became increasingly dependent on and enamored with the
ability of human beings to shape the existing geographical and demographic environments according to their will, to impose new, tangible

'facts' where none had existed" (Chowers 674–675). Sundered history allowed Zionist Jews to believe that there was no set track to Jewish/world history; all they had to do was make their proposed dreams a reality. As Jacqueline Rose puts it, "Violating reality is something that more than one Zionist has been perfectly happy to acknowledge that they do" (15). The very structure of Jewish geography, with the advent of sundered history and the Zionist belief in remaking the Jewish world, was irrevocably altered, from the atopic to the centroperipheral, from diaspora to nation, from heteroglossia to univocality.

We can clearly see this belief in the open possibilities of sundered history at work in Altneuland. Herzl's New Society is created from scratch by a handful of wilful individuals with little struggle or obstacles, rescuing the Jewish people from Europe and curing worldwide antisemitism in one frictionless, "bloodless" push (Altneuland 65). What Herzl imagines in his novel hews closely to Chowers's statement that "Zionists celebrated the human capacity to begin something absolutely new, eventually constructing a demographic, political, and cultural actuality where none had existed before" (654). In this way, Altneuland is set up to show the power of time to change the world. Before Kingscourt and Friedrich embark to their island outside of history, Friedrich gives a telling New Year's Eve speech: "Timelessness begins for us now," he says. Kingscourt heartily agrees, exclaiming: "Die, Time! I empty my glass to your death. What were you? Shame, blood, depravity, progress" (49). It would seem that in leaving society, both men have given up on historical time. When, twenty years later, they re-enter the world and see what time, through an advantageous rent in sundered history, has wrought in Palestine—that "Milk and honey once more flowed in the ancient home of the Jews" (241)—they quickly start to believe in the power of time—in particular, Jewish time—to progress human society. Kingscourt, explaining how time changes, says, "Had I been born into the world today, I should have accepted it just as I accepted the world I was actually born into" (81). In another analogy, Kingscourt says that had they "been away from the world from 1880 to 1900, electric light, the telephone, transmission of electric power by wire would have been even more overwhelming. You show us nothing new in the technical sense, and yet I seem to be dreaming" (81). Here, Herzl shows that utopic futures are possible to imagine because massive historical, social, and technological changes do regularly occur; within a twenty-year period, the world can change irrevocably.

Moreover, Kingscourt's reference to dreaming in the above quote points to another way to conceptualize the temporality of *Altneuland*: as dream time. When Friedrich and Kingscourt sail out of time to their island, Herzl's narrator tells us that "Friedrich heard Kingscourt's words only in a dream. He had fallen asleep. And, dreaming, he sailed through the Red Sea to meet the future" (50). Four pages later, as they make their way to Palestine, Friedrich tells Kingscourt: "I was happy on our island, completely happy. The twenty years passed over me like a dream" (54). The fictional structure of the novel that allows Herzl to project his Zionist hopes into the future can be read as those of dreams, dreaming, dream time, as distinct but not unrelated to lived reality. In the novel's afterword, Herzl famously writes that he "believes Dreams are also a fulfillment of the days of our sojourn on Earth. Dreams are not so different from Deeds as some may think. All the deeds of men are only Dreams at first. And in the end, their Deeds dissolve into Dreams" (296). Herzl's desire for the dream space of *Altneuland* to slip through sundered history and become deeds, become action, is clear.

By the time we arrive in the 1950s, Uris conceives of Jewish history in a very different way. The Zionists were not able to force a new society through the rupture of sundered history; they were able to create a state because—for Uris—the entirety of Jewish history, up to and especially during the Shoah, was a teleologic journey *toward* the state. As Silver exhaustively shows, Uris's main rhetorical goal was to tie the establishment of the state into the same historical current that led to the diaspora and to the Shoah. Silver argues that *Exodus* presents "Israel as the triumphant product of a definable historical process" (21). Tied to this definable historical process is a driving concern for a "particular vision of Jewish empowerment" (36), which is presented in stark contrast to the horrifying scenes of Jewish torture, death, and destruction during the Shoah. "*Exodus*," Silver writes, "is thus simultaneously permeated with an unrelenting awareness of Jewish tragedy and an equally unremitting faith in the Jews' ability to reverse historical fate in the triumphant state of Israel" (40). While this quote makes it sound like *Exodus* conforms to a view of sundered history, Silver misreads Uris's project here: the Jews do not reverse historical fate so much as they *achieve* their historical destiny.

For one example of this from the novel, David Ben-Ami—the character who most consistently compares the Zionist struggle for a state with biblical narratives—tells Ari: "I must never stop believing...that I am carrying on a new chapter of a story started four thousand years ago" (25). Ben-Ami argues for this reading of Jewish history by constantly showing how they are re-enacting biblical stories of Jewish heroism in the very location of those stories: "Right in the same place we fought the Roman Empire we now fight the British Empire two thousand years later" (25). It is Ben-Ami who names the refugee ship the *Exodus*, tying it to the most symbolic event in Jewish history: the Jewish people's escape from the Egyptians.

During the orphans' hunger strike on the *Exodus*, when other characters begin to relent, Ben-Ami gives a long speech on why the strike should continue. The speech's relentless Zionist historicizing of all of Jewish history is central to Uris's rhetorical project:

> Six million Jews died in gas chambers not knowing why they died...If three hundred of us on the *Exodus* die we will certainly know why. The world will know too. When we were a nation two thousand years ago and when we rebelled against Roman and Greek rule we Jews established the tradition of fighting to the last man. We did this at Arbela and Jerusalem. We did this at Beitar and Herodium and Machaerus. At Masada we held out against the Romans for four years and when they entered the fort they found us all dead. No people, anywhere, have fought for their freedom as have our people. We drove the Romans and the Greeks from our land until we were dispersed to the four corners of the world. We have not had much opportunity to fight as a nation for two thousand years. When we had that opportunity at the Warsaw ghetto we did honor to our tradition. I say if we leave this boat and willingly return to barbed-wire prisons then we will have broken faith with God. (182)

This is an excellent example of *Exodus*'s primary strategy: showing how Jewish history—which, in Ben-Ami's formulation, is nothing but violent struggle—inexorably leads to the creation of the state of Israel. Ben-Ami's speech, which is representative of dozens, if not hundreds, of such moments in the novel, shows the truth in Nur Masalha's statement that "Zionists claim that events described in the Old Testament establish the right of twentieth-century Jews to found an ethnic Jewish state in Palestine" (24).[6] What we have, then, with *Altneuland* and *Exodus*, are two conflicting yet related conceptualizations of Jewish time: one where the possibilities for non-violent redemption and utopia are possible, and one where violence and state-making are the only path toward true Jewish individual and national self-hood, respectively.

Because of this, *Altneuland* and *Exodus* narrate the establishment of a Jewish collective in Palestine in tellingly divergent ways. For Herzl, the Jewish New Society came about solely through the organized will of committed Zionists. As Jacques Kornberg shows, in the novel, "Zionist politics were made from above, by exceptional personalities, platonic rulers in the shape of technocrats and financiers" (*Altneuland* xxii). Some of these exceptional personalities include the aforementioned David Littwack; Mr. Steineck, the "chief architect" (*Altneuland* 68), as well as his brother Professor Steineck, a bacteriologist whose famous laboratory is attempting to cure malaria (169);[7] Dr. Marcus, president of the Jewish Academy; President Eichenstamm, an eye doctor, who Friedrich met in Vienna earlier in the book and whose Zionist beliefs were heartily mocked by his fellow Jews (46); and, perhaps most exceptional of all, Joe Levy, the director of the Department of Industry, who was more or less singlehandedly responsible for the establishment of the New Society. Levy is a prototypical New Jew, brilliant, indefatigable, and unstoppable; readers are told that he "understands everything that reveals itself to sound observation and an iron will" (189). These men—needless to point out, they are *all* men—transform Palestine into its utopic Jewish state, through nothing but good planning, organization, knowledge of economics, and the all-important Sultan's charter.

Along with the Jewish characters who enabled the "systemic large-scale colonization" (158) of Palestine, readers are introduced to a wide swath of the New Society, either through conversation or Friedrich and Kingscourt's own touring of the country. A brief catalogue of the universally positive workings of the New Society would include the following characteristics: children do not inherit either their "fathers'" wealth or debt, so that "Each generation is given a new start" (this philosophy of competition is explained, at length, by a stranger who Kingscourt and

Friedrich stop on the street) (275); education through university is free; every member of the New Society performs two years of service for the community, though there "is no army in the New Society" (79); there is no such thing as a career politician, with all political spots being honorary—as David puts it, "politics here is neither a business nor a profession, for either men or women. We have kept ourselves unsullied by that plague" (76); and every service and institution—hospitals, infirmaries, orphan asylums, vacation camps, public kitchens—is centralized. Herzl includes many pages describing the minutia of the New Society's "mutualistic" economic order (see 85–87). The system is based on co-operatives, which provides the mean between individualism and collectivism and creates an economic system where "The individual is not deprived of the stimulus and pleasures of private property, while, at the same time, he is able, through union with his fellows, to resist capitalist domination" (86). To give an example of one of these co-ops, there is a dense discussion of the newspaper co-operatives, which are owned entirely by subscribers (87) and are "truthful and decent" (84). (Readers are informed that there are also private papers.) Perhaps most importantly, it was not until the Jews had a society of their own that antisemitism could actually end: "Only after those Jews who were forced out of Europe had been settled in their own land, the well-meant measures of emancipation became effective everywhere" (178). Finally, when Friedrich and Kingscourt visit Palestine, non-Jews are welcome to join the New Society; however, a small, xenophobic opposition, led by Rabbi Dr. Geyer, is hoping to change this.

We are given the history of the founding of the commonwealth through several speeches and lectures, with the most contrived being when the touring party listens to an audio recording made by Joe Levy, detailing how "a new springtide had risen for humanity" (191). To summarize in very broad strokes, before the colonization began in earnest, antisemitism in Europe was at an all-time high: "Jew-hatred employed its newest as well as its oldest devices," David explains. "Whether Jews were rich or poor or middle-class, they were hated just the same" (65). This time, however, instead of remaining enemies of society—and thanks to sundered history—they had sought out "a refuge for themselves" (66). They did so through the creation of "The New Society for the Colonization of Palestine." Once a charter with the Ottoman government was secured, the society, led by Levy, began to secretly prepare for the mass immigration of Jews to Palestine, a "systematic immigration" that was to take place "immediately after the winter rains" (200). As we were told earlier, "On the whole, it was a bloodless operation" (65), which is, perhaps, the most utopic aspect of Herzl's imagined New Society. Herzl creates a complex economic, social, and technological series of events, beginning with the New Society stock corporation's—modelled on the East India Company and other "such stock companies" used for "colonization" (199)—hiring of Alladino, a Sephardic Jew (no first name is given), to start buying up land in Palestine.[8] Levy, acting as the head of a kind of centralized party Zionism, orchestrates a perfect collaboration between banks, corporations, students, workers, and intellectuals. By the end of the short process, railroads run from Jaffa to Damascus and to points further east, the third temple has been rebuilt (though, as I will discuss below, we are also told the Dome of the Rock still stands), and Jews everywhere live in peace and harmony, including with their Arab neighbours and The New Society's Palestinian inhabitants.

As Jeremy Stolow sees it, "In *Altneuland*, we are presented with the figure of the Jew as the harbinger of a cozy, liberal secularism, as the colonizer for progress, as the defuser of magic and the overturner of moribund traditions, and as the exponent of the sphere of circulation in the modern world capitalist system" (59–60). As David explains it to a flabbergasted Friedrich and Kingscourt, "Only we Jews could have done it... We only were in a position to create this New Society, this new center of civilization here. One thing dovetailed into another. It could have come only through us, through our destiny. Our moral sufferings were as much a necessary element as our commercial experience and our cosmopolitanism" (82). In Herzl's novel, it is the unique historical position of the Jews of Europe that allows them to push their bloodless world-changing plan through sundered history and into reality; by the time Friedrich and Kingscourt arrive, the transformation is complete, and the majority of the novel concerns the two out-of-time sojourners' discovery of the wonders of the Jewish New Society.

Conversely, *Exodus*, from its first page to its last, narrates nothing but the heroic creation of the state. Whether it is a battle scene or a debate scene, a UN vote, or a long flashback to the Shoah, the novel never strays from arguing for, and justifying the need of, a Jewish state—in spite of the Nazis, with or without British approval, and regardless of Arab and Palestinian resentment. Significantly, Uris's narrative is built in such a way that the Jews who wish for a homeland in Palestine are never in the wrong: it is others—namely, the British, and later the Arabs—who force the idealist Jewish settlers to the use of violence. Importantly, Uris's narrator does not regret the use of force but revels in it; still, the Jewish characters are always blameless, and everything bad that happens to them stems from the disease of antisemitism. As the narrator explains, "Jew hating is an incurable disease. Under certain democratic conditions it may not flourish well. Under other conditions the germ may even appear to die, but it never does die even in the most ideal climate" (219–220). Furthermore, Uris continuously hammers home how the events narrated in the novel are the natural conclusion to Jewish history—that, with enough Jewish resistance, force, power, and necessary violence, a state will emerge. The Zionist metanarrative of teleological statehood is presented in full force when the United Nations prepares to vote on the partition plan in the autumn of 1947: "The six-thousand-year-old case of the Jewish people was placed before the conscience of man" (455). Uris draws out the dramatic potential of this scene, going through every country's vote, building suspense even with the vote's foregone conclusion, and ending with Barak exclaiming, "Dear God...I think we have made it" (464). Where Herzl's characters discuss dense socioeconomic systems in policy-wonk detail, Uris's characters go about the work of making a state, from the backroom politicking required to get the votes for the UN plan, to action-laden narratives of battles, battle planning, and battle aftermaths. Uris's other job as a screenwriter means that these scenes are written with cinematic pacing. For example, after David Ben-Gurion declares the state and the second phase of the 1948 War begins, Uris's narrator—in full war reportage mode—zips all over the country, presenting short sections subtitled with their all-caps geographical location. In this way, readers visit the whole country: "NEGEV DESERT" (520), "JERUSALEM" (522), "JERUSALEM CORRIDOR" (523), "HULEH VALLEY—SEA OF GALILLE" (524), "SHARON, TEL AVIV, THE TRIANGLE" (526), and "WESTERN GALILEE" (526). In a parallel moment, after the war, the book lists the numbers of Jews emigrating to Israel from all over the world, declaring that "Israel became an epic in the history of man" (572). From beginning to end, *Exodus* is a novel that narrates at the same time that it justifies the coming into existence of Israel, as both an inevitable outcome of Jewish history and something that had to be fought for.

Since readers of *Exodus* know that the state of Israel was, in fact, created (and especially if they know little else about Israel except this), all the plot, flashbacks, Shoah narratives, and detailed battles have their narrative payoff when the glorious climax of the state's ascension is declared, defended, and achieved. In this way, *Exodus* is a prime example of what Michael André Bernstein calls backshadowing. According to Bernstein: "Backshadowing is a kind of retroactive foreshadowing in which the shared knowledge of the outcome of a series of events by narrator and listener is used to judge the participants in those events *as though they too should have known what was to come*" (16; emphasis original). Against backshadowing Bernstein posits sideshadowing, which is when texts—either historical or fictional narratives—make room for individual choice and the possibility that history did not have to progress the way that we know it did.[9] Sideshadowing is "a gesturing to the side, to a present dense with multiple, and mutually exclusive, possibilities for what is to come" (1), that reaffirms "the primacy of human freedom" (7). Bernstein elucidates the ethical implications of fictional sideshadowing when he writes: "Sideshadowing's attention to the unfulfilled or unrealized possibilities of the past is a way of disrupting the affirmations of a triumphalist, unidirectional view of history in which whatever has perished is condemned because it has been found wanting by some irresistible historico-logical dynamic" (3). For Bernstein, the "remarkably crude foreshadowing that habitually characterizes any global and monolithic way of thinking" (2) can be seen not only in fictional texts, but in histories, and especially biographies. Bernstein looks at a biography of Franz Kafka that includes the birth of Hitler, as if Hitler's role in history was predetermined. Significantly, sideshadowing does not question what *did* happen, but shows how what happened is always one outcome among many: "The one that actually was realized, though, exists from then on with all the weight afforded by the singularity of what we might call its event-ness" (71).[10] Bernstein believes that only a prosaics of sideshadowing, of lived individual lives, can alleviate our tendency to lock the past into monorails. Both the practices of backshadowing and sideshadowing dovetail incredibly well with diasporic heteroglossia: they are both against the teleological, unidirectional singularity of historical time, but are for the ever-expanding possibilities of a lived time that is not closed. In any case, both of the novels under study here engage in back/sideshadowing in telling ways.

Exodus, as is common in most Shoah literature, is rife with moments of backshadowing, particularly where the Jewish characters are blamed for not knowing the future.[11] Uris's narrator flat out blames Karen Hansen's father, Johann, a German-Jewish professor, for not leaving Germany. Shortly after the terrifying events of Kristallnacht, readers are told: "Not only had Johann Clement been a fool, but he had endangered the life of his family as well" (62). Pushing the backshadowing into even more egregious territory, Johann has "visions of his family being trapped and never able to escape the approaching Holocaust" (63). Note the use of the word "Holocaust" here, which would not be the accepted name for the Nazi genocide of European's Jewish population until the 1960s.[12] Two hundred pages later, during the novel's longest historical digression, the narrator states: "In the year of 1933 another great calamity befell the Jews as Adolf Hitler and the Nazis ascended to power. Hitler moved first against the Jewish 'professional' people. The wiser ones among them left Germany immediately and many sought sanctuary in Palestine" (266). Good Zionist characters not only knew what was coming, they escaped. Why else would Dr. Lieberman, the kind, elderly leader of Dan Gafna, tell Kitty: "I came from Germany in 1933. I guess I knew quite early what was going to happen" (342)? When Ari is in Berlin in the "fear-filled" summer of 1939, working "Around the clock as the time ran out" (292), he acts as if the mechanisms of the Shoah are already in place, when in reality, the tenets of the "final solution" were still years away from being put into action. Commensurate with Uris's anti-diasporist Zionism, any Jewish characters' failure to foresee the Shoah is blamed on their diasporic outlook.[13]

Contrary to Exodus, Altneuland's temporal structure operates in a more complex way, especially when read from the vantage point of the twenty-first century. Since Friedrich and Kingscourt leave human society for twenty years, they have no idea what history is doing without them; only upon their return do they learn about the creation of the New Society. I would like to put this forward as a nuanced example of unintentional sideshadowing: reading the novel today, not only do we see how

Herzl thought the future could play out, but we are defamiliarized to how it did play out. Herzl, of course, cannot see the future—and, needless to say, what came after Herzl was not inevitable—but *Altneuland*'s belief in the stability of the old European system, wedded to utopic longing, lets readers today imagine a different path for twentieth-century world history. As Bernstein explains: "The nonlives of the sideshadowed events that never happened are a part of the emotional/intellectual legacy and aura of each actually occurring event, inflecting it in distinct ways" (14–15). From the vantage point of 2023, we can view *Altneuland* and the actual history of Israel as two diverging tracks. Encountering through fiction a Jewish state that does not maintain borders, that does not have an army, and that did not come about through violence, where the "stranger" is "at home among us" (*Altneuland* 276), allows readers critical of Zionist space to apply pressure in order to bring the more ethical aspects of Herzl's utopia to bear on a state that is definitively closer to Uris's version.

It seems to me, then, that the related concepts of sundered history and backshadowing/sideshadowing—theories that both insist on narrative's fundamental relationship to our understanding of chronology and historical time as either opened or closed—can be combined to create a productive lens through which to view the comparison of texts such as *Altneuland* and *Exodus*, texts that imagine the same event—the creation of a sovereign Jewish collective in Palestine—from different points on the temporal scale. Placing together the utopic futuring of Herzl's novel with the euphoric yet dangerous backshadowing of Uris's creates within readers a sense of sundered history: the comparison of the two texts engenders its own sideshadowing, revealing what could have been as existing in between the two poles of utopic hope and ethnocentric historicizing.

To unpack this a little further, it is worthwhile to look at both novels' use of anachrony, or the telling of events out of narrative sequence. Jeremy Stolow shows how the temporal structure of *Altneuland*—the twenty-year blank space between Friedrich and Kingscourt's two visits to Palestine—creates "an emptying out of the chronotopic contents of Palestine in 1902 and their replacement with new contents (in 1923) *without* narrative development" (74). In this way, *Altneuland* is almost entirely narrated in flashforward. Stolow continues:

"The transubstantiation of Palestine from desert to garden, in other words, occurs without conflict, resolution, or mediation" (74). *Exodus*, conversely, relies heavily on flashbacks—there are three major flashback narratives in the novel—to cement its case for the need of a militarized Jewish state. *Altneuland*'s flashforwad anachrony serves the novel's rhetorical project of showing the possibility of revolutionary change in the Jewish world; *Exodus*'s flashback anachrony serves the novel's rhetorical project of justifying the violent establishment of the state as ordained by Jewish history. The former is infused with futurity, the latter with historical revisionism; both believe in the positive effects of European-style nationalism. Going further with our temporal bending, when *Altneuland*'s twenty years of empty time are strapped to Uris's narrative of hardened Jews doing battle for their state, what comes into focus is the fact that the violent conflict at the root of the Israeli/Palestinian crisis was not an historical inevitability, but only one possible option that erupted out of the sundered history of Jewish diasporic time.

Finally, and to conclude this section, I want to turn to a major similarity in how Herzl and Uris conceptualize Jewish time: the way in which the Jews' temporal absence from their biblical home has ruined the land of Palestine. A major tenet of the Zionist worldview holds that only through a new Jewish temporality based on the land of Palestine can the land itself be salvaged from the backwards Indigenous Palestinians, to whom it never really belonged (see Ilan Pappé's chapter "Palestine Was an Empty Land" in his book *Ten Myths About Israel* for a thorough critique of this position). Descriptions of Arab neglect and ruin are constant in *Exodus*. During Barak and Akiva's walk to Palestine, when they arrived in Aleppo, "they received their first taste of the Arab world. They passed through bazaars and dung-filled streets" (211). When they get to Palestine, the Arab village is out of time, static: "The village was as it must have been a thousand years before" (213). Moreover, Uris's narrator blames Arab society for ruining the Middle Eastern water table: "A drop of water became more precious than gold or spices in the unfertile land. The merest, most meager existence was a series of tortured, heartbreaking struggles from birth to death. Without water the Arab world disintegrated into filth; unspeakable disease, illiteracy, and poverty were universal. There was little song or laughter or joy in Arab life. It was a constant struggle to survive" (228). Jeremy Salt describes the arrival of Jewish characters to Palestine in Exodus thusly: "Uris describes the Palestine first encountered by the Zionist settlers as a stagnant land, groaning under the weight of Ottoman and Arab neglect, a land which had once been fertile but which had long since sunk into sloth and decay. The Palestinian people are portrayed as passive, uncaring and fatalistic. Their villages are dirty, their men are stupefied by hashish" (55).

This description is nearly identical to how Herzl describes Friedrich and Kingscourt's first visit to Palestine. Herzl's narrator tells readers that "Jaffa made a very unpleasant impression upon them"; "Everywhere [was] misery in bright Oriental rags"; the landscape "Was a picture of desolation"; the "inhabitants of the blackish Arab villages looked like brigands"; and there were "few traces of present or former cultivation" (42). Friedrich voices the Zionist interpretation, saying, "If this is our land...it has declined like our people" (42). Later on, in a cheap rhetorical move, Herzl has the Palestinian Reschid Bey denigrate the pre-Jewish Palestinian landscape that he himself had presumably been a part of: "Nothing could have been more wretched than an Arab village at the end of the nineteenth century. The peasants' clay hovels were unfit for stables. The children lay naked and neglected in the streets, and grew up like dumb beasts" (123). Stolow's observation about Altneuland—that "Where Arab life is not *already* absent it is represented as an object in *need* of repair, civilizing or, barring these, outright eradication" (63)—holds just as true for Exodus—if not truer because of Uris's sustained assault against the Arabs and Palestinians in the novel. In spite of Herzl's and Uris's distinct historical and cultural worldviews, and their different temporal relationship to the state of Israel—for Herzl, it is a future possibility, for Uris, a past accomplishment and a current reality—they both imbue their fictional narratives with a colonial, Orientalist rendering of Arab time and Arab presence.

While the representations of the pre-Zionist-conquered Palestine in Herzl's and Uris's works are near identical—though in Uris's it is more heavily elaborated—what is not identical is the temporal scope of the Jewish rejuvenation of the land. In Altneuland, the change happens overnight, during Friedrich and Kingscourt's twenty-year dream. As Bey exclaims at the end of his description of the ruined Arab landscape, "Now everything is different" (123). Conversely, in Exodus, Ari, Barak, Yakiva, and all the rest have to wrest their proper destiny from the hands of their enemies in the multiple battles, negotiations, votes, and speeches that make up the bulk of the novel. Both Herzl's and Uris's conceptions of Jewish time—sundered history or teleological inevitability—ignore, reduce, or vilify the Arab presence in Palestine, in order to have the necessary blank slate to play out their visions of Jewish redemption. This erasure—and dehumanizing—of the land's Indigenous inhabitants is one of the strongest hammers in the settler-colonial toolkit. Both novels deploy the same Zionist mythologies of the Arab presence on the land, which is based on time—since Jewish time ended in Palestine, nothing has happened. Arab time, if anything, has denigrated the land, and only Jewish time—through Jewish presence—can rehabilitate it. Stolow's two "distinct operations" that produce the chronotope of Palestine in *Altneuland* are helpful in understanding the rhetorical moves of Uris's novel as well. First, Stolow locates what he calls a cartographic operation, an "imaginative 'mapping' of the land in which a hypothetical colonization has taken place" (62). Second, there's a "detergent" operation, "geared toward excising the presence of a 'native' population (and way of life) resistant or even hostile to the emergence of a Jewish State in Palestine" (63). In *Exodus*, both of these operations that Herzl performs have borne their fruit, but now Uris is committed to narrating the outcome of the mapping and colonization and to presenting it as ethical, necessary, and fundamental to Jewish history.

There are several ways to interrogate this backshadowing of Jewish nationalism into the temporal and spatial fields of Palestine. First, we could refer to the conclusive research that has found that the vision of Palestine as empty, denuded, and degraded is entirely inaccurate—the result of Orientalism, selective readings of the extant literature, and the settler-colonial goals of Zionism.[14] Second, we can look at how Zionist intellectuals have manufactured their readings of the Bible to align with their colonial project. Nur Masalha, in his *The Bible and Zionism*, argues convincingly that from the beginnings of Christian Zionism to the contemporary Israeli state, Zionist biblical studies, archaeology, and geography have all been geared toward linking the Jews to the Palestinian land, erasing the thousands of years of non-Jewish presence in the process. Finally, and most importantly, we can say that regardless of the state of the land and the biblical connections to it, the unavoidable fact is that people lived in Palestine, and had for many generations. The lived reality of Palestinian society can only be viewed as a major obstacle to Zionist colonization. Both Herzl and Uris fold history in on itself, making the implicit claim that since Jews lived there in the Bible, they should still be living there now. With all the differences between Herzl's and Uris's conceptions of Jewish temporality, the insistence on autochthonous claims bolstered by biblical texts read as history and not as religious narratives reveals the damaging sameness of their Zionisms, and their desire to pull the Jewish diaspora into a centroperipheral state.

Publication History and Critical Reception

Having established the importance of theories of time and history in the narrative metaphysics of Altneuland and Exodus, I want to turn to the historical moment of their writing and publication, in order to both place the texts in their contemporary discursive constellation and show how even though the Zionism of these novels ended up being ascendant, diasporic disagreement and critique were with them from the very beginning. Both Herzl and Uris wrote their texts from their own Jewish diasporic positionality and their respective societal contexts of turn-of-the-century Austria and 1950s America. Herzl wrote Altneuland against the backdrop of his waning power in the Zionist movement, and with antisemitism rampant throughout Austria and Europe as the whole region struggled with the centuries-long conflict between liberalism and traditionalism. Uris, conversely, wrote and published Exodus during what historians call the "golden age" of Jewish America, when Jewish diasporic success in the United States was at its zenith; however, with the horrors of the Shoah becoming clear, and the state of Israel clamouring for allegiance, some Jewish Americans were left unsure how to feel about their place in the Jewish world. Both novels received praise as well as harsh criticism from within their respective Jewish milieus. Looking closely at the emergence of these two novels, surprising similarities between the authors' feelings on the Jewish world, on nationalism, and on the role of fiction come into focus. Though writing in vastly different national and diasporic circumstances, both Herzl and Uris were passionate about Zionism's promise as redeemer of the Jewish people, a people whom both authors believed that, due to their statelessness, had atrophied, diminished, and lost the heroism and toughness of their biblical ancestors. Accepting the antisemitic stereotypes that circulated in Herzl's Austria and Uris's America, they both wrote novels extolling the virtues of Zionist ethnic nationalism.

Though he was credited with creating political Zionism, both through the publication of The Jewish State and his role in convening the First Zionist Congress—and despite his nearly complete mythologization as the father of the Israeli state—during his lifetime Herzl had to severely curtail and modify his desired vision of Jewish nationalism. Herzl wanted a centralized, modern state that would yank the Jews into the present; it did not have to be in Palestine, and it did not have to revive Hebrew. Herzl wanted the state to happen immediately, through high level deals with the world powers, but specifically with a charter for colonization from the Ottoman emperor, with whom Herzl met.[15] Herzl's main ideological rivals, the Russian Zionists, however, favoured the slow buying of land and incremental settlement. Influenced by Russian populism, these Russian Zionists, according to historian Jacques Kornberg, "sought to create in Palestine a Jewish peasant stratum close to nature, rooted in the soil" (xi). For them, the rebirth of Hebrew and the land of Palestine was central. As Kornberg puts it: "Differences on these issues could have split the Zionist movement from the outset had not Herzl responded by a combination of substantial concessions as well as vague, deft compromises that would not tie his hands as he pursued his priorities" (xi). In fact, the early Zionist congresses can be seen as a series of ideological battles that Herzl did not exactly win, with opposition to Herzl steadily mounting in the process (xii).[16] "It is against this background of the creeping erosion of Herzl's leadership and his reluctant concessions to an opposition, gradually gaining in strength," Kornberg writes, "that [Altneuland] must be viewed" (xii–xiii). Or, as Stolow puts it, "Novel-writing, for Herzl, became a performance carried out in the corridors of power, not in its inner chambers" (56). Though Herzl was not the first to write Jewish, or even Zionist, fiction that imagines glorious or utopic futures,[17] Altneuland, by the very nature of Herzl's role in consolidating the Zionist movement and his place in the pantheon of Zionist heroes, is the preeminent version.

Herzl's novel was met with blistering criticism from the moment of its publication. As Zilbersheid puts it, "Herzl paid a heavy price for the publication of his utopian novel" (89). According to Stolow, Herzl expected *Altneuland* "to solidify the international Zionist movement and to educate Jews about the practicalities of building a state in Palestine. Instead, it was met with reserved disapproval on the part of Herzl's friends and with derision from his opponents" (70). The critics of the novel lambasted Herzl for a variety of reasons: the novel is not Jewish enough; the changes in Palestine happen too fast; antisemitism disappears too fast; and the novel espouses a simple replanting of European and German culture in Palestine. According to Stolow: "These rejections of *Altneuland* were not only a matter of bitter personal disappointment for Herzl; they also led directly to growing challenges to his leadership," and led to a "series of splits in the Zionist movement" that continued after Herzl's death. Overall, the novel failed to "establish a common front among Zionists vis-a-vis the colonization of Palestine" (71). One of the most vituperative critics of *Altneuland* was Ahad Ha'am, one of Herzl's main ideological opponents.[18] Unlike Herzl, Ha'am believed that the Jewish presence in Palestine should be about spiritual renewal, not state building. In his review—which has not been translated into English—Ha'am wrote that Herzl's vision of a Jewish collective in Palestine was a "monkey's mimicry lacking any independent national characteristics, reeking of 'slavery within freedom,' the result of [the] diaspora in the west, spreading in all directions" (qtd. in Gluzman 103). Ha'am rightly saw Herzl's *Altneuland* as thoroughly Westernized.

One of the more lasting criticisms of *Altneuland* was that it lacked any real Jewish characteristics, textures, or ideas. Ahad Ha'am raised this concern, as does Muhammad Ali Khalidi. Ha'am wrote that, in regard to the New Society's schools: "If Hebrew and other Jewish subjects are taught—we do not know. Because in all matters dealing with education, David tells us only that [schools] attempt to strengthen children's bodies through various sports as is common in England" (qtd. in Gluzman 103). Gluzman reads Ha'am here as revealing "not only the lack of specific Jewish content in the New Society but also Herzl's longing for everything essentially unJewish, including the longing for a culture of the body" (103). For Khalidi, the lack of Jewishness in the New Society proves that Herzl wrote the novel not for a Jewish audience, but for a Christian one. While the insights of Ha'am, Gluzman, and Khalidi on Herzl's relationship to Jewish culture and how he imbued, or did not imbue, that culture in his novel shed light on the inner workings of *Altneuland*, I want to complicate their reading. There are Jewish culture and Jewishness in the novel, just not the kind the above critics are looking for. There are plays on Jewish themes—including the opera on Shabbatai Zee, the false Jewish prophet who led a failed revolution—Yiddish is one of the local languages, the third temple is rebuilt (more on this below), there is a Passover Seder, and stores are even closed on Saturday. The truth is, *Altneuland* is Jewish in the way Herzl expected the future Jewish state to be Jewish: assimilated, secularized, and European. Overall, the criticisms of *Altneuland* reveal how Herzl's diasporic utopic imaginings were, from the beginning, enmeshed within the pre-Israel Zionist debate on what exactly a Jewish state *should* be. Herzl answered in his particular way; the Zionists who actually built the state answered in their own. It is the latter's version that Uris celebrates.

The story of Uris's composition of *Exodus* follows a different trajectory than Herzl's. Uris did not have political ambitions, was not brought up in the cauldron of the Habsburg empire, and he was a proud American. A patriot and a marine raised in a secular, left-leaning household, Uris was not well-versed in Jewish history or religion. When he decided he was going to write *Exodus*, he underwent a crash course not just in Zionism, but in Jewish history writ large. Both Silver and Nadel contend that during the research for *Exodus*, Uris read over three hundred books on Jewish and Zionist themes. Silver also details how Uris travelled across Israel extensively, covering over "12,000 miles" (89) of the new country. Uris vehemently disliked how he saw the Jewish diaspora represented, especially by other Jewish authors. Uris hated most Jewish American writers, including Philip Roth and Saul Bellow, believing that "They spend their time damning their fathers, hating their mothers, wringing their hands and wondering why they were born. This isn't art or literature. It's psychiatry...Their work is obnoxious and makes me sick to my stomach" (qtd. in Nadel 109). Uris, therefore, wanted to write about his version of the Jew: tough, strong, self-sufficient, and ready to fight for what is theirs. "We Jews are not what we have been portrayed to be," he laments. Uris's anti-diaspora Zionism not only misreads the history of Jews living in the diaspora (and takes the antisemitic tropes of Jewish weakness at their word), but also rejects the ethical and positive aspects of a diasporic sensibility for the easy thrills of nationalism and military force. Uris poured large amounts of Jewish history, all filtered through his anti-diaspora Zionism, into the novel.

Uris's publishers may have been uneasy about all this history, but they need not have been, as the book quickly became a literary phenomenon. The unprecedented success of Exodus has been explained in a number of different ways: for Silver, it is because the novel captures a particular feeling of Jewish ethnic empowerment; for Nadel, it has to do with "the moral intensity of [Uris's] writing, which was propelled by hatred of injustice and abuse" (7). While this might seem true when it comes to the subjects of his novels (Jews in Exodus, the Irish in Trinity), it is deeply ironic that what Uris sees as injustice and abuse against Jewish people leads him to act unjust and abusive toward Palestinians, Arabs, Muslims, and anybody else who dares to question the ethicality of an exclusively Jewish nation-state. An additional reason for the novel's success is that it dramatizes the "clash of civilizations" in easy-to-digest writing laced with propulsive action that has clear good and evil. Whatever the reason, the novel's success and importance is immense, historic, and ongoing. It is the most important work of Jewish diasporic fiction focused on Israel, for the simple reason that it helped legitimize the state for countless readers. Uris's novel and Otto Preminger's 1960 film adaptation's massive impact on Jewish diasporic feelings toward Israel show the importance and ethical power of fictional narratives of nation-states written from outside of those nation-states.[19] According to Nadel: "Criticized for sloppy writing, one-dimensional characters, and wooden dialogue, Uris was nonetheless one of the most popular and successful novelists in America, perhaps in the world, for almost thirty years" (9).

Amidst all this fanfare and wild success, there were detractors and critics. In the novel, Uris makes a compelling, forceful argument that Israel could be the impetus for Jewish empowerment, especially in America—but at what cost? One Arab writer's response answers this question definitively: the Jewish empowerment lauded in Exodus comes at the expense of the Arabs and Palestinians. Aziz S. Sahwell's pamphlet, put out by the Arab Information Center of New York City in 1960 and entitled Exodus: A Distortion of Truth, is a major, nearly forgotten, early critical response to Uris.[20] The booklet is a thoroughly researched, well-cited counter-reading. Sahwell argues that Uris has three goals in writing

Exodus: "to justify the violent establishment of a Jewish state on Arab soil, to glorify Israel's military 'valor' in accomplishing its unlawful purpose, and to slander and discredit all Arab people. His tools for the task are untruths, half-truths, deliberate omissions and distortions of events, all blandly presented with an air of historical integrity" (1). The pamphlet is far from perfect—at one point, it says the argument that Jews are returning home to Israel means that New York belongs to "the Indians" (3) (which is a confusion between rightful autochthonous and Indigenous claims and false autochthonous claims, as I discussed in the introduction), and it often confuses Uris himself with Uris's narrator—but as a corrective to the novel, and as a historical document, it is essential.

Another critic of the novel was Philip Roth. Roth gave a speech criticizing Uris's construction of the "New Jew," called "Some New Jewish Stereotypes," which was collected in his *Reading Myself and Others*. It is worth spending some time on Roth's short article on *Exodus*, and not just because the previous chapter was on Roth, but because his incisive critiques of the novel tell us a lot about what was already apparent (to some) in the initial heyday of the novel's (and subsequent film's) success. Roth opens by stating that he suddenly lives in a country "in which the Jew has come to be—or is allowed for now to think he is—a cultural hero" (137). It is the success of the *Exodus* book and film—and the "only authorized version" of the film's theme song (137)—that has brought this new cultural prestige to American Jews. "However you slice it," Roth writes, "there does not seem to be any doubt that the image of the Jew as patriot, warrior, and battle-scarred belligerent is rather satisfying to a large segment of the American public" (137). Roth surmises that this is because, for Jewish Americans, *Exodus* substitutes stereotypes of Jewish weakness for stereotypes of Jewish strength—"there is not much value in swapping one simplification for the other," Roth writes (138)—and for Christian Americans, it allows them to no longer feel guilty for antisemitism and the Shoah. Much of Uris's appeal, Roth writes, is that he helps "to dissipate guilt, real and imagined" (143). "So persuasive and agreeable is the *Exodus* formulation to so many in America," he continues, "that I am inclined to wonder if the burden that it is working to remove from the nation's consciousness is nothing less than the memory of the Holocaust itself, the murder of six million Jews, in all its raw, senseless, fiendish horror" (145). Roth compares the Exodus phenomenon to a piece of popular art that allows Americans to "dispose of that other troublesome horror, the murder of the citizens of Hiroshima" (145). In juxtaposing two covers of Life magazine, one with a picture of the recently captured Adolf Eichmann, the other of Sal Mineo from the following week (who plays Dov in the film of Exodus), Roth regrets that "A crime to which there is no adequate human response, no grief, no compassion, no vengeance that is sufficient seems, in part then, to have been avenged" (146). Finally, Roth laments what Uris has done to the American image of the Jew: "The Jew is no longer looking out from the wings on the violence of our age, nor is he its favourite victim; now he is a participant. Fine then. Welcome aboard" (146). For Roth, what Uris has done, in bringing the Jewish hero into the pantheon of Western colonialism and violence, is what Zionism has done to a diasporic worldview. Roth's thoughts on Uris, tough Jews, and what it means to be powerful and to have access to state violence are in their infancy here in 1961. It would take almost twenty years before they would blossom into book-length form in The Counterlife and Operation Shylock.[21]

Having briefly delved into the publication histories of Altneuland and Exodus, I want to end this section with two brief examples that show how the two discourses orbiting both novels have not lost any of their orbital velocity. Part of the reason for doing this is to make clear the way that Herzl's and Uris's novels transcend their own eras, thanks to Zionism's ongoing ascendancy in the Jewish world, its centroperipheral hold (an ascendancy that is, nonetheless, beginning to feel the disruption of various gravities). First, let us return to the SS Exodus, the actual ship that attempted to run the British blockade with its hull full of Jewish refugees. The historical details of the SS Exodus incident are ones that Uris did not feel it necessary to dutifully record in his novel; however, Gordon Thomas's 2010 Operation Exodus, a monograph focused solely on the ship, its passengers, and its story, toes the same exact ideological line as its fictionalized predecessor. The book's subtitle, From the Nazi Death Camps to the Promised Land: A Perilous Journey That Shaped Israel's Fate, reveals the Zionist narrative that suffuses Thomas's reportage, a narrative that follows the same exact outlines of Uris's book: from the horrors of the Nazi death camps to the renewal, rejuvenation, and historical glory of the Jewish state of Israel. In the prologue, Thomas writes that the 4,500 refugees and the crew of the SS Exodus were "caught up in an event unparalleled in history: a precursor for the foundation of a nation and its people...who fought a sea battle like no other to get to Palestine, their Promised Land, *Eretz Yisrael*" (xv). The story Thomas tells is "of a people pursuing a dream 2,000 years old" that "stands as a judgement on the inhumane treatment of the Jews" (xv), connecting, as Uris so skillfully does, the Nazi genocide of the Jews with the founding of the Zionist state.

The second example involves a recent instance where Herzl and *Altneuland* were in the news. When Marvel Studio's *Black Panther* film came out in February 2018, it was an important moment in African American culture: for nearly the first time, a major blockbuster film written and directed by as well as starring Black people, a film that imagined the uncolonized, Afrofuturistic African state of Wakanda and the proud, culturally intact Wakandans, was everywhere in the public imaginary. It was not long before Zionist writers started to make comparisons between Israel and Wakanda, comparisons that wilfully ignored that Israel was literally founded through the ethnic cleansing and colonization of the Indigenous population. In one such take, Lahav Harkov wrote in *Tablet Magazine* that "*Black Panther* is the most Zionist movie I've seen in a long time...Wakanda is black *Altneuland*—or maybe even Israel" (np). Harkov went on to describe *Altneuland*—calling it "a deeply weird book" for anyone "familiar with the real Israel" (np)— and compared it to *Black Panther*'s Wakanda, claiming that both places have "advanced technology," gendered societies, and political debates about the ethical use of power. We can clearly see here how *Altneuland* is refracted through time. Harkov's article ends with Wakanda's plans, at the end of the movie, to share its technological marvels with the outside world, something, Harkov claimed, Israel already does and that Israelis are "especially proud of."

Palestinian American Yousef Munayyer's response to Harkov convincingly critiqued her equivocation of *Altneuland* and Wakanda. "Beyond the straightforward appropriation of a celebration of someone else's euphoric cultural moment," Munayyer responded, "the 'Black Panther is About Zionism' take is at best untenable and at worst, offensive" (np). His article goes on to show how Herzl's colonial attitude toward both Africa and Palestine directly opposes the anti-colonial thematics of *Black Panther*, points out the Israeli government's support of South African apartheid, and argues that *Altneuland*'s "depiction of

Palestine is a creation of a Zionist imagination, a literary device aimed at justifying the cause of the saviors" (np). Black Panther, Munayyer argued, directly "disrupts" this "fantasy of an impoverished Africa or Palestine in need of saving" (np). What this illuminating exchange between Lahav and Munayyer reveals is the extent to which Herzl's novel still resonates in the culture today, used as a touchstone of Zionist literary production to be celebrated or critiqued.[22] Both Altneuland and Exodus are still relevant, still in the discourse, with their ideologies and implications still circulating, still anchoring Zionist worldviews, and still provoking fierce criticism.

The Palestinians and the Arabs in *Altneuland* and *Exodus*

One of the most important questions we should ask of diasporic novels fictionalizing a Jewish collective in Palestine is: how do they include the Indigenous Palestinian population and their narrative of catastrophe and displacement in their fictional worlds? As I argued in the previous chapter, any Jewish fictional text that wants to engage with Israel/Palestine must make space for the othered and dispossessed Palestinian others if it wants to achieve moral clarity. Operation Shylock, I argued, does this through its robust use of diasporic heteroglossia. As we will see, however, while both Altneuland and Exodus have named, speaking Palestinian characters, what they symbolize, what they speak is not heteroglossic, but univocal.[23] The way both novels confront/distort the presence of Palestinian Arabs is a forceful example of what is at stake in fictional representations of ethnic conflict, especially when it is from the geographical remove of diaspora. Together, they reveal the dangers of writing centroperipheral texts that make no room for the other, that close off their heteroglossic possibilities in order to make their ethnic nationalist case. The two novels, in certain ways, share a similar (Zionist) outlook here: both describe the Arabs as backwards, filthy, unorganized, and untrustworthy, as killers, and as undeserving stewards of the land. This changes in Altneuland when the protagonists return to Palestine, but it only reaches more of a fever pitch in Uris's novel after the state is declared. In both texts, moreover, Palestinians that sign on to the Zionist narrative are given a pass to their Arabness, as it were. Herzl's decisions regarding the Palestinian presence on the land have everything to do with European colonial worldviews of colonial property, and are kept on the peripheral of his utopic Jewish space; for Uris, the Arabs stand for the ultimate obstacle to Jewish statehood, and are therefore painted with a racist, stereotyped brush that has two viscosities: evil, and less evil because they conform to Zionism. Uris's relentless vilification of Arabs and Arabness serves an obvious rhetorical and ideological purpose: to prove that their claim to the land of Israel/Palestine is forfeit in the face of Jewish righteousness. As Jeremy Salt cogently explains: "Unable to find any rational basis for Palestinian opposition to Zionist settlement, [Uris] can only explain it away in terms of the deep and ugly psychoses that grip the Arab mind and that lead them to hate each other and to hate Jews" (58). Clearly, Uris is not afraid to have Arabs appear in his text; their place in Uris's Zionist imaginary is there for all to see. In *Altneuland*, however, the Palestinian question, especially around what happens to the local inhabitants when Joe Levy and David Littwack establish their utopic New Society, is harder to parse. Let us start there, then.

Altneuland has one named, speaking Palestinian character, David Littwack's neighbour and friend, Reschid Bey, and one named, non-speaking Palestinian character, Reschid's wife, Fatima, who is sequestered in her home under strict religious adherence to what David calls "the Moslem customs" (97). Reschid's role in the text is clear: to show to Friedrich and Kingscourt, and therefore to the novel's Jewish and non-Jewish readers, how the New Society has benefited the Arabs as much as it has the Jews. Reschid is a happy member of the New Society, telling Friedrich and Kingscourt that "The Jews have enriched us. Why should we be angry with them?" (124)—a response Herzl and other Zionists assumed they would receive, if they thought about the Arab inhabitants of Palestine at all. Earlier, when readers are first introduced to Reschid (and where David speaks to him in Arabic, and Reschid responds in German), David tells his guests that Reschid's father "was among the first to understand the beneficent character of the Jewish immigration, and enriched himself, because he kept pace with our economic progress. Reschid himself is a member of our New Society" (68–69). This idea, that Zionism would be only positive for those Arabs who embraced it, is still a powerful myth in the Zionist worldview.

This myth, which had not yet come up against the realities of settler colonialism in Palestine, is espoused throughout the novel, by both Reschid and other members of the New Society. During the tour of the rehabilitated countryside, Reschid and the others have a detailed conversation on Jewish enrichment of the Arabs. When Steineck, the chief engineer, mentions that the Jews brought cultivation to the valleys, Reschid says that the Arabs had it, too—"at least there were signs of it"— bringing up his father's orange groves as an example. Steineck concedes this point, going on to claim, "but you could never get full value out of them," which Reschid easily agrees with, stating, "Everything here has increased in value since your immigration" (121). Kingscourt, however, is not satisfied. He asks Reschid: "Were not the older inhabitants of Palestine ruined by the Jewish immigration? And didn't they have to leave the country?" (121). As we will see, this question—if, in the fictional world of *Altneuland*, the Arabs had to leave, i.e., were expelled—is a divisive one. Reschid's response to Kingscourt is that the Jewish immi-gration was a blessing for all Arabs: "Naturally, the land-owners gained most because they were able to sell to the Jewish society at high prices, or to wait for still higher ones. I, for my part, sold my land to our New Society because it was to my advantage to sell" (122). Reschid goes on to give a long, detailed speech, cataloguing everything the Jews did for the Arabs, including plentiful work opportunities and improvements to their villages and livelihoods. The Palestinian inhabitants, accord-ing to Reschid, "benefited from the progressive measures of the New Society whether they wanted to or not, whether they joined it or not" (123). Perhaps this is where Herzl's utopic imagining differs most starkly from today's Israel/Palestine, though, importantly, Herzl admits that the New Society was something that was done to Reschid and his fellow Palestinians, regardless of their thoughts on Jewish colonization.

Judging from Reschid's statements and the statements of other New Society members throughout the text—and against the desires of the xenophobic ethnic nationalists represented by Rabbi Dr. Geyer—it would seem, then, that the Arab does have a place in Herzl's Jewish utopic commonwealth. This is how Shlomo Avineri reads the novel, claiming that "An attempt is made here to involve the Arab residents of the country in a social vision based on universalism" (np). Avineri goes so far as to read the Geyer-Littwack election solely as it pertains to the Arab citizenry of the New Society, instead of through Geyer's wider desire to ban all non-Jewish membership, which is how I read it.[24] Furthermore, the place of the Arab, as embodied in Reschid and his sequestered wife Fatima, is not as simple as critics such as Aveneri desire it to be. In a fascinating queer reading of Altneuland, Michael Gluzman connects the positionality of Reschid with the novel's female characters, arguing how both are used to create the new Jewish male who is not diseased by diasporic femininity. "Herzl's apparently progressive representation of minorities," Gluzman writes, "is undermined by a subtext that relegates both the woman [sic] and the Arabs to the margins of the symbolic order of the New Society" (106). Claiming that the sexual/gender issues in Altneuland have not been properly investigated, Gluzman shows how the New Society is a "narrative of sexual redemption" as well as an ethnic one (90). Gluzman argues that Herzl and other Zionist leaders were trying to cure Jewish masculinity of its "feminized, melancholic" character (96): "Herzl, who internalized the anti-Semitic view of the Jew as having a defective body, describes the diasporic Jewish body as grotesque" (97).[25] Reading the dinner scene where Sarah and David discuss Sarah's ability to participate in the political sphere, but her decision not to, Gluzman writes that David Littwak's views on the place of women are inextricably entangled with his stance on the place of the Arab in the New Society.[26] Women and Arabs are both viewed "as minorities who, in return for equal rights, accept their marginal status within the male Jewish hegemony" (107). Gluzman argues: "The Others in the new society are grateful for their legal equality, but they don't demand that this equality be put into practice. In fact, it appears that legal equality serves as a mechanism to silence resistance" (108). In a convincing reading of Fatima, who we only meet as a hand waving from a window, Gluzman uncovers how Reschid's supposed equality rests on a series of racist and gendered presumptions:

> The equality the Arab enjoys is based on his cooperation and co-optation within Jewish hegemony, because in the public domain he is required to erase his Arabness. In other words, only male Jews are allowed to be whole, unsplit subjects. But it seems that the woman's position is even more inferior, because, while the Arab is allowed to be an Arab at home and a man outside, the woman is encouraged to relinquish

her right to leave home altogether. The Arab in *Altneuland* is encouraged to assimilate; the woman cannot but remain a woman. (110)[27]

Gluzman convincingly shows how Avineri's reading of total equality between Jews and Arabs in *Altneuland* is illusory. However, neither Gluzman nor Avineri helps answer the question of what happened to Reschid's neighbours and cousins.

And it is a question of monumental importance: where did all of the Palestinian villages and Palestinians themselves go in the twenty-year gap between Friedrich and Kingscourt's two visits? Arriving at the thriving port of Haifa, Friedrich and Kingscourt see "many Chinese, Persians and Arabs in the streets, but the city itself seemed thoroughly European" (61), and, later, they both befriend Reschid. Besides these moments, readers are never alerted to a Palestinian presence in the New Society. The travelling companions do not pass through a single Arab village— though, rather enigmatically, at one point David says: "you must not expect to see the filthy nests that used to be called villages in Palestine. Today you will see a new village which is typical of innumerable settlements both to the east and the west of the Jordan" (120). It is quite unclear if the new villages David refers to are Jewish or Arab, or even mixed (though chances are it is the former). One possible reason there are so few Arab Palestinians in *Altneuland* is that since Herzl barely acknowledged their presence in reality, he simply did not include them in his fictional narrative. According to Muhammad Ali Khalidi—and in direct opposition to Avineri's reading—however, the Palestinians have been forcibly removed by the supposedly liberal members of the New Society. "Just as the presence of an Arab population was what rendered the land repulsive to Herzl's narrator in 1901," Khalidi writes, "their absence is what now rehabilitates it" (58).[28] We have already seen the accuracy of the first part of Khalidi's claim, but what of the second? Khalidi reads the Arab question through the lens of Herzl's other, nonfictional writings, including a "little-known" charter between the World Zionist Organization and the Ottoman government that Herzl drafted in 1901–1902 (59). Khalidi's methodology of reading the novel through Herzl's diaries, letters, and speeches is the inverse of critics like Zilbersheid, who read Herzl's politics and plans out of the novel. Furthermore, as historian Derek Penslar points out, in the historiography on Herzl the importance of Herzl's writing on the Arab Palestinians shifts depending on the ideology of the historian. As Penslar puts it, "Herzl's views on the Arabs are a peripheral topic in Zionist historiography yet central in its anti-Zionist counterpart" (51).[29] A telling example of this is Herzl's diary entry where he toys with the idea of forced transfer of the Indigenous Palestinian population; Penslar traces how non-Zionist readers of Herzl focus on this but Zionist ones do not (though pro-transfer Zionists do use it as fuel for their plans of further ethnic cleansing).

Khalidi claims the novel contains the "thinly veiled removal of the indigenous inhabitants," leaving a minority of Arabs "to imbue the society with a cosmopolitan flavor" (62). Referring to the scene in Haifa quoted above, Khalidi writes: "we gather that Arabs continue to be present in Palestine, though in the same way that Chinese and Persians are present, not as native inhabitants but as one minority among others" (58). The idea of a "minority" of Arabs is significant; whether the New Society is emptied of its Indigenous Palestinian inhabitants or not, Herzl's narrator does contradict himself when it comes to the ethnic makeup of the New Society. As one character in the novel states, "Only when the Jews, forming the majority in Palestine, showed themselves tolerant, were they shown more toleration in all other countries" (178). This is a major slip on Herzl's part. If, as Littwack and others proclaim, and as Geyer laments, the New Society lets in anyone who wants to be a member, and we know that Arabs such as Reschid have joined, how is it possible that a Jewish majority was formed without the forced removal of hundreds of thousands of Palestinians? And, without Geyer's ascension, how would a Jewish majority be maintained? In any case, this—Jewish tolerance in the form of a state—is precisely what has yet to materialize in Israel/Palestine, and it gives substantial weight to Khalidi's reading. Significantly, though, neither Khalidi nor Gluzman includes the Geyer election in their reading of the novel. Perhaps this is because for both of them the New Society is already exclusionary, and Geyer's election will change little.

Adjacent to the question of the Palestinian population in *Altneuland* is the geographic whereabouts of the rebuilt third temple in Jerusalem. Readers are informed that "The times had fulfilled themselves, and it [the third temple] was rebuilt. Once more it had been erected with great quadrangular blocks of stone hewn from nearby quarries and hardened by the action of the atmosphere. Once more the pillars of bronze stood before the Holy Place of Israel" (250–251). Herzl uses the existence of the new temple to have his narrator restate the Zionist belief that only with a nation of their own can the Jews redeem their place in world history. "Jews had prayed in many temples, splendid and simple, in all the languages of the Diaspora," Herzl's narrator waxes poetic, "The invisible God, the Omnipresent, must have been equally near to them everywhere. Yet only here was the true Temple. Why?" (253–254).[30] The answer: "Because only here had the Jews built up a free commonwealth in which they could strive for the loftiest human aims" (254).[31] So, clearly the third temple exists somewhere in *Altneuland*'s version of Jerusalem—but where? Khalidi, assuming the temple stands where the first and second temples stood, writes that Herzl "never explains the fate of the Muslim holy places that lay on the site" (57). In my reading, however, Herzl makes it clear that the third temple is not built on the ground where the Dome of the Rock and the mosque of Omar now stands, but in a different part of Jerusalem.[32] Herzl's decision to have rebuilt the third temple is prescient; the Dome of the Rock is one of the most contested geographic entities in the world, and there is a growing movement in Israel to destroy it and rebuild the temple.[33] The ambiguity about where *Altneuland*'s third temple is, while mirroring the unresolved question of where the Palestinian inhabitants of the New Society are, shows how less committed to actually bringing back the Jewish Bible Herzl was compared to subsequent generations of Zionists. The fuzzy geography of Herzl's imagined Jewish commonwealth leaves space for coexistence (a very different outcome than Bezmozgis's fuzzy geography of settlement in *The Betrayers*, as we will see in the fourth chapter). With regard to the status of Arabs in *Altneuland*, the Palestinian presence in Herzl's utopic society, regardless of Reschid's explanations and Khalidi's reservations, remains an open question, the answer to which is in no little part dependent on the political outlook of the reader.

In *Exodus*, Uris includes a plethora of speaking Arab characters; for the most part, however, they are horrible, vicious stereotypes in the worst Orientalist tradition. In fact, *Exodus* has by far the most named, speaking Arab characters out of any text analyzed in this book (with *Operation Shylock* a distant second). As Andrew Furman wryly observes, "one finds oneself wondering, as the novel unfolds, if Uris will ever exhaust his arsenal of new and derogatory ways to depict Arabs" (42). The Arab racism in *Exodus* can be divided into four broad categories: toward historical characters, including the Jerusalem grand mufti Haj Amin al-Husseini, Fawzi al-Qawukji, and Ibn Saud, who the narrator quotes as saying, "*There are fifty million Arabs. What does it matter if we lose ten million people to kill all the Jews? The price is worth it*" (465; emphasis original);[34] toward individualized fictional characters (most significantly Barak's neighbour and friend Kammal and Kammal's son, Taha); toward groups, towns, and Arab landscapes; and toward Arabs and Muslims as either faceless mobs or abstract historical entities (including the historically inaccurate portrayal of Islam as a "religion of the sword").[35] I also include in this schema of negative Arab representation those rare times when Uris's narrator portrays Arabs positively—the Druze, Kammal, Taha, and the residents of Abu Yesha (at least until they turn on Ari and the Jews of Dan Gafna)—because their positive portrayal only deepens the anti-Arab racism of the novel, and fits cleanly into its rhetorical project. While scholars such as Silver and Nadel downplay the importance of Uris's portrayal of the Arabs, the Palestinians, and the refugee crisis, a diasporic-centred reading of the novel must not only place a strong emphasis on the negative representations of Arabs as the ultimate enemy of the Jews and of the West, but also look at how these metanarratives have become deeply entrenched in the Zionist and Jewish worldview.

Uris's handling of the Arab characters, groups, and states in his novel serves a number of ideological functions. First, the Arab is always used as a foil to hold up the unimpeachable yet heroic Jewish characters. As Andrew Furman points out, while Uris "depicts the Jew as a reluctant warrior, he invariably depicts the Arab as a bloodthirsty, savage murderer" (44). In the rare instances where Uris's narrator admits wrongdoing on the part of the Jewish Israelis, it is quickly justified and argued away, with the most egregious example of this being the 1948 massacre of Deir Yassan, which Uris fictionalizes as "Neve Sadij." In the novel, due to "a strange and inexplicable sequence of events a panic broke out among Maccabee troops and they opened up a wild and unnecessary firing"; more than "two hundred Arab civilians were massacred," and the event, which the narrator calls "the blackest blot on the Jewish record," "fixed a stigma on the young nation that it would take decades to erase" (523). However, as Nur Masalha argues, not only was Deir Yassan far from an accident, but it was part of an orchestrated program of ethnic cleansing that involved mass murders in a large number of Palestinian towns (62–64).

Second, the narrative of *Exodus* seamlessly moves the enemy of the Jews from the Nazis, to the British, to the Arabs, and this is done so in such a way that it seems entirely logical, causal, and unavoidable. This is why in the opening pages of the novel, British Brigadier Bruce Sutherland blatantly connects the horrors of the Shoah with the barbarity of the Arabs: "But I can't seem to forget the Arab slave markets in Saudi Arabia and the first time I was invited to watch a man have his hands amputated as punishment for stealing, and somehow I can't forget those Jews at Bergen-Belsen" (31). There is no logical or historical reason to conjoin these two events, except to place the Nazis and the Arabs in the same vanguard of evil. This is also why al-Husseini's connection to Adolf Hitler and Nazi Germany is so central to Uris's characterization of the mufti, and why the narrator repeatedly calls him a "Nazi agent" (467) (more on this below). Third, the Arab Palestinians in Uris's moral universe can only be redeemed if, like Herzl's Reschid, they realize that the Zionist state is in the best interest of the Arabs. As we will see below, Kammal does realize exactly this and is therefore rewarded with humanity; his son Taha does not, and Ari is forced to kill him and destroy his village. (The father-and-son motif when it comes to Arabs who support the Zionist enterprise is noteworthy; first Reschid and his father, and now Kammal and Taha.) It is important to note that this last point—that the only acceptable Arab or Palestinian position is one of acquiescence to the Israeli state, which is why a non-violent movement such as Boycott, Divestment, and Sanctions (BDS) is villainized as much as suicide violence—is still a major element of the Zionist mythos.[36]

The Arabs are constantly generalized, stereotyped, and compared disfavourably to the Jews of the novel. Readers are told that "Greed and lust, hatred and cunning, shrewdness and violence, friendliness and warmth were all part of that fantastic brew that made the Arab character such an enormous mystery to an outsider" (229). The Christian Arabs fare not much better than the Muslim ones. We are told that Nazareth "stank. The streets were littered with dung and blind beggars made wretched noises and barefoot, ragged, filthy children were underfoot. Flies were everywhere" (334). Hiking up Mount Tabor for a party with other Palmach soldiers, Kitty and Ari encounter a Bedouin tribe and are more or less coerced into eating a meal with them: "Kitty looked around. They seemed the dregs of humanity. The women were encased in black robes—and layers of dirt. She was not able to smell the goats but she was able to smell the women. Chains of Ottoman coins formed veils over their faces. The children wore dirty rags" (353). Afterwards, Ari says the sheik wanted to buy Kitty for six camels. It is not just the narrator who lays on the stereotypes. During a debate in the Yishuv during the Arab revolt, readers are told that "Haggling, guilt documents, and the like would never take the place of a gun in an Arab's mind" (255). These off-hand comments are constant throughout the text.[37] Uris's animosity goes beyond description and historical misreadings: the Arabs' refusal to accept a Jewish state turn them whole cloth into rapists and murderers.

During the narrative of Exodus, three female Jewish characters are murdered by faceless Arab mobs. All three of these women—Dafna, Ruth, and Karen—are love interests of the novel's male protagonists—Ari, Akiva, and Dov, respectively—and represent the best of the new Zionist generation in the same way the Arab mobs embody Uris's sense of the Arab polis. "Karen looked the very spirit of the Jews!" the narrator tells readers as she waves an Israeli flag while leading a Shavuot parade (373). Other Jewish women, such as Barak's wife, Sarah, are tortured but are not killed—it is while Sarah is held in captivity by Jemal Pasha's police that she gives birth to Ari, who is quite literally born into struggle (248). When Dafna, who is Ari's first girlfriend and the love of his life, is murdered, readers are told: "Her ears, nose, and hands had been amputated. Her eyes had been gouged out. She had been raped over a hundred times" (281). Ari reacts "in the same way that the Yishuv had learned to accept such things—not by being stirred to violence, but only by deepening his determination not to be thrown from the land" (281). Ruth and her daughter Sharona are murdered during an Arab riot (253); this event is portrayed as the impetus for Akiva to become a terrorist.[38]

Finally, and most significantly, there is Karen's death. Karen, the brightest hope of the new Jewish state, who readers watch transform from a young, scarred Shoah survivor and refugee into a battle-ready, independent young Jewish woman thanks to the ministrations of both Kitty and the Yishuv, moves to a kibbutz on the Gaza border after the 1948 War, and is eventually murdered by marauding Arabs. (Both Dov and Kitty tried to talk Karen out of moving to the border, but she insisted it was her duty as a Zionist and an Israeli.) The death is reported to us in dialogue. Ari informs Kitty, Dov, and others during the Passover Seder scene that closes the novel: "Karen is dead. She was murdered last night by a gang of *fedayeen* from Gaza" (596). The novel ends three pages later, the narrator hinting that both Dov and Kitty will recover from the loss of Karen, due in no small part to the fact that they have the state of Israel. Karen's death is shockingly anticlimactic for a novel full of climactic deaths, and considering that Karen is one of the prime movers of the novel's plot, the nonchalance of her murder is even more strange. As Weissbrod reads the scene: "*Exodus* has a happy ending both for the nation (victory) and for the individuals (Kitty and Ari finally unite). Although evil has not been completely quashed, as evidenced by Karen's death...good certainly has the upper hand, and there is a clearly defined balance of power between the two" (131). Weissbrod christens the close of *Exodus* as a "melodramatic ending *par excellence*" (131). I would further suggest that Uris has Karen's death land as it does to show that nothing has changed: the Jews will always have eternal, non-rational enemies killing their best and brightest. The only difference now, the end of *Exodus* implies, is that there is a state and an army ready to fight those enemies.

Karen's death is a telling example of how Uris fed everything he knew, saw, and read about Israel/Palestine into his own narrow Zionism. As Silver informs us, Uris based Karen's death on a similar event that took place at Kibbutz Nahal Oz in 1956, when an Egyptian ambush killed Ro 'i Rothberg, the kibbutz's security officer. Uris was in Israel researching *Exodus* at the time and attended the funeral. According to Silver, for Uris, "the kibbutz members' determination to carry on under hellish circumstances of desert deprivation and Arab terror symbolized the sabras' capability to overcome everything" (173). The funeral had such an impact on Uris that he often brought it up when talking about the writing of *Exodus*. However, Uris's interpretation of Rothberg's death is not the only one; Rothberg's funeral happens to also be the location of one of Moshe Dayan's most famous speeches, where the general acknowledges the Palestinian narrative. Part of Dayan's speech reads as follows:

> Let us not today cast blame on the murderers. What can we say against their terrible hatred of us? For eight years now, they have sat in the refugee camps of Gaza, and have watched how, before their very eyes, we have turned their lands and villages, where they and their forefathers previously dwelled, into our home. It is not among the Arabs of Gaza, but in our own midst that we must seek Ro'i's blood. (qtd. in Morris 287–288)

Even though Dayan goes on to talk about unending Arab hatred, the eulogy is often read as an early admittance of the effects of Zionist settler colonialism. "To many Israelis, Dayan's Nahal Oz eulogy seemed to point ahead to a future era of mutual political recognition between two peoples," Silver writes. "Whether or not it was Dayan's intention to anticipate a two-state solution in this famous 1956 funeral oration, he spoke eloquently about the need to understand the Palestinians' side of the story" (174). Israeli historian Benny Morris calls Dayan's eulogy "one of the most candid and revealing statements by an Israeli about the crux of Israeli–Palestinian relations" (287). However, as Silver rightly points out, Uris was not interested in that aspect of the story and took his own meanings from the funeral. Even faced with the complexities of the Israeli–Palestinian situation, Uris stuck to his melodramatic worldview of ultimate good and ultimate evil.

Most of Uris's ultimate evil is reserved for one historical figure: al-Hajj Amin al-Husseini, the grand mufti of Jerusalem. Uris turns the grand mufti into the puppetmaster of every instance of Arab revolt, murder, plot, and Jew hatred in the novel, regardless of the complex and nuanced historical reality of Palestine in the Mandate Period. Silver goes so far as to call Uris's narrator's two-page historical summary of the mufti's actions in the 1920s "breathtakingly manipulative" (177). Uris's narrator calls the mufti, among many other things, "the most vile, underhanded schemer in a part of the world known for vile, underhanded schemers...El Husseini was backed by a clan of devils" (253).

Al-Husseini is personified with Uris's usual Arab attributes, as power hungry, and as willing to sacrifice scores of lower-class Palestinians for his political project of killing Jews and taking over Palestine for himself. Uris repeatedly narrates how al-Husseini uses the fellaheen (Palestinian peasants), due to their tendency "to become hysterical at the slightest provocation," as a "political weapon" (253). Even during periods of general quiet in Mandate Palestine, "There was always tension in the air, for the sinister Mufti...lurked in the shadows" (257). It is the mufti and his "tirades" that ruin the "early friendships" between the Jews and Arabs and that made the "destruction of the Jewish homeland" a "'holy' mission of Pan-Arabism" (266), and it is the mufti's men that kill Barak's friend Kammal for cooperating with Jews (274). Most significantly— and most damaging—Uris uses al-Husseini's relationship with Hitler and the Nazis, and his propagandizing during his time in Nazi Berlin, to make a concrete connection between the genocidal antisemitism of the Nazis and what Uris represents as the genocidal antisemitism of the Palestinians.[39] According to *Exodus*, al-Husseini "found a powerful ally for himself—Adolf Hitler" (267). When the British issue an arrest warrant for the mufti, he escapes Palestine "dressed as a woman" (277)— though apparently this is historically accurate, Uris nonetheless uses this detail to further demonize the mufti—and makes his way to Berlin, where "Adolf Hitler greeted him personally as a brother" (296).

As Israeli historian Ilan Pappé explains in his book on the al-Husseini family, "Palestinian historiography was long uncomfortable with discussing" al-Husseini's connection to the Third Reich (315). "However," he writes, "recently they have openly and sensibly revisited this chapter of ill-fated liaisons, describing the players as a few individuals who were detached from Palestine and its politics and no longer attuned to the genuine predicament of the people there" (315). As much as Uris and other Zionists (including Prime Minister Benjamin Netanyahu) want to use the mufti to nullify any Palestinian claim of grievance against the actions of the Jewish state, as Pappé reminds us, "This was not a formative chapter in Palestine's history, but it is one that cannot be ignored given how it has been manipulated by Israeli historiography to Nazify the Palestinian movement as a whole and to justify brutal oppression, ethnic cleansing and occupation" (315). Pappé reads al-Husseini's actions during the war as those of a "hallucinatory figure losing touch with reality and assuming roles and capabilities far beyond those he actually possessed" (315–316).[40] Pappé's book shows, if nothing else, how significant one's ideological lens is when writing historical narratives. While al-Husseini is far from an unproblematic historical figure, Uris uses him as an empty vessel in which to deposit his own anti-Arab sentiment.

For Uris, the moral and human worth of an Arab is entirely contingent on their amiability toward the Zionist project. For that reason, the only Arabs that are represented in a positive way in the novel are Barak Ben Canaan's friend Kammal and the Druze, who are allies of the Jews in their war against the British. Kammal's son Taha, as we will see, is more of a complex character, alternating between his friendship with Ari and his commitment to the Arabs. The Druze are the only Arab group portrayed positively in the novel; this is because they allied with the Jews during the 1948 War. Readers meet the Druze when Ari is taken to the village of Daliyat el Karmil to hide and recover after he is injured in the Acre prison raid to rescue his uncle, Akiva, and Dov, who were sentenced to death for their terrorist activities. Daliyat el Karmil "seemed to sit on the roof of the world": "It was sparkling white and clean in comparison to the filth and decay of most Arab villages." The men, many of whom wear Western clothing, are compared favourably to the other Arab inhabitants of Palestine: "the most dramatic difference was the carriage of dignity and outward pride and the look which suggested that they could be fierce fighters" (435). As Andrew Furman points out, "The Druse, who hide the injured Ari from the British, are allies of the Jews, and this, of course, explains the splendor of their village" (44).

Likewise, Kammal is introduced as an enlightened Arab, "a hater of his own class," who "developed a social conscience" (226) and who admits that the Jewish state is the only way to save the backwards Arab population. And yet, "Despite Kammal's enlightenment he was heart and soul an Arab" (227). In a speech reminiscent of Reschid's, Kammal admits the good of the Jews: "I have watched the Jews come back and perform miracles on the land. We have nothing in common in religion or language or outlook. I am not even sure the Jews will not eventually take all the land. Yet...the Jews are the only salvation for the Arab people. The Jews are the only ones in a thousand years who have brought light to this part of the world" (258). Barak congratulates his friend on accepting the coming Jewish splendour: "I know this is difficult for you to say, Kammal" (258).

After this speech, Kammal sells Barak and the Jewish Agency some land he owns in the Huleh Valley. In return, Barak and the kibbutz help the Arabs, setting up schools to "teach them sanitation, the use of heavy machinery, and new farming methods" (261). As Jeremy Salt describes, Kammal, along with Haj Ibrahim in Uris's The Haj, "are depicted by Uris as moderates who realize that their real enemies are other Arabs and their true friends the Jewish settlers, who have come to live in peace and whose presence can only benefit the Palestinian people" (54–55). Kammal also acts as historical interlocutor for Barak and the early Zionists, teaching them Islamic history, "the magnificent and tragic history of the Arab people" (Exodus 227), though it is the highly orientalized version Uris prefers. Kammal's murder is a direct result of his friendliness with Barak and the other Jewish settlers.

Unlike Kammal, who accepts the Jewish presence in Palestine but still worries about the Yishuv's intentions—Kammal's "mind could not believe that the newcomers would not eventually engulf and exploit the Arabs as all the others before them had done" (229)—Kammal's son Taha has a more complicated outlook. Taha and Ari grew up together and were best friends. However, as the War of Independence heats up, Taha feels the pull of Arab nationalism. Where in the film, Taha does the best he can to avoid helping the Nazis, in the book, after a vicious fight with Ari, Taha declares himself an enemy of the Jews. Taha, who fell in love with Ari's sister Jordana when she was thirteen—the narrator informs us that "Love of a younger girl was not uncommon among Taha's people" (289)—starts to distance himself from Ari. Ari chastises Taha, reminding him of all the good the Jews have done for him: "These stone houses in your village were designed and built by us. Your children can read and write because of us. You have sewers because of us and your young don't die before the age of six because of us. We taught you how to farm properly and live decently" (344). Taha says he will not attack Yad El, but this is the moment that Taha and Ari's friendship begins to break. This is also the first time the narrator takes us into the head of a Palestinian character. What we see is Taha's doubt and skepticism regarding his Jewish benefactors: "Was he really the brother of Ari Ben Canaan or the poor cousin? Taha asked himself this question more often each day. Each time the answer was more certain. He was a brother in name only" (345). While this seems like a reasonable worry, Uris's intent is to show how Taha's Arab nature blocks him from seeing the truth about his Jewish neighbours; nevertheless, Uris has accidentally given us a reasonable thought process of someone who is watching his land erode out from under him. Uris has their friendship end when Taha laments that he could never "declare that he had loved Jordana Ben Canaan quietly and with the heartache that comes with long silence" (345). When Ari and Taha next confront each other, Taha has turned on Ari. They argue about the Arab attacks on the Jewish settlement, which Taha says he cannot prevent. When Taha tells Ari to give him Jordana and Ari proceeds to punch him in the face, their friendship is over. "You have told me everything that I need to know. Get out of my house, Jew" (485), Taha says, reverting to antisemitism. Ari's destruction of Abu Yesha, including ordering the attack that kills Taha, is portrayed as a tough but necessary moral decision for Ari.

A final aspect of Uris's representation of Arabs and Palestinians is how *Exodus* grapples with the Palestinian Nakba and the ensuing refugee crisis of 800,000 Palestinians that Israel would not let go back to their homes and belongings. Uris's narrator makes the same arguments that are still heard all over the Jewish world: that the Palestinians were forced by their own leaders to leave; that the rest of the Arab world is responsible for repatriating them; and that the Palestinians who attempt to access their homes/lands are "infiltrators." Uris's novel, while more forthcoming on the realities of the creation of the state than most novels that have come after, going so far as to acknowledge the refugee situation, still blames the Arabs and the refugees themselves for the loss of their homes and lives. Uris has Barak write up a long report on the refugees and includes it in full at the end of book four. "*The Arabs created the Palestine refugee problem themselves*" (553; emphasis original), Barak's report claims, the villages that were "*hostile*" have been rightly removed, and "*No apologies have to be made for this.*" This language permeates the novel, with whole villages being deemed "*hostile*" and therefore violently removed—as in "*Operation Broom*," which swept the "*Galilee clean of hostile villages*" (515; emphasis original). Letting the Palestinian refugees back in is out of the question, Barak insists: "*it is inconceivable that Israel could even consider resettlement of a hostile minority, pledged to destroy the State*" (553; emphasis original). Barak, paralleling the standard Zionist take, blames the Palestinian and Arab leadership for the plight of the fellaheen, who "*were victimized by men who used them as a tool, deserted* them, and are victimizing them again. Kept penned up, fed with hatred, they are being used to keep Arab hatred of Israel at the boiling point" (554; emphasis original). As Salt rightly notes, "Not only personally but politically, the Palestinians are presented by Uris as the agents of their own destruction" (60).

Barak continues with the victim blaming, stating that "A man who loves his land, as the Arabs profess, will stand and die for it," as opposed to fleeing (554). The hypocrisy here is astounding: first blamed for leaving, the Palestinians are then chastised for not staying to fight, though attempts to return are seen as hostile. Finally, Barak turns the report on refugees into an opportunity for some Zionist back-patting, claiming, as characters throughout *Exodus*—and *Altneuland*—do, that "Israel today stands as the greatest single instrument for bringing the Arab people out of the Dark Ages" (554). Besides the fact that these rhetorical moves against the refugees are still dominant in Zionist discourse and have been thoroughly debunked, I want to briefly show how from the very beginning of the refugee crisis, there were those who did not accept the Zionist narrative. Erskine B. Childers was one of these. In an article published in the late 1950s, Childers thoroughly dismantles the Israeli claim that the Palestinians were instructed to leave by the Arabs. "The fact is that Israel's official charges," Childers writes, "which have vitally influenced the last ten years of Western thought about the refugees, are demonstrably and totally hollow" (np). Childers proves this through a thorough examination of both Arab and Israeli radio and newspaper archives. According to Childers, "These Arabs, in short, are displaced persons in the fullest, most tragic meaning of the term—an economic truth cruelly different from the myth," and the narrative that they were instructed to leave, as opposed to being ethnically cleansed, has been "soothing our highly pragmatic Western conscience for thirteen years" (np).

What we see happening in all the various ways that Uris represents and fictionalizes Arabs, Palestinians, their towns, and their history is Uris fitting them into his cowboys-and-Indians worldview. For the rest of his life, Uris would never stray from his feelings toward the Arabs, and if anything, his animosity and disdain for them only grew in subsequent books. *The Haj*, Uris's 1984 novel that follows a Palestinian family through a number of generations, is stocked with racist, Orientalist views. The plot revolves around a father's incestuous relationship with his daughter.[41] Returning to *Exodus*, there is no shortage of critics and readers of the novel who are aware of the racism. What is missing, as we see with Silver, is a reckoning of what Uris's depiction of the Arabs has meant for the enthusiastic readers of the Jewish diaspora. Uris justifies the Zionist treatment of the Palestinian population through his melodramatic cowboys-and-Indians, settler-colonial, paradigm, arguing that the Arabs were an obstacle to Jewish rejuvenation that needed to be vilified, delegitimized, and dehumanized, and that deserved to be removed from the Jewish state.

"A Solution Is Still Possible": Conclusion

In this chapter, I have compared *Altneuland* and *Exodus* as two novels of the Jewish diaspora that fictionalize a Jewish collective living in Palestine through a univocal Zionist modality. Having unpacked how both novels engage with different models of Jewish time, I have analyzed the two novels' publication history and some contemporary critical responses, and critiqued how the Arab and Palestinian narrative is presented. Overall, I have argued that, despite their similarities, *Altneuland*, as a settler-colonial utopic novel, shows us a Zionism that still believed it could create a Jewish presence in Palestine without bloodshed, whereas *Exodus* celebrates the violence used to create Israel, and set a dangerous precedent for how the Jewish state has been viewed by the diaspora and world at large. I would like to end the chapter by making the case that the sundered history of novels like *Altneuland* can be powerful correctives to the racist national narratives of authors like Uris. The elections that take place in *Altneuland* during Friedrich and Kingscourt's visit show us how the fate of nations, peoples, and the world can always be altered for the better.

The Geyer election subplot is the clearest indication that Herzl was aware of the issues that a Jewish nation-state could generate. Even though politics are mostly frowned upon in the New Society, when Friedrich and Kingscourt return to Palestine after their twenty-year absence, general elections are underway. There are two factions running: one represented by David, Steineck, and others, and the other by Rabbi Dr. Geyer, "the patriot, the nationalist Jew" (138), the former representing what Avineri calls the "liberal ethic" (np), the latter a reactionary, xenophobic ethnic nationalism.[42] The main issue in the election is the place of the non-Jew in the New Society. Geyer and his followers wish to exclude non-Jewish people from the Jewish commonwealth, while his opponents, the current ruling elite, want to keep the New Society open to all who wish to join. The novel, and therefore Herzl, quite clearly comes down on the side of inclusiveness. As President Eichenstamm says to David: "You must be steadfast in your fight. You are right. Geyer is wrong...The stranger must be made to feel at home in our midst" (111). At the Neudorf debate, Geyer's representative, Mendel, proclaims: "What we made with our own hands must remain ours" (141). Steineck responds: "you must hold fast to the things that have made us great: to liberality, tolerance, love of mankind. Only then is Zion truly Zion!" (139). David himself rebuts Mendel, expounding on the novel's theme that the wonders of the New Society were not built solely by Jewish pioneers. "It would be unethical for us to deny a share in our commonwealth to any man, wherever he might come from, whatever his race or creed," David says, "For we stand on the shoulders of other civilized peoples. If a man joins us—if he accepts our institutions and assumes the duties of our commonwealth—he should be entitled to enjoy all our rights" (152). At the end of the debate, the narrator tells us: "That day Dr. Geyer lost the votes of Neudorf" (154). And sure enough, at the novel's end, just as Kingscourt and Friedrich make their decision to become members of the New Society, Geyer loses the election.

Thinking of the Geyer election alongside sideshadowing and temporality, Geyer's defeat at the ballot box solidifies one of Bernstein's main claims about how we narrate history: that every decision, every debate, every election could have gone in a different direction. From every historical moment, heteroglossia blooms. Unfortunately, Geyerism has been present in Israel since its founding, and is only becoming more ascendant; but, as sideshadowing insists, as a contrapuntal exegesis of *Exodus* and its multiple scenes of elections, votes, and decisions reveals, and as the utopic yearning of *Altneuland* breaks through our temporal status quo, it is still possible for the Jewish collective in Israel/Palestine to change course. The Jewish philosopher Martin Buber, who in the 1930s and 1940s was a founding member of IHUD, a group of progressive Jewish

Zionists—including Judah Magnus and Henrietta Szold—who believed that cooperation with the Palestinians was a necessity and that declaring a state was the wrong way to achieve what even then they referred to as binationalism, had a similar temporal awareness, arguing for the immediate need to redirect the course the Zionist leadership in Palestine was pursuing. In his 1947 article "The Bi-National Approach to Zionism," Buber, discussing the need for rapprochement with the Palestinians and the opportunities for it that had already been lost, writes: "More emphatically than ever has it to be shown that a solution is still possible. To bring this solution about will be more difficult and less satisfactory now, than at any earlier stage, but its realisation is still within our reach: it will bring us back to our path of constructive work" (13). Buber's words are as true today as they were seventy years ago. Instead of looking at the violent Jewish past and trying to justify it through an ethnically exclusive Zionist teleology, as Uris does, we need to start new dialogues, accept new narratives, open new possibilities, and look toward the utopic possibilities of the future. Yes, the possibility of justice, of binationalism, is harder now than it was yesterday—than it was in the 1940s or in Herzl's own time—but its realization is still within our reach. Any time can be a moment of sundered history.

Arab Jews, Polycentric Diasporas, Porous Borders

Israel/Palestine
in the Short Fiction
of Ayelet Tsabari

WE HAVE NOW REACHED A POINT OF transition in the book. This transition runs on a number of different tracks. Track one: moving from major, canonical Jewish authors—Herzl, Uris, and Roth—to younger, contemporary writers—Ayelet Tsabari and David Bezmozgis—who are not only still alive, but in the early to mid stages of their writing career. Track two: moving from the American (and Austrian) context to the Canadian one, with all the differences that entails. Track three: moving from large, formative novels to shorter fictional forms; for Ayelet Tsabari, the short story and the short story collection, for David Bezmozgis, the short novel. The implications of these generic differences will be addressed throughout the subsequent chapters. The fourth and final track: both Tsabari's *The Best Place on Earth* and Bezmozgis's *The Betrayers*, unlike the texts that came before, filter their fictional worlds through one specific subsection of the Jewish diasporic world and their impact on/place in Israel/Palestine. Instead of attempting to perform a wide-scope societal reckoning of Israel in their fiction, Tsabari and Bezmozgis confine themselves to the perspectives of Arab Jews and Soviet Jews, respectively. What will not change in the following two chapters is the exploration of Jewish diasporic writing centred on Israel/Palestine. With Tsabari and Bezmozgis, however, we move definitively into the twenty-first century.

Though the eleven stories in Tsabari's *The Best Place on Earth* take the form of traditional, realist short fiction—each story has a handful of central characters, a central conflict, some sort of resolution, and adheres cleanly to its narrative point of view, either first or third person—taken together, Tsabari has crafted a story collection that deeply challenges the common narratives told about Israel. The stories' Israeli characters—Arab Jews from Yemen, Egypt, Iraq, Tunisia, and Jerusalem—allow a vantage point into Israeli society that has been absent from Canadian or American fiction, where the Ashkenazi viewpoint and narrative remains dominant.[1] Tsabari's characters consist of multiple, shifting identities, and are constantly on the move, passports in hand, humming along diasporic routes: three of the eleven stories begin in an airport;[2] virtually all of the characters have immigration in their recent past; and the settings are as diverse as the Tel Aviv suburbs, Jerusalem, the Negev desert, but also India, Montreal, Toronto, and BC's gulf coast. However, Tsabari is interested in much more than simply detailing the diasporic lives of Arab Jewish Israelis around the world. The fluid, dynamic identities that people the stories in *The Best Place on Earth* disrupt any sense of clean national belonging, whether to Israel, Canada, or elsewhere (and mirror Tsabari's own peripatetic nature). Rather, the characters in the collection resonate with a specific, and powerful, sense of *diasporic* belonging (or unbelonging).

While on the surface the stories in *The Best Place on Earth* can seem to be mostly about characters falling in and out of love, family dramas, and slices of life from Israel and the Israeli diaspora, one does not have to dig too deep to find a perfectly balanced mixture of emotion, politics, critique, and hope. These are truly stories that *enact*: enact their politics, enact their theorization of contemporary life in the Jewish world, and enact the possibility for moving beyond ethnic nationalism to something more like justice. This enactment, this bringing-into-being, can be read as an instance of diasporic heteroglossia, with each story speaking from an ever-enlarging perimeter of diasporic positionalities, within and without the centroperipheral centre of Israel/Palestine. The stories reveal a range of tensions present in life in Israel, in diaspora, and in what it means to be Arab Jewish in a European Jewish country. Tsabari's fiction brilliantly and carefully communicates the contemporary realities of Israel's Arab Jews; through a close engagement with her stories, we can hopefully begin to loosen the Zionist demand that a strict ethnic nationalism is the only way to keep the Jews of Israel—and, implicitly, the Jews of the world—safe.

In this chapter, then, I argue that in giving voice to characters who have diasporic or unclear origins, who belong to the ethnic, racial, economic, and geographic margins of Israeli society, and who are in constant struggle with the ethnic and national boundaries of Zionism, Tsabari uses her fiction to make the diasporic heteroglossic argument that Israel and Zionism's—and, in a more general sense, the nation-state's itself—insistence on overly defined and patrolled modes of national identity can only be enforced through limiting and violent enclosures. Tsabari, through the diverse situations she brings to life in The Best Place on Earth, thoroughly demolishes Zionism's claims of pure national origins, of the need for—and efficacy of—borders political and social, and of the eternal animosity between Jew and Arab. The overriding element that ties all of the stories together, besides the characters' Arab Jewishness, is their belief in fluid identity, in overcoming differences through desire and love, in the diasporic insistence on relating ethically to the stranger, the Other, the supposed enemy. The collection as a whole, therefore, embodies what Ella Shohat compellingly calls a "diasporic polycentric perspective" ("Introduction" 14). In a complimentary and nuanced parallel to diasporic heteroglossia, Shohat claims that this poly-centric perspective "situates post-partition Arab-Jewish/Mizrahi history within a constellation of multidirectional and palimpsestic and porous cross-border movements" ("Introduction" 14). As we will see, the stories, characters, and situations of The Best Place on Earth do exactly this.

Ayelet Tsabari and her work vividly reveal the possibilities of diasporic Jewish writing in our contemporary moment. Born in Israel to what she calls a "large family of Yemeni descent,"[3] Tsabari grew up in what Zionists claim is the negation of Jewish diaspora, Israel, while belonging to a partic-ular, non-European outpost of that diaspora: the Yemeni Jewish diaspora. Jews have lived in Yemen since the third century, and have a varied and rich cultural, religious, and sociological tradition—a tradition that was down-played, scoffed at, and eradicated by the Zionist state institutions after their mass emigration to Israel in the early years of the state (as we will see below). The bare facts of Tsabari's positionality as a Yemeni Jew in Israel already challenge received wisdom on Israel, the Zionist "ingathering" of the Jews, and the simple binary of diaspora/home. Tsabari, however, pushes the shape of the diasporic continuum even further. After travelling and residing all over the world—her recent memoir, *The Art of Leaving*, details some of these experiences—in the 1990s, Tsabari made Canada her home, first in Vancouver, and then in Toronto, writing and publishing her fiction in Canadian journals and presses beginning in 2006. Written in what Melissa Weininger terms "Hebrew in English" (18), Tsabari's work is a perfect example of what Rebecca Walkowitz calls the born-translated novel—or, in this case, the born-translated short story collection—containing as it does multiple languages, linguistic registers, and linguistic competencies, always already translating and being translated. "Rather than Hebraizing her English," Weininger explains, "Tsabari frequently imports Hebrew (and occasionally Arabic) words into the text, often translating them simultaneously" (20). Tsabari thus places her English narratives "outside of Hebrew," where "Hebrew must be imported" and where it is "always artificial, requiring translation and explanation" (20). What this denaturalization and deterritorialization of Hebrew— as Weininger calls it—accomplishes is to relocate Hebrew "back to the Diaspora" (20). In other words, by moving Hebrew out of its national context and into a foreign—here, English—linguistic structure, modern Hebrew can be detached from the Zionism that engendered it, can be diasporized. On the same page of a Tsabari story, characters can be speaking in English, Hebrew, or Arabic, with the tensions between these languages constantly brought to the fore. While Canadian literary institutions claim Tsabari as one of their own, it can just as easily be said that Tsabari is an Israeli writer, a Yemeni writer, a Jewish writer, a writer of colour, a woman writer.

To complicate matters further, in late 2018, Tsabari, her husband, and their young daughter returned to Israel for what Tsabari calls a "trial move to Israel" ("After 20 Years in Canada" np). In *The Globe and Mail*, Tsabari writes about her decision to return to Israel, how Toronto has become home, and how "Leaving is messy, a fracture, an unravelling." "Returning does not fix it," she realizes: "It's possible that this is not return at all, but another phase in a series of departures" ("After 20 Years in Canada" np). Tsabari may have returned to Israel, but her diasporic consciousness after twenty years in Canada means that there will forever be a tension between home and away. Importantly, Tsabari's multiple identities speak to not only her own personal and familial history, but the entangled, complex networks of Jewish diasporic movements. Tsabari, with her ancestral roots in Yemen, her diasporic distance from Israel during her decades of travel and living in Canada, her return to Israel with Toronto now becoming a new home that she is distanced from, and the originary Jewish diasporic attachment to Israel, reveals how complex, fluid, and ever-changing the Jewish diasporic situation is, and productively troubles Zionism's binaric insistence on the dominant Israeli state and the subservient diasporic condition.

Tsabari, in her early career, has achieved a high level of success, in both the Jewish and non-Jewish literary world. *The Best Place on Earth* won, among other prizes, the Sami Rohr Prize for Jewish Literature and the Edward Lewis Wallant Award, two major Jewish literature awards (with major purses attached). Tsabari's second book, the memoir-in-essays *The Art of Leaving*, was released in spring 2019. The memoir, which explores themes and issues familiar to readers of her fiction, including growing up as an Arab Jew in Israel, losing loved ones (Tsabari's father died of a heart attack when she was very young), Tsabari's experiences in the army, partying and travelling in India, and relocating to Canada, is a fascinating window into the raw material that Tsabari uses to craft her fiction.[4]

The stories in *The Best Place on Earth* evocatively bring to light the inter-Jewish hierarchies and tensions present in the state of Israel. The story "Say It Again, Say Something Else," for example, is about a female Yemeni Jewish teenager whose family has recently returned from America and who falls in love with another young Jewish woman, a recent immigrant from the Soviet Union; the story revolves around the differences between them and their assigned place in the Israeli collective. The collection also critiques the role gender plays in the militarized Zionist culture, which appears in most of the collection's stories in various guises. In "Casualties," the protagonist's boyfriend cannot handle his army service deployment in Gaza, and, readers are led to believe, kills himself. "Warplanes" explores what it means to lose a father not to the army but to heart disease in a society that celebrates its war heroes but basically ignores those who die from natural causes. "I wish my father had died in the army instead of in a hospital," the first-person narrator admits, after listing all the benefits that accrue to a "bereaved Israeli Defense Forces family" (201). "There is no Remembrance Day for people who died of a weak heart" (201), the narrator laments. In "Below Sea Level," David and his recently retired IDF (Israeli Defense Forces) commander father are estranged because David chose not to serve in the IDF, convincing the army's psychiatrist that he would kill himself if they made him enlist, a betrayal that David's father, a career army man, finds unforgivable. Weininger glosses the gender politics interrogated in the collection thusly: "Tsabari's male Israeli characters struggle with and suffer from the expectations associated with the image of the New Hebrew Man" (27). The stories also expose the affective economies at play in Israeli society. In "Tikkun Olam," for example, the collection's opening story, readers witness the ways in which a suicide bombing in a Jerusalem cafe reunites a nihilistic Israeli man with his ex-girlfriend, who has become religious.[5]

The stories also explore the distances between generations of Yemeni, and other Arab, Jews. In "Brit Milah," when Reuma visits, for the first time, her daughter Ofra and Ofra's infant son in Toronto, she has to confront the fact that her daughter has grown away from her family. Ofra and her half-Jewish husband Matthew did not circumcise their son, a religious transgression Reuma finds near impossible to forgive. Growing up, Ofra rejected Reuma's Yemeni culture and adopted the dominant Ashkenazi culture of Israel: Ofra "despised anything Yemeni...She even changed the way she spoke; as a little kid she spoke like her parents, with guttural hets and ayins. Reuma lost her daughter over and over again: first she became Ashkenazi, then Canadian" (54). It takes Reuma the majority of the story to understand that Ofra has made Canada her new home: "Reuma looked at her, surprised: Ofra was smitten with the weather, with the naked trees, with the season; she felt at home in this cold, strange country. Reuma felt a sharp, quick pinch in her heart. Her daughter wasn't coming home" (59–60).

Tsabari, unlike any of the authors investigated thus far, has intimate knowledge about what it was like to grow up on the margins of Israel's Jewish collective.[6] Yet she also captures daily life in Israel: the constant presence of Nescafé in the kitchen, men with beat-up cigarette packs in their back pockets, the smells and sounds of the falafel stands, the omnipresence of the sea in Tel Aviv, the even greater omnipresence of the army. A story like "The Poets in the Kitchen Window," for example, captures life in Tel Aviv during the Gulf War, when Iraq bombarded the city with Scud missiles. The stories do not take national borders as an immutable feature of life in the Middle East, however. Tsabari integrates throughout the collection images that defy the logic of national borders. In "Say It Again, Say Something Else," to take one example among many, a heat wave "travels from Libya and Sudan" to Tel Aviv (34); the very earth systems of the Middle East connect Arab and Jewish geographies.

I will focus my analysis of the collection on three stories. These three stories—"Invisible," "A Sign of Harmony," and the aptly-named "Borders"—best exemplify the ways in which the collection, as a whole, shows how unnatural strict national identities are, especially when they are predicated on originary ethnic, religious, cultural, gender, and historical matrices. "Invisible," I will argue, reveals the commonalities between Filipina foreign workers in Israel and Yemeni Jews, forcing readers to reshape their understanding of Israel from a nation of Jews and their national other, the Palestinians, to a nation-state in a system of nation-states where the elite have power and the marginalized do not. "A Sign of Harmony," in its confrontation between two different diasporic identities, Yemeni and Indian, reveals the similarities and differences in navigating the colonial and postcolonial world as a person of colour. Maya's ability to mix elements of Indian culture with her Yemeni and Israeli identity, furthermore, is a telling example of diasporic fluidity predicated on having non-white-coded skin. Finally, "Borders," the most politically forward of the stories in the collection, acts to collapse the various borders of Israeli and Zionist identity, most significantly that between Arab and Jew. Na'ama, in literally crossing the Israel/Egypt border at the story's end to try and find her Bedouin father, demolishes numerous binaries fundamental to the Zionist narrative. My reading of "Borders" will bring in Judith Butler's discussion of Moses as the

quintessential Arab Jew—an idea that germinates in Freud, blooms
in Edward Said, and is harvested in Butler—a notion that allows us to
rethink Zionism's most pernicious claims and replace them with a diasporic cultural and ethnic capaciousness.

Tsabari's fiction shows that the binaries essential to Zionist thinking, Arab/Jew, home/diaspora, citizen/infiltrator, are not only collaps-
ible, but are so muddled, the slash between the two terms so porous, that
their existence must be called into question. The stories taken together
are a powerful argument for the multitude of diasporic gradients, middle
spaces, and compromises, for Shohat's "diasporic polycentric perspective," all of which contradicts Zionism and its insistence on a pure
Hebrew Jew. I would like to suggest that the ability the form of the short
story collection gives Tsabari to present her readers with eleven different
manifestations of Arab Jewish diasporic positionalities makes a strong
claim for the genre of the short story collection as one that best fits the
diasporic mould, and one that can—and here, does—utilize the elements
of diasporic heteroglossia. Moreover, out of all the texts under study in
this book, it is *The Best Place on Earth* that, however obliquely, posits a
way out of Zionism, ethnic nationalism, and border policing.

In order to perform my readings of the three stories, I will first
discuss the Arab Jew through their place in Zionism. I will then move
on to contextualize the histories of the various Arab Jewish communities before honing in on the Yemeni one. My overarching argument for
this chapter is that *The Best Place on Earth*, through the multiplicity of
perspectives, situations, and geographies of its stories, reveals that far
from there only being one Jewish diaspora that has now been succeeded
by Israel, there have always been numerous, proliferating Jewish diasporas, and the nation state of Israel is just one place where the constant
enfolding and expanding of these diasporas plays out. No matter how
violently Zionism attempts to negate the diaspora, it continues its
dynamic movement through time even within the walled confines of
its state.

The Arab Jew as Diasporic Possibility

As hinted at above, the figure of the Arab Jew explodes from within
the binary between Jew and Arab that is essential to Zionist thinking.

Arab Jews, or Jews from Arab/Muslim countries, sometimes also called Mizrahi (which can be translated as "easterners" or "Orientals") or Sephardic Jews, make up the Jewish majority of Israel.[7] Smadar Lavie defines who she calls the Mizrahim as "Jews with Israeli citizenship whose genealogical origins lay in non-Yiddish-speaking countries" (24), in particular "the Arab and Muslim World and the margins of Ottoman Europe" (1). This would make Mizrahim a less capacious term than Arab Jew, which does not stipulate Israeli citizenship as one of its conditions; according to this definition, all of the Arab Jews in *The Best Place on Earth* are Mizrahim, but this is not necessarily true for other Arab Jews, such as those that immigrated to North America or elsewhere instead of to Israel.

Astonishingly, for a country where the Ashkenazi (or Jews of European descent) are the members of Israeli society with visibility, agency, and power—in other words, the ruling elite—50% of Israeli citizens are Arab Jews or Mizrahim (Lavie 1). With Palestinians who have Israeli citizenship (as differentiated from the Palestinians who live in the Occupied Territories, refugee camps in surrounding Arab countries, or further afield in the Palestinian diaspora) making up 20% of Israel's population, that means that only 30% are of Ashkenazic origin. As Lavie puts it: "Overall, approximately 85 percent of world Jewry is Ashkenazi, but only a small percentage of them live inside the State of Israel. Conversely, only 15 percent of world Jewry is Mizrahim, yet a great majority lives inside the Israeli state" (3). This majority status is not equitably represented in Israeli society. As Yehouda Shenhav writes, Arab Jews "account for only a quarter of the students in the country's universities, and their proportion among university professors, judges, leading media figures, writers, and in the arts remains substantially below their ratio in the population" (*The Arab Jews* 8–9). In order for the Zionist ideology to subsume the vast numbers of Arab Jews that emigrated to Israel, whether voluntarily or through Israel or state-of-origin coercion, the "Arabness" of the new immigrants had to be "underscored, erased, and otherwise managed in order to fit [them] into the Jewish collectivity" (*The Arab Jews* 2). This is one reason why Arab Jews are considered a single, undifferentiated mass, in spite of their varied cultural and national origins, not to mention the unique migration histories of the Yemeni, Iraqi, Persian, Moroccan, and Egyptian Jews, histories that are elided by, and subsumed into, the Zionist narrative of the "ingathering" of the Jewish exiles.

These unique diasporas—many centuries old, with their own customs, histories, literatures, geographies, and even languages—had to be shorn of their uniqueness in order to fit into the Zionist state.

Tsabari attempts to re-complicate the heritage of Arab Jews in her stories, through characters that have definite historical and familial ties to varied Arab Jewish collectivities. There are Egyptian Jews (Na'ama and Mira in "Borders"), Iraqi Jews (Uri's mother, a very minor character, in "The Poets in the Kitchen Window"), Tunisian Jews (Naomi and Tamar's mother in "The Best Place on Earth"), Palestinian Jews who have lived in Jerusalem since the sixteenth century (Tamar and Naomi's father in "The Best Place on Earth"), Moroccan Jews (Yael in "Causalities"), and Arab Jews with unclear origins (Samir in "Borders"). Most of all, however, there are Yemeni Jews: Savta in "Invisible," Maya in "A Sign of Harmony," Lily in "Say it Again, Say Something Else," Reuma in "Brit Milah," and Uri and his father in "The Poets in the Kitchen Window." What all these characters have in common is a tense relationship with their Arabness, which varies from story to story but is always present.

The Arabness of the Arab Jews was a contradiction for a Zionism that situated Arabs as the eternal Jewish enemy. As Ella Shohat describes it, for the first time, the two elements of Jewish Arab identity, Arab and Jewish, were forced into becoming antonyms ("Sephardim in Israel" 47, 66).[8] What for centuries had been an unquestioned mixture of cultural Arabness and religious Jewishness was suddenly torn asunder. Shohat writes that "Zionism...brought a painful binarism into the formerly peaceful relationship between the two communities. The Sephardi Jew was prodded to choose between an anti-Zionist 'Arabness' and a pro-Zionist 'Jewishness'" ("Sephardim in Israel" 47). This mutation-into-antonym is dramatized throughout The Best Place on Earth and is one of the book's recurring tropes. A short scene in "The Poets in the Kitchen Window" shows how, within Israel, "Arab" has become shorthand for the impermissible, the out-of-bounds: "At school," the narrator relates, "everybody said Sima Landau fucked Arabs, which Uri supposed was another way of saying she was a whore who'd sleep with anybody" (83). Likewise, the story "Brit Milah" opens at the border control at Toronto Pearson Airport, where Reuma, who does not speak much English, is being interrogated by a border agent. "Born in Yemen?" the border guard asks, to which Reuma answers in the affirmative (42).

This troubles the border agent, who starts studying Reuma's passport intently: "She thinks I'm an Arab," Reuma worries, quickly mentioning that she is Jewish (42). In "Say It Again, Say Something Else," when teenaged Lana tells her new friend Lily to be suspicious of any Arabs on the city bus, Lily tells Lana (whom Lily has a crush on) that her grandmother came from Yemen, "so we are Arabs in a way, Arab Jews" (35). Lana responds by laughing: "No, that's impossible," she says, "You're either an Arab or a Jew" (35). Lana here reminds Lily, who has only recently returned to Israel after living in Canada, about the Zionist division between Arab and Jew. When Lily pushes back, saying Lana is a Belarussian Jew, so why can't Lily be an Arab Jew, Lana states "I'm Israeli now…And so are you" (35), evoking the Zionist mythos that Israel eradicates all Jewish (diasporic) identities except for one: your Israeliness.[9] I agree with Weininger, who reads this scene as reflecting "the way in which Zionist discourse erases or elides the historical specificity of Jewish cultures, particularly those from the east, or Arab lands, in its movement toward a monolithic and uniform Israeli identity" (24). Far from Israel being a homogeneous country of Jewish people, therefore, the "ingathering" of Arab Jews into a country designed for/by Ashkenazi has created a highly stratified state, one where the European-Jewish minority enjoy a place of privilege, power, and access to state and national resources, and the Arab Jewish majority are far down the social, political, cultural, class, and economic ladders.

The Israeli state forced Iraqi, Moroccan, Yemeni, Tunisian, and other Arab Jews to shed not only their Arabness, but their particular cultural history and their Jewish difference: in other words, their diasporaness. In the Zionist framing, therefore, the Arab Jew is a figure of the past, gone, erased, melted away in the purifying bath of Israeliness. A small example: the title of a book published in 1984 under the "Social Orders" imprint of Harwood Academic Publishers, The Last Arab Jews, speaks plainly to this teleological rendering of Arab Jewishness.[10] Concomitant with this idea of the Arab Jew existing only in the past is the historical belief that the Arab Jews escaped their violent Muslim-majority homes and were welcomed with open arms by the Israeli state. In reality, the Arab Jews were brought to Israel to further the Zionist project, to increase demographic superiority over the Palestinians, and to be used as cheap labour (again to the detriment of Palestinian workers), while the myth of their glorious return to the Jewish homeland was used as a shield to deflect from any criticism, rebellion, or yearning for their old countries. As Shohat writes, "The pervasive notion of 'one people' reunited in their ancient homeland actively deauthorizes any affectionate memory of life before the State of Israel" ("Sephardim in Israel" 49). Since the stories in *The Best Place on Earth* are focused on first and second-generation Israeli Jews who emigrated from Arab countries, it is necessary to look broadly at the place of Arab Jews in Israeli society. In the following section, I will discuss the Arab Jews generally, and then look at the Yemeni Jewish community, before, during, and after their immigration to Palestine, and later Israel.

The histories of the Arab Jews, both before and after the rise of Zionism and the establishment of the Israeli state, are as varied as their geographical origin. Diasporic communities like those in Yemen, Jerusalem, and elsewhere in Palestine have existed since the time of Jesus. Others, what could properly be called Sephardic Jews, came to the Ottoman empire after being expelled from Spain in 1492.[11] In their new communities, they continued to speak and write in Ladino and Judeo-Arabic, both languages that are written using the Hebrew script. Arab Jews lived in their diasporic communities for hundreds and hundreds of years, usually in relative harmony with their Arab and Muslim hosts. These broad trajectories of Arab Jews are thoroughly diasporic, and represent a thriving, non-European version of Jewish cultural fluidity and resilience, one that shows the power of the Boyarins' concept of rediasporization, of living diasporic lives many times over.

To the early Zionists, however, the Arab Jewish newcomers, seen through Eurocentric, Orientalist eyes, were one undifferentiated, primitive mass. Lital Levy, in her groundbreaking monograph on Arab Jewish writers who continued to write in Arabic after immigrating to Israel (as well as Arab Palestinian writers who write in Hebrew),[12] describes it thusly: "In the massive waves of immigration, craftsmen from tiny hamlets in the Atlas Mountains or Kurdistan arrived alongside educated, white-collar professionals from cosmopolitan Cairo and Beirut; the Ashkenazi-led establishment did not differentiate between them.

Sephardi and Arab Jews were treated as social inferiors, collectively stigmatized as 'Asiatics' and 'Levantines'" (40). I agree wholeheartedly with Shohat when she writes that "While the positing of a singular 'Jewish History' (with a capital H)...has been seminal for the Jewish nationalist narrative, the work here argues for the plural—'Jewish histories.' And while 'Jewish Diaspora' (with a capital D) has been perceived as originary and unique, I have tried to narrate multiple diasporas, scattered across various geographies" ("Introduction" 21). These multiple diasporas threading throughout multiple Jewish histories are exactly what Tsabari captures in her heteroglossic stories, powerfully chipping away at the monolithic, univocal Zionist version of capitalized Jewish History and Diaspora.

According to the Zionist-inflected version of Jewish history that is currently still dominant in the Jewish world, Muslim and Arab animosity toward their Jewish citizens was eternal, ongoing, and constant. Shenhav calls this the idea of the "ancient, insurmountable conflict between Arabs (who are not Jews) and Jews (who are not Arabs)" (The Arab Jews 2). This is far from the historical truth, and stems from the grafting of European antisemitism onto the Arab world, in order to further the Zionist claim that only in their own state can Jews be safe. The golden age of Sephardic Judaism, was, after all, in the Muslim kingdom of Iberia. Levy describes how "Hebrew-Arabic bilingualism and translation date back at least to the tenth century CE. The interplay of the two languages was a defining feature of Sephardi Jewish civilization" (53). More broadly, Levy writes that

> In memoirs of both Jews and non-Jews from Ottoman
> Palestine and in Hebrew-language short stories and novellas
> by "native" Palestinian Jewish writers, relations between
> Sephardi and Moghrebi Jews and their Christian and
> Muslim neighbors are typically depicted as cordial or warm,
> replete with mutual exchanges of food and gifts on holi-
> days, shared extrareligious customs and practices, and even
> shared wet nurses. (29)

While Jewish Arabs lived in relative harmony with their Muslim neighbours and rulers, we also have to be careful to not (over) idealize the Jewish diasporas in Arab lands. Jews lived as Arabs, yes, but that does not mean there was not discrimination, and occasional violence. As Shohat states: "While it is true that Zionist propaganda exaggerated the negative aspects of the Jewish situation in Muslim countries, and while the situation of these Jews over 15 centuries was undeniably better than in the Christian countries, the fact remains that the status of *dhimmi* [non-Muslim minorities] applied to both Jews and Christians as 'tolerated' and 'protected' minorities was intrinsically inegalitarian" ("Sephardim in Israel" 45). However, it is imperative that we remember that this is utterly different—and utterly unrelated—to the Jewish experience in Europe. A diaspora existence is not necessarily an existence free of violence and discrimination; at its best, it is a mode of living not predicated on exclusive land ownership, ethnic superiority, or xenophobia.

One of the most frequent examples of Muslim hostility toward their Jewish populations deployed by Zionists to prove the eternal hatred of the Jews is the *farhud*, when Iraqis rioted in Baghdad in 1941 and killed anywhere from 175 to 780 Jews. The two-day riot is listed in The Holocaust Museum in Washington, tying it directly to Nazi Jew hatred. Both Shohat and Shenhav deal carefully with the *farhud*. Shenhav explains how the riot occurred shortly before the British conquered the city, and writes that it was "the only event of its kind in the history of Iraqi Jewry, was confined exclusively to Baghdad and did not spread to other cities. Historians agree that it was indeed an exceptional event in the history of Jewish-Muslim relations in Iraq" (43). However, the Zionist narrative took what was an exceptional event and cast it as the norm to further their political ends. Shohat implores us to consider that "One can denounce the violence of the *farhud* without instrumentalizing it to forge a discourse of eternal Muslim anti-Semitism" ("Introduction" 5). Shohat refers to the use of the *farhud* and other scattered events of Jewish killing in Arab countries to prove that Jews were not safe there as the creation of a "narrative of perennial Arab hostility to Jews and a trace-the-dot history of pogrom-like episodes" ("Introduction" 1), and warns that this narrative obscures more than it reveals. "There is very little room in this 'pogromatic' discourse," she writes, "for examining the entangled implications of Zionism, Palestine, and Israel for 'the question of the Arab-Jew'" ("Introduction" 1). Diasporic life always has its problems, but this does not, and should not, negate the diasporic existence in its entirety, especially not when this is done to further ethnic nationalism. The need to "pogromatize" Jewish Arab history, to turn it into a theatre of European antisemitism, to substitute one diasporic history for another, makes this clear.

In any case, what is undeniable is that the Arab Jewish situation changed absolutely with the rise of Zionism, culminating in the declaration of the state, the 1948 War, and the expulsion of the Palestinians. Palestinian scholar Joseph Massad explains how the creation of Israel engendered a "complete overhauling of the ethnic identities of the population" it had jurisdiction over (54). Arab Jews were "juxtaposed" to Yiddish-speaking Ashkenazi Jews; Palestinians were categorized into "Druze, Bedouin, and Christian and Muslim Arabs" (54). The Arab Jews were viewed through a colonialist, Orientalist lens; it was through this lens of "Jewish orientalism" (Shenhav, The Arab Jews 37) that the Arab Jews were brought to Israel, through propaganda, false promises, and at times, coercion. Shenhav contends that "the discovery of the Arab Jews and their ethnification within the Zionist enterprise can be understood only as a distinct product of the colonial paradigm" (The Arab Jews 25), a paradigm, moreover, that "Zionist historiography shies away from addressing" (22). Shenhav writes that "the colonial setting is the place from which any discussion of the Arab Jews must begin...the remnants of this colonial logic vis-a-vis the Arab Jews remain embedded in Israeli culture and politics to this day" (14). As a case study, Shenhav, using extensive archival research, details the story of the Solel Boneh (the national, major Israeli construction company) outpost in the Iranian city of Abadan, which Zionist emissaries used as their basecamp to entice the Jewish communities of Iraq, Persia, Turkey, and elsewhere to make aliyah (Abadan is right on the Iran-Iraq border). Shenhav argues that "this was the first time all the Jews from the Islamic countries were subsumed under a single category identifying them as one homogeneous group subject to an immigration plan" (The Arab Jews 22).[13] The letters, diary entries, and public remarks of these emissaries are a stunning collection of racist, Orientalist stereotyping. The Ashkenazi elite in the Yishuv, and later the Israeli state, wanted the Arab Jews to be used as labourers, and to ensure the Jewish demographic majority, but they did not accept the Arab Jews as "Jewish," because they did not conform to their European-centred notions of religiosity. Shenhav points out the irony of avowedly secular Zionists claiming the Arab Jews did not perform their religion correctly.

These Zionist emissaries were willing to do whatever was in their power to convince the Arab Jews to leave their homes and immigrate to Israel. Yet, as Shohat writes, "it was not an easy task for Zionism to uproot the Arab-Jewish communities" ("Sephardim in Israel" 48). Even after the state of Israel was created, and the Iraqi government was allowing Jews to leave, the majority of Iraqi Jews stayed, until a series of bombings targeting synagogues and Jewish schools catalyzed the community into flight. Shohat argues that these bombings "appear to have been the product of a collusion between two groups—Israeli Zionists (including a small group of Iraqi Zionists), and factions in the Iraqi government...who were pressured by the international Zionist-led campaign of denunciation and who had an immediate financial interest in the expulsion of the Iraqi Jews" ("Sephardim in Israel" 48). If Shohat is correct that Zionist agents were involved in the bombing of Jewish Iraqi buildings, this is a shocking example of a nation-state using violence in order to end a diaspora it claims as its natural property. In any case, the promises the Zionist emissaries made to the potential immigrants were not delivered once they arrived in Israel, often after leaving their belongings and savings behind. Arab Jewish immigrants arrived to disorder, lack of materials, and racism. They were deloused with DDT, housed in immigration centres or development towns, and had any number of indignities forced on them.

The colonial and Orientalist attitude toward the Arab Jews existed (and exists) both on the labour Zionist (the "left") and revisionist Zionist (the "right") ends of the spectrum; this racism from the Zionist centre to the diasporic periphery would dictate how Arab Jews were treated in the Zionist state. As Tikva Honig-Parnass explains, "According to the dominant Orientalist ideology, Mizrahim have been perceived as descendants of undeveloped countries and as members of inferior cultures. This perception has enabled the Ashkenazi Zionist Left governments to subordinate Mizrahim in the economy and society" (15).[14] David Ben-Gurion, leader of the Labour Zionists, spoke often on this topic. The Jews "from Morocco," he wrote, "had no education. Their customs are those of Arabs...We do not want Israelis to become Arabs. We are in duty bound to fight against the spirit of the Levant, which corrupts individuals and societies, and preserve the authentic Jewish values as they crystallized in the [European] Diaspora" (qtd. in Massad 57). Ze'ev Jabotinsky, the leader of the Revisionists, agreed with Ben-Gurion on at least this point, writing in 1926 that "Jews, thank God, have nothing in common with the East. We must put an end to any trace of the Oriental spirit in the [native] Jews of Palestine" (qtd. in Massad 55). Lest we think this is a phenomenon of the early state and pre-state past, Golda Meir, prime minister of Israel from 1969 to 1974, was known for greeting Soviet Jewish immigrants at the airport, an activity that she never did for Arab Jewish immigrants, famously saying things to them like: "You are the real Jews. We have been waiting for you for twenty-five years. You speak Yiddish!...Every loyal Jew must speak Yiddish, for he who does not know Yiddish is not a Jew. You are a superior breed—you will provide us with heroes" (qtd. in Massad 61–62). Arab Jews rightly took this as demeaning; in response, at one of the first Israeli Black Panther protests, demonstrators apparently shouted with gleeful irony, "Golda, teach us Yiddish" (qtd. in Massad 62). These Jewish colonial beliefs of the ruling elite were a central part of the government's policies toward the Arab Jewish majority in Israel, affecting them economically, culturally, and socially. Part of the reason Arab Jews in Israel flocked to Menachem Begin's Likud party in the 1970s and 1980s was in reaction to the discriminatory attitudes of the ruling Labour party.

A significant role in the homogenizing process for the Arab Jews was the erasure of their culture, tradition, and language. Shohat damningly encapsulates the phenomenon: "In many respects, European Zionism has been an immense confidence trick played on Sephardim, a cultural massacre of immense proportions, an attempt, partially successful, to wipe out, in a generation or two, millennia of rooted Oriental civilizations, unified even in its diversity" ("Sephardim in Israel" 74). Levy, likewise, explains the difficulties faced by Arabic-speaking Jews newly arrived in Israel:

> While all new immigrants experienced hardships, while all Diasporic languages were suppressed, in practice, the dilemmas of Arabic speakers were compounded by the added misfortunes of arriving on the scene long after the Ashkenazi founders, of being socially marginalized and

stigmatized as a minority population, and, worst of all,
of being associated with the language and culture of the
enemy—an utterly intractable problem. (40)

Needless to say, Arab Jews' Arabness did not simply disappear, even if it
was suppressed; we are reminded of this repeatedly in Tsabari's fiction.

For example, in "Brit Milah," we hear about the older "Yemeni
women from the neighbourhood who held on to the old ways, resisted
modern appliances, still dressed as though they were in Yemen" (52).[15] And
in "The Best Place on Earth," the protagonist's Jewish Tunisian mother,
living in Israel for decades, "remained removed from Israeli culture,
always a little critical of Israeli bluntness and informality"; it is not until
the suicide attacks of the second Intifada that she begins thinking of
herself as Israeli, and Arabs as the Other (226). Likewise, Shenhav writes
about how his father and his father's friends spoke Arabic, read the Arabic
press, and listened to Arabic radio stations; some of them spent time in
other countries and "identified themselves as Arabs" (3). Nonetheless, as
Massad puts it, "the Arabic of the Arab Jews became the language of the
enemy" (53). Tsabari fictionalizes this to devastating effect in "The Poets
in the Kitchen Window," when Uri's father stops writing poetry: "Uri
understood. The poetry they taught at school, the books he found in the
school library, were mostly written by old Ashkenazi men. He had never
heard of a Yemeni or Iraqi poet, or any Mizrahi poet for that matter" (70).
Later in the story, when Uri discovers a book of poetry by the Jewish Iraqi
poet Roni Someck, he himself starts writing poetry again, after stopping
because he was bullied by his classmates—even Uri is put off when he
finds out that Yasmin's new boyfriend is Palestinian (82). Shenhav, while
acknowledging the damage of stripping the Arab Jews of their national
and cultural heritage, also notes how, after the "shared life-experience
of the Arab Jews in education, the army, the development towns, the
factories, or on the margins of the lower middle class," Arab Jews in
Israel have, in fact, achieved a "homological sameness" (15).

The Arab Jewish relationship to the Palestinians is a fraught one,
especially when considering the Israeli government's use of Arab Jews as
pawns in their oppression of the Palestinians. Shohat lays it bare when
she states: "The same historical process that dispossessed Palestinians
of their property, lands, and national-political rights was linked to the

process that dispossessed Sephardim of their property, lands, and root-edness in Arab countries (and within Israel itself, of their history and culture)" ("Sephardim in Israel" 48). The theory of the "spontaneous population exchange"—that Israel "exchanged" its Palestinian popula-tion for the Jewish population of Arab countries—is deployed in order for Israel to not have to redress the Palestinian refugees. As Shenhav explains, the population exchange theory "was proposed with the aim of denying Israel's responsibility for the expulsion of Palestinians from Palestine in 1948 and 1967, to alleviate demands to compensate the Palestinian refugees, and to serve as a bargaining chip against the so-called right of return" (111). Shenhav argues that, "For all practical purposes, the population exchange initiative was used to legitimate Israel's wrongdoing with regard to the mass exodus (not to say expulsion) of the Palestinian refugees in 1948" (111).

Significantly, the stories in The Best Place on Earth do not have any Palestinian characters, which has been noted as a deficiency. Lorraine Adams, for one; in her New York Times review of the collection, writes that a character detailing his army unit's raid on a Palestinian house in "Causalities" (and the character's inability to participate in the raid) is "the collection's only brief detour into the Palestinian point of view" (np).[16] While I am not convinced that detailing a raid consti-tutes a Palestinian point of view, Adams misses other moments where Palestinians, or Arabs that are impacted by Israel, appear, or are alluded to, in the stories. There is Tariq, a Bedouin man we never see on the page, but who is pivotal to the action of "Borders." There is the suicide bombing that is the central event of "Tikkun." As I argue elsewhere, the suicide bombing is the closest we get to having a Palestinian character present ("Jewish Affect During the Second Intifada"). There might not be any Palestinian characters in the collection, but the stories themselves are always aware of the settler-colonial reality of Israel (and, as we saw in Exodus, having Palestinian characters is not necessarily a good thing). The stories hum with it. The entire argumentative thrust of this chapter rests on the belief that having Arab Jews in fiction forces an awareness of the Palestinian presence—diasporic heteroglossia from a different angle. As Shohat has it, "Just as all communities, traditions, and identi-ties may be said to be 'invented,' the idea of 'the Arab-Jew'...provides a post-partition figure through which to critique segregationist narratives while also opening up imaginative potentialities" ("Introduction" 4).[17] In light of the goals of this chapter, I want to further Shohat's belief in the power of affinity and analogy by arguing that by uncovering how Zionism and its hegemonic institutions treated, and treats, its own Jewish citizens who happen to come from diasporas in Arabic lands, *The Best Place on Earth* shows how Zionism is not even an ethical ideology in regard to those it claims to represent, let alone the Indigenous Palestinians. In this way, the Arab Jew acts as a hinge that allows a new political order to be imagined in Israel/Palestine, one where Jew and Arab have equal political efficacy.

One final factor I want to address here is the widespread belief that the Arab Jews living in Israel are all right wing, hate Arabs and Palestinians, and are passionately loyal to the Israeli state. While it is true that the Mizrahi vote in 1977 helped Likud get into power for the first time,[18] Arab Jews, whether Yemeni, Iraqi, or Moroccan, have always fought back against their treatment at the hand of the Ashkenazi elites. As Joseph Massad puts it, "Over the years, Mizrahi resistance has ranged from outright revolt to peaceful demonstrations and political organization" (65). Whether it was protests at the immigration centres and development towns (see Bryan K. Roby's *The Mizrahi Era of Rebellion*), protests like The Wadi Salib Uprising over unfair housing practices, or the organized activities of the Israeli Black Panthers, Arab Jewish resistance has always been either ignored or explained away. Moreover, it was a Yemeni-led armed uprising that led to the commission looking into stolen Yemeni babies (more on this below). Finally, there is organized Arab Jewish support for the Palestinian cause. In 1989, a "historic meeting" (Massad 65) between Arab Jews and Palestinians was held in Toledo, Spain, with thirty-eight Mizrahi intellectuals and a "large Palestinian delegation," including the Palestinian poet Mahmud Darwish. Several of the Arab Jewish speakers presented in Arabic, their "native tongue" as Joseph Massad puts it (65).[19] Overall, Arab Jewish resistance has been around since the beginning of the Zionist project. So, while the Arab Jews of Israel support the right-wing political parties, they also fight against them. The Arab Jewish community in Israel/Palestine, no matter how homologized they have been through the army and other state apparatus, still do not speak with a single voice, nor should they be expected to.

The Yemeni Jewish Diaspora, its Dissolution, and its Treatment by the State

Moving from a more general discussion of Arab Jews in Israel/Palestine to the specific history of Tsabari's Jewish Yemeni diaspora, we will see that the Yemeni Jewish diasporic experience correlates to the narrative(s) analyzed above, but also deviates from it/them in significant ways.[20] Yemeni Jews had been living their diasporic existence in Yemen for two millennia, and had always maintained a religious and spiritual connection with Palestine. During the times that Yemen was under Ottoman control, Yemen and Palestine were provinces of the same sprawling empire; in this way, Yemen and Palestine were more connected than Palestine and European Jewry. Unlike other Arab Jewish collectivities, Yemeni Jews started to immigrate to Ottoman-era Palestine in significant numbers in the 1880s (Shenhav, *The Arab Jews* 28). As Gershon Shafir explains, "Jews from Yemen had arrived in Palestine continuously, parallel to, and independently of, the Eastern European stream, during the whole period of the First and Second Aliyot" (92). Yemeni Jews started migrating to Palestine for a number of reasons, including "the opening of the Suez Canal in 1869, and the reconquest of Yemen by the Ottomans in 1872, which integrated Yemen into world commerce and exposed the Jewish artisans to the ruinous competition of European industrial products" (Shafir 92). Shafir also stresses that Yemeni Jews were drawn to Palestine for religious reasons "rooted in spiritual bonds with the Holy Land" (92), and not in order to create a viable Jewish state like so many of their European cousins. At the time, then, political Zionism was not a motivating factor for Yemeni Jews.[21]

After the state of Israel was established, the Yemeni Jews were the first Arab Jewish community to be brought to Israel en-masse, with around 50,000 arriving between 1948 and 1951 (Meir-Glitzenstein 150), in a mission with the Orientalist codename Operation Magic Carpet. It was a dangerous journey; many died along the way and while waiting in the British protectorate of Aden to be flown to Israel. The Yemeni Jews had to walk for days and weeks through the desert—and for those who lived in the rural areas outside of the main cities the trek was further and more dangerous—to Aden, where they were kept in horrific conditions in poorly-run camps before being flown to Israel in overloaded planes.

Once in Israel, they were housed in transit camps, treated as inferior, and not invited into the Jewish collective on equal and open terms. Seen as primitive and backwards, the arriving Yemenis had their religious artifacts stolen by the government, and even had their children kidnapped and given to Ashkenazi families for adoption. The Yemenis immediately entered the solidifying inter-Jewish ethnic hierarchy at the bottom of the ladder, assumed to be "inferior culturally, religiously, and nationally" (Shenhav, *The Arab Jews* 71). This is not how the Yemeni immigration to Israel is remembered, however. In the dominant myth of the early-state period, the "rescue" of the Jews from Yemen is seen as a high-water mark.

Joseph B. Schechtman's 1952 article "The Repatriation of Yemenite Jewry" is a typical example of how Zionist historiography looks at the Yemeni Jewish exodus from Yemen and their ingathering in Israel. Schechtman states that, "Since the sixth century, when Yemen adopted Islam, the Jews have suffered almost uninterrupted persecution," and describes the Yemeni Jewish existence as "wretched" and full of "longing for the lost homeland" (209). We see here the phenomenon Shohat delineates, where European-style antisemitism is grafted wholesale onto the non-European Muslim world. Yemeni Jews did not suffer "uninterrupted persecution," and when they did long for the "lost homeland," it was for the holy sites of Jerusalem, not an ethnically pure nation-state.[22] Even things like the Orphans' Decree, where Jewish orphans were forced to convert to Islam, have a more complicated history than simple uninterrupted persecution (more on the Orphans' Decree below, in my analysis of Tsabari's story "Invisible"). Furthermore, a diasporic ethics would point out that, even if the status of Jews in Yemen as *dhimmi* (a protected minority under Islamic law) had drawbacks, the Yemeni Jews nevertheless lived a vibrant, religiously and culturally alive communal life, and had good relations with their Muslim neighbours, governors, and elites. The tone of Schechtman's article is condescending and paternalistic, downplaying anything that could make Israelis or Jews look bad, including the state of the refugee camps and the stealing of artifacts, the latter of which he waves away as the government taking stewardship over the grateful newcomers' religious objects. This is the version of Operation Magic Carpet that also appears in the end of Uris's *Exodus*, where the benignly antisemitic American pilot, Foster J. MacWilliams (could there be a more American name?), gets involved in Operation Magic Carpet, flies "four hundred missions covering millions of miles and bringing in nearly fifty thousand Jews to Israel," falls in love with the Jewish state, sheds his earlier animosity toward the Jews, and marries a Jewish Israeli woman and settles in Tel Aviv (570). MacWilliams is yet another American whom Uris imagines as being seduced by the Zionist dream. Uris's narrator tells us that the fact that "the Jews of Yemen remained Jews was incredible" (562), and the pages dedicated to their history and their journey to Israel are, not surprisingly, full of racism, Orientalism, and primitivism. The narrator tells readers that "The Yemenites could not comprehend things like water taps, toilets, or electric lights," and that in one of the planes flying them to Israel, "The smell was horrible" (it was so bad that MacWilliams throws up) (566–567). It is the romanticism of the journey, the view of the Jewish Yemenis as arriving from the biblical era, that lends Operation Magic Carpet such a powerful narrative role for Zionism, as evinced in both Schechtman and Uris.

Recently, Operation Magic Carpet has begun to be re-evaluated from outside the Zionist mythic narrative. Esther Meir-Glitzenstein's take on the Yemeni immigration is a little more even-handed than Schechtman's. Significantly, she explains how there was no anti-Jewish violence in Yemen when the Jews started to leave; she also spends significant time debunking the myth of the Yemeni Jews' primitiveness. "Operation Magic Carpet," she writes, "is an example of a tragic failure, that, with the help of a myth, became a tale of rescue and redemption, a constitutive myth that Israeli society tells itself about itself and on which generations of young people have been reared" (168). She describes the horrific conditions at the transit camps in Aden, which were meant to accommodate 1,000 people but ended up housing around 14,000. "Significantly," she writes, "most of the deaths occurred not in Yemen, where the Jews were protected by the authorities, but in the British protectorate and in Aden, where they arrived sick and hungry" (152). Meir-Glitzenstein places most of the blame on the Joint Distribution Committee (JDC), the Jewish American organization that ran the camps, excoriating it for its treatment of the Yemeni Jews. "By no means," she writes, "can this operation be considered a success or deemed a credit to the organizers" (150). Meir-Glitzenstein spends most of her essay investigating why the reality of the Yemeni immigration has been so successfully erased, replaced with the mythic, glorious return we encounter in Schechtman and Uris. What she discovers is that the narrative about the Yemeni Jewish migration to Israel was created before the mission had even been carried out. Some of the responsibility for the mythic tones belong to two JDC leaders, Edward Warburg and Dr. Joseph Schwartz. The JDC's reports, made in real time, completely ignored the disastrous elements of the operation, including the deaths of Yemeni Jews and the horrendous conditions of the camp. Meir-Glitzenstein concludes that the JDC wanted to "be the first to tell the story, to give the JDC credit for the operation and to make it clear that the role of the Israeli government and the Jewish Agency was secondary" (155). In other words, the desire of the American Jewish organization to take credit for the operation led to a sanitizing of its more negative aspects, a sanitizing that the Israeli government and other Zionist figures were more than happy to run with. This is a fascinating example of American and Zionist organizations fighting over who gets credit for helping to end a Jewish diaspora. In the resulting narrative, therefore, "The price of the immigration is downplayed or concealed; what remains is the hardship in Yemen, the messianic yearning, the exhausting trek on foot through the desert, and the wondrous arrival in Israel" (163). The collapsing of a diaspora not in immediate danger is cleaned of its ugly details and held up as a myth of glorious Zionist return.

Once they arrived in Israel, things did not improve for the recent immigrants. Their treatment lands at the nexus between Orientalism and colonialism, embodying Shenhav's concept of "Jewish colonialism." Denigrated as backwards, biblical, and both too religious and not religious enough, the Yemeni Jews were placed in transit camps, had their Torahs and other ceremonial belongings stolen, and were otherwise mistreated. The Yemeni Children Affair is a harrowing example of how Yemeni Jews were treated by the Ashkenazi elite in Israel. In the late 1940s and 1950s, hundreds if not thousands of Yemeni babies were stolen from their families, who, as Shohat puts it, "Traumatized by the reality of life in Israel," fell prey to "a ring of unscrupulous doctors, nurses, and social workers" ("Sephardim in Israel" 56). The stolen babies were then given up for adoption to Ashkenazi parents in Israel and elsewhere. The hospital would tell the mother that the child had died, often producing no death certificate, and not allowing the parents to see the bodies. Three official government inquiries later, there are still no clear answers as to who was responsible; the full extent of the affair has yet to be elucidated, and most likely never will be. According to a February

2018 *New York Times* article on the Yemeni Children Affair, it was not until the rise of DNA testing that parents, children, and siblings were able to find each other and reconnect. Overall, there are more than 1,000 officially reported cases, but according to Malin Fezehai, "estimates from advocates are as high as 4,500" (np).[23] The article tells the surreal story of Leah Aharoni, who had twin daughters, Hagit and Hannah. The hospital told Leah that Hannah had died at birth. However, when Hagit turned seventeen, the family received *two* draft documents from the army: "one for [Hagit], and for her twin sister, Hannah" (np). This naturally led Leah Aharoni to the conclusion that her daughter was still alive. What happened to Aharoni—receiving a military draft notice for a child assumed dead—has happened to numerous Yemeni parents, in what must be a truly surreal and emotional experience, one that only further exemplifies the disregard the Israeli state has for Arab Jews. This is the kind of story that can only exist in a national context where one group of people is considered dispensable.[24]

It was not just children that the authorities stole from the Yemeni immigrants; an unknown number of valuable religious artifacts and books, including centuries-old Torahs, were stolen from the new arrivals. The best source for information on this episode is the book *Ex Libris: Chronicles of Theft, Preservation, and Appropriating at the Jewish National Library*, by Gish Amit. Unfortunately, the book—which, alongside the case of the stolen Yemeni artifacts, looks at the thousands of Jewish books stolen by the Nazis, and the untold thousands of Palestinian books that were left behind in 1948 and all appropriated by the Israeli national library—is currently only available in Hebrew.[25] As Arie M. Dubnov writes in his review of *Ex Libris*: "As with the controversial kidnapping of Yemenite children, the missing Yemenite books affair, [Amit] concludes, will forever remain an unresolved puzzle, especially given the fact that valuable archival material has been destroyed over the years, even during the 1990s, before the State Commission of Inquiry summoned to investigate the kidnapping allegations could examine it" (96). The negative responses to Amit's book speak to the ongoing negation of Arab Jewish life in Israel. Zeev Gries's lengthy, virulent response to Amit's book blames Muslims and Muslim culture for the same crimes Amit critiques in his book; even if this were true, it does not negate how the early Zionists treated the possessions of the Shoah victims, Palestinians, and Arab Jews. Gries also draws false parallels to the mass immigrations to America, saying that "This type of migration inherently involves the abandonment of property: houses, land, belongings, and cultural artifacts, including books" (74).

To summarize, the Arab Jews, who lived in their diasporic communities for centuries, were treated as inferior Jewish material by Zionist emissaries, brought to Israel under false promises of land, wealth, work, and safety, and were forced to abandon the Arab parts of their identity in order to achieve the homologized "Jewishness" integral to the claims of the Israeli state. Yemeni Jews, in particular, were treated as colonial subjects, having their children and religious and cultural artifacts stolen from them, and in general not being given the life opportunities their fellow Ashkenazi citizens enjoyed. The Arab Jewish situation is different than other colonialist ones in at least one major respect: they were needed by the state in order to achieve a demographic majority over the Indigenous Palestinians, but were still relegated to the margins of Israeli society. This is the world Tsabari delves into—and cracks wide open—in her fiction. In the stories that make up The Best Place on Earth, the layers of Orientalism, diaspora, postcolonialism, majority-minority politics, erasure, and sunken history that Arab Jews live with in Israel rise to the surface for the first time in English literature.

Visible Minorities, Invisible Diasporas: The Seen and the Unseen in "Invisible"

In fictionalizing the lives of Arab Jews who live in Israel, the stories in The Best Place on Earth reveal the complex social hierarchy of the country; in the story "Invisible," Tsabari goes further, unearthing the diasporic connections of marginalization, ethnicity, and labour in the era of the nation-state and globalization. "Invisible" tells the story of Rosalynn, a Filipina foreign worker living in Israel whose temporary worker permit has expired. Significantly, Rosalynn is the only non-Jewish protagonist in the collection, and one of only a few non-Arab Jewish protagonists. When "Invisible" opens, Rosalynn is working as a live-in caregiver for Savta, an elderly Yemeni Arab Jew who spent her childhood in Yemen (savta is the Hebrew word for grandmother).[26] Since Rosalynn's worker visa has expired, she is considered, in the eyes of the Israeli state apparatus, as an illegal foreign worker. Tsabari's third person narrator draws a powerful parallel between Rosalynn's situation in Israel as an undocumented worker at a time of government crackdown and her employer Savta's childhood as an orphaned Jew in Yemen, where she was at the mercy of the Yemeni government. This has the unsettling effect of revealing how the concept of invisibility can be a powerful form of resistance to the bureaucratic violence of the nation-state toward those it deems unwanted.

In "Invisible," therefore, the global connections between foreign workers, the nation-states' others, and gendered aspects of both state violence and domestic work are highlighted. When Rosalynn hides from the Israeli police during a raid in the story's ambiguous final scenes (ambiguous since readers are left uncertain as to whether Rosalynn gets caught or evades capture), the material consequences of the ethnic nationalism of states like Israel are painfully exposed. That the country that Savta immigrated to in order to escape minority persecution in Yemen (as a Jew) is now persecuting members of its non-Jewish minority such as Rosalynn—to say nothing of the treatment of the Palestinians—who are a vital part of Israel's economic, social, and cultural fabric, makes a powerful case for the violence that ensues whenever a state apparatus has the ability to decide who belongs, and who does not. Moreover, Rosalynn's diasporic consciousness—she has a family in the Philippines where she sends her money—echoes that of Savta, her Filipina friends, and a score of other characters in the collection's stories. Even though they are separated by citizenship, class, and race, their diasporic bond supersedes that of both the nation-state and its violent border maintenance.

The global network of Filipino foreign workers is an example of a precarious, economically driven diasporic community, with collectivities in numerous countries that exist under the aegises of dehumanizing national and international policies, and makes plain the tensions between the diaspora and nation-state. The Filipino foreign worker diaspora, including both male and female workers, is truly a global phenomenon. There are Filipino workers in over 130 countries (Parreñas 1129). According to the Philippine Overseas Employment Administration, in 2015 there were a total of 1,844,406 foreign workers, both on land and on the sea (Gavilan np). And these are just the numbers for the legal workers.[27] According to Rhacel Salazar Parreñas, there are in total over six million Filipino labour migrants, with about 60% of them, around three and a half million, being women.[28] The major beneficiaries of this global diaspora of workers are the nations where they are employed, because they get cheap labour—and, depending on the country, do not have to trade things like citizenship, health care, or workers' rights in order to procure it—and the Philippines, which can continue the status quo; if there were no labour migration, it is estimated that unemployment in the Philippines would increase by 40% (Parreñas 1136). The money sent back by the foreign workers to their families, called remittance, keeps the economy afloat. The women, for their part, join the labour diaspora for any number of reasons. These include: the ability to make money for their families; to escape abusive relationships; and to strive for a better life. Parreñas, in her study of a Filipina labour workers' international magazine, writes that "It is not surprising that migrant Filipina domestics do not go home even though they articulate the desire to do so" (1140). Conversely, the Filipino government encourages the labour diaspora.[29] Parreñas, after Saskia Sassen, evaluates the Filipina labour diaspora as the result of the "opposite turns of nationalism," which are the "denationalization of economies" and the "renationalization of societies" (Sassen qtd. in Parreñas 1129). As such, "these migrants emphasize both their nationalist and diasporic identities, thus simultaneously reinforcing and transgressing the nation-state" (1130). When this happens in a country like Israel/Palestine, which bills itself as the negation of the Jewish diaspora, the nation-state is further reinforced and, through the actions of people like Rosalynn, transgressed.

While the situation of Filipina workers differs on a country-by-country basis, the situation of Filipina workers in Israel is particularly fraught.[30] This mainly stems from the tension between the desire in Israel for cheap, non-Palestinian labour, and the Zionist imperative of maintaining a pure, Jewish national space. Or, as Claudia Liebelt puts it, "Subject to a migration regime which excludes non-Jews from citizenship and, since the ousting of Palestinians from the labour market in the early 1990s, depends on the recruitment of overseas workers, Filipinos in Israel live in a state of economic, legal and social precariousness" (76). Tsabari writes about the shift of worker demographics in Israel in "Brit Milah," when Reuma remembers that "Growing up she'd never seen Chinese or blacks in Israel, but now they were everywhere, migrant workers who were filling positions Israelis were too lazy for, jobs Palestinians used to have before the intifada, and Yemenis before them, in Israel's early days...cleaning homes, washing dishes, picking oranges" (42–43). Filipina caregivers were brought into Israel in the mid-1990s, after the Israeli government decided to subsidize in-home care, instead of hospitals and public institutions (Liebelt 76). However, many Filipinas decided to stay after their work visas expired, having made familial, economic, and cultural connections with the country. In response, the Israeli government periodically attempts to evict them. As recently as February 2019, the Population, Immigration and Border Authority in Israel arrested eighteen Filipina mothers, two fathers, and their children, with plans to deport them in the summer (Yaron np). According to Lee Yaron's *Haaretz* article, "The children facing deportation were either born in Israel or have spent most of their lives in the country, and Hebrew is their first or only language" (np).[31] In response to the deportations, Filipino activists started a group called the "United Children of Israel." "We came to Israel many years ago, and have been taking care of the elderly and people with special needs with great dedication," the organization's statement reads, "Our children were born and grew up in Israel. Don't let the deportation happen. Join the fight" (qtd. in Yaron). It is not difficult to imagine Rosalynn and her friends as members of this group;[32] in any case, "Invisible," in fictionalizing one particular life out of the thousands of Filipina foreign workers in Israel, puts a human face on the phenomenon that readers can easily empathize with, and perhaps reconceptualize how they view foreign workers in their own countries.

At the time of the story, Rosalynn's presence and status in Israel is highly precarious. The government is in the midst of a frenzy of nationalist rhetoric, and is rounding up undocumented workers and sending them back to their "home" countries. Rosalynn's Filipina friend Beatrice—who is safe from the immigration police, having married an Israeli and having therefore been granted Israeli citizenship—warns Rosalynn: "Nowhere was safe anymore...the new government was determined to catch and deport illegal workers: there were so many of them now" (125). Another friend, Vivian, confirms that "It's getting bad...They're doing random searches in markets and bus stations now" (124), which acts as foreshadowing for the story's final scenes. As Liebelt shows, this is not a fictional element of Tsabari's story. In 2002, for example, there was a

"large scale deportation campaign" with "tens of thousands of illegalized workers from the Philippines and elsewhere...arrested and the most
outspoken community activists chosen for deportation" (76).[33] Not only
does Rosalynn not want to leave Israel because working for Savta is how
she economically maintains her family in the Philippines—including her
mother and young daughter, Carmen, who Rosalynn has heartbreaking
phone conversations with—but because Israel has become a second home.
This is the double turn that Parreñas theorizes, where Filipina migrants
constitute the Philippines as their originary home, but also "create an
international community" that acts to extend their "sense of place and
sense of community...into a transnational terrain" (1131). Rosalynn exists
in the diasporic tension between the Philippines as home, the transnational terrain of Filipina foreign workers, and her sense of belonging to
Israel; she both fantasizes about being in her small Philippines town with
Savta's lodger Yaniv and walking the Tel Aviv seawall with her daughter,
Carmen (121, 124). As the narrator of "Invisible" tells us, Rosalynn
"couldn't pinpoint when Israel had started to feel a bit like home, when
she figured out the way of the seasons, when the conversations on the
streets were no longer gibberish. And yet, she was still a stranger, probably always would be" (125).

Just because Rosalynn feels a sense of belonging to Israel, in particular to Savta and the small town of Yemeni elderly they live in, it does not
mean that she is welcomed with open arms.[34] "Some days," we are told,
"she felt invisible in Israel: she had heard people speak about her—or
people 'like her'—in her presence before. Other times it was as though she
was walking around with no clothes on: everyone stared" (131). Rosalynn
both belongs and does not belong; feels at home, but also worries that her
daughter in the Philippines does not understand why she is not with her;
experiences the heightened racism geared toward anybody non-Jewish,
but also feels a familial bond with Savta. The story exists at the intersec-
tion of diasporic tensions, precarious work, capitalist systems of global
commodity exchange, and Zionist ethnic-nationalist policing.

When Rosalynn begins to fall in love with Yaniv, who is a friend of
Savta's grandson Ilan, and they begin a tentative romantic relationship,
Rosalynn is further imbricated in the daily life of her adopted country.
Yaniv moving into the shed in the back of Savta's yard is the catalyst
that starts the story. This is one of Tsabari's great themes: the power of

mutual attraction and cohabitation to break down strict boundaries of ethnic mixing. In some countries with a large Filipina workforce, it is actually illegal for Filipinas to get pregnant or get married to a citizen (Singapore is one such country; see Parreñas 1134); this is not the case in Israel. Yaniv, who moves into the shed in Savta's backyard on the story's first page, is, unlike Savta and Ilan, of Ashkenazi heritage, and is suffering from post-traumatic stress disorder after half of his army unit died during the first Lebanon War. He moves into Savta's backyard in order to try and escape from the pressures of normal militarized Israeli existence.[35] Interestingly, readers are told that the tenants prior to Yaniv were a "young Ethiopian couple" (110). Ethiopians, Arab Jews, foreign workers such as Rosalynn, those Israelis like Yaniv who have been damaged by the militaristic character of the country—all share a marginalized space in Savta's house. Yaniv's apology after he is rude to Rosalynn communicates clearly that it is not just the ethnically different who need a space to be invisible in the Israeli nation-state: "I just…I came to Rosh HaAyin thinking this was the one place I could…I don't know, disappear I guess. Here no one would bother me or get on my case" (129). Rosalynn starts feeding Yaniv, and Yaniv gives Rosalynn an iPod for her to send to her daughter; in a climactic moment, they kiss.

Yaniv and Rosalynn's burgeoning relationship, as so many in *The Best Place on Earth*, breaks down ethnic and nationalist barriers that are supposed to keep people separate. Tsabari's insistence on the inevitability of people from different ethnic groups starting relationships, being attracted to each other, and falling in love directly challenges Zionism's belief in a pure Jewish state, as well as enacting a diasporic belief in a borderless world. Just as Bakhtinian language grows from unique utterance to unique utterance, human society enlarges with every new connection, even when in tension with the boundary dictates of the national centre. A truly diasporic outcome.

However, the story does not end there, with a burgeoning relationship between the illegalized Filipina worker and outcast Israeli ex-soldier. Shortly after they kiss, Rosalynn goes to the market to buy ingredients to make Filipino food for Yaniv, and it is there that the authorities catch up to her when they perform a raid of the market looking for illegal workers. It is deeply ironic that when the police catch up to her, Rosalynn is at the market to make the cuisine of her home country, which Yaniv teases her for not making, and that now she presumably will be deported to. Big raids such as this are not uncommon in Israel. As David V. Bartram explains, "Large sections of Tel Aviv, in particular, are well known as foreign worker neighborhoods, and Israeli police are not encumbered by constitutional provisions that would inhibit massive checks for identity papers" (317). In other words, without a constitution, the Israeli police have free rein to perform these raids and weed out inhabitants without the proper paperwork. This exact situation is narrated in flashbacks in "Invisible." "Back when Rosalynn lived in Tel Aviv," readers are told, in "an aging, decrepit part of Tel Aviv that was now claimed by migrant workers as their own," Rosalynn had often gone to a Filipino club near the old Tel Aviv bus station. "Whenever the immigration police raided the area, the party would come to a halt, everyone lining up to produce passports and visas. Rosalynn had seen friends who worked illegally, like her, escorted into vans, from which there was no coming back" (123). Since at the story's end readers are not explicitly told if Rosalynn is apprehended or not, Tsabari leaves it uncertain whether Rosalynn is caught or manages to escape.

Whether Rosalynn escapes from the immigration police or not at the story's end, Tsabari deliberately has her precarious legal position in Israel parallel Savta's own experiences as a Yemeni Jew. Rosalynn's employer, an elderly Yemeni woman in a wheelchair, tells the traumatic story of her childhood in Yemen in several dialogic parcels staggered throughout the text. We learn about how her parents died when she was a young child, how the Yemeni authorities "threatened to convert her to Islam" (111–112), how eventually "she had walked for weeks through the desert, from San'a to Aden, with a group of Jews on their way to Israel" (111–112). Savta's journey parallels that of many Yemeni Jews who emigrated to Israel through Aden, an experience that Zionist historians like Schechtman celebrate and that Meir-Glitzenstein troubles. The policy of converting Jewish orphans in Yemen to Islam is also historical reality, and an example of how minorities in Muslim-majority countries did live under rules and laws that they did not necessarily have any control over. However, the Yemeni Orphans' Decree, as it is known, has recently been revisited by scholars, and a new consensus on the law and its implementation is emerging. A brief detour into the new scholarship on the Orphans' Decree reveals how Savta's life experience is dictated by the diasporic reality of Yemeni Jews, at the same time it makes clear that the Orphans' Decree was not the epitome of antisemitism that Zionist historiography claims it to be.

The reinstatement of the Orphans' Decree happened sometime in the 1920s (it is unclear exactly when) and was a result of a power struggle between the Yemeni Zaydis, led by Imam Yahya, who became the new ruler of Yemen, and the Ottoman empire. Imam Yahya, in an attempt to assert his sovereignty against Ottoman claims, reinstated Zaydi law, a Shia variation of Islamic law that had been defunct under Ottoman rule; the Orphans' Decree, which was a part of Zaydi law, was therefore reintroduced. The original version of the law is believed to be about helping Jewish orphans, which the Yemeni Muslim elite were responsible for, by taking them into their house and raising them as their own (now Muslim) children. Both Bat-Zion Eraqi-Klorman and Ari Ariel agree that the Orphans' Decree was not designed to persecute the Jews in Yemen per se, but was all about the function of power.[36] Where Eraqi-Klorman and Ariel disagree is around how the Orphans' Decree and power actually operated. For Eraqi-Klorman, the decree was carried out almost exclusively in the parts of Yemen where Yahya held sway, mostly Central Yemen; for Ariel, the decree was actually used by Yahya to *assert* power over the periphery of his rule.[37] What is certain is how the Yemeni Jewish community responded to the Orphans' Decree. They did all they could to prevent orphans from being converted, including hiding them, helping them escape, and, as in the case of Savta, through marriage. As Eraqi-Klorman thoroughly details, most often the community would try to marry orphans to each other, but sometimes the young women would also be married off as second or third wives to older men. This is important in light of "Invisible," in that Savta makes it seem like it was her husband who acted as an individual and saved her, while the reality is that it was almost definitely the Jewish community as a collective that married Savta to her older husband as a way to save her from conversion.

Both scholars insist that, overall, the Jews in Yemen coexisted with the Muslim majority, and their *dhimmi* status more often than not protected them from harm rather than harming them. They also both point out how Zionists, both Yemeni and not, blew the Orphans' Decree and its consequences out of proportion in order to persuade Yemeni Jews to immigrate. As Eraqi-Klorman points out, "The impression made by the Orphans' Decree seems, moreover, to have been heightened by the Palestinian-Jewish conflict" (43). I would suggest that the Jewish status of dhimmi in Yemen and the complex reality of Jewish life in the villages and cities of Yemen are typical examples of the diasporic trade-off. The Jewish communities were a working, respected part of Yemeni society, but sometimes they had to deal with minority persecution, to which they responded with collective action, not to mention the numerous Muslim Yemenis who also fought against the decree. This does not mean that Jewish existence in Yemen was catastrophic, just that diasporic existence is not necessarily easy. Moreover, the Jewish organized response to the Orphans' Decree is a profound example of creative diasporic resistance. This is the complex historical situation that engendered Savta's narrative of state persecution, marriage as a way to remain Jewish, and escape to Israel.

Further connecting her life story to that of Rosalynn's, Savta details how "she too had worked in people's homes when she arrived, cleaning and doing laundry for the rich Ashkenazi" (112). Tsabari makes clear the linkage between Savta and Rosalynn here: though Rosalynn is not Jewish (or Arab), the two women have more in common as immigrants on the lower rungs of the social ladder than with others who share their religion or ethnicity. Rosalynn adds yet another lens to the diasporic polycentric perspective that Savta and Tsabari's other Arab Jewish characters embody. Moreover, just as Yaniv can bestow Rosalynn with citizenship through marriage—as some of Rosalynn's other Filipina friends have done—we eventually learn that an older Jewish man saved Savta from the orphanage and from conversion. "I was in love once too, you know," Savta tells Rosalynn. "My husband, he take me when I was twelve. He was eighteen. He married me so the government won't take me. He saved me" (128).[38] The fact that Savta was clearly mistreated by the Yemeni authorities should remind us of Shohat's warning not to view Arab Jewish existence pre-Zionism as utopic, while, at the same time, rejecting the view that it was constant abuse and violence. Moreover, Savta is only allowed to continue her Jewish identity because the rights of a patriarchal society override those of religious and gender considerations. In a similar vein, Rosalynn is aware that one way she can become an Israeli citizen is through marriage to an Israeli man, yet another parallel between the two women.

Another major node of commonality between Rosalynn and Savta, one which the story emphasizes in its climax, is their need to hide from the state authorities. This need to hide, to be "invisible," evokes the perilous position of the nation-state's marginalized. It is at dinner with Rosalynn and Yaniv that we first hear of how Savta escaped the Yemeni authorities:

> "In Yemen they take the Jewish orphans, the government. Make them Muslims. I was hiding when they came. I go downstairs...Hide where the donkeys lived, in the corner. I hear them walk in the house...and then they come and they open the door and they look...I pray to God, please make me disappear. And then I close my eyes and make myself very small, like you can't see me, like I'm not there."
> "Invisible."
> "Yes." (119)

Counter to what we originally believed, it was not just her husband that saved Savta, but her managing to become "invisible" during this search. (The story echoes several testimonies discussed in Eraqi-Klorman's article.) Savta gives several reasons for why the authorities did not find her, including the mystical one of God and the more pragmatic fact that it was dark where she was hiding (119). When compared to Rosalynn's own encounter with the state apparatus that closes the story, the potential benefits of being invisible, unseen, in a country based on ethnic nationality, are brought into terrifying focus. This is yet another aspect of the diasporic condition: not only to be at the mercy of the national governments, but to have the ability to go unseen within its decrees and alleyways.

"Invisible" ends with Rosalynn's (supposedly) narrow escape from the immigration police during their early-morning raid on the market where she is shopping. Rosalynn manages to run at first, hiding in an alcove "filled with junk, littered with cigarette butts and stinking of urine and mould" (132). Notice the parallels to Savta's own hiding spot, "where the donkeys lived." The narrator explains that Rosalynn "wasn't ready to leave Israel. She needed more time. Savta needed her. Her daughter's future relied on the money she sent. And there was Yaniv" (132–133). The short, declarative sentences help to under-score Rosalynn's fear. When a female police officer starts looking into Rosalynn's hiding space, it seems like Rosalynn's imminent capture and expulsion from Israel is fast approaching. The tension rises again when Rosalynn drops the ring Savta gave her, and it clatters on the floor: "Rosalynn froze. The police officer turned around, and Rosalynn could see her eyes squinting in the dark" (133). It is a material symbol of the two women's connection—a ring—that alerts the police officer to Rosalynn's presence. However, in a telling echo of Savta's evasion of the Yemeni authorities, Rosalynn manages to make herself unseen: "She closed her eyes and willed herself to disappear. She…felt her body shut down, become small and quiet and limp, her breath soft and light, her clothes a vacant, bodiless heap on the dusty floor" (133). This is how the story ends, with Rosalynn invisible, the army officer either about to find her, or about to walk away. Tsabari's meaning here rings out as clearly as the ring Rosalynn dropped: Rosalynn and Savta are connected through their need to hide from the state. Unlike the Zionist or other nationalist worldviews, where it is people of the same nationality that are at odds with other national others, here it is one's place in the national, ethnic, gender, and class hierarchies that determines affiliation. The Yemeni and Israeli authorities, one Muslim, the other Jewish, operate as the nearly indistinguishable face of the national state, where Rosalynn and Savta, with their differing life stories, represent the diasporic.

In these final moments of the story, Israel is shown to be just another iteration of the nation-state, the same as Yemen, where there is a clearly defined hierarchy of those who belong, and those who do not. What Tsabari suggests with Rosalynn and Savta's disappearance—their skin colour, economic status, and gender connecting them more than their belonging to different ethnicities and countries (and age groups) sets them apart—is that as long as there is a nation-state, there will be a need to police its borders, to label certain groups as citizens and others as illegal, unwanted, disposable.

Travel, Return, Skin Colour:
The Collision of Colony and Diaspora
in "A Sign of Harmony"

If "Invisible" investigates the diasporic encounter between a Yemeni Jew and a Filipina caretaker that takes place in Israel, Tsabari's story "A Sign of Harmony" focuses on the complex collision between an Arab-Jewish Israeli woman and a Britain-born Indian man outside of the borders of the Israeli nation-state. In the story, which is set entirely in India,[39] we see that national belonging is far from wholly constitutive of one's identity; rather, skin colour, cultural competency, language, class, gender, and ancestry all feed into how one is perceived, by others as well as by oneself. The story, therefore, challenges the pervasive belief of the nation-state as location for identity formation, presenting instead diaspora, skin colour, and community as possible sites of identity creation, which is nonetheless a fluid, dynamic process. "A Sign of Harmony" centres on the relationship between Maya, an Israeli of Yemeni heritage who lives in India for half the year, spending the summers selling Indian goods at European festivals, and Ian, a British man of Indian heritage who travels to India for the first time to visit Maya, in order to continue the intensely sexual affair they started in London. The differences between Maya and Ian and their feelings toward India help readers map out the always already compromised processes of belonging/becoming inherent in the contemporary globalized world, and implicitly make the case for the power of fluid, multivalent cultural and ethnic identities not hamstrung by notions of ethnic purity. Once again, we see the fructifying diasporic difference of the Boyarins win out over the univocal staticness of Zionism and all the ethnic superiority that comes along with it.

That this diasporic encounter takes place in postcolonial India, between an Indian man who lives in the colonial metropole and a Yemeni Jew who hails from the settler-colonial state of Israel, is no accident. What Maya and Ian very quickly discover is that India means two very different things for them. For Maya, India is an adopted home; for Ian, it is the distant land of his ancestors, a rundown place of poverty and decrepitude he looks at through the eyes of an upper-middle class British man. Both Maya and Ian have complex identities: Maya, never fully able to shed her Israeliness, still takes on the identity of an Indian, and Ian, though aware of his Indian heritage, does not want to compromise his Britishness; finally, both cannot escape the fact of their dark skin. Using Homi Bhabha's conceptualization of the third space, I will show how Ian's and Maya's differing personal configurations of the global and the local, and of the colonized and the colonizer, make their relationship predestined for failure. In a world made up of nation-states and the ongoing trauma of empire, the way Maya and Ian decide to navigate their diasporic identities, one detaching from any sense of national belonging, the other clinging to their Britishness, reveals the damaging closing-off of identity.

Maya, like many Israelis, first travelled to India after her army service. In fact, there is a significant Jewish Israeli diaspora in India, centred in the north of the country in the summer and in the province of Goa in the winter. It is common practice for Israelis to travel abroad after their army service, to "decompress," often using their discharge bonus to fund it; India is one of the main destinations. These Israelis are known for their drug use and their partying; Tsabari's essays about India in The Art of Leaving confirm this, as does the documentary Flipping Out, which is about post-army-service Israelis who have drug-induced psychotic episodes while in India.[40] As Shalev Paller puts it in an article he wrote in The Times of Israel, after proudly stating that he participated in Operation Protective Edge, where over two thousand Palestinians were killed and over ten thousand were wounded in Gaza: "I'd had three years of alarms each morning, of always having an assignment, of constant uncertainty as to when I'd be home next. Three years of my days not really belonging to me. Now that they did, once again, I was going to fill them with flute lessons, mantra-humming monks, and as much India as possible" (np). There is something perverse about serving in an occupying army and then flying to India in order to "decompress" without any responsibilities or worries.[41] Maya lives half of every year in India, has business and near-familial connections there. "India feels like my home," she says to Ian when he questions what she does there all year (162).[42] Due to Maya's dark Yemeni skin, she is able to nearly become Indian. Ian, on the other hand, privileges the British parts of his postcolonial identity, and does not connect with the India Maya has attached herself to.

Nonetheless, it is Maya and Ian's non-white skin that brings them together in the first place. Tsabari complicates the global diasporic networks of skin colour and (post)coloniality again and again in this story. When Ian and Maya first see each other at a loft party in London (which is given to us in a flashback), Maya "mistook him for an Israeli, maybe of Yemeni heritage, like her" (160). Likewise, "later [Ian] told her he'd thought she was Indian" (160). It is the possibility of a shared history, marked by their skin colour, that initially compels them toward each other. During their fast and furious romance, they both discover that they come from troubled families—Ian's Rajasthani father married his British mother "against his parents' wishes" (161) and was disowned; Maya, in an echo of Ian's father, was also disowned by her highly traditional, religious family when she joined the Israeli armed forces.[43] Ian's parents are prime Tsabari: an Indian man and a British woman falling in love, breaking the binary of colonized and colonizer, with Ian as the mixed offspring of these divergent histories. Furthermore, Maya uses Ian's outward appearance to convince him to come visit her in India. "Imagine what an experience that would be," she implores him, "being in a place where everyone looks like you" (162). Even so, Ian comes to India more as a British person than as an Indian returning home, a diasporic consciousness thoroughly imbued with the prejudices of the host country.

From the moment Ian steps off the plane, Maya sees how out of place he is: "Despite his dark skin, long eyelashes and thick eyebrows, he stands out, overdressed in his stiff jeans, his gelled hair, his fluorescent green backpack" (155–156). Ian goes on to perform inappropriate public displays of affection; be overwhelmed by the pushiness of the cab drivers, with Maya intervening in Hindi; and "watch the chaos" of the streets of New Delhi "with huge eyes, forgetting to blink" (157). In another moment of understated cultural incongruity, "Ian rips a piece of roti and dips it in his saag as if it were a biscuit in a cup of tea" (163). Maya rationalizes Ian's reaction to the cultural difference on display, the narrator telling us: "She understands how he feels. There was no reason to assume it would be different for Ian simply because he is Indian. He grew up in London, after all" (157). Even so, Maya is still disappointed by Ian's negative reaction, and the relationship immediately begins to sour.

Ian's discomfort at the reality of urban and rural life in India only intensifies as his stay lengthens. He is disgusted by the hostel Maya resides at—even though she took out a more expensive room for his visit than the usual one she rents—prompting him to remark "I think you've been spending too much time in India" (159). Ian is completely overwhelmed by the cacophony and poverty of the Chandi Chowk bazaar, which Tsabari describes in descriptive, unsentimental sentences:

> ...tangled wires, chains of coloured bulbs and large banners
> hanging between dilapidated buildings. The heat is at its
> peak and everything smells stronger, ripened. As soon as
> they step out of the rickshaw, people brush against them,
> push them, touch them...Ian and Maya turn into an arched
> alleyway and beggars latch on to them. Ian is hugging his
> camera like it might leap from his chest. A barefoot child
> wheels a man with no limbs on a plywood board past them.
> A blind woman, her eyes excavated, waves flies from her
> listless baby. Another woman's nose seems to be eaten away
> by leprosy. A little girl with an amputated arm tugs on Ian's
> sleeve. Ian dispenses rupees at a panicky pace. (163–164)

After they leave the market, Ian voices his disgust. "You've been there before. Couldn't you have warned me," he says to her in an "accusing tone" (164). Though Maya responds by saying "It will get easier, you'll see," she still compares his reaction to her first time at the market: "She was mesmerized by it; she'd bought fabric and strappy sandals, sampled food from street vendors, walked until her feet blistered" (164). The class differences between Ian and Maya are becoming apparent, another fathom in the distance growing between them. When they travel to Jaipur, Ian insists on taking a train that is "air conditioned and a lot fancier than the second-class sleeper she usually takes" (164).[44] They also stay at a higher-end hotel, because, as Ian puts it before they leave New Delhi, "I wouldn't mind having a real toilet" (164). When Ian takes Maya to eat at an expensive restaurant, "Maya adds the bill up in her head and thinks of how many days she could have lived in India on that amount of money" (166). Clearly, Ian and Maya expect different things out of India. Ian is there as a tourist, not wanting to suffer from a lack of modern-day convenience and comfort. Maya, conversely, wants to belong to India, to blend in and adapt to the culture of her adopted home. Ian's diasporic distance from India is one of unease and distrust, where for Maya, India allows her to access parts of her identity that Israel had forced her to sublimate.

Exemplifying this difference, Maya's first experiences in India are in stark contrast to Ian's. India literally and metaphorically strips Maya of certain parts of her Israeli identity and remakes her—or allows her to remake herself. Like so many Israelis, Maya left Israel after her army service to travel, and headed straight to India. However, two weeks after arriving, "her backpack was stolen on a train to Varanasi: her passport, her traveller's cheques, her address book, her clothes, her travel guide. Gone. She had nothing but the clothes on her back. It was as if someone had erased her" (158). This erasure of the outward manifestation of her Israeliness—her Israeli passport, her traveller's cheques from an Israeli bank, her address book and travel guide most likely written in Hebrew—powerfully represents how national identity is fabricated. What is not fabricated is Maya's adeptness at gaining cultural competency (unlike Ian); what cannot be erased is Maya's dark Arab-Jewish skin, which will forever link her to the global south. Without money or identification, Maya starts to work at the hostel she is staying at (the same hostel she takes Ian to in the story's present day), where she babysits the owners' daughter. At the hostel, Amrita, one of the owners, takes Maya under her cultural wing, giving her clothes and helping her dress. When Maya, wearing Amrita's shalwar kameez and a bindi, looked at herself in the mirror, "she was stunned by her reflection. Her small frame, her dark skin, her straight black hair. 'Like Indian girl,' Amrita gasped, wobbling her head from side to side, in that gesture Maya later adopted, somewhere between yes and no" (158). Shortly after this moment, readers are told that now, when Maya walked "the streets of New Delhi, the city made space for her" (159), a striking change from when she first arrived, was marked as a tourist, and was immediately robbed. Unlike Ian, who holds on to his Britishness as a defense against what he finds off-putting in India, Maya, stripped of her markers of identity, and happening to have dark skin, eagerly takes on this new identity. Now, unlike Ian, Maya "has learned to navigate between her personas, her borrowed and inherited identities" (156). Note that it is not that Maya becomes less Israeli per se, but that she can switch between her various personas, which impact and leave traces within each other.

Maya and Ian embody two different manifestations of what Homi Bhabha calls, after Frederick Jameson, the third space of cultural identity. This third space exists between the national and the globalized, between the colonizer and the colonized, and is a fluid, dynamic space, where both elements—here, Ian's Indianness and Britishness, and Maya's Arabness and Israeliness—hold varying degrees of sway. Bhabha writes that the "non-synchronous temporality of global and national cultures opens up a cultural space—a third space—where the negotiation of incommensurable differences creates a tension peculiar to borderline existences" (312). Similar to the diasporic, the third space is constantly shifting:

> Hybrid hyphenations emphasize the incommensurable elements—the stubborn chunks—as the basis of cultural identifications. What is at issue is the performative nature of differential identities: the regulation and negotiation of those spaces that are continuously, contingently, "opening out," remaking the boundaries, exposing the limits of any claim to a singular or autonomous sign of difference—be it class, gender or race. (313)

When Maya and Ian, who met in the colonial centre of London, reunite in India, the particular mixtures of their third space identities—the stubborn chunks of their mixed heritages—prove combustible. Maya, in reclaiming her identity as a woman of colour, has her Arabness, and her acquired Indianness, at the forefront; Ian, on the other hand, has the British ascendant over his Indianness. Their disastrous experience together in India is, then, a kind of third space squared. Maya's sense of herself—what we could call a diasporic sense—is incredibly dynamic, not static as Ian's is, and is always open to new contingencies and borderlines.

In fact, throughout her life, Maya has set herself apart in order to control her identity. In wanting to wear makeup and skirts, and go dancing and flirt with boys, she deceives her very religious family, actually living two selves: the chaste, religious daughter, and, as soon as she leaves the house, the rebellious teenager. Maya remembers the "double life she had led all through high school, how she carried a pair of jeans and an eyeliner in her bag and changed in the bushes before heading off to parties in Tel Aviv" (161). Maya's estrangement from her family and their way of life was finalized when she insisted on joining the Israeli army, which she used as a final escape from their constricting religiosity. Furthermore, once she adopts India as her home, Maya feels the need to distance herself from the other Israelis in India. Through putting down roots in India, Maya does not see herself as just another Israeli spending a year abroad, as the subjects of Flipping Out do, and when Oren—one of the Israeli tourists Maya spends the last night of the story with—points out that she is the same as him, she bristles at the suggestion: "as if she's just another one of those backpackers who come here for a few months after army service and then return to their real homes, start university, rent an apartment in Tel Aviv, hang a series of stylized photographs of barefoot Indian children on their living room walls" (170). (This is a pretty good approximation of Yasmine in "The Poets at the Kitchen Window.") What Tsabari reveals in "A Sign of Harmony" is that the ability to take on multiple identities is not necessarily an outcome of simple international movement in a globalized world, but rather, for people who can more easily move through cultures and contexts than others, the globalized world allows for the constant reinvention of the self. Even Maya's name relates to her taking on of identities: "In Hindu philosophy, Maya was the illusion we veiled our true selves with" (158). Maya "had never expected to experience a spiritual revelation in India," we are told, "had thought it a cliché, yet here she felt she was unveiling her true self, stripping off the illusion" (159). It is perhaps a similar unveiling of his true self that she hopes Ian will undergo on his first trip to India.

Unlike Maya, Ian's sojourn to his ancestral homeland does not turn him into an "Indian" (if such a thing is even possible), but instead throws his difference into sharp relief, especially for Maya. This is one of the many reasons their relationship wobbles, and finally, in Jaipur, collapses. At the fancy restaurant in Jaipur, with Ian "starting to feel human again," as he puts it (166), the sexual attraction starts to reignite. Maya thinks that Ian finally "looks like the man she remembers from London" (166). However, the brewing sexual tension evaporates when Ian sees a rat, freaks out, and hurriedly pays the bill. Ian gets angry at Maya for attempting to negotiate with the rickshaw driver on the way home, and they have a fight in the hotel room:

> "You realize you were bargaining for the equivalent of less than a pound."
> "It's not about that...It's how it works here. They expect you to bargain. Didn't you read about it in your guidebook?"

"Well, you don't have to talk to him like that."

"Like how? It's called negotiating."

"I don't know. You seemed a little harsh."

"I'm Israeli, this is how we talk…What?…You guys are just as patronizing as Israelis. We're just more direct about it."

"I'm Indian," Ian says.

"I'm more Indian than you are," she says and immediately regrets it. (167)

Here we are, then, at both the climax of the story and the crux of the issue. Maya, a Yemeni Jew who grew up in Israel, estranged from her orthodox family, has told Ian, a first-generation Brit of Indian heritage, that she is more Indian than he is. In a moment of interpersonal anger, Maya claims that her cultural competency outranks Ian's heritage. This is a crucial encounter between two people who have been irrevocably marked by the nation-state and colonialism, whose third space identities do not mesh and yet who both no longer cleanly belong anywhere.

Ultimately, despite their discovered differences, "A Sign of Harmony" revolves around the unavoidable connection of being dark-skinned in a global world where white is coded as dominant. The title of the story comes from a barista in London, who tells Maya and Ian during their early courtship that they "look like brother and sister" (161). When Maya reacts negatively to the suggestion, the barista states, "No, it's a good thing…It's a sign of harmony" (161). At the narrative's end, Maya returns from her aborted sexual encounter with Oren and sees Ian sleeping in the hotel bed, and is "taken by how handsome he is, like a Bollywood actor." "He could be a local," she thinks to herself, "especially now, undressed, stripped of his accent, his guidebook, his backpack. He looks the part, just like she does; both wear the right skin colour, the right features, yet neither of them belongs here, not really. She wonders if this is all they ever had in common" (174). Just like Maya, when the trappings of capitalism and outsiderness—a guidebook, a backpack—are removed, Ian's Indian heritage, marked on his skin, becomes the prime identifier. Maya's realization that neither of them belong in India, though for opposing reasons, opens up the possibility of diasporic (non-)belonging. As in "Invisible," Tsabari uses her fiction to show that, even with all the differences, it is Ian and Maya's skin colour that unites them. The story, like so many in *The Best Place on Earth*, once again flips the national script: Maya realizes that neither she nor Ian belongs in India, but for very different reasons. Nor do they cleanly belong in Israel or Britain. Their third space diasporic identity puts them on the outside of national belonging.

"Egyptian, Israeli, It Was All the Same": Collapsing Borders in "Borders"

The final story of Tsabari's I read in this chapter is the phenomenal "Borders." Here, Tsabari most profoundly disrupts the racial and ethnic hierarchy that is so well established yet so hidden in Israel. I will focus on three distinct ways "Borders" achieves its effects. The first is through the character of Samir, an Arab Jew who worked as a spy during his army service, an experience that had the paradoxical outcome of allowing him to see outside of Zionist hegemony. The second way is through the central narrative of the story, where the protagonist Na'ama, with help from Samir, discovers that Tariq, a Bedouin man Na'ama knew as a friend of her mother's when they lived in a settlement in the then-occupied Sinai Peninsula, is actually her biological father. Na'ama's mother, by having a child with Tariq, has clearly transgressed the boundaries of Jewish/ Arab ethnicity. Finally, I will use the ending of "Borders"—where Na'ama crosses the border from Israel into Egypt to attempt to find Tariq—as a jumping off point into a discussion of Moses as an Arab Jew, a concept that I will trace through Freud, Edward Said, and Judith Butler. What Moses-as-Arab-Jew allows us to see in Tsabari's fiction is how Arabness and Jewishness, far from being the antonyms Zionism insists they are, have been with the Jewish people for millennia, perhaps even from the beginning, and can be used as a catalyst for a more just future in Israel/ Palestine.

The Israeli resort town of Eilat, the setting for "Borders," is an important symbol of Jewish geography. Located at the very bottom of Israel, on the shores of the Red Sea, bordering Egypt and Jordan, within sight of Saudi Arabia, Eilat is used by Tsabari to symbolize how national and ethnic borders do not stop people from moving across and within them, regardless of what the national narrative insists are immovable, uncrossable boundary lines. Eilat, once the "southern outpost of the Limes Palestine, the line of border fortresses established by the Romans and Nabateans" (Gradus 87), is now Israel's most popular and well-known resort destination. In other words, Eilat exists within and outside national borders, and national time.

Likewise, Na'ama's childhood—and beyond—exists within the shifting national borders of Israel. When the Israeli army occupied the Sinai Peninsula during the 1967 War, fourteen civilian communities were established there, especially along the coastline of the Gulf of Aqaba ("Israel-Egypt Relations"). In the late 1960s and 1970s, these settlements attracted counter-cultural Israelis, who wanted to be far from the authorities. It is at one of these settlements, a small collective farm—called in Hebrew a *moshav*—named Nuweiba, that Na'ama was born. Na'ama's mother, Mira, was posted to the Sinai during "her army service, a couple of years after the peninsula was seized in the Six Day War" (177). Na'ama's mother "had fallen in love with it—the remoteness, the simplicity, the unbearable beauty—and decided to stay, undisturbed by the fact that it was Egyptian land, taken over in an act of war" (177). The narrator here clearly locates the geography of the peninsula as geopolitical, as something that *should have* disturbed Na'ama's mother, and can be seen as subtly implying that Mira's disregard for the colonial reality of Nuweiba echoes the general Israeli disregard for the colonial reality of Israel proper, which was no less "taken over in an act of war." "There weren't many Egyptians living in the peninsula," the narrator tells us, moreover, "just Bedouins, who lived in tents, adhered to tribal laws and didn't care which government ruled them. The land itself didn't change, they said. Egyptian, Israeli, it was all the same" (177). The Bedouins, including Tariq, do not believe in national borders, or the nation-state and its governments. The nomadic, like the diasporic, represents another configuration of human life that does not rely on borders, land-owning, or states.

In any case, Na'ama is a product of this geography. The narrator writes that Na'ama was "a child of the desert, her feet callused by hot, white sand, her eyes used to squinting through the fog of sandstorms, her body accustomed to moving slowly, preserving its energy on hot summer days" (177). Na'ama's identity is inherently connected to the landscape. After the evacuation of the Sinai settlements—a condition for the

Israel–Egypt Peace Treaty signed in March 1979 was the total withdrawal from the peninsula ("Israel-Egypt Relations")—Na'ama and Mira move back to Israel proper, and return to Tel Aviv. There, Na'ama's grandmother—Mira's mother—bemoans this facet of her granddaughter's personality: "We left Egypt to come to Israel, but somehow we ended up with a Bedouin granddaughter" (189). Na'ama's heritage as an Egyptian Jew further complicates the Jewish geography of her life. Significantly, Na'ama is literally named after the land, Na'ama Bay in Sharm el-Sheikh (177), further exemplifying her hybridized identity, being named after a landmass that once politically belonged to Israel but no longer does.

The Jewish geography at play in Eilat is a major source of action and tension in the story, acting as it does for Na'ama as a reminder of her childhood on the Sinai Peninsula, just on the other side of the heavily surveilled border. Unlike some of their fellow ex-moshavites, neither Na'ama nor Mira return to the Sinai to visit after their removal (178). Nonetheless, once Na'ama and her friend Karin go down to Eilat for a scuba diving trip on Coral Beach, at a scuba place and hostel near the Egyptian border called The Deep, Na'ama gets re-hooked on the desert landscape and the ocean, being so close to her birthplace. "Coral Beach wasn't Sinai," Tsabari's narrator writes, "but it was close enough to trigger her body's memory: the same red, jagged mountains towering quiet and majestic behind her, the same warm sea licking her feet...It was as though her body had retuned itself, resonating with an old melody" (176–177). Is this the old melody of her childhood on the peninsula, or the even older memory of her heritage as an Egyptian Jew? Possibly, it is a mixture of both. As Na'ama explains to Samir, "My mom was born in Israel, but my grandparents came to Israel from Alexandria. Totally different from Sinai, though. Two different continents" (189). After their first trip to Coral Beach the summer before, Na'ama and Karin had returned as often as they could, spending the various Jewish holidays there. In the summer between high school and the start of their army service, they hitchhike down to The Deep for the season, which is where Tsabari begins the story. Na'ama imagines their summer at Coral Beach as an "old Israeli" movie: "A summer of firsts and lasts, of falling in love and saying goodbye, skinny-dipping in the sea and staying up until sunrise" (175). Notice how the spectre of the army hangs over these expectations. Due to the presence of Samir, who works the front desk and is a friend of The Deep's owner, Ari, what starts out as a typical story of the summer after high school, with Na'ama and Karin wanting nothing more than a place to work and go scuba diving, expands into a life-changing event for Na'ama.

As mentioned already, Samir, like Na'ama, is an Arab Jew. This, however, is the extent of Na'ama's, and therefore our, knowledge of Samir's ancestry. Samir is not his real name, but was his "Arabic name in the army" (184); the fact that he still goes by it implies his ongoing sympathies for the Arab/Palestinian perspective. Na'ama, thinking about Samir's name, remarks that she was "pretty sure he wasn't an Arab" (179). Besides this, nobody in the story knows much else about Samir's ethnicity. Karin immediately thinks Samir and Na'ama should sleep with each other; Na'ama is a virgin and hopes to not be by the time she gets called up for army service. (Karin herself is sleeping with Ari.)

Samir serves a much greater purpose in the text than a potential sexual partner, though: he embodies, he *enacts*, the false borders put up between Arab Jews and Arabs, in particular Palestinians. He brings the most fecund diasporic heteroglossic, polycentric perspective to the story, the collection, and perhaps all the texts under study in this book. For his army service, Samir went undercover—a *mistarev*, in Hebrew— as a spy. However, as Ari sarcastically puts it, Samir "spent too much time pretending to be an Arab in the army. It made him all fucked in the head" (186). (That diagnosis, of course, depends wholly on what side of the political spectrum you stand on.) Significantly, Ari says this after a heated discussion about the moshav where Na'ama was born. It is worth quoting the exchange in full:

"How old were you when you had to leave?" Ari propped his sunglasses on his head.

"Eight," she said.

"That must have been hard."

"They were settlers," Samir said. "They must have known that it was temporary."

"I wouldn't call them settlers." Na'ama shifted in her seat. Settlers made her think of gun-toting fundamentalist Jews living in the West Bank. "It was different then. They didn't go there for ideological reasons."

"Still, they settled on occupied land," Samir said. "Everyone makes it sound all romantic, but facts are facts. That famous guest house in Nuweiba that everybody talks about? That was built on Bedouin land."

"It wasn't like that." She sat on her hands, annoyed. "They were just a bunch of hippies looking for a place off the grid."

"Hippie settlers." He grinned. (186)

Tsabari suggests that Samir's time living as an Arab—and even, possibly, as a Palestinian—regardless of its falseness, has allowed him to view the conflict from outside of Israeli hegemony. Furthermore, while Na'ama is right that there were "hippies" in the Sinai, there were also right-wing religious fundamentalist settlers, which Na'ama, in the above exchange, insists there were not. In fact, Yamit, the biggest of the Jewish settlements, put up a large fight against the army when they came to evacuate them.[45] Settlers could call themselves left wing or right wing, but it does not hide the fact that, as Samir is so well aware, they are living on land that is not theirs, and for political purposes. Na'ama and her hippie settlers are to the Sinai what the gun-toting fundamentalist settlers are to the West Bank, are to the Israeli settlers living in Israel proper, regardless of the defenses Na'ama and other Israelis have put up to ignore this fact.

Samir's experience as a spy fictionalizes Shenhav's discussion of the phenomenon of the Israeli government using its Arab Jewish citizens as spies. As his main example, Shenhav writes about Eli Cohen, who rose through the ranks of the Syrian army, was caught, and executed.[46] Shenhav writes: "Such is the logic of the Israeli state: top-heavy with contradictions. On the one hand, it wants to strip its Arab Jews...of their Arabness, while on the other, it implores some of them (like my father and his friends) to go on living as Arabs by license" (3). Arab Jews like Eli Cohen, Shenhav's father, and Tsabari's Samir, with their knowledge of Arabic, their cultural competency, and the fact that they could pass as Arabs (because they *were* Arabs), were tapped by the Israeli state solely to act as spies. Shenhav laments that although "Arab Jews were routinely used as spies, their cultural skills were never used to forge positive links with Arab countries" (5). As we have seen, since Zionism dictates that Arabs and Jews are eternal enemies, it was ideologically impossible to envision a scenario where Arab Jews could represent the possibility of a totally different political configuration. Instead, the state's "practices were used to separate Arab Jews from their Arab backgrounds" (5). However, as we see with Samir, being a spy among Arabs can backfire, at least ideologically, and result in a kind of contrapuntal reading of the strict us-and-them dogma of the Israeli government and army, not to mention of Zionism writ large. Throughout the story, Samir points out the absurdity of the borders that separate Arabs and Jews, remarking, for example, about Jordan's King Hussein's occasional visits to the border in his yacht: "Wouldn't it be cool if he could just keep sailing and dock right here? Sit and have a beer? It seems so strange that there's this invisible border you can't cross" (188). This borderless ideology is doubly significant in the context of "Borders," because it is Samir's unusual connection with his Arabness, attained through being deployed as a spy, that allows him to see through the ideological blinders that keep even Na'ama from realizing that Tariq, the Bedouin who lived near Nuweiba, is her father.

When Na'ama arrives at The Deep at the beginning of the story, she is under the impression that she does not know, nor has ever met, her biological father. Mira, Na'ama's mother, told Na'ama that her father was a tourist from Spain named "José Louis" (183), which is a Spanishized version of Joe Louis, the famous American boxer with the name that is now perhaps better known as a prepackaged dessert food. The name seems like a bit of a cruel joke on Mira's part. Regardless, Na'ama arrives in Eilat with no real knowledge of her father; he had become "an empty pit she learned to walk around" (183), a metaphor based on land and landforms. What Na'ama does arrive in Eilat with is a series of photographs from the moshav that she recently found in her mother's belongings. They are mostly of Mira, and a few are of Tariq, who Na'ama knew as a Bedouin man who lived nearby and who was a regular, well-liked fixture on the moshav. Tariq and Mira were particularly close, and Na'ama has fond memories of him, including of a visit she went on with Tariq to his family's tent, which, unbeknownst to her (or to readers at the time), was her own extended family's tent. In one of Na'ama's photos, Tariq is "sitting in his galabeya on a frayed rug with Na'ama in his arms, his shoulders hunched as if to protect her" (180). Looking through the pictures, Na'ama "missed Sinai, now more than ever, and she missed Tariq, who had been a big part of her life growing up" (181). After Samir engenders

Na'ama's realization, Na'ama rethinks her memories of the moshav, of her mother, of Tariq: "She lay awake considering every quirk of her character that she couldn't trace back to her mother, revisiting every memory she had of Tariq" (193). Just like Na'ama, we as readers can also reread these memories of Tariq once she discovers the truth. This rereading mimics, in a way, the need to rehistoricize Arab Jewish history from beyond the limits of Zionism. This is another feature of the short story: as a short fictional unit, a short story can be read multiple times in a short time span, deepening its fictional power. When further combined into a short story collection, each fictional unit can act as a different voice, deepening the heteroglossic potential of the work.

Over the course of the story, two people other than Na'ama look at the photos, Karin and Samir. Karin, as a typical Israeli teenager brought up on stories of Arab enmity, is incredulous: "Seriously...Your mom let a Bedouin babysit you?" Na'ama responds by saying, "He was our friend... It was different over there" (181). Karin's response is indicative of the Israeli fear of the country's Arab other, whether Palestinian or Bedouin. Likewise, Na'ama is so entrenched in the Zionist hegemony that the thought that her mother could be in love, have sex, and have a child with Tariq is inconceivable. Nonetheless, Na'ama still understands that outside of the borders of Israel, in the occupied land of the Sinai, it was "different" enough for Bedouins and Israeli Jews to be in community with each other. It will take the outsider perspective of Samir to break down Na'ama's more insistent internal borders.

When Samir sees the photo, on the other hand, he immediately asks if Tariq is her father (190). Though a standard enough question, the colour of Tariq's skin and the unspoken borders of Arab and Jew make Samir's surmise—the polar opposite of Karin's—not only incredibly loaded, but incredibly perceptive. Having broken free of Zionist ideology, the possibility of cross-cultural and ethnic interaction becomes commonplace, a possibility enacted throughout The Best Place on Earth. Na'ama's initial response is denial: "'What?' She snorted. 'Of course not.' She paused. 'Why would you say that?'" (190). The idea that Tariq is Na'ama's father is so new to her, so foreign, that at first she cannot accept it as even a possibility, yet the movement from "snorted" to "paused" initiates the possibility of acceptance; when her stomach "caved in as [if] from a direct blow...Her body [going] numb," the possibility has solidified. Samir answers Na'ama's question by saying, "I don't know. The way he's holding you, I guess. And you said before you were like a little Bedouin when you came back" (190). This time, Na'ama responds to the impossibility of Tariq being her father by kissing Samir, instigating their first sexual interaction (and, since we know that Na'ama is a virgin, her first sexual interaction as well). Samir starts to perform oral sex on Na'ama, but she is both too nervous and too close to allowing herself to accept that Tariq is her father, and she has Samir stop. "Whatever," Samir says after Na'ama apologizes, "It's my fault. I should have known. You're just a kid" (192). Samir and Na'ama's sexual encounter is aborted, but Samir has sent Na'ama on a new path, and his role in the story is complete.

Once Samir opens the possibility of Na'ama's parentage, Na'ama is confronted with the vast amount of evidence she has carried around as memories for all of her life, and she accepts that Tariq is her father. She looks at the photographs again, "trying to see what Samir had seen" (192). Not surprisingly, her thoughts mostly focus on her mother: "Had her mother lied to her all these years?" she wonders (191). In the after-burn of realization, Na'ama sees that Mira must have truly loved Tariq. "All those years," she thinks, "Mira had been searching for somewhere she'd be as happy as she was in Sinai, longing for the one man she must have really loved" (193). Just as Samir can now see from the Palestinian and Arab perspective, Na'ama acknowledges that Mira and Tariq being in love is "[a] story" that makes "so much sense" that she can't believe "it [took] her so long to figure [it] out" (193).[47] This encapsulates one of Tsabari's most destabilizing and constant moves in The Best Place on Earth: the belief that people loving each other across ideological, national, and racial borders is natural, organic, and the best remedy for hatred and ideological boundaries.

Once Tariq's fatherhood is known, Na'ama decides to leave Israel and cross into Egypt to try to find him. Na'ama crosses not only the political border between Israel and Egypt, but the Zionist-patrolled border of Jewish-Arab miscegenation. As it turns out, Na'ama had unconsciously been preparing for her journey to Egypt: "Now she wondered why she had packed not only her passport, but the photos and the one thing she had from Tariq: a cone shell necklace he had given her the day she and her mother left" (194). Unfortunately, even if Na'ama finds Tariq, the chances of a problem-free happy ending are slight. If Na'ama remains in Israel, she will have to continue living the precarious balance between Arab and Jew. Not only that, but she still has her looming army duty: will she stay in Egypt as a deserter? Will she return to Israel and refuse to enlist? Or will she return from her search for Tariq and join the army, where she could quite possibly be involved in destroying Bedouin villages and forcibly removing the inhabitants?[48] Seeing how Na'ama is half Bedouin, this would be a strain, to put it lightly. Whatever Na'ama chooses on the other side of "Borders," she will inevitably have to contend with the deeply divided elements of her identity as manifested in the political, cultural, and ethnic reality of daily life in Israel.

As we see throughout *The Best Place on Earth*, diasporic Jewish identity is never whole or static, but is always fluid, multi-variant, dynamic, historically contingent: in a word, heteroglossic. Na'ama, already an Arab Jew of Egyptian heritage, discovers—or rediscovers— that her father is a Bedouin Arab, therefore making the Arab side of her identity that much more prevalent. The history of Israel/Palestine and Egypt is fundamental to Jewish religion, myth, and historiography, not least of which is through the figure of Moses. Moses was not only the leader of the Jewish people's freedom from Egyptian bondage and arrival in Canaan, but the one who brought God's laws to the Jewish collective. Na'ama, by crossing into Egypt, reverses Moses's original journey, not to find a homeland promised by God—and that must be emptied of its original inhabitants—but to find a father. It is worth taking some time, then, to look at how Moses has been read as an Arab Jew. The thread I will unravel starts with Sigmund Freud, who in his later book *Moses and Monotheism* runs a thought experiment that imagines Moses as an Egyptian, goes through Edward Said's reading of Freud, and ends with Judith Butler's reading of Said's reading of Freud. Tracing this intellectual trajectory, we witness how a revisioning of Moses's place in Jewish history as a diasporic one can be utilized in the pursuit of justice within and without the Jewish world.

In *Moses and Monotheism*, Freud makes three main claims about Moses. The first is that Moses was not Jewish at all, but a highborn Egyptian who ended up leading the Jewish people to Canaan. The myth of Moses and the exodus from Egypt, therefore, "undertakes to transform [Moses] into a Jew" (13). The second claim is that the monotheism

Moses brings to the Jewish people is actually an offshoot of a shortly lived Egyptian religion. And the third is that Moses was murdered by the Jewish people (which has something to do with the fact that, according to Freud, there were two original Jewish people, the one led by Moses and another group that merged with them later). Reading the book today, Freud appears to be partaking in pretty wild conjecture, though it is exhilarating to watch a mind like Freud's dabble in biblical scholarship. Put in historical context, though, Freud can be read as engaging with the German biblical scholars who, starting in the nineteenth century, began historicizing and contextualizing the biblical texts; Freud's reading is just a particularly fanciful one. For Freud, the Jews's murder of Moses is the original sin they had to repress. For the purposes of this book, Freud's conjecture that Moses was an Egyptian just further shows how no group has pure origins.

Said, in his essay "Freud and the Non-European," sees in Freud's excavation of Moses's origins the beginnings of the possibility of moving past xenophobia, the nation-state, and ethnic puritanism. Said's reading of Freud, like his readings of other canonical European writers such as Jane Austen, is careful, contrapuntal, generous, yet thoroughly critical. Said is both ruthless and generous in his reading of Freud, noting Freud's narrow thinking when it came to most of the rest of the non-European world, but also lauding Freud for not holding the European up as an ideal of humanity. Said finds Freud's discussion of Moses and his place as both the originator and that which must be hidden in the Jewish people particularly fecund. Reading Freud's complication of identity through the figure of Moses, Said concludes that a group's identity "cannot be thought or worked through itself alone; it cannot constitute or even imagine itself without that radical originary break or flaw which will not be repressed, because Moses was Egyptian, and therefore always outside the identity inside which so many have stood, and suffered—and later, perhaps, even triumphed" ("Freud and the Non-European" 517). Said uses Freud's undetermined history to ask, can such an outlook "aspire to the condition of a politics of diaspora life? Can it ever become the not-so-precarious foundation in the land of Jews and Palestinians of a bi-national state in which Israel and Palestine are parts, rather than antagonists of each other's history and underlying reality? I myself believe so" ("Freud and the Non-European" 517). Said raises the radical possibility of binational coexistence here; however, he does not discuss how the Arab Jew already embodies this possibility of coexistence. It is Butler who teases out that particular thread.

In the chapter entitled "Impossible, Necessary Task" from her 2012 book *Parting Ways: Jewishness and the Critique of Zionism*, Butler reads Said's essay on Freud as having two relevant theses. The first is that "Moses, an Egyptian, is the founder of the Jewish people, which means that Judaism is not possible without this defining implication in what is Arab," which leads Butler to rightly conclude that "Such a formulation challenges hegemonic Ashkenazi definitions of Jewishness" (28). The second thesis is that "'displacement' characterizes the histories of both the Palestinian and the Jewish peoples and so, in [Said's] view, constitutes the basis of a possible, even desirable, alliance" (29), what I referred to above as the possibility of a binational existence. These two ideas correlate perfectly with what Samir stands for in "Borders," with what the love between Mira and Tariq, as embodied in the birth of Na'ama, can create. Butler calls Moses a "figure of cathexis, a living conjuncture" (30). This living conjuncture means opening up the Jewish people's concept of itself to those groups such as the Arab Jews who do not have a European origin.

For Butler, the figure of the Arab Jew "constitutes conjuncture, chiasm, and cohabitation (understood as coarticulation with alterity) as a founding principle of Jewish life" (30). In other words, Butler claims Jewish life as diaspora, polycentric, and heteroglossic. Shohat speaks similarly when she states that the Arab Jew can seen as a form of "utopic longing" ("Treyf"). Besides Arab Jews such as Samir—as well as Maya, Savta, and other major characters in the stories of *The Best Place on Earth*—whose mixed identity runs throughout their heritage, there is Na'ama, whose mother, an Egyptian Jew, crossed the Zionist-mandated lines and procreated with an Arab Bedouin. The moshav in the Sinai, then, even though it is located on "stolen land," as Samir puts it, can be seen as a place of "conjuncture, chiasm, and cohabitation." Thus, Na'ama represents the opportunity that comes from two peoples that are supposed to be at unending odds with each other coming together and embracing the multinational character of Israel/Palestine. Freud turns Moses into an outsider who leads the Jewish people to monotheism and Canaan; Said takes Freud's Moses and uses him to question the possibility of a diasporic, binational existence in Israel/Palestine; and finally, Butler takes Said's gloss of Freud's radical conjectures on Moses and invites us to think of Moses as the first Arab Jew, full of potential justice. The Zionist-induced antonyms of Arab and Jew collapse, due not only to the existence of Arab Jews and the hundreds of years of coexistence they are the products of, but to Judaism's originary break/flaw, Moses, a break/flaw that Na'ama re-enacts in crossing the border into Egypt at the end of "Borders."

"The Irreversible Conditions of Social Life": Conclusion

In this chapter, Tsabari's stories of Arab Jews living in Israel/Palestine have been analyzed in order to show how they refuse to accept the borders between ethnicities, histories, cultures, and nations, whether they manifest in a single person or in vast geopolitical formations. Moreover, the stories in *The Best Place on Earth* successfully give voice to those who have historically been voiceless, and represent the complex problems of being an Arab Jew in today's Jewish world, both inside and outside of Israel. Along with this, the stories reveal how a nation that is supposed to be the end of diaspora just ends up being a collection of different diasporas, engendering new diasporas and setting the ground for polycentric diasporic heteroglossia, regardless of the hegemonic violence used to poison that ground.

Arab Jewish writers, activists, and scholars are at the forefront of challenging Zionist hegemony. Even Moses, the forefather of the Jewish religion, can be deployed in this way. To return to Butler, I agree wholeheartedly that "If Moses stands for a contemporary political aspiration, it is one that refuses to be organized exclusively on principles of national, religious, or ethnic identity, one that accepts a certain impurity and mixedness as the irreversible conditions of social life" (31). As I hoped to show in this chapter, we can see that Tsabari has created a diverse array of characters, placed in a wide range of social and political situations—a feat only possible in book-length form through the multi-voiced comprehensiveness offered by the short story collection—who embody the radical potential that Butler locates in Moses. Tsabari's fiction brilliantly and carefully communicates the contemporary realities of Israel's Arab Jews; through a close engagement with her stories, we can hopefully begin to loosen the Zionist demand that a strict ethnic nationalism is the only way to keep the Jews of Israel—and, implicitly, the Jews of the world—safe. Rosalynn, Maya, and Na'ama represent a contemporary world of movement, interpersonal relationships, and fluid and accepting cultural difference that does not need to be policed, walled-off, or punished, and that can come from a place of radical diasporic hope.

"The Jewish Semitone"

Zionism and the Soviet Jewish Diaspora in *The Betrayers*

IN THIS CHAPTER, I analyze David Bezmozgis's novel *The Betrayers*, focusing on its representation of the massive migration of Soviet Jews to Israel in the latter half of the twentieth century, an event that reshaped the demographic, political, and cultural landscape of Israel/Palestine. In *The Betrayers*, Bezmozgis creates a convincing picture of the Soviet Jewish impact on Israeli society and culture at the same time the novel laments the dying Jewish diasporas of the former Soviet Union (FSU); however, by formulating the politics of the novel as exclusively Jewish, by leaving out any sense of a Palestinian narrative or perspective, Bezmozgis feeds—whether inadvertently or not—the Zionist consensus in the Canadian Jewish community. Bezmozgis himself refers to the novel as a "Zionist" text ("An Afternoon with David Bezmozgis"), and even though it seems to explicitly critique the country's rightward political drift, it implicitly condones Israel's Zionist ethnic nationalism. In this way, while the novel at first glance may appear to conform to the attributes of diasporic heteroglossia, upon closer inspection it is only an ersatz diasporic heteroglossia; this is because *The Betrayers* is a text that firmly roots itself in the Zionist centre, shutting itself off from heterodox Jewish voices, as well as any and all Palestinian ones. The supposedly antithetical Zionisms of Baruch Kotler, the novel's protagonist (liberal, secular, moral), and his son Benzion (right wing, religious, zealous), which come to a head in the novel's final sections, end up being simply two manifestations of the same ideology: settler-colonial, ethnic supremacist, and violent. Add in the fact that the novel's supposed central conflict between diaspora and home is played out by characters who are both Zionist, as well as the novel's brutal depictions of life in the dying diasporas of the FSU, and it is clear that *The Betrayers* is committed to the centroperipheral relationship between the Jewish diaspora and Israel. Nonetheless, through a contrapuntal, anti-Zionist reading of the text, we can adduce how xenophobic ethnic particularism does not perform well when transferred into positions of state power, a fact that speaks to the ethical power of diaspora over ethnic national nation-states.

The novel is preoccupied with the journey from diaspora to nation-state. When Kotler reminisces about his triumphant arrival in Israel after over a decade spent in the Soviet Union's gulags, he literally calls it the "high point of his life" (224). He "had been filled with joy," the narrator tells us: "The entire country had been astir. The prime minister had sent an official plane. They flew from Prague to Tel Aviv, just the Israeli aircrew, two diplomats, Miriam, and him...He had never felt such promise, such optimism" (224). This is *aliyah*—referring to Jewish immigration to Israel, aliyah is a Hebrew word that translates as "rising up" and comes preloaded with ideological baggage—as personal transcendent journey. The novel that precedes this closing moment acts to trouble the convergence between oppressed diasporic minority and hegemonic powerholders that hinges on Kotler's private flight to the Zionist state. By unpacking various significant aspects of the novel, including contextualizing the mass migration of Soviet Jews at the end of the twentieth century, the novel's vague and problematic geopolitics, and the lack of Palestinian voices or narratives in Bezmozgis's fictional world, I argue that Bezmozgis, in attempting to capture the collapse of Soviet Jewry, also ends up inadvertently revealing the contradictions and paradoxes of liberal Zionism. Because of this, I read the novel as a telling example of a counter-diasporic-heteroglossic text: closed instead of open, univocal instead of polyvocal, interested only in the narratives of the winners, dismissive of Zionism's others, and teleological to the extreme.

Bezmozgis, who immigrated to Canada with his family from Soviet Latvia as a young child, has written four award-winning books that mine the joint themes of Jewish exile, Jewish diaspora, and the Jewish immigrant experience, all from the perspective of the last great wave of Soviet Jewish immigration. In *The Betrayers*, his third book and second novel, Bezmozgis pits two divergent Jewish trends against each other: the Zionist ethnic national, embodied in the character of Soviet refusenik/Israeli politician Baruch Kotler, and the diasporic, embodied in the character of the disgraced, ailing, former KGB informant Chaim Tankilevich, the man who betrayed Kotler to the Soviet authorities. As much as Kotler's arrest and imprisonment dictate the direction his life will take, so too does Tankilevich's act of betrayal impact the rest of his life. When Kotler—who is not so loosely based on Natan Sharansky, the world-famous refusenik and Israeli politician—and Tankilevich come across each other by chance in the decaying coastal city of Yalta in *The Betrayer's* central conflict, they confront each other against the backdrop of what Bezmozgis figures as the final death rattle of the Soviet Jewish community.

Unlike Bezmozgis's two earlier books—the short story collection *Natasha and Other Stories* and the novel *The Free World*—where he mines his family's immigrant past and his own autobiography for fictional material, in *The Betrayers* he explores the Soviet Jewish present, in Israel and Crimea. Bezmozgis himself calls *The Betrayers* a novel "in real time." In his aptly-named essay "The Novel in Real Time" (which was originally published in *The New Yorker*, but is included in the paperback edition of *The Betrayers*), Bezmozgis writes provocatively of the experience of composing a novel set in contemporary Crimea, even as the political situation there, and in Ukraine as a whole, was changing day to day, due to the 2014 Russian invasion and subsequent annexation of the peninsula.[1] As Bezmozgis puts it, "I felt frustrated that world events conspired to undermine my designs for the book" ("The Novel in Real Time" 3). It is not just Crimea that exists in an ever-changing present, but Israel/Palestine as well. Unlike earlier texts explored in this book—*Altneuland*, with its belief in sundered history and the eruption of Zionist time, *Exodus*, with its teleological sense of Israel's creation—*The Betrayers* is concerned with the Jewish present. Looked at this way, the novel's oddly undeveloped sense of geography when it comes to the settlement withdrawal central to the novel's plot is a striking aspect of the novel, which I will spend a fair amount of space critiquing below. The fact is that *The Betrayers* is indeed a novel in real time, but as we will see, this real time is thoroughly national time, Zionist time: just as the Israeli geography of the novel is purposefully fuzzy, the Palestinian narrative is nonexistent in Zionist time.

Alongside his status in Canada, Bezmozgis's work is considered part of the burgeoning worldwide genre of Soviet Jewish literature, produced from wherever former Soviet Jews live—Israel, North America, Europe, Australia—and written in Russian, English, Hebrew, and German. Adrian Wanner, in his monograph *Out of Russia: Fiction of a New Translingual Diaspora*, defines Soviet Jewish literature as being produced by "contemporary Soviet-born emigres who left their country of origin to become writers in languages other than Russian" (3) and who maintain some aspect of Russianness in their work. Wanner calls this Soviet Jewish literature a "growing and understudied phenomenon of translingual diaspora literature" (3). Formulating Soviet Jewish writing as a worldwide diasporic phenomenon, which it certainly is, reveals once again the fact that Jewish diasporas continue to proliferate, instead of being consumed into Israel. Even the Soviet Jews who immigrated to Israel, what Zionists would call a return to home, can and should be considered diasporic. The networks of Jewish diaspora, even for those Jews who currently reside in Israel, are dynamic, constantly changing, and not disappearing anytime soon.

In all of his published work, Soviet Jewish immigration is Bezmozgis's central theme. In *The Betrayers*, Bezmozgis takes his fiction to the country where the greatest number of Soviet Jews from the last major wave of Soviet Jewish immigration landed: Israel. Parallel to this, *The Betrayers* is also the first time Bezmozgis's characters are no longer new immigrants en route to their destination or attempting to adjust to their new adopted home; Bezmozgis has turned his attention to Jewish immigrant characters who have attained major state power. It is not only Israel that Bezmozgis visits in *The Betrayers*, but the actual FSU. In fact, the entirety of the novel—which takes place over one eventful weekend—is set in Ukraine, though Israel is a constant subject, coming up frequently in Kotler's flashbacks and intermittent phone and email communication with his family. At the time of the writing of this book, there has been no scholarly work published on *The Betrayers*. As such, I will rely a little more on particularly insightful book reviews, and Bezmozgis's prodigious interviews, articles, and filmed talks on the novel. By focusing on a diasporic reading of *The Betrayers*, I hope to jumpstart the conversation on this important novel.

It is possible to read *The Betrayers* as a flawed but significant example of the Jewish diasporic novel, imagining as it does a dying nexus of the Jewish diaspora (the FSU) filtered through the consciousness of an Israeli-cum-Russian-Jew, written from the burgeoning, vibrant diasporic node of Jewish Canadian literature. Indeed, I will be reading the novel as partly that. However, when placed under deeper scrutiny, a counter-reading of the novel is possible that productively troubles the above description, revealing the text's lack of diasporic heteroglossia. *The Betrayers*, therefore, becomes an important example of what is at stake in fictional accounts of Israel written from the diaspora that do not allow other voices in, especially voices that challenge or trouble Zionism. In order to make this argument, I will spend significant time in this chapter discussing the immigration of Soviet Jews. Overall, I suggest that while Bezmozgis understands the immigrant experience in Canada and the depleted Jewish world of the FSU, his Zionism and elision of Palestinian narratives lead to a flawed, and troubling, fictional representation of Israel/Palestine that wishes for nothing if not the maintenance of the violent status quo.

The frame narrative of *The Betrayers*, which is the stuff of political thrillers, is what connects the novel's two geographical locales, Israel (figured in the novel as "home") and Crimea (figured as "diaspora"). Kotler, the "world's most illustrious refusenik" (105), is famous throughout the Jewish world, and especially in the Soviet Jewish world, and is considered an important voice in the Israeli Russian Jewish community.[2] As Kotler's (much younger) mistress and travelling partner Leora reminds him, "If there is a Russian Jew in the world who doesn't know who you are, I haven't met him" (17). Kotler is also a successful Israeli politician. His political party, which represents Soviet Jewish interests and has eight seats in the Knesset, is a part of the unnamed prime minister's ruling coalition, and Kotler himself holds a cabinet position.[3] In the events leading up to the novel's start and told to readers in flashback, Kotler runs afoul of the Israeli prime minister[4] when he refuses to go along with the prime minister's plan to unilaterally dismantle an unspecified settlement bloc in the West Bank and withdraw the settlers with force, if necessary. Kotler's outspokenness against what he sees as a foolish unilateral withdrawal leads him to publicly criticize the prime minister's plan in an op-ed in *The New York Times*, where he threatens to resign his cabinet position. Kotler's position against the withdrawal, as the political voice of Soviet Jews in Israel, can be taken as representative of the general anti-Palestinian worldview of the Russian Jewish community. Moreover, even this little detail of Kotler's defiance shows the importance of the Jewish American diaspora: why would Kotler write an op-ed in the *Times* if not for the importance, both political and financial, of the American Jewish (and non-Jewish) community to the ruling elite of Israel?

When Kotler, in a surreptitious meeting with one of the prime minister's operatives, refuses to keep quiet and to pretend that the cabinet is not divided, even in the face of blackmail, the operative leaks photos of Kotler's affair with his young assistant Leora—also a Soviet Jew, Leora immigrated to Israel with her parents when she was a young child—to the Israeli press. Suddenly mired in scandal, Kotler and Leora leave Israel to hide out in Yalta, a Crimean resort town in Ukraine where Kotler vacationed as a child, to wait for the scandal to blow over. While in Yalta, the Knesset votes to go ahead with the settlement withdrawal; Kotler voted against the withdrawal before leaving, "not wanting to be on record as merely abstaining" (24). A newspaper article Kotler reads summarizes the various reactions to the planned pullout: it was the "same choir singing the same song. The prime minister cited defensible borders and the welfare of the Israeli state. The chief of staff spoke of the army's inviolable discipline. The Left rejoiced. The Right seethed. The Americans applauded. The settlers pledged bloody insurrection. And the Palestinians complained" (25). Notice how the metaphor of the "same choir" singing "the same song" functions here, presenting this next (fictional) step of the unfolding Israel/Palestine crisis as yet more of the same, all the relevant actors performing their expected parts, with the implication that nothing has changed, and nothing will change. Notice also how the Palestinians "complained." Not only is this oversimplified—which Palestinians? Complained how? Is there any possibility that their complaints were legitimate?—but it is also more or less the only direct action Bezmozgis gives to any Palestinian character or entity throughout the novel. The lack of representation of a Palestinian narrative in the novel, especially one concerned with the West Bank, is a dangerous elision.

While all this is unfolding in Israel, Kotler runs smack into another, even more fateful conflict from his past. Needing a place to stay in Yalta, Kotler and Leora end up billeting at the house belonging to Chaim Tankilevich, a fellow Soviet Jew and apparent KGB agent who betrayed Kotler. Publishing an article in *Izvestia* calling Kotler a CIA spy, and then testifying at Kotler's trial, Tankilevich delivered Kotler to thirteen years in the gulag. As the narrator poetically describes it, Tankilevich's betrayal of Kotler was the beginning of Kotler's "third life" (101). The narrator explains: "First life: rank-and-file Soviet citizen. Second life: rank-and-file dissident. Third life: the chosen among the chosen" (101). The "chosen among the chosen" refers to Kotler's notoriety and fame while in the gulag, which translated directly into political power once he arrived in Israel. Kotler was a prisoner of the Soviet gulag from age twenty-five to thirty-eight: "He had gone into prison a young man, newly wed, and he had come out a gaunt, desiccated saint" (55). Unlike Kotler, ever since the trial Tankilevich has lived a life of shame and obscurity, hated by the Jewish people who remained in the FSU as the one who betrayed the world's most famous refusenik. Sasha Senderovich rightly sees Tankilevich as "a pitiful figure symbolic of what remains of the Jewish community in Crimea" ("Autobiographical Rut" np). Conversely, it was while Kotler was in the gulag engaging in hunger strikes and refusing to give in to the Soviet authorities—with Kotler's wife Miriam agitating on his behalf from Israel—that Kotler became world famous. Kotler's fame is not undeserved; he withstood tremendous violence and oppression from the Soviet authorities. "Simply," readers are told, "he was forced to discover hidden reserves of strength. And once he rose, it was hard to return to the man he'd been before—a fairly ordinary man, with no grand designs" (138). Tankilevich's betrayal is presented as the pivotal event in both of their lives, catapulting Kotler to the height of cultural and political power, and sinking Tankilevich into disgrace, resentment, and obscurity.

When Kotler lands at Tankilevich's Yalta doorstep, Tankilevich is involved in a drama of his own. Though compared to Kotler's political intrigue Tankilevich's dilemma is smaller, more personal, it nonetheless is symbolic of the state of the Soviet Jewish diaspora. No longer part of the KGB's witness protection program, in order to survive Tankilevich is being supported with a subsidy from the Jewish Hesed, which itself is reliant on donations from wealthy American Jews. However, the woman in charge of the Hesed, Nina Semonovna, knows who Tankilevich is, calling him a "notorious traitor to the Jewish people" (80), and demands that in exchange for her continued support, Tankilevich makes the four-hour round-trip trolleybus journey every Saturday morning to Simferopol in order to attend Saturday services at the synagogue, which is in desperate need of enough Jewish men to maintain a minyan. Tankilevich, in order to receive his Hesed-funded discount on food, must also shop at the Simferopol market. Semonovna strikes this deal with Tankilevich—who needs both the financial support and the secrecy she can offer—even though she says it disgusts her; this, readers are led to believe, is the sorry state of affairs for what is left of the Jewish community in Crimea. The Simferopol synagogue not having enough Jewish men for a minyan is a sad comment on the remaining members of the Soviet Jewish community.[5] Tankilevich calls the fact that the Hesed needs to ship him in every week for the minyan "a bizarre and inadvisable thing to disclose" (60).

When Kotler and Leora arrive in the Crimea, Tankilevich, who is in ailing health and understandably no longer wanting to make the difficult journey every Saturday, is attempting to get out of the arrangement. On the Saturday of the novel, which Tankilevich calls a "day of frustrations" (93), readers watch as he begs Semonovna, and as Semonovna refuses to relinquish Tankilevich's duties. According to her, he wants to "retain the disguise of Vladimir Tarasov [the alias given to him by the KGB], keep the subsidy, and retreat from [his] obligations to the community and the synagogue" (82). Afterwards, Tankilevich experiences a nasty incident of antisemitism at the market—with the offending antisemite yelling "The hell I'll beg forgiveness from the likes of you! While you get special money and I have a hole in my pocket. The Germans could have lined up a few more of you in '41!" (89)—and heads home to his wife Svetlana in disgrace. Earlier, on the bus to Simferopol, Tankilevich feels his usual remorse at the fact that he is a Jew who has been left behind: "This pitiless monotony, this drone of a life, to this he had been condemned. Especially in this land, to this they had all been condemned. The fortunate among them were able to shirk the knowledge, to keep it in abeyance. But this was denied him. Deliberately and vengefully denied him. He was forced to look, to contend with the unremitting dreariness of existence" (60–61). Tankilevich, "a seventy-year-old man afflicted with cataracts, arrythmia, and sciatica, captive of the trolleybus, tormented body and soul" (61), is a depressing vision of the Soviet Jewish community that remains in the FSU, relying on financial support from American Jewry, experiencing bald-faced antisemitism when in the public commons, barely able to enact a minyan, deteriorating in body, mind, and soul.

These are the two respective crises Kotler and Tankilevich are in when their paths cross in Yalta. Face to face for the first time since Kotler's trial, the two men are forced to come to terms with what happened in the past, what it means that the Soviet Union no longer exists, how both of their lives have turned out, and who, if anybody, is to blame. Their confrontation also allows Bezmozgis's narrator to muse on large questions of morality, human character, forgiveness, and fate. These large questions include: will Tankilevich admit why he betrayed Kotler? Will Kotler forgive Tankilevich? Were they both just victims of the unjust Soviet system, or does Kotler have the moral high ground? Will Kotler give Tankilevich and Svetlana the thing they want most of all, the opportunity to immigrate to Israel? What will become of the Soviet Jews who remain in the FSU? The scenes that narrate Kotler and Tankilevich's reunion, arguments, pleadings, accusations, judgments, and explanations are the most successful of the novel; Bezmozgis captures the tragic effects and aftereffects that living in a totalitarian system imparts on both those who flourish in spite of the system and those who languish within it, to be "ordinary [men]...ensnared in a villainous system" (172). In the end, Kotler does not exactly forgive Tankilevich, but he does use his power and fame to convince Semonovna to allow Tankilevich to no longer need to travel to Simferopol every Saturday yet still receive his stipend. The betrayed forgives the betrayer; the Israeli politician lessens the suffering of the nearly destitute Jew trapped in a disappearing diaspora.

Kotler and Tankilevich's reunion is the central plotline of the novel, with Kotler's political problems and Tankilevich's personal problems acting as side plots that feed, refract, and parallel their own interpersonal conflict.

A byproduct of the frame narrative is the fact that the entirety of the novel's present tense takes place in Crimea, leading scholars such as Norman Ravvin to be inclined to downplay Israel's significance in the metaphysics of the novel, to, as he himself admits, "push...the Israeli material...into the background" ("A Refusenik Returns" np).[6] I disagree with Ravvin here: while the Crimea-set sections are the more successful of the two, the Israel material is nonetheless of paramount importance in unpacking the nuanced ramifications of this novel, particularly the government's planned pullout from the unnamed settlement bloc. Allowing the two parts of the novel to hold equal weight reveals how Bezmozgis's stated commitment to write a novel in real time fares better when set in the fading Jewish geography of Crimea than when it shifts to the problematic Jewish geography of Israel/Palestine. Near the novel's end, readers find out that the settlement withdrawal that Kotler so vehemently opposes has begun. Kotler laments that the Israeli government, which he is still nominally a working member of, "had tasked young men—somber children with long limbs and smooth cheeks—to undertake this ugly job. To smash the work of their brothers and expel the brothers too. To do it and continue to believe that, afterward, they could still be brothers. And to trust that this served the greater good" (116–117). For Kotler, it is not that these long-limbed and smooth-cheeked "young men" are conscripted into an army that is imposing military occupation on millions of people that agitates him, but that they are being ordered to remove Jewish people from their (illegal under international law) homes; the dangers of ethnic in-group thinking are painfully apparent.

Moreover, even though Kotler thinks that withdrawing the settlers is a mistake, he still reacts with chagrin when he finds out that his son, Benzion—whose name is no accident: literally translating to "son of Zion," it is also the name of Benjamin Netanyahu's father, who worked as the personal secretary for Ze'ev Jabotinsky, the father of revisionist Zionism—has decided to disobey army orders and, for ideologically rightwing religious reasons, not participate in forcibly removing the settlers.[7] Kotler implores Benzion to act out his army orders, chain of command apparently outweighing political and moral convictions in Kotler's worldview. Nonetheless, Benzion refuses to evict the settlers. As Kotler puts it, "The son had gone against the wishes of the father. It was nothing new. It accounted for the greater part of human history" (185). When Kotler and Leora return to Israel in the novel's closing coda, aboard a plane that "contained a mingling of humanity that now existed only on a flight like this...a little flying shtetl...A Sholem Aleichem story come to life" (223), Kotler's son is going through his own battle against the state, having shot himself in the hand in order to be exempt from army duty. Senderovich, in his insightful review of *The Betrayers*, is right when he says that "The novel makes us consider how the legacy of Soviet Jewish dissidence can become, in the hands of the new generation, a blueprint for a kind of heroism that can inspire the continuation—rather than the end—of the occupation" ("Autobiographical Rut" np). Benzion has taken on the dissident values of his father, except where Kotler fought against the all-powerful Soviet state on behalf of Soviet Jews, Benzion fights on behalf of right-wing ethnonationalist settlers against the possibility of a slightly-less expansive military occupation.

In terms of its form, the novel embodies the tensions between Israel and the diaspora in its very structure. The first section, "Sanctuary," follows Kotler; the second, "Hostage," follows Tankilevich. The third section, "Reunion," takes up the two characters' confrontation, with the final section, "Ascent," reverting back to a third person that is tight to Kotler's perspective. (There is also a brief final section, entitled "Coda.") The entire novel unfolds over a busy, claustrophobic weekend. Bezmozgis mentions Philip Roth's *The Ghost Writer* (among works of other authors) as a model for the constrained spatial and temporal qualities of the text ("Reading Group Guide" 10). Which raises the question: if Bezmozgis had looked to Roth's Israel-situated novels as models instead of the first Zuckerman book, would he have opened up more space in his novel for the Palestinian other? In terms of style, the humour in the book successfully captures a particular Soviet and Israeli dryness. For example, when Svetlana convinces Kotler and Leora to stay at her house, she uses indoor plumbing as a selling point; when they get to the house, the narrator remarks that "between the desk and the dresser was the door to the celebrated toilet" (16). In another instance, Kotler reminisces about his pre-gulag self in typical Soviet self-deprecation:

"A former musical prodigy with small hands, a degree in computer engineering, and a desire to live in Israel. This described nearly every Zionist in Moscow" (138). Kotler is also constantly making fun of Soviet style thinking, what Senderovich calls "Kotler's near-parodic Soviet dissident-turned-Israeli-politician rhetoric" ("Autobiographical Rut" np). Though Tankilevich does have his own scenes, the most sustained of which is his Saturday of misadventures in Simferopol, and there are a few short scenes where it is just Svetlana and Leora, Kotler really is the protagonist of the novel. One way of reading this narrative fact is that Bezmozgis is acknowledging Israel's—as represented by Kotler, famous Zionist refusenik and member of the Knesset—current dominance in the Jewish world.

In fact, Bezmozgis often remarks on his feeling of Israel's centrality to the Jewish world. Though a celebrated chronicler of Soviet Jewish life in the Canadian diaspora, Bezmozgis seems to have no place for North America in his personal Jewish geography: "Implicitly," he writes, *The Betrayers* "advances this particular formulation: The Jewish future is to be found in Israel. The Jewish past in Europe. Where in this equation is North America? Neither the future nor the past. Which begs the question: What kind of literature can be made of a place that, for Jews, represents neither the past nor the future? What role does America play in Jewish life, and by extension what kind of Jewish literature can be created here?" ("End of American Jewish Literature, Again," np). I would like to suggest that through a diaspora-centred reading of Bezmozgis's novel, a possible answer to this question can be found. And that answer has to do with privileging the dynamic, non-power-holding versions of Jewish collectivity over the Zionist ethnic nationalist one. While Bezmozgis evocatively mourns the dying Jewish diasporas of the FSU in *The Betrayers*, the novel's Zionism allows him to paint a misleading picture of Israel/Palestine.

The Dispersion of the Soviet Jewish Diaspora

The massive departure of Soviet Jews from the USSR at the end of the twentieth century is the subject that undergirds not only *The Betrayers*, but all of Bezmozgis's work. The emigration of Soviet Jews out of the

Soviet Union in the 1970s, 1980s, and 1990s is an event of profound importance and significance, forever changing the terrain of Jewish geography. From 1971 to 1981, approximately a quarter of a million Jews left the Soviet Union (Wanner 6). This first Soviet wave was the most ideologically driven, with Zionism being the prime mover. For the rest of the 1980s the gates closed, but from 1989 until after the fall of the Soviet Union, 1.6 million Jews left the Soviet Union and the FSU. Out of these 1.6 million, "more than 950,000, or 60 percent," settled in Israel; this cohort is known as the Great Aliyah.[8] With 378,000 Soviet Jews immigrating to North America after 1988, and Germany and other places receiving smaller numbers, Israel is home to the largest Soviet Jewish diaspora (Remennick, *Russian Jews* 5, 210).[9] The reasons Soviet Jews left Russia vary greatly, but include antisemitism, Zionism, daily life under Soviet totalitarianism, and—especially after the fall of communism—economic opportunity. From an estimated 2,279,000 Jews in the FSU in 1959, in 2002 the number was down to 400,000. According to Larissa Remennick, "the major potential of emigration of former Soviet Jewry has already been exhausted" (*Russian Jews* 19). In general, Soviet Jews felt like they could not fully participate as Russian people, due mainly to antisemitism; yet, in their new world diaspora, including in Israel, they were able to hold on to and even expand their Russianness. As Adrian Wanner pithily puts it, "Ironically, and sadly...the wish of the Russian Jews to be Russians could only be fulfilled outside Russia" (7). This is a thoroughly diasporic phenomenon.

Remennick's *Russian Jews on Three Continents* is an important monograph that explores the sociology of the new Soviet Jewish diasporas, in particular the Israeli one.[10] In her sociological study of the Soviet Jewish communities in Israel, America, Toronto, and Germany, Remennick paints a multifaceted group portrait of these Jewish diasporas, utilizing statistics, interviews, literature, and historical sources to bolster her findings. According to Remennick (writing in a different text), the Soviet Jewish migration to Israel "was rather distinctive on the global landscape of recent migration waves generally and ethnic return migrations specifically" ("Former Soviet Jews" 208). Remennick notes, however, that "The 'return' in the Israeli case is purely symbolic, as one cannot return to the land that one's ancestors left 2,000 years ago" ("Former Soviet Jews" 209), which seems a pointed, if implied, jab at the Zionist mythos of return.

The impact that Russian Jewish migration had on Israel, culturally, sociologically, economically, and politically, cannot be overstated.
Wanner is right when he claims that the new Russian-speaking Israelis
"have profoundly transformed the country's demographics and culture"
(89). Russian Jews in Israel have held onto their Russianness to a considerable degree; instead of "coming home," they have, like the Arab Jewish
diasporas discussed in the previous chapter, become their own diaspora.
Russian culture—which, it is important to note, was not vilified or
suppressed the same way Arab Jewish culture was—is thriving in Israel.
There are over three hundred Russian book, video, and music stores
across Israel, several national daily and weekly newspapers in Russian,
popular magazines and literary almanacs, and several Russian TV chan-
nels (Remennick, "Former Soviet Jews" 216–217). The large number of
Jewish doctors in the FSU translated into large numbers of Soviet Jewish
doctors in Israel: "As a result of their mass entry into Israeli medicine,
doctors with a Russian accent comprise today fully half of all Israeli
practitioners under the age of forty-five and one-quarter among those
aged forty-five to sixty-five" (Remennick, *Russian Jews* 82). This is a
truly phenomenal statistic, and it speaks to the relative ease with which
Jewish immigrants from the FSU (or, at least, certain portions of them)
were integrated into Israeli society. According to Remennick, Russian
is the most "common" second language in Israel (*Russian Jews* 164); *The
Betrayers* acknowledges this astonishing fact when Leora jokes that
"Even the Arab storekeepers" speak Russian now (126). For one further
illustrative example, when Soviet Jews arrived in Israel, they wanted to
have Christmas trees on New Year's Eve; in the FSU, with outward trappings of religion banned, having a Christmas tree on New Year's Eve was
a culturally acceptable thing to do. Though there was resistance at first,
now many Israeli homes have New Year's Eve trees.

Politically speaking, the Russian Jewish Israelis have also made
a major impact, mostly being a voting boon for the right-wing parties.
Fifteen to twenty percent of Russian Israelis call themselves "nationalists." Remennick describes the general political outlook of the majority
of Israeli citizens from the FSU succinctly, "summed up as three antis":
"anti-socialist, anti-Arab/Moslem, and anti-religious" (*Russian Jews*
127). Remennick continues: "Most of them agree on these three negative
tenets, while their positive political beliefs may broadly vary, including

a large portion of those with no clear political outlook at all" (127). Bezmozgis represents this fact in his novel through Kotler's centre-right Zionist politics, as well as Benzion's move to the extreme settler right. Finally, and perhaps most importantly, is the major role the FSU Jews played in the Zionist necessity to keep a Jewish demographic majority over the Palestinians. Writes Remennick: "they have shifted the shaky balance between Jewish and Arab Israelis, fortifying the Jewish majority and bringing it to 80 percent" (*Russian Jews* 162).[11] Describing the racial and ethnic prejudices of the Soviet Jews in Israel, Remennick reports: "about 30 percent of Russian immigrant respondents consistently admitted to having prejudice against Moroccan and other Mizrahi Jews; 40 percent expressed negative opinions about Ethiopians and over 80 percent strongly disliked the Arabs" (67). The numbers alone make a strong case for the impact of Soviet Jews in Israel, where they are 20% of the Jewish population (Remennick, *Russian Jews* 7); in the other countries where they immigrated, meanwhile, "Russian-speaking Jews comprise a tiny minority" (Remennick, *Russian Jews* 7). Referring back to the previous chapter, the differences between how the Arab Jews are seen in Israel versus the FSU Jews further reveal the Eurocentrism of the ruling Ashkenazi elite.

Where the Soviet Jewish mass immigration landed, as well as those Soviet Jews who travel between the FSU, Israel, and America, exemplifies both the dynamism and tensions of the Jewish diaspora. As is well known, American Jewish institutions, activists, and wealthy individuals played a major role in the battle to allow Soviet Jews to leave the USSR. What is less discussed is the fact that where the Soviet Jews would immigrate to once they were able to leave was far from predetermined: American Jewish institutions and Israeli institutions, as well as influential individuals and activist groups, fought a series of heated battles over where they would end up.[12] In the end, America severely limited the number of Soviet Jews it would accept per year, and the majority of Soviet Jews landed in Israel. What this saga reveals is the intensity of the debates in the Jewish world about where Jewish refugees should go, and if the refugees themselves should be able to make the choice; the fact that so many Soviet Jews wanted to come to America as opposed to Israel is a definite blow to the Zionist mythos and narrative. Moreover, an established, wealthy Jewish diaspora giving aid to a less well-off Jewish diaspora is a common phenomenon. We see it in *The Betrayers* itself, where the Simferepol Hesed, run by Semonovna, is entirely reliant on Jewish American donations. The importance of the Soviet Jewry movement in America post World War II is hard to downplay. Stuart Altshuler goes so far as to call the "Soviet Jewry narrative" the "antidote to the harrowing tales of murder, apathy, and evil that surround the lessons of the Holocaust" (xiv). While this is stretching the significance somewhat, it is, indeed, a major event in Jewish history.

Remennick, in her book, talks about the Soviet Jews who return from Israel to the FSU, who live in both places, or who leave Israel for North America or elsewhere. "With their emigration, Russian Jews discovered a freedom of movement unthinkable in Soviet times," she writes (*Russian Jews* 156).[13] Bezmozgis also includes this in *The Betrayers*, through the minor character of Moshe Podolsky, one of Tankilevich's synagogue friends who immigrated to Israel in the late 1990s, but returned to Ukraine after three years. This fact, of the movement of Soviet Jews throughout the Jewish world, shows the longevity of diaspora to the detriment of the Zionist project. The multiplicity of diasporic homes in the Soviet Jewish imaginary punctures the Zionist claim of Jewish telos in the return to Israel, as does the large community of ex-FSU Israeli expats.

The Last Jew in Crimea, Withering Away: Kotler and Tankilevich, Israel and Diaspora, Betrayal and Forgiveness

As seen through the inclusion of a character like Podolsky, part of Bezmozgis's rhetorical project in *The Betrayers* is to enter into the ledger of fiction what Soviet Jewish immigration did to both the places the Soviet Jews landed *and* the places they left. Bezmozgis himself confirms this, claiming in an interview included in the paperback edition of the book that "In the novel, I wanted to show where the ex-Soviet Jews had had their greatest impact. The answer to that was in Israel—where they transformed the country by their massive influx—and in the countries of the former Soviet Union, where, to a significant extent, they transformed those countries by their absence" ("A Conversation" 17). In the novel, we see the impact of the departure of Jews from the FSU most clearly through Tankilevich's experiences, both during his long life living in the Soviet Union and on the Saturday that Tankilevich's portion of the novel occurs. His confrontation with an antisemite at the Simferopol grocery store, his necessary presence in the minyan of older Jewish men in Simferopol—Tankilevich is what is left of a once vibrant Jewish community.[14] Through his experiences, readers learn how the Jewish institutions survive solely on the largess of American Jewish donors, how the Jewish population, mostly departed for Israel or America, barely ekes by. As Semonovna puts it, "This is our predicament. Our people go and we can't replace them" (76). Tankilevich takes a poetic view on the old Crimean Jews who remain: "History had laid its heavy hand on them but they had burrowed, eluded, resisted, and remained. One needed only to look at their faces—expressive Jewish faces—to see that they had known the depths of life. Let no one say that he lacked feelings for these people and this place" (65). Taken together, Kotler and Tankilevich are Bezmozgis's personification of what he calls the "answer" to the Soviet Jewish impact in the FSU and Israel, respectively.

Both Kotler and Tankilevich have historical, real-life analogs. As mentioned above, Kotler's life story is strikingly similar to Natan Sharansky's. It seems that, no longer using his own life or family as primary fuel for his fiction, Bezmozgis has turned to historical figures, in this case a historical figure who is still alive, in order to compose his novel in real time. Where Kotler is a musical prodigy on the piano, Sharansky was a chess prodigy. Where Kotler was accused in the newspaper *Ivetsia* by a friend (Tankilevich) who was a dentist, Sharansky was accused in *Ivetsia* by a friend who was a doctor. Sharansky married his wife the day before she emigrated to Israel; Kotler marries his wife under similar circumstances. Kotler's memoir, like Sharansky's, is named after a quote from the Psalms.[15] Their lives, post Gulag, are near parallels as well: both are hailed as nationalist heroes, both create political parties catering specifically to the Soviet Jewish vote and get swept into the Knesset, and both leave their government posts in protest.[16] Tankilevich is also based on the doctor who betrayed Sharansky, Sanya Lipavsky, though Bezmozgis is able to take more fictional liberties in exploring what his life post-betrayal was like.[17] These two main male characters are at opposite ends of the Soviet Jewish spectrum; what is common to both men is that neither will outlive the social and mental conditioning of living under the Soviet system. Kotler's time in the gulag, for one, will never leave him: "He knew the year was 2013 and that the Soviet Union no longer existed, but he felt the cold menace of the KGB, sensed the nearness of his old tormentors. He knew he was an Israeli citizen, a husband and father, a dissident champion, but he felt isolated and vulnerable, helpless to stave off the horror" (47). Tankilevich, to an even greater extent, is permanently marred by what the Soviet system put him through, what he says he "forfeited his life" (151) for. As Joel Martineau reads it, "Kotler realizes that his betrayer has led a shamed, hollow life, unable to reveal his true identity, his Zionist dreams extinguished by existence within the witness protection program, while the vitality of the Crimea crumbles around him" (125–126). Both men will forever carry the scars of living under a totalitarian system, and reveal the possible dangers of a diasporic existence, especially one that exists under the aegis of powerful state apparatuses.

The reunion and encounter between Kotler and Tankilevich do not actually occur until halfway through the novel. "Here it was," the narrator tells readers: "The moment [Kotler] had fantasized about had finally arrived" (109). In a moment of dark humour, Kotler greets Tankilevich by saying "boker tov," Hebrew for good morning. They argue about how they have both changed their names, with Kotler Hebraicizing his, and Tankilevich getting a new name when he went into witness protection. Tankilevich is immediately distrustful of Kotler. "What do you want?" he asks Kotler, "You have come to collect? Well, I have paid and paid for my sins. I have paid in excess. I am paying still. And I have nothing for you" (111). He tells Svetlana to give their money for the room rentals back.

In the pages where Kotler and Tankilevich converse, the power differential between the two men is palpable. Kotler is philosophical, magnanimous; Tankilevich is embittered, mistrustful, emotional. Kotler learns for the first time the circumstances behind Tankilevich's espionage and betrayal of Kotler, how Tankilevich forfeited his life and became a spy and witness in order to save his criminal brother from execution. Even though Tankilevich was sent to Kotler and the other refuseniks as a spy, he still claims to have become, in the process of spying, a Zionist: "It so happened I discovered Zionism through the KGB.

But the things I learned, the people I met—those were the best days of my life. You say I pretended to care about Israel, but I cared as much as anyone else. I too dreamed of living there even though I knew that for me it was a futile dream" (153).[18] Tankilevich wants to blame the Soviet system for what he was forced to do, but for Kotler that is not enough of an exculpating justification: "It was the Soviet Union; who wasn't forced?" Kotler asks. "Everyone was forced. Some nevertheless managed to resist" (147). Tankilevich then turns to the specious reasoning that "if they hadn't used me to hang those years on you, they would have used someone else," going even further by saying that he was just as punished as Kotler: "I got the same thirteen years and however many more" (150). Bezmozgis portrays the act of betrayal as one that has a double effect, altering the life trajectory of the one who is betrayed as much as that of the one who has done the betraying. The promise of Israel in the life of Soviet Jews is also made apparent; even somebody like Tankilevich, a KGB spy, felt the paradisiacal pull. The fact that the fictional character embodying Bezmozgis's dying Soviet diaspora is a Zionist shows the centroperipheral Zionist gravity at the centre of the book: everybody, and everything, is being pulled toward Israel.

In the end, it is Kotler who must decide if he will forgive Tankilevich or not. At first, it appears that Kotler will not grant Tankilevich the one thing he and Svetlana want; without a public apology from Kotler, Svetlana believes that she and Tankilevich will never be able to immigrate to Israel. Kotler, however, steadfastly refuses to absolve Tankilevich publicly: "I can't go before the world and say that he was not culpable for his actions. Because the world would misunderstand" (173). Tankilevich, bitter to the end, says he would do it all again. Kotler says he would never have done it at all. It is Kotler who holds the ultimate power over Tankilevich, unlike earlier when Tankilevich's actions helped send Kotler to the gulag. And Kotler's judgment? Israel has no need for people like Tankilevich. "Here is what I will say to you, Volodya," Kotler intones:

> And I say it without malice. Israel doesn't need you. It has
> thousands like you. Thousands of old generals on park
> benches plotting the next war with the Arabs. It can do
> without another. So why go to a place where you are not

needed? Why not ask instead: Where am I needed? Where do my people need me? And choose that place. Choose that place, for the first time in your life, of your own free will. (174)

Putting it a bit more bluntly on the next page, Kotler tells Tankilevich to "Choose to wither away, the last Jew in Crimea" (175). However, after leaving Tankilevich and Svetlana, Tankilevich on the couch after suffering a brutal panic attack, Kotler does soften his stance, travelling out to Simferopol to visit Semonovna to get Tankilevich out of his subservience to her. As Leora puts it to Semonovna in words that close out the book proper, "Let him live" (218). So, while nothing is resolved between the two men, Kotler does attempt to lessen Tankilevich's suffering. The betrayed has absolved the betrayer; the character representing the Zionist home has forgiven the character standing in for the duplicitous diaspora. Kotler will now return to Israel to try to deal with his own personal and political crises, the Soviet Jewish diaspora will continue to die, with Tankilevich, symbolic of "the last Jew in Crimea," "wither[ing] away" (175), and Israel will continue its rightward drift.

Fate, God, and the Face:
Authorial Power and Confrontation

Bezmozgis is well aware of the major coincidence that brings Kotler and Tankilevich together, and uses it as a springboard into an exploration of fate, religious belief, ethics, and authorial power. A number of theories for the two men's improbable reunion are presented throughout the novel. To Kotler himself, it is nothing but "A very strange coincidence" (211). However, as an incredulous Leora puts it to Kotler when Kotler first glimpses Tankilevich, "You've stumbled upon the man who betrayed you forty years ago. The odds of this, of ending up a boarder in his house, are almost nil. But so? Now what? Is it that you want to exact vengeance? What is it?" (53). Tankilevich, for his part, believes Kotler was sent to Tankilevich to further humiliate him. The literal reason for their reunion, of course, is the fact that Kotler and Leora planned their trip in haste, which leads to the hotel reservation they thought they made falling through, and the need to rent a room from Svetlana, which leads Kotler directly to Tankilevich.

The most sustained explanation, however, comes from Svetlana herself, who, as a practising Christian, believes it is divine providence that has brought the two men together, that it was God that sent Kotler to them (97).[19] At first, Svetlana frames the reunion as unavoidable fate. "If it is fate," she says to Kotler, "your disapproval will not change it. Standing instead of sitting in my kitchen will not change it. Even walking out the door will not change it. A tree will fall across your path. Because if fate has ordained to bring you here, it will conspire to keep you here" (114). As Svetlana confides to Leora when the two women are alone, however, it is much more than fate for Svetlana. Svetlana is convinced that Kotler and Leora are the answers to Svetlana's prayers for a better life, a better life that entails immigrating to Israel. Svetlana takes it as a given that God himself has arranged the events of the novel, telling Leora:

> Only He could contrive to bring us together at such a time.
> When we are all in such need. It is clear as day that every-
> thing is according to His will. I am surprised you don't see
> it. He brought you here not only for our sake but also for
> yours. You say that Baruch's forgiveness will be of no benefit
> to my husband, but how can you be so sure? If he is fulfill-
> ing God's plan, then it will be to everyone's benefit. And if it
> seems improbable, that is further proof that it is ordained. I
> see by your face that you still don't believe. You think I am a
> lunatic. But half the miracle has already happened. You are
> here. If half the miracle has already happened, it is lunacy to
> deny the other half. (132)

Svetlana wants to see reconciliation between these two estranged products of the Soviet system, which will benefit both of them. In this way,
not only is she religious, but she is also an idealist who believes it is God's
plan to ingather the Jews—or, at the very least, her husband—to Israel.
It is possible, I suppose, that in the fictional world of The Betrayers it was
God that contrived to bring Kotler and Tankilevich together, that it was,
as Svetlana refers to it, "Divine Providence" (113); nonetheless, in another,
more pressing way, it is not God that brings them together, it is Bezmozgis

himself, the author-as-godhead. Whether Bezmozgis gives Svetlana this speech to slacken readers' suspension of disbelief or to further the novel's investigation of faith, fate, and the possibilities of forgiveness, it is nonetheless necessary to read it as a reminder of the very real power an author wields over their fictional world. Bezmozgis wanted to bring together accused and accuser, betrayed and betrayer, hero and disgraced, and he did so; he holds the ultimate authorial power.

The novel's seeming insistence on the need for former enemies to confront each other face to face can be seen as a productive fictionalization of the theory of Emmanuel Levinas, where the encounter with the face of the Other, combined with the ethical imperative to not kill, supersede any other considerations. John Wild calls Levinas's theories of the face a *"phenomenology of the other"* ("Introduction" 13), and this is an important aspect of Levinas's philosophy, most developed in *Totality and Infinity: An Essay on Exteriority*.[20] For Levinas, emphasizing the face is a way to approach the Other, which is not just a negation of the self (as it was for Hegel) or an object to my self's subject (as it was for Sartre) but an alien, totally other being, the stranger. The only way to connect with the face is through speaking, is through language. "The face is a living presence; it is expression," Levinas writes: "The face speaks. The manifestation of the face is already discourse" (*Totality and Infinity* 66). Wild glosses this as an "ethical choice to welcome the stranger and to share his world by speaking to him" ("Introduction" 14). This bears a striking resemblance to the ethical nature of diasporic heteroglossia, where the multiple voices of a novel push back against a nationalist centre, where strangers are able to speak and challenge dominant ideologies.

Moreover, the face of the Other presents itself "and demands justice" (*Totality and Infinity* 294). This justice is not only about acknowledging the alterity of the Other, but the moral necessity to not kill: the "ethical resistance" to killing the Other, an "infinite resistance to murder," which "gleams in the face of the Other, in the total nudity of his defenceless eyes, in the nudity of the absolute openness of the Transcendent," paralyses power (*Totality and Infinity* 199). In *Ethics and Infinity: Conversations with Philippe Nemo*, Levinas states that exposure of the face, its nudity, means that "The face is exposed, menaced, as if inviting us to an act of violence. At the same time, the face is what forbids us to kill" (86). Levinas explains: "The first word of the face is the 'Thou shalt not kill.' It is an order. There is a commandment in the appearance of the face, as if a master spoke to me. However, at the same time, the face of the Other is destitute; it is the poor for whom I can do all and to whom I owe all. And me, whoever I may be, but as a 'first person,' I am he who finds the resources to respond to the call" (89). It would seem, then, that in Levinas's theory of the face, the ethical obligation to acknowledge the Other, to speak to the Other, to not kill the Other, is paramount. While it is unclear if Tankilevich manages to get over his bitterness and see Kotler as a human with a face, Kotler does see the suffering humanity of Tankilevich, and decides to alleviate it (while not offering a full pardon of Tankilevich's actions). Kotler, in seeing the face of Tankilevich, "renders possible and begins all discourse" (*Ethics and Infinity* 87).

Considering the novel's interest in confrontation, in the centrality of Kotler and Tankilevich's discourse, is it possible, then, that the novel's belief in the benefits of the face-to-face encounter between Kotler and Tankilevich, between betrayer and betrayed, offers a way forward for the Israel–Palestine crisis through a Levinasian insistence on the face of the Other? Perhaps not. In *Parting Ways*, Judith Butler performs a necessary intervention into Levinasian ethics, holding Levinas to account for what she reads as his anti-Palestinian pronouncements. According to Butler, "to make use of Levinas for a left politics is precisely to read him against his own Zionism and his refusal to accept that Palestinians make a legitimate ethical demand on the Jewish people" (39). Butler laments that in Levinas's thought "The ethical obligation toward the face of the other is not an obligation one can or does feel toward every face" (39).[21] Nonetheless, Butler makes a strong case that "it is possible to read Levinas against himself, as it were, and arrive at a different conclusion" (47), namely that Jewishness is unavoidably about living together with non-Jews. This diasporic rendering of Jewishness is one that, as we will see, *The Betrayers* does not endorse. That Kotler is able to see the face, the humanity, of his betrayer, the man responsible for his thirteen years in the gulag, but is not able to see or accept the humanity of the Palestinians in the West Bank, who would benefit most directly from the settlement withdrawal Kotler is adamantly opposed to, reveals the dangers of a Levinasian outlook that does not "arrive at a different conclusion," as Butler puts it. For Kotler, only other Jews are predetermined to have faces; the Palestinians under military occupation by his own government do not.

Zionism(s), Morality, and the Palestinians

Turning from the confrontation between Kotler and Tankilevich—the main narrative trunk of the narrative—to the Zionist politics of the novel, Bezmozgis creates a dangerous-yet-telling tension between Kotler and his son Benzion. The novel sets up Kotler as a sort of old guard Zionist Israeli political intelligentsia, while his son Benzion is part of the religious settler zealots. This generational rift is symbolic of what Bezmozgis sees as the country's rightward drift. Where the conflict between Kotler and Tankilevich is between two men of the same generation who dealt with their different situations under the Soviet system in different ways, with Tankilevich giving in to Soviet pressure and Kotler refusing to give in, the brewing conflict between Kotler and Benzion is one between father and son, between somebody who yearned for a national home and somebody who was born into a national home, between a Zionism that is (supposedly) secular and a Zionism that is (fanatically) religious. Sasha Senderovich actually sees the conflict between Kotler and his son as central to Bezmozgis's rhetorical project. "The question at the heart" of the novel, Senderovich writes, "is the legacy that one generation bequeaths to another. The novel...asks us to consider how the heroism and political stoicism associated with Soviet-era Jewish dissidents get translated into a blueprint for political action by their children who, now planted in a different place, interpret this legacy in their own ways" ("Autobiographical Rut" np).

This is a specific example of Jonathan and Daniel Boyarin's warning about the dangers of transferring techniques of diasporic survival into structures of hegemonic power. The Boyarins provocatively claim that "Capturing Judaism in a state transforms entirely the meanings of its social practices. Practices that in Diaspora have one meaning—for example, caring for the feeding and housing of Jews and not 'others'—have entirely different meanings under political hegemony" ("Generation and the Ground" 713). For the Boyarins, the ethnic specificity and inwardness that allowed the Jewish diaspora to function and flourish in Europe mutate when combined with political and state power. They conceptualize this thought as an evocative equation: "Particularism plus power yields tribal warfare or fascism" (706). Explaining how Jewish institutions in the diaspora did not attempt to Judaize the Others who lived with and around them (unlike Christianity), they write that this fact "also meant that Jewish resources were not devoted to the welfare of humanity at large but only to one family. Within Israel, where power is concentrated almost exclusively in Jewish hands, this discursive practice has become a monstrosity whereby an egregiously disproportionate measure of the resources of the state is devoted to the welfare of only one segment of the population" (712). They conclude, in a harsh renunciation of Zionism, that "Insistence on ethnic specialty, when it is extended over a particular piece of land, will inevitably produce a discourse not unlike the Inquisition in many of its effects" (712).[22] We can see this clearly in the case of Kotler and his fellow Soviet refuseniks, who fought against the oppression of their Jewish particularity while in the diaspora only to be installed in a state where Jews have hegemonic power, and where, to quote the Boyarins one more time: "The inequities—and worse—in Israeli political, economic, and social practice are not aberrations but inevitable consequences of the inappropriate application of a form of discourse from one historical situation to another" (713). Kotler's battle against the Soviet state has turned into Kotler refusing to withdraw illegal Israeli settlements from Palestinian land.

The novel seems to want to show how Benzion furthers the "Particularism plus power yields tribal warfare or fascism" equation through his religious belief that sole Jewish ownership of the West Bank is a transcendent, God-given right. While Senderovich is right to point to the differences between Kotler and his son as central to the novel, with a little further analysis from an anti-Zionist perspective, and with the words of the Boyarins in mind, I want to bring into focus the novel's more troubling ideas when it comes to Israel/Palestine, morality, and the treatment of the Palestinians. What I uncover is that the different Zionisms of Kotler and Benzion—one secular, one religious; one "liberal," one far right—are not as wide as Bezmozgis intends them to be, or as the standard Zionist discourse insists they are. The supposed heteroglossic urge behind Kotler's and Benzion's differing politics collapses with the slightest application of non-Zionist pressure.

To start this excavation, it is necessary to discuss how the novel takes an essentialist view of morality. In the world of *The Betrayers*, some people are just born with morals, like Kotler; others, like Tankilevich, simply are not. This almost Calvinist ethical framework is evident throughout the novel, but most baldly during the novel's climax, when, with Tankilevich ailing on the couch after his panic attack—a panic attack everybody thinks is something more serious—Kotler tells Svetlana that "We are born as we are" (171). Kotler claims he holds Tankilevich "blameless" before expounding on his—and, more generally, the novel's—moral philosophy:

> I accept that he couldn't have acted differently any more
> than I could have acted differently. This is the primary
> insight I have gleaned from life: The moral component is
> no different from the physical component—a man's soul, a
> man's conscience, is like his height or the shape of his nose.
> We are all born with inherent propensities and limits. You
> can no more be reviled for your character than for your
> height. No more reviled than revered. (171)

On the next page, Kotler pushes the point further: "Just as there are people in this world who are imparted with physical or intellectual gifts, there are those who are imparted with moral gifts. People who are inherently moral. People who have a clear sense of justice and cannot, under any circumstances, subvert it" (172). The fact that Kotler is one of these people who are born "inherently moral" is alluded to throughout the text. In an earlier phone conversation with his daughter Dafna—who is naturally disgusted with her father for letting the family be dragged through the scandal of his affair instead of acquiescing to the prime minister's demands—Kotler tells her: "There are matters of principle where you cannot compromise. Under any circumstances. If I'd compromised, it would have been worse. Far worse for all of us. For our country and for our family, which is part of our country" (45).[23] At the end of the novel, Leora calls Kotler an "exceptionally moral person" (197), and says she is more like Tankilevich, thereby aligning her in-born morality with the weakness we are meant to see in Tankilevich.

Not only does Bezmozgis himself believe in Kotler's exceptional morality, but he appears to wholeheartedly endorse Kotler's moral philosophy as well. Bezmozgis claims in the interview at the back of the paperback edition that not only is Kotler "empirically more courageous and principled than I am," but that he is "exceptionally lucid about what is

morally correct and unapologetic about acting according to his principles"
("A Conversation" 13, 14). Bezmozgis explains that writing The Betrayers
entailed reaching "a point where I felt that I clearly understood his moral
precepts, the rationale that guided his actions" ("A Conversation" 13).

What are we to make of this seemingly rigid worldview that
divides the inherently moral from the inherently immoral? Even more
pressing, how does this worldview impact the conflict between Israel
and the Palestinian people that the novel is at least obliquely concerned
with? It is not difficult to take issue with the presentation of Kotler as
unambiguously moral. (Nowhere, for example, does Bezmozgis explain
how Kotler's infidelity with Leora fits into his moral framework.) If
Kotler is an unimpeachably moral person, he is moral with regard to
only one thing: his fellow Jewish Israelis (but not, it bears mentioning,
those Jewish Israelis on the left). An important question for this book is
whether part of Kotler's morality and Zionist territorial maximalism is
a product of him reading a "samizdat translation" of Exodus (49), as so
many Soviet Jews did, and which I discussed in the first chapter. With
the knowledge of the horrors of the Israeli occupation, of the ethnic
cleansing and oppression of the Palestinian people, how can Bezmozgis
continually insist Kotler is a moral person? The answer is that Kotler is
moral purely in a Zionist framework, his morality contingent on Jewish
ethnic nationalism.[24]

We see this in mutated and exaggerated form with Kotler's son
Benzion, who himself couches his religious-settler ideology in the
language of ethics, of morals.[25] "I'm talking about a person's soul,"
Benzion tells his father in the first phone conversation they have after
Kotler absconds from Israel. "When it screams, No. What are you
supposed to do? Ignore it? If you see that your country is on the road to
ruin, do you not do something about it? Before it's too late" (119). A little
before this moment, Benzion compared his ethical dilemma—to obey
army orders and evict the settlers, or to disobey orders and do what he,
and his rabbi, think is right—to Kotler's own struggle against the Soviet
Union, to which Kotler gently chastised his son: "Despite what some
people say, the time has not yet come to compare Israel to the Soviet
Union" (119). Israel might not be the Soviet Union from the viewpoint
of its Jewish citizens, but from the viewpoint of its Palestinian citizens
and, more importantly, from that of the citizenship-less Palestinians that

Israel has military control over, the comparison is at least worth entertaining. At the novel's end, Kotler and readers find out that Benzion has indeed disobeyed the orders of the IDF.

Significantly, Benzion goes beyond simply refusing to participate in dismantling the settlement bloc: he, along with two of his fellow religious right-wing soldiers, shoot themselves in the hand. The group of dissenters start calling themselves "the Brotherhood of the Right Hand" (200), in reference to the fifth verse of Psalm 137, where the speaker says he would cut off his right hand for forgetting Jerusalem. This speaks to the dangerous Zionist (and other religious groups') literal reading of biblical-era texts. Moreover, Benzion's use of the Psalms as justification for religious fanaticism is the opposite of how Kotler used the Psalms, which he read when he was in the gulag and which connected him "with his people from deepest antiquity, with King David himself, who was made palpable through his verse as a man of flesh and blood racked by the same fears as Kotler was" (184). Kotler bemoans, at the same time that he rationalizes, his son's rebellion against the diktat of the state: Kotler's "time had passed. The country desired a different kind of hero. Perhaps he should be proud, for he had supplied it with one" (224). We can see here the Boyarins' dire warnings about the combustive violence of ethnic particularism and power coming into effect. Moreover, Benzion's dissent neatly maps onto Remennick's discussion of the "movement among recruits and soldiers declining to serve in certain problem-ridden locations" (Russian Jews 132), with left-wing soldiers refusing to police "the controlled Palestinian territories" and the "nationalist and religious soldiers" refusing to participate in the "evacuation of the Jewish settlements from Gaza and Samaria" (132). As Remennick puts it, "These young refuseniks prefer imprisonment to participation in the violent actions that go against their beliefs" (132).

The novel clearly wants us to side with Kotler here: even though he disagrees with the settlement withdrawals, he also disagrees with Benzion's refusal of army orders for national-religious reasons. Kotler—and the novel—sees Benzion as the new face of the Israeli zeitgeist, and asks us to grieve this fact. In "The End of American Jewish Literature, Again," after stating that "Israel doesn't need the Diaspora so much as the Diaspora needs Israel" (a highly questionable statement), Bezmozgis wonders what it would mean for American Jews if Israel became "a theocratic and/or totalitarian state" (np), in other words, the kind of state Benzion, the Brotherhood of the Right Hand, and his rabbi wish to implement. Bezmozgis sees this eventuality as just as "catastrophic for secular American Jews as for their Israeli counterparts...for a secular humanist Jew, it would be impossible to identify with such a country" (np).[26] This is the liberal Zionist worldview in action: always seeing illiberalism or disaster in the future. We see the same formulation in Peter Beinart's *The Crisis of Zionism*, which is likely the best encapsulation of liberal Zionism of the past decade. Beinart, speaking of the tension between Zionism and liberal democracy, writes that "If Israel fails in that struggle [to reconcile the two], it will either cease being a Jewish state or cease being a democratic one" (12). The belief driving this position is that if the occupation (rightly seen as immoral) spills over the green line into Israel proper (seen as a flawed democracy, but as a democracy nonetheless), Zionism will have lost its moral centre. Beinart calls this "the illiberal Zionism beyond the green line," which "destroys the possibility of liberal Zionism inside it" (27). Both Beinart's and Bezmozgis's positions seem difficult to maintain, considering that Israel already de facto rules over millions of Palestinians who do not have the democratic right to vote, and considering the ethnic cleansing at the birth of the state and the refusal to let the refugees back in. This form of Zionist thinking is as dangerous, if not more so, than revisionist Zionism.[27]

I want to suggest that *The Betrayers*, read contrapuntally through an anti-Zionist lens, actually reveals that things are quite different than Bezmozgis presents us with here. Kotler and Benzion, despite Kotler's disappointment in his son (as well as in Benzion's religious fanaticism), are not as far apart, ideologically speaking, as the novel purports. From the viewpoint of the occupied, refugee, and diasporic Palestinians, Israel is already an oppressive, indeed totalitarian, state. A Jewish-only democracy does not a democracy make, especially when that democratic state rules over millions of stateless Palestinians, and when it achieved its Jewish majority through ethnic cleansing. By paying particular attention to the novel's presentation of the prime minister's plans for settlement withdrawal, which readers can deduce is taking place in or near Hebron, the novel's total lack of Palestinian narrative, and the novel's failed attempt to imagine other ways to live besides ethnic nationalist ownership of land, I will spend the rest of this chapter arguing that *The*

Betrayers is in fact a novel that deeply resists a diasporic ethics when it comes to Israel/Palestine. The supposed dispute between Kotler and Benzion, not to mention the diaspora/Israel tension between Kotler and Tankilevich, which has the gloss of heteroglossia on it, is, in this reading, only surface deep: the novel, in its iron belief in Zionism, deploys a false diasporic heteroglossia, when in actuality it is deeply univocal, deeply centroperipheral, and deeply committed to the Zionist time of maintaining Jewish ethnic supremacy in Israel/Palestine.

The Jewish Geography of Hebron

Throughout the novel, the details of the settlement bloc withdrawal are purposefully kept vague, including, bizarrely, not informing readers which actual settlements are being withdrawn. From the start, this is problematic. There is a massive difference between the dismantling of an ideological settlement (where settlers believe they have a religious national claim to exclusive ownership of the land) and an economic settlement (where the incentives of moving to the territories—including lower rent, fewer taxes, and other subsidies—are the prime factors for its residents). According to Bezmozgis, he wanted the inciting incident of the pullout to be both "prescient and oblique" ("A Conversation" 14). While this is in line with Bezmozgis's intention of writing a novel in real time, I am doubtful of its prescience—we seem a very far distance from any Israeli government giving up land in the West Bank. It is most definitely oblique, though. What settlements the prime minister pulls out of and what Kotler takes his moral stand against are of incredible importance to the overall rhetorical project of the novel—or at least, they should be.

Even though the withdrawal from the settlement bloc is spoken about and referred to at numerous points in the novel, readers are left to piece together what it actually entails themselves. The only direct allusion to the geography of the withdrawal appears in Kotler's religious gloss on the situation in the novel's very first sentence, which helps us place the settlements as somewhere in the West Bank: "God was banging His gavel to shake the Judaean hills" (3).[28] The West Bank is a large area of land, under various jurisdictions, and with many different settlement blocs, including East Jerusalem (which the Israeli government considers part of Israel proper). The description of the actual withdrawal that Kotler sees on the television from Crimea, the "full shameful, histrionic, heartrending pageant" complete with "Stricken, grieving, furious settlers facing columns of distressed and stone-faced Israeli soldiers and police," a young Orthodox woman "thrusting her squalling infant into the face of a young female soldier," and settlers dressed in concentration camp garb (replete with the yellow star of David), does not help us situate what we are actually watching, which settlements, or how many settlers, though it does suggest that it is an ideological settlement being dismantled (181–182). Instead, we are given no concrete details at all: no numbers, no names, no landmarks, no locations. In a text where the geographical details of Crimea are so clearly mapped out—particularly Yalta and Simferopol, and the trolley/car ride between them—this is a striking and troubling omission. Because of this, readers of *The Betrayers*, in order to grasp the political implications of the central event of the novel—it is, after all, Kotler's reaction to the planned withdrawal that sets the action rolling—have no choice but to dig for clues as to the details of the withdrawal.

What reveals itself after such digging is that Hebron is the most likely location for where the offending settlements are located. Not only is Hebron the only named West Bank location in the entire novel, but when it is mentioned, it is in connection to Benzion, who is apparently stationed near the contested city (23). Since readers know that Benzion and his unit are an active part of the withdrawal, and with nothing else to go on, it seems safe to assume that it is in fact the settlements in or adjacent to Hebron that are slated for withdrawal. Without any other hints, and a lot riding on the location of the withdrawal, we must assume that this is the case. If it is the settlements near Hebron that Kotler is against withdrawing from, looking at the history and reality of the Hebron settlements will help to reveal the major flaws of Kotler's moral superiority.

Hebron is important in both the Jewish and the Muslim religious traditions, being the supposed burial place of Abraham. Palestinian Jews lived in Hebron for hundreds of years before the advent of political Zionism. The 1929 riot, where sixty-seven Jews were killed, was a dark moment in the city's history. The current political reality of Hebron is the result of the 1967 War and Israeli occupation of the West Bank, and the 1994 Hebron Protocol, which was the last part of the Oslo Accords

to be implemented. Shuhada Street, once the bustling main thorough-
fare of Palestinian Hebron, is now a ghost street, with the stores closed
and the army constantly patrolling; in 1994, 322 Palestinian shops were
permanently closed (Fishbain np). The settlement closest to Hebron,
Kiryat Arba, was started illegally by right-wing religious settlers and has
around seven thousand residents. These same ideological settlers also
started an illegal occupation in the old city of Hebron itself, where they
are protected by the Israel army from the 270,000 Palestinians who live
in the city.

The story of the establishment of Kiryat Arba is a shocking and
upsetting example of settler colonialism in action. A year after the 1967
War, a group of young religious students and their families obtained
a permit from Israeli Central Command to spend 42 hours in Hebron,
ostensibly to celebrate Passover. Once inside the city, they rented out
the Palestinian Park Hotel and refused to leave. They squatted in the
hotel for six weeks; the Israeli government "responded by deferring any
binding decision on whether these settlers could remain permanently"
(Neuman 50), going so far as to relocate them to Hebron's military headquarters, where they lived for three years, until the government finally
granted them permission to build Kiryat Arba.[29] Shortly after, these
religious settlers were also allowed to create a Jewish Quarter in Hebron
proper, supported by the IDF. This was more or less the status quo situation—with Jewish settlers claiming more and more land and buildings, the IDF backing them up, and severe limitations being placed on
Palestinians—until 1994, when Jewish settler Baruch Goldstein massacred twenty-nine Palestinians who were at prayer at the Tombs of the
Patriarch during Ramadan. The Goldstein Massacre is a pivotal event in
the last days of the peace process; Goldstein is hailed as a hero by many
in the religious national camp. Moreover, the first Palestinian suicide
bombing, by the newly formed Hamas, was claimed as a response to the
Goldstein Massacre (Abunimah "Hebron Still Under Siege"). None of this
is mentioned in The Betrayers.[30]

Another indirect outcome of the Goldstein Massacre was the
1997 Hebron Protocol. The protocol divided Hebron between Israeli and
Palestinian control, with Israel controlling the section labelled H2 and
the Palestinian Authority H1. The protocol was one of the last parts of the
Oslo Accords implemented by the Israeli government. Ostensibly a way

to peacefully divide Hebron and its environs, the Hebron Protocol ended up allowing the settlers to remain in Hebron, supported by a large army presence.[31] Significantly, Benny Begin, Menecham Begin's son, resigned from the Knesset and his post of science minister in protest of the protocol, because he felt it was relinquishing too much of the city. Begin was quoted as saying "The handing over of Hebron to the hands of the enemy and foe is a signal of despair. The air carries the bitter taste of capitulation, the spicy smell of embarrassment and the scratching and grating sound of unavoidable attack" (Schmemann np). Seeing how Bezmozgis cites Benny Begin as a source on the novel's acknowledgements page (228), it is fair to say Kotler and his resignation are based, at least in part, on Begin; why not, then, include the details of Hebron? Finally, it is important to remember that the Hebron Protocol, like the entirety of the Oslo Accords, is, as Yehuda Shenhav puts it, a "procedural mechanism that sentenced the historical origins of the conflict (e.g. the Palestinian refugees, the Jerusalem question, the problem of the Jewish settlements) to oblivion" (Beyond the Two State Solution 2).[32]

Is this what Bezmozgis had in mind? Regardless of one's political affiliation, what is happening in Hebron right now cannot be regarded as ethical, moral, or tenable. Can somebody like Kotler, who is purposefully meant to be morally brilliant, seriously condone the current situation in Hebron? Reading the soldier testimonies in Breaking the Silence's (BTS) most recent testimonial document on Hebron, Occupying Hebron: Soldiers' Testimonies from 2011 to 2017, would convince any moral person of the Hebron occupation's horrible, dehumanizing violence. As the intro to the testimonies clearly explains,

> A close, sober look at what goes on in Hebron today, depicts
> the reality of Israeli control over the occupied territories as
> a whole: a reality wherein the division between rulers and
> inferiors is crystal clear and rests upon each individual's
> national and ethnic belonging. A reality in which violence
> is the only means of existence. A reality that steadily erodes
> the values of law and justice until they lose all meaning.
> From within this reality, soldiers' testimonies paint a
> self-portrait of the occupation. (5)[33]

The booklet—which is the fourth such document BTS has released that focuses on Hebron (*Occupying Hebron 4*)—is a truly upsetting, and enraging, portrait of how the act of military occupation corrupts the occupiers and severely mistreats the occupied. It also forcefully communicates the unethical relationship between the right-wing settlers and the soldiers tasked with protecting them. The settlers bring the soldiers gifts and cakes, and feed them elaborate meals, all in a (successful) effort to make the soldiers feel even more beholden to the settlers. After a soldier would shoot a Palestinian or put down a riot, settlers would give them gifts of a knife, an axe, or other such "cold" weapons (20).

Occupying Hebron shows the cascading, overwhelming power of collating anonymous testimonies in this fashion. Here is part of the testimony from a First Sergeant stationed in Hebron in 2014:

> They (the settlers) know that they can do whatever they want, and they do whatever they want. They know that we can't do anything. The cops are their friends, friends of their families. They know that nothing will happen to them. They know they can say what they want, they can say "death to Arabs," that they all deserve to die. They know that they can slap them, they know that they can hit them, they know that they can steal from them if they want and nothing will happen to them. It's true, they know that the soldiers can't do anything. In order for the soldiers to further accept this behavior, they hand out gifts. (22)

As a soldier in the Judea Regional Brigade succinctly summarizes it: "There's no rule of law, no justice and no judge" (27). (There is a productive resonance here with *Operation Shylock* and what Philip witnesses in Ramallah.) In another testimony, we hear of settler children who ask the soldiers why they are not killing the Palestinians walking by (32). These soldiers that are telling their stories could be in Benzion's unit; Benzion, of course, would not give a testimonial to BTS, and would most likely think the organization is a traitor and terrorist sympathizer. In any case, the booklet's testimonials paint a grim picture of Hebron. Kotler claims that he does not want to give up any settlements until there's a final "peace settlement"; he actually imagines himself at the scene of the eviction, carrying a sign that reads "*Peace Settlement Before Settlement Withdrawal!*" (135). Picturing Kotler standing on the edges of Kiryat Arba holding this sign, with the testimonies of BTS in mind, can one not help but question Kotler's supposed morality? Furthermore, Kotler's claim that he wants a peace settlement before a settlement withdrawal, in this light, can be seen as a similar delaying tactic to what Shenhav refers to as Oslo's "procedural mechanism" (*Beyond the Two State Solution* 2). Kotler's similarity with Benzion is also now more apparent, with their only difference being their chosen tactics—political power or military rebellion, respectively.

Bezmozgis bases his fictional withdrawal from the Hebron settlements on the 2005 pullout from Gaza. Kotler directly compares the novel's forthcoming withdrawal with Gaza: "And what did they [the Gaza settlers] get in return? They got what Kotler had predicted. From the Arabs they got rockets—some people had apparently expected bouquets. Not that he blamed them for their optimism. They hadn't had his education" (136). The "education" Kotler refers to here is being a Jewish Zionist dissident in Soviet Russia; what this has to do with Gaza is unclear (not to mention that claiming that the Arabs immediately started firing rockets is a gross historical simplification). Kotler continues:

> This is what they had done when they withdrew from the
> Gaza settlements in 2005, and they were doing it again, as if a
> mistake stubbornly repeated could yield different results. To
> uproot thousands of your own people. To make casualties of
> them for no discernible purpose. It was gross incompetence.
> If you were not willing to protect your people, you should
> not have encouraged them to live in that place, you should
> never have held the territory. There was no middle ground.
> Once you had committed to one, you had committed to all.
> The time for simply walking away had long passed. Now you
> stayed at any cost or exchanged a pound of flesh for a pound
> of flesh. That was all. Nothing else. (137)

This line of thinking, standard enough in Zionist circles, utterly elides the real makeup of power in Israel/Palestine. First, it suggests that the Hebron settlements were encouraged by the government, when in reality they were spearheaded by the right-wing religious settlers themselves. While the government and military were undoubtedly complicit in the settlement of Hebron, it was by no means created through their initiative. It is also important to remember that transferring a civilian population to an area under military occupation is illegal under the Geneva Conventions: article 49 of the Fourth Geneva Convention declares: "The Occupying Power shall not deport or transfer parts of its own civilian population into the territory it occupies" (Geneva Convention 185). Accepting the Palestinian narrative would mean accepting that the Palestinians, regardless of poor leadership and certain decisions, have been the victim of Zionist and Israeli aggression since at least 1948, as Rashid Khalidi narrates in *The Hundred Years' War on Palestine: A History of Settler Colonialism and Resistance, 1917–2017*; Israel is objectively the all-powerful hegemon in the conflict. Kotler's above attitude utterly disregards the historical reality of Israel/Palestine, and thus can hardly be labelled as ethical in its all-or-nothing territorial maximalness.

Moreover, Kotler's above narrative also buys into the standard liberal Zionist reading of the Gaza pullout: that it was done with peace in mind. The reasons for the Gaza pullout could not be further from a desire for peace. Prime Minister Ariel Sharon and his government removed the settlers from Gaza in order to further cement their hold on the West Bank and to maintain a Jewish demographic majority. In any case, Gaza is still very much occupied by Israel, just not from within, but through settlements and army bases. As the Israeli group Gisha argues in their 2007 position paper, "The alleged end to occupation in Gaza, and the disengagement which accompanied it, only mark the continued colonization by other means. The pretense of ending occupation in Gaza has only deepened the political and humanitarian disaster which Israel has brought upon it" (Bashi and Mann 19). They go on to state that the "completion of the disengagement plan has not absolved Israel of its obligations to permit and to facilitate the proper functioning of civilian life in the Gaza Strip" (19). The authors explain how Israel continues to control Gaza through an "invisible hand": "control over borders, airspace, territorial waters, population registry, the tax system, supply of goods, and others. Gaza residents know that their ability to use electric lights, to buy milk, or to have the garbage collected depends on decisions made by Israel. At times, soldiers operate in the streets of Gaza, but even after they leave, Israeli control over the lives of Gaza residents remains constant" (9). Since Gisha's paper was written, there have been at least two major military invasions of Gaza, both with substantial death tolls for Gazans. Yehuda Shenhav concurs with the members of Gisha, writing that, "As colonial history has taught us, occupation can be administered from a distance, without permanent military presence and without settlers. Israel is still operating an occupation regime in Gaza, as it denies the Strip a legitimate government, controls its economy, held the border crossings exclusively until 2011, prevents access from the sea and air and wages an ongoing campaign for the elimination of the leaders of the struggle" (Beyond the Two State Solution 19).

It is important to remember what modern Gaza is: the majority of Palestinians (80%) who live in what is now known as the Gaza Strip are refugees from Israel proper who fled or escaped there in 1948. Gaza has become, in the words of Max Blumenthal, "a warehouse for a surplus population" (3).[34] Avi Shlaim, likewise, writes that the Gaza settlement withdrawal "was not a peace plan but a unilateral move to redraw the borders of Greater Israel" (94). Shlaim continues: "Sharon did not submit it to the Palestinians as a basis for peace talks, and later refused even to discuss with them practical coordination relating to the pullback itself. Withdrawal from Gaza, completed in September 2005, was not a prelude to a comprehensive settlement but a prelude to further expansion on the West Bank" (94). The situation in Gaza has further deteriorated: during the writing of this book, Gazan residents have participated in weekly protest marches, which have been met by Israeli sniper fire, killing journalists, children, and medics.

Finally, The Betrayers offers no hint as to the political reasons for the prime minister engaging in the withdrawal, leaving readers to once again make their own inferences. In the current political situation in Israel, a settlement withdrawal from the West Bank is literally unthinkable; if Bezmozgis was serious about imagining an Israel where something like this was possible, he did not do any of the groundwork to set it up. Again, the attention to detail Bezmozgis expends in The Betrayers naming and representing the geography of Crimea is entirely absent in the novel's treatment of the settlement withdrawal, which is not only the instigating incident of the novel, but its entire background, and at times foreground. Moreover, in the frame of the novel, is there any reason to doubt that the prime minister's withdrawal is part of what Yehuda Shenhav describes as the "staggering 'peace process'" that is "part of a sterile simulation-game of peace, which has gone on since the early 1990s, all around the 1967 paradigm" (*Beyond the Two State Solution* 20)? This is why any actual withdrawal from the West Bank would constitute a stunning about-face for the Israeli government, and would deserve much, much greater detail if it were to be imagined in novelistic form. Fiction writing is a series of choices; *The Betrayers* itself admits as much through Svetlana's discussion of the author-as-god. Bezmozgis chose to play Jewish geography—crystal clear in Crimea, imprecise and vague in Israel/Palestine—this way.

Part of the answer to why Bezmozgis imagines a settlement withdrawal but leaves its details fuzzy can be found in the novel's treatment of the Palestinian narrative. The lack of Arab characters or Palestinian narrative of any kind is the novel's biggest—and most dangerous— shortcoming. Before turning to the major oversight of the absence of Palestinians from the novel's narration of the Hebron withdrawal, it is worth it to briefly catalogue the times Arabs or Palestinians do appear in the text. I have already mentioned the Arabs "complaining" and the Palestinians "throwing rockets." Elsewhere, Kotler watches an old Soviet movie when first arriving at Svetlana's, *White Sun of the Desert* (directed by Vladimir Motly and released in 1970), describing the film's Arab characters thusly: "The women in their burkas, the somnolent bearded elders, the crusading Western liberators, the primitive Muslim insurgents, the flaming oil wells; who could have predicted the immutability of this unhappy subject?" (49).[35] The choice of the word "immutability" is highly significant here, and highly troubling. It assumes that these supposed characteristics of Arab people are not historically contingent, based on political and social structures, or predicated on decades of Western imperialism and resource extraction (and are not just a product of viewing the Arab world through an Orientalist lens). If Arabs are immutable "primitive...insurgents," than peace is unachievable. These are the hallmarks of Orientalism, and a justification for maintaining the Israeli status quo.

The most significant space given to Arabs or Palestinians in the novel does not involve Kotler at all, but occurs when Tankilevich is at the Simferopol synagogue attending Saturday services. With the other elderly Crimean Jews, Tankilevich takes part in a derogatory, Orientalist—and slightly antisemitic—conversation. Moshe Podolsky, the Crimean Jew who immigrated to Israel in the late 1990s but after three years returned to Ukraine, blames the "Arabs" for all of Israel's ills.[36] "What do the Arabs do?" he intones. "They throw rocks. They attack innocent women and children. They shoot rockets. If they pay a few shekels in tax, where does the money go? To their crooked Palestinian officials, who, if such a thing is possible, are more corrupt than our Ukrainian ones" (65). Podolsky also has considerable scorn for the current Israeli government, which he sees as bowing down to the Arabs: "Meanwhile, the Jews pay money to the state. In Israel, they pay taxes, and from America they send how many millions. And what does the state do with this money? It commands Jewish soldiers to evict Jews from their homes" (65). Another of the elderly Jewish synagogue-goers responds to the news of the settlement withdrawal by saying that "it's only in Israel if a Jew builds a house it's a crime" (65). This is, of course, not true: the occupied territories are not Israel, and it is Palestinians who constantly have their houses demolished. Podolsky's rant gains in intensity, capping off with a tirade against the Israeli government, comparing them to the Judenrat, the Jewish council that liaised between the ghettos and the Nazis. "The Americans and the Arabs issue the order," he pontificates, "and their Jewish servants carry it out. They deceive themselves with the same rotten Judenrat logic" (67). This parallels Kotler's own position, and the one that the book implicitly takes, that unilateral engagement with the Palestinians is antisemitic. Podolsky continues: "And when the Arabs take over? When the Judenrat gives them Jerusalem? Then what will happen to this Yad Vashem?" (68). This is an encapsulation of another aspect of the Zionist narrative: that Israel and the treatment of the Palestinians is warranted because of the horrors of the Shoah. Podolsky does not understand the difference in power between these two contexts. In any case, the Palestinians who throw rocks and rockets, and who will apparently destroy Israel's Holocaust museum and memorial, are the only Palestinians in the entirety of the novel.

It is likely that readers are meant to disagree with Podolsky, perhaps even see him as racist, but without space left in his fictional world for a different viewpoint to counter Podolsky's (and Kotler's and Tankilevich's and Benzion's), it is hard to be certain. This is one place where the novel's lack of diasporic heteroglossia is crystal clear. Bezmozgis took a different, more successful tact in his prior novel,

The Free World, where the grandfather and patriarch is a staunch, still-believing communist, but his ideologically-rigid viewpoint is just one among many, which helps put it into historical and political context, and is a good example of diasporic heteroglossia. However, though Podolsky's stance is not necessarily endorsed by the narrator—though how different is it really from Kotler's position against giving up any land for any reason?—the Jewish state as the telos of Jewish history is explicitly endorsed later in the same scene, when Tankilevich, through the narrator, asks:

> What was the point of Jewish prayer? What was the point
> of it from the very beginning? One point: Zion. A return
> to Zion. The ingathering of the scattered people of Zion.
> The arrival of the messianic age and the rebuilding of the
> temple in Zion. When there were millions under the tsar,
> it was for Zion. Now that there was but this puny remnant,
> it could only be for Zion. Even in London, New York, and
> Dnepropetrovsk, where they were not living under the
> shadow of extinction, it was still for Zion. Only in Zion
> was it not for Zion. (68)

This also raises the question of who Bezmozgis's intended reader is meant to be. A typical Canadian Jewish person with mild Zionist leanings could read the above, could read the whole novel, and not be bothered by the fact that the Palestinian perspective is utterly absent. Liberal Zionists could read and agree with everything the novel purports; right-wing Zionists would find Kotler's betrayal of his son the most damning betrayal in the novel.

If we are assuming that Bezmozgis intends for readers to see through Kotler and Benzion's Zionism, it must be noted that this would require specific knowledge and ideological openness that simply does not currently exist in the general Canadian Jewish readership. When, for example, in 2017 Mira Sucharov—an associate professor of political science at Carleton University—wrote an article in *The Canadian Jewish News* (CJN) making connections between the Canadian government's treatment of First Nations and the Israeli occupation, she received such a negative and "aggressive" (Verman np) response that she quit her position as columnist at the newspaper (which is the only national Jewish paper in Canada). The Jewish public who responded to the article could not stomach the use of the word occupation; Sucharov writes that she "felt like a geologist who had been hired to write a column for the community paper of the Flat Earth Society" (qtd. in Verman np). As Alex Verman points out, Sucharov was the only left-leaning regular columnist at the CJN. The CJN, in presenting the occupation as a matter up for debate, does a disservice to its readers; moreover, the paper routinely excludes left, anti-occupation voices from its pages while allowing right and far-right views.[37] As Verman puts it, "when a newspaper operates on a flatly pro-Israel editorial stance, it becomes impossible for readers to expect anything different. If the editorial guidelines argue that some things and some voices just should not be published, it's no wonder that publishing them can make life difficult for the sole writer who is tasked with doing so" (np). It is not a stretch to imagine these readers finishing *The Betrayers* without any reaction to Kotler's position, or to the missing Palestinians. In as much as fictional texts on Israel/Palestine have the ability to change diasporic Jewish opinions on Zionism and Israel, how novels such as *The Betrayers* address, or do not address, the Palestinian side of things is of utmost importance.

This gets to the root of the issues I have regarding how the Hebron withdrawal is handled in the novel. The settlement withdrawal is presented as a crisis simply *for* Jews—for Israeli Jews, for diaspora Jews, between Kotler and the prime minister, between the settlers and the army, between Benzion and his father, between Podolsky and his dream of an entirely Jewish, Arab-free Palestine, between what the narrator terms "the enforcer and the resister," with "the nation of [Jewish] onlookers who sat wringing their hands in front of their televisions" (117). The nearly 300,000 Palestinians who live in Hebron, the millions who live in the West Bank, Gaza, Israel, and the Palestinian diaspora, are entirely outside the scope of the crisis; they are not agents in this drama, they do not have a say. They barely register as human. Far from it; the action is simply being done to them. It is not just the lack of Palestinian characters; even a Jewish character that puts forward a Palestinian or non-Zionist perspective would help alleviate the poorly weighted political architecture of the novel (as we saw in *The Best Place on Earth*). If Bezmozgis truly wants to write a novel in real time that presents to the

world "true facts" and that "pushes the world in a certain direction" as
he puts it ("An Afternoon"), if he wants to look at Israel/Palestine as it
is, should he not have opened up space to include the Palestinian narrative?[38] How the Palestinians who live in Hebron feel about the withdrawal matters (does it not?), but Bezmozgis does not even acknowledge
that there are other, non-Jewish people living in Hebron (and if they are,
they are rock-throwing, evil landgrabbers, a la Podolsky). Considering
the novel's interest in author-as-god, is it not fair to say that it was totally
in Bezmozgis's authorial power to include the Palestinian narrative
in his fictional, well-mapped-out Crimea? Bezmozgis mirrors the religious settlers' own ideological erasure of Palestinian presence on the
land—which is yet again a new iteration of the Zionist erasure of their
presence—and undermines whatever restorative effect the book might
have engendered. The fact is that The Betrayers is indeed a novel in real
time, but it is Zionist time. The Palestinians are faceless in Zionist time,
and without a face, they cannot speak, closing any potential for heteroglossia. Compare this to Tsabari's stories, which achieve a powerful
diasporic heteroglossia through their dedication to diasporic identities that are in constant push/pull with the national centre of Zionism;
Bezmozgis's novel, on the other hand, only sees in one direction, and is
what Bakhtin would call univocal, even though on its surface it appears
to take the guise of multiple voices. This, in the end, is the kind of morality Kotler is supposedly so brilliantly endowed with: the morality of the
settler-colonialist, which erases Indigenous presence in its claim of sole
autochthonous and Indigenous belonging to the land.[39] In his attempt to
write a novel in real time that purports to be reasonable, to mourn the
country's rightward drift, and to be heteroglossic, Bezmozgis has instead
written a deeply Zionist text that uses the trappings of multiple voices in
order to mask its univocality.

Bezmozgis's own writing and thoughts in regard to The Betrayers
are instructive here. Bezmozgis writes that: "Technically speaking, the
age of Jewish exile is over. It ended, if not precisely with the establishment of the state of Israel, then with the collapse of the Soviet Union,
when practically any Jew in the world could live in Israel if he so chose"
("A Conversation" 15). Though an interesting way to think of Jewish exile,
this belief takes for granted the Zionist claim that Israel is the telos of
Jewish diaspora. As a diasporic, anti-Zionist Jew, this is a problematic

statement, to say the least. In the novel, Kotler waxes poetic about the uniqueness of the Jewish situation, what he calls "the Jewish semi-tone" (125). If Israel is the natural home—the natural end of exile—that Bezmozgis says it is here, then how can that not significantly diminish the multitudinous notes of this "Jewish semitone"? It is in the varied, dias-poric manifestations of Jewishness that this semitone rings at its most affirmative; it is in the world of the diaspora, where Jewish collectivities did not wield political power, after all, that the semitone was engendered, shaped, and refined. As George Steiner succinctly puts it:

> The survival of the Jews has no authentic parallel in history.
> Ancient ethnic communities and civilizations no less gifted,
> no less self-conscious, have perished, many without a trace.
> It is, on the most rational, existential level, difficult to believe
> that this unique phenomenon of unbroken life, in the face
> of every destructive agency, is unconnected with the exilic
> circumstance. Judaism has drawn its uncanny vitality from
> dispersal, from the adaptive demands made on it by mobility.
> (23).

It is this diasporic mobility that allowed the Jewish semitone to be sounded in the first place. The ethnic nationalism of Israel is only one possible timbre among many, and, I would suggest, is a highly discordant one, especially when it is the only one given room to sound off.

"Land! The Land!":
The Possibility of Coexistence

Even with the novel's concrete Zionism, the possibility of different ways of living on the land do manage to sometimes push up through the text. Or, as Kotler, through the narrator, exclaims, "Land! The land!" (196). Due to Kotler's position as a politician, he has seen various political recon-ciliations. He went on a UN-sponsored mission to see how the Cypriot Turks and Greeks had buried "their hatreds. Deep enough for radishes, Kotler had felt. In a generation or two, maybe deep enough for olives" (39). Tankilevich himself muses on ownership and the vicissitudes of history.

The old Torah Talmud building in Simferopol, the reclaiming of which Tankilevich knows is Semonovna's "big ambition" (70), was the Nazi Gestapo headquarters, and after the fall of the Nazis had been the Institute of Sport. Even though in the 1990s the government had returned

> some buildings to local communities...there was little
> chance it would return this one. The state was poor and
> the Jews were poor. What did moral and historical claims
> matter in such an equation? So the Gestapo had used it as
> their headquarters. So they had collected Jews there before
> sending them to their macabre deaths. But the innocent
> students of the Institute of Sport hadn't done this. Why
> should they be dispossessed? (71)

Tankilevich answers his own question: "A crime demanded rectification! That was why. But it would never happen" (71). The language of coexistence also crops up in smaller, more personal moments, such as when Kotler reminisces about the time his family shared a small apartment with another Russian family: "They had coexisted peaceably, without conflicts, for the entire month, sharing among them not only the kitchen but also the toilet" (7). Between the Greeks and Turks, the language of peaceable coexistence, and Tankilevich's belief in rectification, it would seem that the novel does make space, however minor, for the possibility of justice.

The most significant account of land, besides those directly related to the Middle East, is when Kotler and Leora are driving through territory that has recently seen the return of the Crimean Tatars, an ethnic group that had been ethnically cleansed during the Soviet era. Apparently, the same land now belonging to the Tatars was once considered for a Jewish autonomous zone in Crimea. Bezmozgis himself states that Crimea is "a land that could have rivalled Israel, a land that, in its own way, is as contested as Palestine" ("An Afternoon"). Kotler compares the Tatars' land and shoddy houses to an earlier period in Israel, and to "the Arab parts of the country in the north and south" (196), before saying to Leora: "Imagine...this could have been the Jewish homeland. Then the Tatars and the Russians could have demanded we go back to where we belong, as the Palestinians do now" (197). The casual comparison between the Tatars and Palestinians, made by Kotler to prove the universal hatred of the Jews, is actually a pretty astute observation, seeing how both were ethnically cleansed.

The history of the Muslim Tatars in Crimea is one of genocide, forced relocation, suffering, and the creation of a diasporic conscious- ness. As Brian Glyn Williams relates in his history of the Tatars, in the wake of World War II, Stalin forcibly transferred a quarter of a million Tatars—mostly women, children, and the elderly, with the men either still fighting in the Red Army or collaborators who had retreated west with the Nazis—to central Asia.[40] Fully expecting to be murdered, the Tatars were loaded onto poorly vented cattle cars and carted east; as Williams puts it, "This 'removal' was carried out with a cold efficiency that resembled the deportation of Jews to camps in Nazi Germany" (333). It was not until the collapse of the USSR that the Tatars were allowed to return to Crimea, and around half did, but their towns and fields had been transformed into resorts and hotels, and they had no choice but to set up squatter camps; it is these camps that Kotler and Leora see. According to Williams, and as seen in *The Betrayers*, all Crimean cities are "surrounded by distinctive Crimean Tatar settlements made up of simple rough-hewn brick houses, covered with corrugated tin roofs, often lacking running water and elec- tricity, located on dirt roads" (346). Stalin's war crimes against the Tatars created a vivid diasporic consciousness, which the Tatars refer to as *pitme- gun surgun*, or "continuing exile" (346): "the brutal deportation and exile of the USSR's entire Crimean Tatar population has shaped this people's contemporary collective identity," Williams explains (335).[41] The idea that Crimea itself could have been a Jewish homeland comes up a few times in the novel, but is never fully addressed; nonetheless, the successful return of the Tatars shows that there is hope of a Palestinian return.[42]

Even with the language of coexistence, however, Kotler's response to the reality of the Tatar villages shows his true feelings on the matter. Kotler is only able to think of inhabiting land through the prism of exclu- sive ownership, through private property, through ethnic nationalism:

A measure of earth under your feet that you could call your own. Was there a more primitive concept? But nobody lives in the ether. Man is a physical being who requires physical space. And his nature is a prejudicial nature of alike and unalike. That was the history of the world. How much earth can you claim with another's consent? How long can you hold it if you haven't consent? And is it possible to foster consent where none exists? Kotler didn't know the answers to the first two questions, but the essential question was the last, and the answer to that was not favorable. (196–197)

Kotler's Zionism—tempered with his horrific experiences in the Soviet Union—has blocked from his view any other kind of land-dwelling, whether that be diasporic, Indigenous, nomadic, or pluralistic. Kotler's above gloss also severely misunderstands the situation regarding the Tatars. In being violently expelled from their homes, the Tatars have more in common with the Palestinians than with Israeli Jews (though of course, in the context of Europe, the parallels are all too clear). It is a sad tragedy of Kotler's way of thinking that once the only way to live is through violent force, violent force becomes all you know. Connected to violent force, of course, is the othering of the Indigenous, non-wanted population, which in the case of Israel is the Palestinians.

"History's Joke" and The Dying Jewish Diasporas of the FSU: Conclusion

Ultimately, The Betrayers offers its Canadian audience a flawed, dangerous, univocal narrative about power and land in Israel/Palestine side by side with a moving look at the dying Jewish diaspora of Crimea, representative of the FSU more generally. My diasporic heteroglossic reading of the novel argues that even though Bezmozgis critiques the Israeli nation-state's rightward drift through the generational rift between Kotler and Benzion, the novel, in its refusal to address the causes and systemic imbalances of the situation in Israel/Palestine, in its fuzzy geopolitics, and in its complete elision of the Palestinian narrative, actually ends up espousing the violent Zionist status quo. Kotler's very-much-impeachable morality ends up being the byproduct of the dangerous transfer of diasporic defence mechanisms to positions of hegemonic power. For Kotler, Tankilevich, and Bezmozgis, the political situation in Israel is all about Jewish power and Jewish conflict; the real victims of the Zionist state, the Palestinians, are not even treated as agents in their own occupation and oppression. I agree strongly with Judith Butler in *Parting Ways*, when she reminds us that the solving of Israel/Palestine cannot come from Jews exclusively. *The Betrayers*, then, can be taken as a telling example of what happens when Jewish diasporic authors with an interest in Israel/Palestine forget that they are not the only people whose livelihoods are at stake.

Of course, *The Betrayers* occupies two very different geographies. The novel must be given credit for its nuanced rendering of not only the last remnants of the Jewish collectivity in the FSU, but of the crumbling post-communist countries where these remnants exist. Bezmozgis describes the FSU with satire, irony, and love, from the statue of Lenin that is looking "peripherally at a McDonald's" (23), to the blasphemies of Russian TV: "The game show was offensive, but there were no words for the newscast. Every lie starched and ironed" (98).[43] However, it is Jewish Crimea that Bezmozgis most successfully imbues with fictional form. He does this in the small detail of Kotler's description of Svetlana and Tankilevich's house, "an ordinary village house. A plot of land and its modest yield. A life of shtetl dimensions" (14). He also does this through the big, emotional speech. Here is Svetlana talking candidly about the Soviet treatment of the Jewish people who resided in the FSU:

> I understand very well how it is. We didn't treat the Jews fondly here. The Russians and the Ukrainians. We were terrible anti-Semites. With repressions and pogroms, our fathers and grandfathers drove the Jews from this country. Because we didn't want them here, the Jews had to make their own land. They shed their blood for it. A hundred years later and the Jews are nearly gone. So this is a great triumph! But how do we celebrate? By bending over backward to invent a Jewish grandfather so that *we* can follow the Jews to *Israel*! Ha! There is history's joke. But tell me who is laughing. (165–166)

Besides the admittance of societal guilt, Svetlana refers here to the phenomenon of Russians feigning Jewish ancestry in order to immigrate to Israel.

Tankilevich's experience of antisemitism at the Simferopol grocery story reveals that the hatred of Jewish difference has not vanished in the FSU. However, a young woman and her daughter do approach Tankilevich after the attack, and, in a kind of apology for the man's behaviour, the woman gives a speech of her own, regretting all the Jewish people who have left for Israel: "*How many such valuable people did we lose? Intellectual people. Specialists. Thousands. I don't blame them. Because this country is still primitive, full of primitive people. In front of my daughter, I'm embarrassed for this country*" (92; emphasis original). Both this woman and Svetlana acknowledge, while at the same time idealizing, the Jewish absence from the FSU. Tankilevich calls this interaction the day's "single redeeming moment" (92).

Finally, we have Kotler's gloss on the history of Jewish people in Crimea. The catalyst for Kotler's thoughts here is Tankilevich: "Capricious fate had cast him [Tankilevich] as the final link in the long chain of Crimean Jewry. A chain that stretched back more than a thousand years…Now it was coming to a close, like all Jewish stories came to a close, with suitcases" (180). As pointed at here, the Jewish story continues, but in new diasporic spaces. Though Kotler laments that "all Jewish stories" end with suitcases, a diasporic ethics would insist that a story that ends with a suitcase is far more desirable than a story that ends with checkpoints, an oppressed national Other, or a nuclear arsenal (or, of course, with a gas chamber, the other extreme Kotler does not address here). This essentializing of the "Jewish semitone" to a simple Zionist reading, even with Bezmozgis's deep knowledge of Jewish diasporic spaces—both in the FSU and in Toronto—is emblematic of the novel's major failure. While *The Betrayers* is enlightening on certain aspects of the Jewish world, overall, it helps keep the Jewish diaspora in the dark when it comes to the reality of settler colonialism in Israel/Palestine. While Kotler and Tankilevich argue about who behaved worse under the defunct Soviet system, millions of Palestinians remain under brutal military occupation in their names, and are not given a second thought.

Conclusion

Diasporic Heteroglossia,
Second Cousins,
Learning to Be Each Other's Guests

IN THIS BOOK, I have been concerned with Jewish
American and Canadian fiction that turns its narrative gaze toward
Israel/Palestine. In performing readings of my five primary texts—
Operation Shylock by Philip Roth, *Altneuland* by Theodor Herzl, *Exodus*
by Leon Uris, *The Best Place on Earth* by Ayelet Tsabari, and *The Betrayers*
by David Bezmozgis—I have made a case for the importance of fiction in
mapping out the complexities of Jewish geography. Through the readings
of these five texts, we can learn a lot about the state of the Jewish world,
of the diaspora's relationship with Israel/Palestine, and of the possibilities of fiction to imagine ethical alternatives to Zionism's violent ethnic
nationalism as manifested in the nation-state. I have argued that Jewish
diasporic fiction had a role in cementing Zionism's hold on the Jewish
world, moving from an atopic to centroperipheral relationship, and that
it can—and should—likewise have a role in moving toward an antagonistic relationship with Israel, one that celebrates the possibilities of

diasporic consciousness; in fact, the same deeply Zionist texts, when read contrapuntally from a position of diaspora ethics, can unintentionally perform such productive work.

One way that fiction can challenge Jewish ethnic nationalism, I have argued, is through what I term diasporic heteroglossia, the ability of the novel (or short story collection) to house multiple voices and narratives that, taken together, push back against a Zionist centre. In *Operation Shylock*, Roth deploys diasporic heteroglossia, including Philip's refusal of diasporic heteroglossia in the novel's missing final chapter, to mount a multi-pronged, nuanced, and complex attack on not only Zionism, but on national belonging of any kind. In comparing *Altneuland* and *Exodus*, using the creation of the Israeli state as the fulcrum to bend both texts toward each other, I showed how these texts utilize two different concepts of Jewish time—sundered history and teleological Zionism—to wish for a state and to cement that state in the Jewish world; both novels, therefore, act as dangerous examples of univocalism. The short stories of Ayelet Tsabari's *The Best Place on Earth* perform their own kind of diasporic heteroglossia, fictionalizing the borderless, shifting diasporic identities of a wide range of Arab Jewish characters and situations. In my reading of three of the stories—"Invisible," "A Sign of Harmony," and "Borders"—I made a case for the stories' enactment of diaspora politics, what Ella Shohat calls a "diasporic polycentric perspective" (*On the Arab-Jew* 14). Finally, I argued that *The Betrayers* reveals the pitfalls of a Zionist rendering of Israel/Palestine in diasporic fiction, where the situation of the diaspora is clearly and devastatingly articulated, but where the reality of Israel/Palestine is left woefully undeveloped. In this way, *The Betrayers* is a telling example of a univocal novel dressed up in diasporic heteroglossic clothing. In sum, throughout *Leaving Other People Alone*, I have revealed, analyzed, and pushed the stakes of playing Jewish geography in diasporic fiction. It is my hope that, in doing so, novels such as *Operation Shylock* and short story collections such as *The Best Place on Earth* will continue enlarging the scope of what is possible to imagine, in the Jewish world and beyond; likewise, I hope that I have begun to develop the tools for critiquing Zionist texts such as *The Betrayers* and *Exodus*, texts that substitute ethnic dominance and Jewish supremacy for the diasporic consciousness and ethics that the Boyarins and others celebrate.

A brief look at the ever-growing number of Canadian and American Jewish novels and story collections that are preoccupied with Israel/Palestine makes the clear case that the Jewish diasporic world is taking the problems of its centroperipheral relationship seriously. In the past ten or so years, there has been an outpouring of fictional texts, whether Zionist or not, that interrogate the relationship between the North American Jewish diasporas and Israel. In Canada, we have Nora Gold's *Fields of Exile* and Alison Pick's *Strangers with the Same Dream*; in the US, there is a much bigger output: Shelly Oria's *New York 1, Tel Aviv 0*, Nicole Krauss's *Great House* and *Forest Dark*, Moriel Rothman-Zecher's *Sadness is a White Bird*, the novels of Joshua Cohen (*Moving Kings, The Netanyahus*), the short story collections of Nathan Englander (*For the Relief of Unbearable Urges, What We Talk About When We Talk About Anne Frank*), and Rebecca Sacks's *City of a Thousand Gates*. Along with the fictional texts themselves, there are anthologies such as *Kingdom of Olives and Ash: Writers Confront the Occupation*; edited by novelists Michael Chabon and Ayelet Waldman, *Kingdom* is a collection of essays by fiction writers from across the globe who toured the West Bank and Gaza Strip.[1] The anthology looks the horrors and violence of both the occupation and the Israeli state square in the face.

Pick's, Rothman-Zecher's, and Sacks's novels all exhibit traits of diasporic heteroglossia, with named, three-dimensional, significant Palestinian characters, and plenty of room for the Palestinian narrative. Matti Friedman, writing on some of these recent novels, argues that "Jewish American writers of a few decades ago might have poked around the strange Jewish country in the Middle East, but they knew that the real literary action for them was back home. The novelists of 2017 don't seem so sure" ("Distant Cousins" np). Friedman also astutely points out that where American and Israel Jews used to be siblings, riven apart by the destruction of Europe, they are now, in these novels, second cousins (the fact that Friedman is an ardent Zionist and still sees this shows the power these texts have when it comes to shifting relationships). This move, from siblings to second cousins (skipping, interestingly, the closer alignment of first cousins), is part of the diaspora demanding more space in the playing field of Jewish geography, and is hopefully setting the groundwork for a major shift in the Jewish world.

This leaves the question: why now? Why are all of these books being written, published, and read in the first decades of the twenty-first century? While I do not think there is one clear answer to this, there are several important aspects to consider. The first is simply that challenging the hegemony of Israel and Zionism in the Jewish world is not as taboo as it once was (not that all of these texts are so ripe with critique, because some, such as *Fields of Gold*, are clearly not); the rise of Jewish anti-Zionist and anti-occupation groups such as Jewish Voices for Peace, If Not Now, and Independent Jewish Voices are corollaries in the activist/political sphere. As Zionism loses its narrative and mythological hold, we will see more and more books that search for alternatives, that side with the Palestinians. The more Jewish voices pushing back against Zionism, the wider diasporic heteroglossia gets, the higher the chance of reinserting ourselves into diasporic time. Second, the Jewish literary scene has also changed. The immigrant experience, except for Soviet Jews like Bezmozgis, is far enough in the past, and has been mined so thoroughly, that North American Jewish writers are beginning to branch out in their interests and subject matter. Finally, I think this can be seen as representing an ethical turn in Jewish North American writing. Jewish authors such as Rochman-Zecher are hungry for Jewish narratives, lives, and communities that are not based on Zionism. It is my prediction that these authors will start to be drawn toward diaspora, that invention of the Jewish people refined and redefined over thousands of years, as an ethical place to start remaking the Jewish, and wider, world.

I will end this book, then, with a reassertion of the importance of changing how we live, of the ethical possibility of diaspora, with its concomitant demand to abolish all borders, militaries, and nation-states. With the end of oil approaching, with the climate disaster worsening, with the growing refugee crisis, with the vast inequities between rich countries and poor (poor usually from colonialism, capitalism, and resource extraction), a world free of borders, of the violent policing of national adherence, is the only just option. As the Boyarins, Edward Said, Judith Butler, and others quoted in this book passionately demonstrate, it is through a diasporic relationship to land and to each other that we can find a way forward. It is through leaving other people alone, in all senses of the phrase. I hope to have made the case that the writing, reading, and studying of fiction has a role to play in working toward a better world.

There is something of incredible value in the fact of the Jewish diaspora and its millenia-long existence. The value is that of the

Boyarins' leaving other people alone, of borderless existences, of group survival that still acknowledges the existence and validity of other groups. As George Steiner movingly puts it, "I cannot shake off the conviction that the torment and the mystery of resilience in Judaism exemplify, enact, an arduous truth: that human beings must learn to be each other's guests on this small planet, even as they must learn to be guests of being itself and of the natural world" (24). This "humbly immediate" yet "terribly abstract, morally and psychologically exigent" truth is one that humanity "will have to learn...or [it] will be made extinct in suicidal waste and violence" (24). The Boyarins concur when they write that: "The renunciation of difference seems both an impoverishment of human life and an inevitable harbinger of oppression. Yet the renunciation of sovereignty...combined with a fierce tenacity in holding onto cultural identity, might well have something to offer to a world in which these two forces, together, kill thousands daily" ("Generation and the Ground" 723). The renunciation of sovereignty, living as each other's guests, leaving each other alone, these are the powers of a committed and ethical diasporic existence.

Notes

Introduction

1. A note on terms. I will be using Israel/Palestine for the region where Zionism and the Palestinian struggle against Zionism are rooted, unless Israel or Palestine fits the context. For the various wars Israel has fought in, I will use the designation the 1948 War, the 1967 War, etcetera. For events in Palestinian history, I will be using the appropriate Palestinian term: the Nakba, the first Intifada, the second Intifada, and so on.

2. In a 1974 interview with Joyce Carol Oates, Roth remarked that "Sheer Playfulness and Deadly Seriousness are my closest friends" (Why Write 120).

3. Additionally, there is Alvin H. Rosenfeld's 1997 article, "Promised Land(s): Zion, America, and American-Jewish Writers," which briefly surveys the literature before performing a reading of Philip Roth. All three of these texts are hedged by the borders of the United States. There are no books or articles as of yet on Canadian literature that deals with Israel/Palestine.

4. Anti-Zionism differs from positions such as post-Zionism in its core belief that the Jewish settlement of Palestine is based on the ethnic cleansing and colonization of the Palestinian people, and that this is a wrong that is ongoing and in urgent need of restitution and repair. Where post-Zionism questions the founding myths of Israel and takes into account the narrative of the Palestinian, but still asserts the need for a Jewish-majority state, anti-Zionism declares that Jewish supremacy in Israel/Palestine must be demolished, making way for a society that treats all of its members as equal. Where postmodernism is a continuation of modernism, post-Zionism is, in many ways, just a continuation of Zionism.

5. However, being an anti-Zionist is not just about Jewish nationalism. It is about opposing any form of group belonging that predicates itself on military domination. As Salaita puts it, "It is never a good idea, even through the trope of

243

strategic essentialism, to link an ethnic group to a military apparatus" (*Israel's Dead Soul* 23).

6. I was alerted to the concept of citational practices when I encountered a Twitter conversation between Indigenous scholars Daniel Heath Justice and Chelsea Vowel on April 25, 2017: @âpihtawikosisân, "This. I think citational practices are super value-loaded, and it is a really key part of any work I do," *Twitter*, 25 April 2017, 11:06 a.m., https://twitter.com/ apihtawikosisan/ status/856887245936177153; @justicedanielh, "Absolutely. Citational politics are often under-appreciated but very revealing about who we truly value in our intellectual genealogies," *Twitter*, 25 April 2017, 12:01 p.m., twitter.com/ justicedanielh/status/856900996290588672.

7. As Butler points out, the lessons of the Jewish European genocide should be, rather, "that nation-states should never be able to found themselves through the dispossession of whole populations who fail to fit the purified idea of the nation" (*Parting Ways* 24).

8. Stéphane Dufoix adds some nuance to the word's origins: "In the so-called Septuagint Bible, 'diaspora' is used twelve times" (4). But it did not necessarily mean "galut" or dispersion after the first temple was destroyed: it "always meant the threat of dispersion facing the Hebrews if they failed to obey God's will, and it applied almost exclusively to divine acts. God is the one who scatters the sinners or will gather them together in the future" (4–5).

9. Dubnow's entry is a fascinating historical document. Written in 1935, Dubnow's survey of Jewish history and diaspora is before the Shoah, before the Zionist success in creating a state. Dubnow is unabashedly celebratory of the Jewish diaspora, writing: "The nature of Jewish emigration and wanderings is not peculiar in itself. It is the persistence of the Jewish people as a recognizable group through centuries of such wanderings in countries where they constituted a compact minority, which never enjoyed the powerful and dependable protection or support either of a homeland or of any foreign ally, that makes the Jewish Diaspora a rare and significant phenomenon" (127). Dubnow writes how—thanks to colonialism and the spread of the European global empires— "By the twentieth century the Diaspora had spread to all quarters of the globe" and states that "The Diaspora has left a deep imprint on all aspects of Jewish life" (129). Dubnow was murdered in a Nazi ghetto in 1941.

10. Chariandy's list of the "difficult and important" questions scholars of diaspora explore "with great subtlety" is an excellent encapsulation of the field: "Is there an 'ideal' or 'original' conceptualization of diaspora? Are racial and ethnic groups automatically diasporas? Can diasporas be created through voluntary migration, rather than traumatic exile? Must a diaspora have an extant homeland culture before dislocation, or can it develop or invent one

retrospectively? How does generational difference impact the imagining of a diaspora? Must people in a diaspora long to return home? If so, what type of return is this: physical or symbolic?" (np).

11. Safran did rework his list after critiques from various scholars. See Robin Cohen's *Global Diasporas*, pages 6–8.

12. A note on the term "Shoah": there is no word or phrase that properly captures the enormity of the Nazi genocide of the Second World War, nor can there be. Though Holocaust is the accepted word in English, the religious and sacrificial connotations make it grossly inappropriate for an attempted genocide. As George Steiner puts it, "the noble Greek word, 'Holocaust,' signifying a solemn burnt offering, has no legitimate place in this matter" (12). I will be using the Hebrew term *Shoah*—which means calamity—for the Nazi genocide. (There is also the Yiddish phrase *Khurbn Eyrope*, which translates to destruction of Europe).

13. See Gabriel Gabi Sheffer's "Is the Jewish Diaspora Unique? Reflections on the Diaspora's Current Situation" and David Landy's *Jewish Identity and Palestinian Rights: Diaspora Jewish Opposition to Israel* for a thorough exploration of the changing aspects of the relationship.

14. Chariandy, for one, writes that "Indeed, it would be difficult to overstate the influence of Jewish thought upon many other peoples who have later come to understand themselves as traumatically displaced diasporas," and that "Articulators of the postcolonial diasporas need to be sensitive to the origins of diasporic thought in Jewish histories and commentary" without needing to make it the "definitive model" (np), a phrase Chariandy quotes from James Clifford (see Clifford 249).

15. Dufoix, Sheffer, and many others take at face value that Israel is the originary home of the Jewish diaspora.

16. For the Boyarins, "the biblical story is not one of autochthony but one of always already coming from somewhere else" (715). "Israelite and Jewish religion is perpetually an unsettlement of the very notion of autochthony" (715), they write, yet "Israeli state power, deprived of the option of self-legitimation through appeal to a divine king, discovered autochthony as a powerful replacement" (718).

17. The Boyarins write that "The dream of a place that is ours founders on the rock of realization that there are Others there just as there are Others in Poland, Morocco, and Ethiopa. Any notion, then, of redemption through Land must either be infinitely deferred...or become a moral monster" (714).

18. The Boyarins, likewise, do not let Christianity off the hook: "Christian universalism, even at its most liberal and benevolent, has been a powerful force for coercive discourses of sameness, denying, as we have seen, the rights of Jews, women, and others to retain their difference" (707).

19. Significantly, the Boyarins mention that the Rabbis of the Talmud declared the biblical command to wipe out the city of Jericho in the Israelites' conquering of Canaan as "no longer applicable" (710). Therefore, the Israeli settler movement "to refigure the Palestinians as Amalek and to reactivate the genocidal commandment is a radical act of religious revisionism and not in any way a continuation of historical rabbinic Judaism" (710).

20. As Melanie Kaye/Kantrowitz puts it in her poem "Notes from an Immigrant Daughter: Atlanta," "I can't go back / where I came from was / burned off the map // I'm a Jew / anywhere else is someone else's land" (qtd. in *Colors of Jews* np).

1 | Philip Goes to Israel

1. As Michael Holquist explains, by the novel Bakhtin means much more than the long prose genre that rose to prominence in the eighteenth century, but is referring to any literature that pushes against dominant currents.

2. Of course, as Furman implies, Roth does not always readily align with progressive, leftist politics. For an impassioned critique of Roth's Jewish individualism as embodied in *American Pastoral*, see Michael Lerner's "The Jews and the 60s: Philip Roth Still Doesn't Get It."

3. There has been some recent discussion on the question of Roth's feelings toward Zionism. Louis Gordon, for one, in his essay on Roth and Zionism in *A Political Companion to Philip Roth*, argues that Roth was clearly aligned, in both his literary output and personal life, as a liberal Zionist. Though Gordon admits that Roth has displayed "considerable and, at times, serious skepticism toward Zionism and Israel in his fiction and nonfiction" (119), he nonetheless argues, through bringing in a variety of Roth's nonfiction works, open letters, and stories from friends and acquaintances, that "the three voices of Roth—Roth the author, Roth the character, and Nathan Zuckerman—share the same political views with the Israeli Civil Rights and Peace Movement," in other words, a centre-left liberal Zionism (120). Gordon's mixture of literary criticism (which is more cherry-picking from the pertinent texts) and biographical reading bolsters his conclusion, though it does not make for an overwhelmingly convincing case. For example, Gordon writes that since Roth signed an open letter in the *New York Times* denouncing "the policies of Prime Minister Shamir" through a liberal Zionist lens, it is impossible therefore that Roth himself was more critical of the Israeli state than the letter he signed (123). Gordon offers cursory readings of the two Israel-situated novels, picking particular speeches and scenes and isolating them from the diasporic heteroglossia of the texts. For Gordon,

since neither Zuckerman nor Philip are anti-Zionists, Roth himself could not have been an anti-Zionist, which is an interpretive leap Gordon does not even attempt to justify. Gordon seems to read "the confession" of *Operation Shylock* as a confession of liberal Zionism: "If we understand *Shylock* as a function of Roth's 'confession,'" he writes, "then the so-called missing chapter at the novel's end that details the character of Roth's secret mission for the Mossad can be understood for what it really is: a literary device in the service of his confession" (129). Gordon does not explain this or unpack it in any way. Later, he writes that "the fact that the Philip Roth character skeptically undertakes the mission to Greece on behalf of the Mossad is symptomatic of this line of political thinking"—that Roth held progressive Zionist and not anti-Zionist views. In any case, whether Roth would have called himself a Zionist, a liberal Zionist, or an anti-Zionist has no bearing on what the fictional texts themselves do, what they allow, and what they fictionalize.

4. For the sake of clarity—and to insist on the wide gulf separating Philip Roth the author from Philip Roth the narrator—I follow the established convention (started by Debra Shostak) of referring to *Shylock*'s narrator as Philip, the book's author as Roth, and the imposter/double as Pipik.

5. The similarities between the two novels would be worth exploring further. Compare the following quotes from *Shylock*—"Yes, I thought, this is how to prevail—forget this shadow and stick to the task" (56); "I had managed despite everything to do the job" (216); "I'm seeing double, I thought, doubles, I thought, but because of not eating, because of barely getting any sleep, or because I'm coming apart again for the second time in a year?" (302); "I am an American citizen...I am here on a journalistic assignment for an American newspaper" (347)—with these lines from *Fear and Loathing*: "I was, after all, a professional journalist, so I had an obligation to *cover the story*, for good or ill" (4); "The only way to prepare for a trip like this, I felt, was to dress up like human peacocks and get crazy, then screech off across the desert and *cover the story*. Never lose sight of the primary responsibility" (12); "I recognize this feeling: three or four days of booze, drugs, sun, no sleep and burned out adrenalin reserves—a giddy, quavering sort of high that means the crash is coming. But when? How much longer?...The possibility of physical and mental collapse is very real now" (89).

6. Of the three scholars mentioned above, McLoughlin comes closest, by actually mentioning the West Bank trial as well as the trial of Shylock in *The Merchant of Venice* as the trials referenced in the novel. Beyond pointing to them, however, she does not give any more space to them (and she also misses Smilesburger's future Palestinian trial of Israeli Jews). Likewise, in the introduction to the *Tikkun* round-table the editors acknowledge that "The theory of 'Diasporism' is

espoused in the context of the Demjanjuk trial on the one hand and the Intifada and the miscarriage of justice in regard to Palestinians on the other" (Ezrahi et al. np), but they do not mention Ramallah or the scenes set there specifically.

7. Demjanjuk comes up even before the novel begins: in the Preface, Philip discusses the outcome of the Demjanjuk trial, at least up until the point of publication. "As of this date," he writes, "the Supreme Court is still deliberating the appeal" (14).

8. Roth is not the only Jewish North American writer to have used the Demjanjuk trial as source material. The Canadian Jonathan Garfinkel's 2004 play *The Trials of John Demjanjuk: A Holocaust Cabaret*—a true cabaret, with songs, accordion music, elaborate costumes, choruses, and jokes—touches on many of the same elements of the trial that Roth does in *Shylock*, including the defense's obsession with the veracity of the paperclip on the Trawniki ID card and Rosenberg's memoir. Most significantly, the play questions the possibility of Demjanjuk being both a mass murderer and innocent American autoworker. In a song called "Two Faces Are Better Than One," John sings "Oh yes it's true / a good possibility / That a man is a man / with many personalities / But can two faces / be one?" (scene 27, p. 24). In a move that Roth would surely have approved of, Garfinkel creates a separate character named Ivan, who is Ivan the Terrible at the age he would have been during the Shoah, who speaks with John, and does a song and dance number with the "Survivor" character. At the end of the play, when John has been acquitted in Israel, but his second denaturalization is under way, John asks Ivan if they were criminals. "We were gods," Ivan answers, in a chilling moment of unsettling truth-telling. Garfinkel, without the knowledge of what happens at the German trial, does not come down conclusively one way or the other on John's identity during the war.

9. Demjanjuk was the first American citizen to be denaturalized twice, a detail that both Philip and Roth would no doubt savour.

10. When Douglas follows the Demjanjuk case to its Munich trial, a different set of juridical problems are brought to bear on the question of prosecuting Nazi perpetrators. Where Israel enshrined into law its right to try Nazi perpetrators, Germany decided it did not have legal standing to do so. Douglas explains: "German courts rejected the concept of crimes against humanity; and while Germany incorporated genocide into its domestic criminal code in 1954—some thirty-four years before the United States got around to it—its jurists concluded that the crime could not be applied to atrocities committed during the Nazi era, including the extermination of Europe's Jews" (144). One of the main reasons for this decision was how many Nazi judges were still active in the German court system. Douglas claims that "In the early years of the Federal Republic as many as 80 percent of the judges in the BGH, Germany's highest appellate court, had

served in the judiciary or as state officials during the Third Reich" (175), which is a shocking and sobering statistic.

11. The trial was further complicated when the German Literature Archive in Marbach took on Israeli lawyers in order to make a case that they should have the cultural right to Kafka's work, because he wrote in German. Butler believed that either outcome of the trial would have problematic consequences: if Israel kept the archives, they would further strengthen their spurious claim as the rightful owner of Jewish cultural and literary production; if Germany won, they would show how nationality is predicated exclusively on language (since Kafka's work would belong in Germany simply because he wrote in German) ("Who Owns Kafka?" np). Frustratingly, in August 2016, Israel won the court case, with the Supreme Court deciding that the documents belonged in the National Library. The decision read, in part, that "Max Brod did not want his property to be sold at the best price, but for them to find an appropriate place in a literary and cultural institution," by which they meant an Israeli one ("Franz Kafka Literary Legal Battle Ends" np). For a book-length exploration of the trial, the prior trials that led to the Supreme Court one, the personalities involved, as well as biographical sketches of Kafka, Brod, and others, see the 2018 *Kafka's Last Trial: The Case of a Literary Legacy* by Benjamin Balint. Balint reveals that it was the same handwriting expert who examined Brod's handwriting who examined Demjanjuk's ID card (196). While critical of most of the actors in the drama around Kafka's papers, Balint does write about how the trial in Israel "threw into stark relief the country's ambivalence toward Diaspora culture. Throughout the trial, Israel acted as though it can lay claim to any pre-state Jewish cultural artefact, as though everything Jewish finds its culmination in the Jewish state, as though Jewish culture has been driven by a teleological thrust toward Jerusalem" (101–102).

12. Ziad, true to his paranoid nature, tells Philip that Shmuel works for the Mossad. "It isn't enough that Shin Bet corrodes our life here by buying an informer in every family," Ziad says, "It isn't enough to play the serpent like that with people already oppressed and, you would think, humiliated quite enough already. No, even the civil-rights lawyer must be a spy, even that they must corrupt" (146). Readers are never given any proof of Ziad's assertion.

13. For the two most nuanced takes on Philip's double, see the works of Debra Shostak and Timothy Parrish.

14. The two most troubling of these being Diasporism's joint assumptions that a Jewish collective living in Israel/Palestine could only and always lead to ethnic nationalism, and that Arab hatred of Jewish people is uniform, unexplainable, and unavoidable.

15. The bulk of readers' knowledge of Diasporism comes from two places in the novel: the article in a Hebrew newspaper that Aharon Appelfeld reads to Philip

over the phone (31–33), and Philip's own phone interview with Pipik, where he pretends to be the freelance French journalist Pierre Roget (39–48). Both of these exegeses take place in the early pages of the novel, before Philip leaves for Israel. Philip also gives a lengthy monologue on Diasporism when he pretends to be Pipik to both the Ziads (155–162) and to Gal, the soldier (168–171).

16. As Pipik tells Philip-as-Pierre-Roget: "Zionism undertook to restore Jewish life and the Hebrew language to a place where neither had existed with any real vitality for nearly two millennia. Diasporism's dream is more modest: a mere half-century is all that separates us from what Hitler destroyed. If Jewish resources could realize the seemingly fantastic goals of Zionism in even less than fifty years, now that Zionism is counterproductive and itself the foremost Jewish problem, I have no doubt that the resources of world Jewry can realize the goals of Diasporism in half, if not even one tenth, the time" (44). There is nothing untrue in this statement, showing not only how surprising Zionism's actual success was, but that a movement that wishes to undo Zionism's worst trespasses—not necessarily Diasporism—has a chance of success, however improbable.

17. It is an open secret that Israel has nuclear weapons, contrary to international law.

18. According to Rashid Khalidi, "The Palestinian people, facing as before an array of forces stronger than they, have also once again been victimized by poor leadership when they most needed to make the right choices" (The Iron Cage xiv). This should not excuse Israel from its role in oppressing the Palestinians.

19. It is interesting to compare Pipik with Ziad's more empathetic take on Mizrahi Jews: "Sephardic boys…Moroccans. The Ashkenazis prefer to keep their hands clean. They get their darker brethren to do their torturing for them. The ignorant Arab haters from the Orient furnish the refined Ashkenazis with a very useful, all-purpose proletarian mob. Of course when they lived in Morocco they didn't hate Arabs. They lived harmoniously with Arabs for a thousand years. But the white Israelis have taught them that, too—how to hate the Arabs and how to hate themselves. The white Israelis have turned them into their thugs" (139).

20. Pipik pushes the satire even further: "And what a historic day for Europe, for Jewry, for all mankind when the cattle cars that transported Jews to death camps are transformed by the Diasporist movement into decent, comfortable railway carriages carrying Jews by the tens of thousands back to their native cities and towns" (45). As if a Jewish return to Poland could erase the horrors of the Shoah. Whatever happens next in the Jewish narrative, whatever the coming reshuffling of Jewish geography, the Shoah will—and should—loom, just as the injustices of the Jewish attempt at a state should remain a fixture in the Jewish cultural memory.

21. Dickstein goes on to say that he does not take Diasporism seriously because "Philip Roth doesn't propose it seriously," saying that it is simply "an apologia for the secular, assimilated American Jew" (np).

22. In a terribly ironic twist of history, the supposed homecoming of the Jewish diaspora had the effect of engendering a *new* diaspora, the Palestinian one. According to William Safran, "In several respects, the Palestinian diaspora resembles the Jewish and Armenian ones" (87). Safran writes that "the physical fact of a growing Palestinian diaspora and a collective diaspora consciousness cannot be denied; and while that consciousness may be diluted in the case of relatively prosperous Palestinians who have settled in Western countries, it is strongly perpetuated among the children of refugees and expellees" (88). Likewise, Robin Cohen writes that the "midwife" of "The 3.9 million-strong Palestinian diaspora" was "the homecoming of the Jewish diaspora" (3–4). Though I disagree with the conceptualization of the birth of Israel as a "homecoming," Cohen's point about the emergence of the Palestinian diaspora is nonetheless a valid one.

23. In the *Tikkun* round-table, Daphne Merkin takes umbrage at the conflation of Jewishness with Zabar's: knishes at Zabar's, she writes, no longer "speak to our current sense of things" (np). She continues: "The vexed issue of assimilationist, proto-ethnic Jewish identity has undergone changes since the glory days of Lenny Bruce and Catskill hotels, although you wouldn't know it by reading *Operation Shylock*." Merkin feels similarly about Roth's presentation of Israel: "there is still little of the Israel I know that is recognizable in these pages, despite the carefully transliterated Hebrew phrases, just as neither Israeli nor American Jewry seem true-to-contemporary-life" (np). Somewhat counter to the above reading, Merkin goes on to state: "If I were living in Israel—if I were my sister, say, who lives in Jerusalem with her American husband and four American-born children despite ongoing doubts and criticism—I would despise this book. As someone whose emotional investment is safely tallied from these shores I merely dislike it" (np).

24. Abunimah believes that "The ideological collapse of the two-state solution leaves no alternative but to shift our discourse and practice toward democratic and decolonizing alternatives" (*Battle for Justice* 47). "There has never been a more opportune moment for Palestinians to put forward their demands for decolonization, equality, and justice in clear, principled, visionary, and inclusive terms," he writes (234).

25. Omer-Sherman is referring in particular to Philip's spying, not the chapter excision per se. Besides this pithy statement, he does not have much else to say about the missing chapter, except to call the novel's ending "hastily contrived" (233).

26. The epilogue opens with Philip's extended musings on the excised chapter, and ends with the long final scene detailing Philip's meeting with Smilesburger at an Upper West Side deli, where Smilesburger implores Philip—through a number of different rhetorical strategies—to cut the eleventh chapter. The rest of the epilogue is taken up with Philip's imagined scenario of receiving a letter from Jinx, and his epistolary response (this part of the ending bears a striking resemblance to the ending of The Counterlife, where Nathan and his British wife Maria exchange fictional letters).

27. According to Shostak, Roth's papers reveal that Roth had numerous working titles for the novel, including "'Split,' 'Duality,' 'The Other One,' 'You Are Not Yourself,' 'Cured of Myself,' 'A Life Not My Own: A Fable,' 'Haunted,' 'Schizo: The Autobiography of an Antithesis,' and, alternatively, 'Against Itself: The Autobiography of an Antithesis'" (728). That he went with Operation Shylock suggests that Roth decided to place the spy mission on a higher thematic ground than Philip's battle with Pipik.

28. Smilesburger "would like to know the names that are signed on those checks. I would like to have a chance to talk to these people and to ask what they think they are doing. But first I must find out if they truly exist other than in the hate-filled imagination of this mischievous friend of yours, so bursting with troublemaking ticks and lies. I never know whether George Ziad is completely crazy, completely devious, or completely both" (342).

29. David Biale, writing ten years after Pollard was sentenced, writes that, for progressive Jews, "the case of Jonathan Pollard evokes the kind of moral ambiguity that makes us much more uneasy than confident." Biale believes that "Whatever one might think of Pollard, Israel's behavior toward him since his arrest has been nothing short of shameful" and that "Unfortunately Pollard has become a poster boy for the right-wing settler movement and their U.S. supporters," calling the settlers' championing of Pollard's cause—as well as Pollard's actions themselves—a "brew of ideological hubris" (np). In November 2015, Pollard was released on parole after serving thirty years in prison (Baker and Rudoren np).

30. The foreshadowing is even more forceful: when listening to Ziad rail against Israel, Philip "studied him with the coldhearted fascination and intense excitement of a well-placed spy" (129). Later, at the Ramallah military court, Philip wonders if Ziad is a collaborator: "He's an Israeli spy—and who he is spying on is me...No, he's a spy for the PLO. No, he's a spy for no one. No one's a spy. I'm the spy!" (149).

31. Fascinatingly, as Gerard O'Donoghue relates in his analysis of the setting of the Hebrew school in Roth's work, Operation Shylock was actually conceived as the final book in Roth's loose tetralogy of books that straddle the divide between

fiction and autobiography. The other three books in the tetralogy are *The Facts: A Novelist's Autobiography* (1988), *Deception* (1990), and *Patrimony* (1991), which is about the death of Roth's father and is the closest to true memoir in all of Roth's oeuvre. According to O'Donoghue, "Despite a remarkable variety of subject matter and tone, the working papers for these books and *Operation Shylock* demonstrate that Roth conceived of them as a coherent work, what he tentatively envisioned as 'An Autobiography in Four Acts'" (161). Roth's engagement with the boundaries of autobiography in this phase of his career shows how cognizant he is of the dangerous slippages possible between character and author.

32. A glaring example of this slippage in the scholarship occurs when Idit Alphandary writes that "The real Philip Roth is a Zionist" (59), leaving it unclear who exactly she means (and either way, it is an unproven statement). Likewise, O'Donoghue writes that he is going to "leave the ambiguity of whether we are talking Philip Roth the author, or Philip Roth the character hanging in the air, where it ought to remain suspended" (155).

33. Budick goes further in her discussion of *The Counterlife*, writing that she took "offense at *The Counterlife* when it first came out. It seemed to me indelicate, to say the least, and perhaps even endangering to me and my family personally living in Israel, for Roth to use the dire political reality of Israel in order to play frivolous postmodernist games with Jewish identity" (72). This statement of offense raises an important question: if agitating against the more horrendous consequences of an ethnically based national ideology really endangers the people living in the state founded by that ideology, does that not speak to the precarious nature of the ideology and its state more so than it does to the author's frivolity? (And if the postmodern games *are* frivolous, then why take offense?) Budick works past her initial offense by staging a reading of the novel that centres on what she sees as Roth's belief that "Israel was a reality for which people gave their lives" (72).

34. I don't have the space here to explore the confessional issues at play in *Shylock*. The novel is subtitled "A Confession," and is purported to be nonfiction by both Philip and Roth, yet it ends with the disclaimer that "This confession is false" (399). According to Alan Cooper, "When review copies were being sent out in January and February 1993, Simon & Schuster kept changing the designated review categories from fiction to nonfiction and back again to fiction, and reports from within the walls of the publisher had a frenzied Roth haunting the precincts with changes and expressions of anxiety" (qtd. in Kaplan, *Jewish Anxiety* 65). For more on the issues of confession, nonfiction, and fiction in the novel, see Alphandary.

35. A possible reading of both of these moments is through the symbolism of circumcision. At the end of *The Counterlife*, Zuckerman has a long passage on

how he will circumcise his unborn son, claiming circumcision as a marker of the original loss that is Jewishness. Philip himself, when mulling over what to do with the eleventh chapter, thinks that he should—since he is now labelling (according to him, mislabelling) the book as fiction—"Publish the manuscript uncut" (361), a word with deep ties to circumcision. In this reading, both Henry and Philip are declaring their fidelity to the Jewish collective through the ritualistic circumcision of fiction.

36.   As Shostak informs us, "among Roth's manuscripts and notes currently on deposit at the Library of Congress, there is no trace of a deleted chapter, certainly nothing like the 'twelve thousand words' (357) the narrator claims here" (747). Shostak rightly points out that this does not necessarily mean the eleventh chapter was never written, though for our purposes here the excision of the chapter is the chief concern, not its existence outside of the text.

37.   Significantly, Kaplan writes that "there is a dialogic openness about Roth's work; and in this very openness (ironically given how harshly raked over the coals Roth has been for not always portraying Jews in a positive light), some scholars have identified a Jewish/Talmudic sensibility, the rabbis arguing with each other over the centuries as a model for how ultimately unanswerable the questions he raises resolutely remain" (8). This dovetails well with my diasporic heteroglossic reading of Roth, and its similarities to Talmudic hermeneutics.

2 | Herzl Meets Uris

1.   With Herzl and Altneuland, I depart from the national boundaries of Canada and the United States that I set up as the scope for this book. I do this for a number of reasons. First, including Altneuland reinforces my commitment to diaspora over nation. Second, Altneuland's importance for my project—a novel imagining a Jewish state in Palestine—helps reveal what is at stake in Jewish diasporic fiction on Israel. Third, the comparison between Altneuland and Exodus garnered some surprising results, and not including them here because of artificial national boundaries did not make much sense to me.

2.   Nur Masalha's The Bible and Zionism: Invented Traditions, Archaeology and Post-Colonialism in Israel-Palestine is an excellent book-length study of how the Bible has been used by Zionists—both Jewish and Christian—to justify the Jewish colonization of the Holy Land. In particular, Masalha explicates how biblical archaeology has been deployed by the Israeli state and its academic institutions to "de-emphasize the Arab and Muslim connection to the land, to foster Jewish nationalism and state-building, and to legitimize the dispossession of the

indigenous inhabitants of Palestine" (4). Likewise, Yehouda Shenhav, in his important *Beyond the Two State Solution: A Jewish Political Essay*, shows how thinking on the Israel/Palestine situation is often framed temporally. Shenhav's explication of "1967" time shows how the Zionist discourse pivots on the 1967 borders, effectively erasing the realities of "1948 time."

3. All of *Altneuland's* critics agree that it is a utopia. For example, Stolow writes: "Taken on its own, *Altneuland* falls rather unproblematically in that genre of nineteenth century utopian literature" (57). Or, as Shlomo Avineri puts it: "Like all utopian novels, this is a didactic and slightly boring work that contains long speeches and descriptions of social institutions that, of course, weigh down on the plot" (np).

4. According to Chowers, the Nietzschean strand within Zionism focuses on individual, secularist redemption in the face of the decline of the hegemony of Jewish religion and tradition, where the Marxist–socialist strand believes that there is no economic or social space in Europe for the Jews, and so they therefore need a total territorial and economical transformation. Chowers concludes: "We may say, then, that Zionism involved a singular mixture of Nietzschean and Marxian themes; its success depended on both a metamorphosis and conscious reshaping of the self, and the inauguration of new economic and social conditions" (665).

5. A heteroglossic sense of time is diasporic to the core: lacking national time; open; constantly fructifying difference; and aware that history, from the viewpoint of those who have lived it, is anything but certain.

6. Masalha goes on to argue: "Contrary to the archaeological and historical evidence, the view that the Bible provides Jews with a title deed to the 'whole land of Israel' and morally legitimises the creation of the State of Israel and its 'ethnic cleansing' policies towards the native Palestinians is still pervasive in Jewish Zionist circles" (24).

7. The main reason Professor Steineck and his team are trying to eradicate malaria is for the "opening up of Africa" (169). According to the professor during the tour of his laboratory, "The white colonist goes under in Africa. That country can be opened up to civilization only after malaria has been subdued. Only then will enormous areas become available for the surplus populations of Europe. And only then will the proletarian masses find a healthy outlet" (170). Most important, in regard to this rather amazing endorsement of resource extraction and economic warfare, is the simple fact that Herzl did not shy away from his belief that colonization is a universal good, and exactly what the Zionists were attempting in Palestine.

8. Uris has a character who operates in a similar vein as Alladino: Joab Yarkoni, a Moroccan Jew with "intimate knowledge of the Arab countries" (37). Among

other exploits, Yarkoni smuggles one hundred date palm saplings from Iraq into Palestine. For his part, Alladino is far more successful in buying Palestinian land than the historical Zionists were; on the eve of the 1948 War, only 6% of the land was owned by the Jewish community in Palestine (Masalha 5). The place of Arab Jews in Israel and Jewish diasporic fiction will be addressed at length in chapter 3.

9.   As Bernstein discusses, he developed his theory of backshadowing based on the work of Gary Saul Morson, who originally coined the term "sideshadowing" (xi).

10. Much of Bernstein's monograph critiques the backshadowing present throughout the fiction of Shoah survivor and Israeli novelist Aharon Appelfeld.

11. Uris also engages in backshadowing that is not directly linked to the Shoah. In the Barak/Akiva history narrative, readers are introduced to Herzl thusly: "But as Yakov and Jossi lived in apparent aimlessness in Palestine, dramatic events were taking place in another part of the world which were to shape their destiny and the destiny of every Jew for all time" (219). These "dramatic events" refer to Herzl's conversion to Zionism. Uris's novel makes it seem unavoidable that Herzl would become a Zionist and have the profound effect on Jewish history that he has had. At times, Uris's narrator hides this historical certainty around Herzl in the form of rhetorical questions: "What had brought him to Paris, really? What unseen hand guided him into that courtyard on that winter's day? Why Herzl? He did not live or think as a devout Jew, yet when he heard the mobs beyond the wall shout, 'Death to the Jews!' his life and the life of every Jew was changed forever" (221). Continuing to tie the events of early Zionism in with the biblical sweep of Jewish history, the narrator tells us that "Nothing like" the First Zionist Congress "had happened since the second Temple had been destroyed" (221). Remarkably, in Uris's narrative of Herzl, he leaves out the writing of Altneuland. It seems the Herzl of Uris's imagination did not waste time writing fiction. In any case, the "unseen hand" that turns Herzl into a Zionist is the unseen hand of Jewish history as Uris conceptualizes it, moving people, places, countries, and armies into place for the glorious transcendence of the Jewish state.

12. For a fascinating look at the history of the word Holocaust to describe the Nazi genocide, see Steve Friess's "When 'Holocaust' Became 'The Holocaust'" in The New Republic.

13. Or, as Bernstein eloquently puts it: "Just as the first Christians condemned the Jews for having seen the Savior, witnessed his miracles, and still choosing to reject him, so the contempt of writers projecting backward from their knowledge of the Shoah convicts all those who failed to heed the initial signs of Nazism's reign. It is as though the Jews, initially cursed for not recognizing the Messiah, are now to be scorned again, two millenia later, for having failed to recognize the anti-Christ" (34).

14. Salt reads contemporaneous nineteenth-century travel logs, often by "clergymen with no sympathy for Islam" (56), to see if Uris's picture of a "denuded and neglected land" carries any truth (56). After looking at the writings of W.F. Lynch, J.L. Porter, J.M. Thomson, and John Lloyd Stephens, Salt concludes: "They certainly found poverty and neglect, but they also write of a beautiful, fertile, and, in places, intensely cultivated land" (56). Stephens, in particular, Salt writes, sees a land flush with blooming growth, prosperous villages, and oceans of wheat.

15. For a look at Herzl's travels in search of a deal for Jewish colonization in Palestine, see Desmond Stewart's "Herzl's Journeys in Palestine and Egypt." Also see Amos Elon's Herzl for the standard biographical take on Herzl's life.

16. At the First Congress, the centrality of Palestine to Zionism was put into the Basel Program. At the Third Congress, Herzl rewrote the Jewish Colonial Trust to "restrict its tasks to Palestine" (Kornberg xi). At the Fourth Congress, Herzl was still able to continue avoiding the question of Hebrew and its place in the Zionist project; however, by the Fifth Congress, he had conceded. When Herzl brought the Uganda Plan to the Sixth Congress—put forward by the British, the Uganda Plan would have given the Jews a piece of colonial Kenya for Jewish immigration—the Zionist movement was almost torn in half; it was Herzl's personal charisma that kept it together, though the plan, which had passed by a slim margin, was forgotten.

17. For the history of Jewish utopias, from the Jewish Messianism of the seventh-century Book of Zerubbabel and onward, see Miriam Eliav-Feldon's "'If You Will It, It Is No Fairy Tale': The First Jewish Utopias."

18. For a scholarly look into the debate between Herzl and Ahad Ha'am, see Yossi Goldstein's "Eastern Jews vs. Western Jews: The Ahad Ha'am-Herzl Dispute and Its Cultural and Social Implications." For a recent discussion of the contemporary ramifications of the dispute, see Hillel Halkin's 2016 article in Mosaic, "What Ahad Ha'am Saw and Herzl Missed—And Vice Versa," as well as the published responses. Halkin's article is a juicy read, detailing the major scandal that Ha'am's review of Altneuland—and Max Nordau's virulent response to it—created in the Zionist world. The divisions in the organized Jewish world, between Ha'am's cultural Zionism and Herzl's political Zionism, between Eastern European Jewry and Western (though, as Halkin explicates, these were not as clearly demarcated as Goldstein believes), bubbling under the surface since the First Zionist Congress, exploded. The article also narrates another scandal: the Sixth Zionist Congress, where Herzl put forward the infamous "Uganda Plan."

19. The filmic version of Exodus, like the novel, had an enormous impact on diasporic views of Israel/Palestine. At the same time, the film reveals several

tensions between Uris's and director Otto Preminger's view of Zionism and the Jewish diaspora. As Silver explains, Preminger, who had a successful life in Vienna before immigrating to America in 1935, "was unlikely to embrace the Zionist attitude of unyielding criticism of Jewish Diaspora life that laced through Uris's text" (74). Nonetheless, *Exodus* the film still played a significant role in mainstreaming Zionism, especially through its particularly American embrace of Israel. For more on Preminger's film, see Silver's book, Weissbrod's article, or Stephen J. Whitfield's "Israel as Reel: The Depiction of Israel in Mainstream American Films."

20. Throughout the scholarly discourse on Uris and *Exodus*, the only mention of Sahwell's booklet I came across is in Nadel's biography, yet even there, he does not offer a reading of the text.

21. In Nathaniel Rich's *The New York Review of Books* review of Roth's 2018 collection of nonfiction, Rich, discussing our contemporary political moment, wrote: "Readers and critics, distraught at the nihilism of the current political nightmare, have sought comfort in fiction that affirms their principles and beliefs, fiction in which victimized peoples rise triumphant. They desire a new *Exodus*, new Leon Urises. And they will get them. But we should hope for something more. We should hope for new Philip Roths" (np). While I agree with much of this sentiment (as evinced in the previous chapter on Roth and *Operation Shylock*), I am unclear as to who the "they" are that Rich seems to have pinned down so cleanly.

22. *Black Panther* is not the only Marvel film that is of interest to the concerns of this book. *Thor: Ragnarok*, written and directed by the Jewish Maori filmmaker Taika Waititi, is a fascinating exploration of ethnic cleansing, of the possibility of surviving without a home, and of diaspora. When Thor's homeworld of Asgard gets destroyed, its inhabitants left stranded on a spacecraft, Thor emphatically states that "Asgard is a people, not a place." It would not be a stretch to say that this is Waititi acknowledging the Jewish, and diasporic, aspects of his identity.

23. In the following two chapters, I will show how the number of speaking Arab characters in the texts under study diminish into nonexistence. Why this occurs will be a running question.

24. Avineri writes: "The land belongs exclusively to the Jews, argues Geyer, and he establishes a political party whose platform calls for denying the Arabs the right to vote. This is not a report on Israel circa 2002; these words were written 100 years ago" (np). This interpretation of Geyer's platform is a massive stretch: nowhere in the text does Geyer, or any of his representatives, mention the Arabs or their right to vote.

25. Gluzman reads Friedrich and Kingscourt's relationship as a homoerotic one, which gets replaced by a "dormant heterosexual desire" once they arrive in

the New Society (99). "As the plot unfolds," Gluzman writes, "land and woman become entirely enmeshed in Friedrich's imagination: his budding desire to be a useful member of the New Society and his nascent heterosexual desire for Miriam are linked time and again" (99). Gluzman unearths a hidden paradox at play in *Altneuland*: that Herzl's Zionism, as espoused in the novel, is supposed to cure Jewish diasporic femininity, but at the same time result in equality of the sexes.

26. Significantly, we are told that before Sarah married David, she was part of the "radical opposition," which must mean Dr. Geyer's party. Is Herzl suggesting that women would not necessarily choose the correct, liberal universal mindset—perhaps because of their lack of rationality? Though David proudly states that women "have active and passive suffrage as a matter of course" (75), he also claims that Sarah has forgotten "a bit about her inalienable rights" and that she no longer goes to political meetings (75). Sarah seems to agree with her husband, telling Friedrich and Kingscourt: "If my husband wished it, I should live just as Fatma does and think no more about it" (97). Uris also includes this kind of conservative gender dynamic in *Exodus*, with the narrator writing that "Many women who fought for their independence" in the kibbutz movement "didn't like it once they had it" (257).

27. It is worth quoting Gluzman's thoughts on Fatima further: "The Arab woman is nothing but a floating hand waving silently goodbye, cut off from the body that it represents synecdochically. Her total absence—seeing but not seen—and absolute passivity are manifested also by lack of voice: she does not greet but is rather greeted; she does not utter a word but serves as an invisible receptacle to the greetings sent to her from afar. But is the difference between the Jewish woman and Arab woman as significant as it first appears?" (109).

28. Ahad Ha'am had a similar question in his own review of *Altneuland*: "How... could the New Society obtain sufficient land for Jews from all over the world if the arable land that previously belonged to the Arabs remained in their hands as before?" he asks (qtd. in Rose 89).

29. Penslar explains that "Herzl himself paid but little heed to Arabs during his 1898 visit to Palestine, but he was made aware of the spectre of Arab as well as Ottoman opposition to Zionism from a brief exchange of letters in 1899 with Youssuf Zia al-Khalidi, a former mayor of Jerusalem and veteran senior Ottoman bureaucrat" (52). Writing with regard to *Altneuland*, Penslar points out: "The consensus among pro-Zionist historians is that Herzl, speaking through Bey, intended there to be a substantial Arab presence in the future Jewish state, which would both include Arabs as equals in civil society and respect their religious culture" (53). As we have seen, Avineri would agree with this stance; Khalidi would not; and critics such as Zilbersheid would seem to have no opinion.

30. Passages such as these, even if they were written merely to appease Herzl's critics, certainly help refute the claim that *Altneuland* is not a Jewish text.

31. Significantly, the third temple is only one of the major buildings Herzl includes in *Altneuland*. Others include the Jewish Academy, modelled after the French Academy, and the Peace Palace, "an international center for great undertakings," its programs and activities by "no means limited to Palestine and the Jews, but includ[ing] all countries and all peoples" (249). Together, these three buildings represent the religious, intellectual, and humanist aspects of the Zionist rebirth Herzl hoped for.

32. The desire to rebuild the temple appears elsewhere in diasporic Jewish fiction. A major plotline in Michael Chabon's alternate history *The Yiddish Policemen's Union*, for example, involves a radical religious Jewish sect who wants to blow up the Dome of the Rock and build the third temple. Also see Tova Reich's *The Jewish War*.

33. See the work of journalist David Sheen on the religious leaders, politicians, and military personnel involved in agitating for the destruction of the Dome of the Rock and the building of the third temple.

34. The populations of the Jews living in the Yishuv compared to all of the Arab countries combined is a repeated motif for Uris, which he uses to prove the miraculous nature of the state's survival. Near the end of the book, during the 1948 War, the narrator asks rhetorically: "Could a half million ill-armed people hold back a flood of fifty million hate-crazed Arabs? They would not only have to face the Arabs inside Palestine, all around them on a hundred fronts, but the regular national armies as well" (466).

35. For the most part, Uris does not distinguish between Christian and Muslim Arabs, unless it is to further disparage Muslim Arabs.

36. BDS, as a movement to exert financial and cultural pressure on the Israeli state, is one of the most important contemporary elements in the Palestinian struggle for justice. Launched in 2005 by more than 170 Palestinian civil society groups, BDS is modelled on the South African anti-apartheid struggle, and "urges nonviolent pressure on Israel until it complies with international law by meeting three demands": ending its occupation and colonization of all Arab lands; recognizing the fundamental rights of Palestinians; and allowing the return of Palestinian refugees ("What is BDS?" nd).

37. Kitty makes a direct comparison to Jewish and Arabic children: "Once a week Kitty went down to Abu Yesha with the doctor to hold morning clinic for the Arabs. How pathetic the dirty little Arab children were beside the robust youngsters of Gan Dafna. How futile their lives seemed in contrast to the spirit of the Youth Aliyah village. There seemed to be no laughter or songs or games or purpose among the Arab children. It was a static existence—a new generation

born on an eternal caravan in an endless desert. Her stomach turned over as she entered the one-room hovels shared with chickens, dogs, and donkeys. Eight or ten people on the same earth floor" (348). Part of Kitty's burgeoning Zionism is her disgust at the Indigenous Palestinians.

38. Akiva, Barak's brother, is one of the founders of the underground Maccabees, a paramilitary organization based on both the Irgun and the Stern Gang, which Uris combines. The novel, while making space for discussions of different Zionist tactics—including the terrorist bombing of the King David Hotel—and while Akiva's embrace of confrontational violence leads to his and Barak's estrangement, comes down on the side of Akiva.

39. The film version of *Exodus* handles the connection between the Nazis and Palestinians somewhat differently. In the film, actual, literal Nazis are in Palestine pushing the Palestinian leadership, represented by Taha, to kill the Jews. Taha vacillates, but decides to not cooperate with the Nazis. This difference in representation comes down to the differing worldviews of Uris and Preminger.

40. From al-Husseini's election as mufti in 1921, to the 1929 Arab Revolt, to al-Husseini's actions during World War II and the War of Independence, Pappé tells a nuanced story, a much-needed antidote to Uris's one-sided demonization of the mufti. The mufti was stuck in a complex historical situation, with the British on one side and the Zionists on the other. Pappé shows how al-Husseini's friendship with the Nazis, while not excusable, came from these historical circumstances. Al-Husseini had lost his place of power by the end of the revolt. According to Pappé, "the Palestinian political elite as a whole ceased to play a significant role in Palestine's destiny" (301). Netanyahu and other prominent Zionists still present a picture of the mufti virtually unchanged from Uris's version; in a 2015 speech at the World Zionist Congress, Natanyahu went so far as to make the mendacious claim that it was al-Husseini who had given Hitler the idea for the final solution. This claim has been widely critiqued. As historian Christopher R. Browning puts it, "Netanyahu's latest lie is part of a persistent campaign to portray the grand mufti as a major Holocaust perpetrator. It's not true" (np).

41. In Elia Zureik's review of the novel, he writes that "what emerges from the book is a highly vindictive and historically distorted account of the conflict in which history has been abused beyond recognition and used as a tool on which to hang an elaborate edifice of hate. The book reveals very little about either Arabs or Jews, but much more about Leon Uris's distorted perception of the world" (118). As Salt puts it, "*The Haj* is a profoundly racist work not just because it reduces Arabs once again to a series of ugly stereotypes, but because it appears to be a conscious attempt to show that the culture of an entire people is rotten to the core" (61–62).

42. We never see Geyer directly—whose name, according to Avineri, is German for "vulture" (np)—only those who speak for him, such as Mendel, who Steineck and David debate at the Neudorf settlement. Significantly, Herzl describes Geyer as a rank opportunist, as a "rabbi of immediate advantage" (137). Apparently, before the creation of the New Society, Geyer was a vocal anti-Zionist: "He and his ilk invented the myth of the Jewish mission. The function of the Jewish people was asserted to be to instruct the other peoples. Therefore, they alleged, we must live in the dispersion...And Zion was not Zion!" (138). In other words, before migrating to Palestine and becoming a xenophobic ethnic nationalist, Geyer was, of all things, a defender of diaspora! (Among other things, Herzl is satirizing the Reform movement position here.) In this way, Herzl attempts to delegitimize diaspora consciousness at the same time as xenophobia, by joining them together in Geyer. Surprisingly, Gluzman, Khalidi, Stolow, and Zilbersheid—who offer four otherwise important and productive readings of Altneuland—do not address how the Geyer faction and its failed electoral bid complicate their readings of the novel.

3 | Arab Jews, Polycentric Diasporas, Porous Borders

1. Even the title, The Best Place on Earth, points to the importance of Jewish geography in Tsabari's work. The title, which is taken from the old British Columbia license plates, where the eponymous story takes place, also can be seen as posing a question: is Israel the best place on earth?
2. Two of the stories are about Israeli Jews flying to Canada to visit their relatives (in "The Best Place on Earth," Naomi visits her sister Tamar on a BC gulf island, in "Brit Milah," an older Yemeni Jewish woman from Tel Aviv visits her daughter in Toronto) and one is about an Israeli visiting their relatives in Israel ("Below Sea Level," where David, who lives in Montreal with his girlfriend, visits his ex-general father in the Dead Sea region of Israel).
3. See Tsabari's website at ayelettsabari.com/about.
4. See my review of the memoir. Comparing Tsabari's fiction with her nonfiction reveals some interesting differences between the two genres. Even though both The Best Place on Earth and The Art of Leaving cast a wide geographical net, set in Israel, India, and North America, in The Art of Leaving Tsabari narrows her lens in certain ways; Tsabari's fiction seems more attuned to the larger political situation of Israel/Palestine. For example, in a chapter in the memoir where Tsabari is mourning the loss of her childhood home, which her mother decided to sell and which is being demolished, there is no sense that just a few miles

away, Palestinian homes are also being destroyed, but without their owners' consent. This is something that would not escape the gaze of Tsabari's fictional narrator.

5. For a reading of this story where I use Sara Ahmed's theorizations of affect and Talal Asad's incisive investigations into the ideological uses of terror and suicide violence, see my chapter in the collection *All the Feels*.

6. This is, of course, partly due to the constraints I've put on this book. The fact remains, though, that Tsabari is a Canadian writer with extensive knowledge of Israel.

7. There is some debate about which is a better umbrella term for this diverse population. Smadar Lavie uses the term Mizrahi (plural Mizrahim) because this was the term forced on the new immigrants, and one that, starting in the 1980s, was reclaimed by Arab Jewish intellectuals and imbued with political agency. As Lavie points out, however, "Most non-Yiddish-speaking Jews originating in Asia and Africa refer to themselves with a designation of their family's country of origin" (1). Shenhav prefers the phrase Arab Jews, because, as he puts it, the phrase "challenges the binary opposition between Arabs and Jews in Zionist discourse, a dichotomy that renders the linking of Arabs and Jews in this way inconceivable" (*The Arab Jews* xi). Ella Shohat, on the other hand, uses the term Sephardim, highlighting the origin point of medieval Spain (but seemingly ignoring those Arab Jews who do not originate from the Iberian Peninsula). Without making a claim for the supremacy of one term or the other, but with the aims of this chapter in mind, I will use "Arab Jews" throughout this book, unless the scholar I am discussing has a different preferred term.

8. One of the most significant scholars of Arab Jewish issues, Shohat's monumental 1988 article "Sephardim in Israel: Zionism from the Standpoint of its Arab Jewish Victims" (notice its obvious allusion to Edward Said's famous title) was the first major intervention of Arab Jewish critique in English.

9. For a different reading of this exchange, one that deploys Sara Ahmed's concept of affective economies, see my essay on "Tikkun Olam" in *All the Feels*.

10. As the book's summary has it, "The once numerous and vital Jewish communities of Morocco, Algeria and Tunisia have disappeared, succumbing during the past century to the assimilating temptations of French culture, or, more recently, to the pressures of migration" (np). As if assimilating or migrating erases one's identity.

11. Ella Shohat brilliantly shows how so much of our global situation stems from 1492: the expulsion of the Muslims and Jews from the Iberian peninsula had a direct impact on the European colonization of North and South America. For Shohat, the *Reconquista* and the *Conquista* are two sides of the same colonial, Orientalist coin. Or, as she provocatively states, "The extension of a ready-made

ideological apparatus that crossed the Atlantic could be viewed as the beginning point for Orientalism in the Occident" ("Introduction" 15).

12. Writing about Iraqi and Egyptian Jewish writers who never let themselves be absorbed into the Zionist body, Levy shows how these authors ended up in what she calls a linguistic no-mans-land: "As historic subjects who fit neither the master narrative of Zionism nor that of Arab nationalism, their contributions to Modern Hebrew and Arabic literatures languish unrecognized, indeed virtually unknown" (67).

13. Shenhav's book also contains some personal reflections. One of the more striking of these is his recollection of his grandmother, who immigrated to Israel from Iraq in 1950, saying that "the uprooting of more than 100,000 Jews from Iraq in the 1950s, along with the erasure of their past, was a barbaric act" (*The Arab Jews* 7). It is not difficult to imagine one of the elderly characters in a Tsabari story saying something similar.

14. Throughout her book *False Prophets of Peace*, Israeli activist Honig-Parness absolutely excoriates Labour Zionism and its version of socialism: "The labor movement's version of socialism was a tool for implementing colonization rather than a means of creating a new social order. It demanded absolute subservience of all class interests and individual aspirations to the Zionist project" (10).

15. Significantly, the narrator is describing these women only to show us how the story's protagonist, Reuma, has moved away from these traditional Yemeni women. "Many years ago," the narrator writes, "Reuma had taken off the head scarf and learned how to drive; she even drove on Shabbat" (52). As usual with Tsabari, Reuma's decision to move "with the times" is put into both cultural context and cultural tension.

16. Apparently, a number of publishers did not accept *The Best Place on Earth* for publication because of its lack of focus on the Palestinian–Israeli conflict. According to Adams, Tsabari responded by arguing "that she was drawn to the schisms between Mizrahi…and Ashkenazi…because their divergent loyalties have been overshadowed or downplayed" (np). In any case, I do not necessarily agree that the stories do not focus on the "Palestinian–Israeli conflict." The very first story revolves around a suicide bombing, and as I discuss throughout this chapter, the animosity between Israeli Jews and Arabs is a constant subject of the stories. Moreover, what we learn from Tsabari is that Jewish diasporic literature on Israel/Palestine can include the Palestinian narrative without necessarily having Palestinian characters; this is the inverse of what we see in texts like *Exodus* and even *Altneuland*, where having Palestinian characters does not mean the novels are sympathetic, or even conscious of, the Palestinian point of view.

17. Shohat is careful to emphatically state that she is not attempting to equate Palestinian and Arab Jewish suffering. Obviously, Shohat writes, "Palestinians

are those most egregiously wronged by Zionism," but the point of interrogating the relationship between Arab Jews and Palestinians "is one of affinity and analogy rather than perfect identity of interests or experience" ("Sephardim in Israel" 75).

18. Lavie blames the Arab Jewish support for the Israeli right on "the foundational role" played by "the Zionist left political parties that established and maintained the intra-Jewish racial formations of Zionism" (22). For Lavie, Zionism is able to convince a percentage of Arab Jews to turn to ethnic nationalism because "While intra-Jewish racial formations divide Mizrahim and Ashkenazim, the theological binary classification of the world as Jews vs. Goyim…unites Mizrahim and Ashkenazim as Jewish citizens of Israel—the self-proclaimed homeland of all world Jewry in the midst of the Arab World" (22).

19. See Ella Shohat's article, "A Voyage to Toledo," on the conference, which she attended, for a personal reflection on the event.

20. This should not come as a surprise, seeing how the Yemeni Jewish diaspora is its own unique entity, as are the Iraqi Jewish, the Moroccan Jewish, the Libyan Jewish, the Syrian Jewish, the Iranian Jewish, and the Turkish Jewish diasporas.

21. Yemeni Jews were a part of the Zionist colonization of Palestine at this time, however. Shafir details in his book how Yemeni Jewish labour was used instead of Arab labour by the first aliyah immigrants. For more, see Shafir, chapter 4.

22. See Jews and Islamic Law in Early 20th-Century Yemen by Mark S. Wagner for a more objective look at how Jews were treated in Yemen.

23. The New York Times article also points out how child abduction and out-group adoption is a common practice in settler-colonial nations, citing Australia and the "Sixties Scoop" in Canada as examples.

24. The website www.edut-amram.org is a moving collection of testimonies from Yemenite and other Mizrahi families who have had their children abducted (The Yemenite, Mizrahi, and Balkan Children Affair).

25. Arie M. Dubnov, in his detailed review, writes that "Amit's book expounds the dialectical dynamic by which Zionism appropriated the cultural inheritance of the three cultures it sought to silence and negate, namely the 'Galutish' tradition of Jewish life in the Diaspora, the indigenous Palestinian culture, and that of the 'Oriental' Jews originating from Arab and Islamic countries…Furthermore, it reveals how often looting, confiscation, unlawful appropriation, and crude theft were conducted under the guise of cultural rescue, relief, and preservation" (93–94). Dubnov, while praising the book overall, takes issue with how Amit handles the "heirless" books from Shoah victims.

26. Tsabari foreshadows the plot of "Invisible" when, in the earlier "Brit Milah," Reuma tells her daughter Ofra that she is getting old, and that "Soon you'll have

to hire me a Filipina, or maybe put me in a home" (48). This is a possibility of the genre of the short-story collection that Tsabari utilizes to excellent effect: the ability to mention a situation, a problem, a setting, a relationship dynamic, in one story, and then have it appear as a central aspect in another story. (This is only heightened in a collection that has recurring characters.) The overall effect is one of capaciousness, thoroughness, and the author's ability to create a fully realized and dynamic world, and has a similar affect as diasporic heteroglossia.

27. In the same year, Saudi Arabia had 406,089 Filipino workers, the UAE had 227,076, Taiwan had 62,598, and America had 17,234 (Gavilan np).

28. Parreñas explains that: "The outflow of women from the Philippines represents one of the largest and widest flows of contemporary female migration. As the quintessential service workers of globalization, Filipino women provide entertainment, childcare, elderly care, and companionship to men and families around the world" (1133).

29. Though, as Parreñas puts it, "The Philippine government is caught in a deleterious situation: it deploys workers around the world to generate foreign currency while it simultaneously lacks strength to protect citizens working in richer nations. Although international rights codes may declare the rights of transnational citizens, the fate of migrant Filipina domestic workers is for the most part dependent on the receiving nation-state" (1138).

30. For a look at how this operates in an American context, see *Empire of Care: Nursing and Migration in Filipino American History* by Catherina Ceniza Choy; for a list of studies done in particular national contexts, see Claudia Liebelt (75). For a general, descriptive history of foreign labour in Israel, see David V. Bartram, who analyzes the mass influx of low-level foreign workers after 1993, when Israel started replacing the "Traditional Palestinian labor force" (303). In Shmuel Amir's "Overseas Foreign Workers in Israel: Policy Aims and Labor Market Outcomes," Amir analyzes the residential construction industry, "in which most foreign workers are employed" (42), and investigates "the reasons for the failure of the governmental policy to reduce significantly the presence of foreign workers since 1996" (42). Finally, Liebelt's "On Gendered Journeys, Spiritual Transformations and Ethical Formations in Diaspora: Filipina Care Workers in Israel" is a fascinating anthropological study of Filipina care workers in Israel who maintain a spiritual dimension, through their Christianity, while working in Israel.

31. Filipinas are far from the only demographic currently facing the fear of expulsion in Israel. In recent years, African refugees, mainly from Eritrea and Sudan, have been faced with removal from Israel as well.

32. Weininger describes "Invisible" as Tsabari exploring the challenges of the situation of foreign workers in Israel "from the perspective of one of these

foreign workers, perhaps currently the most marginalized and invisible population within Israeli culture and society" (25). The "perhaps" in this sentence is doing a lot of work, and seems to exclude Palestinians and Arabs.

33. After the governmental campaign, the Filipino workers' union dissolved; according to Liebelt, it was after the union dissolved that churches became the prime sites of Filipina organization and resistance (76).

34. The relationship between Rosalynn and Savta is a common one in Israel. "The image of an elderly person resting on a Filipina's elbow," Liebelt writes, "as well as public parks and squares in Israel where the elderly sit in one corner chatting and their Filipina carers sit in another, became a recurrent motif not only of Israeli daily life but also of its films and arts" (76). This exact scene occurs almost verbatim in "Invisible," when Rosalynn, Savta, and Yaniv walk past "the elderly Yemenis, sitting in their wheelchairs with their Filipina caretakers in a parallel row on a park bench" (119), though Yaniv's presence confuses the Yemenis. This just shows how tuned in to the Israeli daily routine Tsabari is.

35. This is not the only place in the collection where Tsabari confronts the fallout of militarism in Israel. "The Poets in the Kitchen Window," "Casualties," "Below Sea Level," and "Warplanes" all reveal how the machismo, gender hierarchies, and violence of the ever-present army colour not only daily life in Israel, but the personalities and worldviews of anyone who grew up in the country.

36. The articles from Eraqi-Klorman and Ariel, spaced ten years apart, are an excellent introduction to the historical debate surrounding the Orphans' Decree. Eraqi-Klorman's article, in particular, is an excellent re-evaluation of the situation, and includes firsthand accounts from both Yemeni Jews and Muslims.

37. Ariel raises the important point that Yahya seems to have known about the existence of Jewish orphans who were being hidden in Sanaa and who escaped to Aden—and allowed it to continue.

38. Interestingly, the narrator mentions that the story of Savta's husband is her "favourite story, one she never tired of relating" (111). More so than her migration to Israel, Savta's husband is her origin story.

39. Several stories in the collection perform similar work of looking at how identity changes/adapts/splits when Israeli Jews of Arab background leave Israel. In "Brit Milah," a Yemeni mother visits her daughter and non-Jewish husband in Toronto, to find out they are not planning on circumcising their son; in "Below Sea Level," a son and his girlfriend travel from Montreal to visit his estranged father, a recently retired general, at his home near the Dead Sea; and, in "The Best Place On Earth," two sisters—one still living in Israel, the other on Hornby Island on BC's Gulf Coast—reunite in Canada.

40. *Flipping Out* is a sobering film. Director Yoav Shamir uses edits of army raids on Palestinians intercut with Israelis saying they did nothing wrong or immoral

during their army service to devastating effect. The racism of some of the Israeli tourists is also highlighted, with one Israeli, in a particularly egregious moment, after saying the Indians are "like Arabs" states that "They're children. Retarded children." Flipping Out is a damning portrayal of entitled ex-soldiers getting high in a foreign country, and those of them who end up having to face the consequences.

41. Besides the ex-soldiers, other Israelis also spend significant amounts of time in India, and constitute a diaspora in their own right. Around eighty thousand Israelis visit India every year (Lafontaine np). The most travelled route is apparently called "The Humus Trail," where signs are in Hebrew (and English) (Lafontaine np). An article called "The Karma Kosher: Far from Their Drugged-Out Image, Goan Israelis are the New Entrepreneurs," published in Outlook India, claims that "Things have changed among the Israelis of Anjuna, and markedly. The old, hard-to-die stereotypes of Israelis in Goa as a partied-out, drugged-out, loud and uncouth crowd is finally fading, with long-time Israeli residents, as well as new arrivals, upgrading their crafts and trades" (Ginsburg np). In "A Sign of Harmony," Maya rests somewhere in between the two poles of drugged-out escape and entrepreneurial expatriate.

42. Maya is not the only character in The Best Place on Earth who travels to India after the conclusion of their army service. Uri's sister Yasmin in "The Poets in the Kitchen Window" returns from a year and a half in India during the course of the story, showing up "clad in an Indian outfit," putting a poster of a guru named "Osho" on her bedroom wall, bearing the "sannyasi" name of "Tatagat," and filling the apartment with the smells of "Indian spices, brewed chai, and incense" (66, 73, 76, 72–73).

43. The fact that Maya disappoints her family by wanting to join the IDF is a neat inversion of the norm in Israel, where—for non-Orthodox Jews—enlisting in the army after high school is the expected, undeviating norm. Once again, Tsabari flips the script.

44. The narrator abstains from mentioning that Jaipur is in Rajasthan, which is where Ian's father's family is from. It would seem that Ian has no interest in exploring or reconnecting with the land of his father.

45. According to the Jewish Virtual Library, "The Yamit evacuation...was met with resistance by right-wing Jews, mostly followers of Rabbi Meir Kahane, who threatened to fight back against the IDF and even to blow themselves up if soldiers entered their bunkers" ("Israel-Egypt Relations"). Kahane himself flew to Yamit from Brooklyn to convince the settlers not to detonate any explosives. For a satirical re-enactment of the Yamit evacuation, see Tova Reich's The Jewish War, 112–121.

46. The recent Netflix miniseries *The Spy* is based on Cohen's life, and stars Sascha Baron Cohen.

47. The realization also allows a more nuanced understanding of Mira to click into place for Na'ama. Mira's constant moving from apartment to apartment after leaving the moshav, and her never staying with a man for more than a year all now make sense. Interestingly, Mira's post-Sinai life is framed as one of nomadism, directly paralleling the Bedouin lifestyle. Na'ama goes so far as to think of Mira as "the eternal nomad" (194). Nomadism, like diaspora, is another mode of life that is antithetical, and therefore dangerous, for the nation-state, which is not only another connection between Jews and Bedouins, but explains why one of the first things new nations do is force the nomadic populations under their control to stop moving and to settle.

48. The Israeli army regularly destroys Bedouin villages. According to the BBC, the United Nations considers "18 Bedouin communities" as being "at risk of forcible transfer because they are located in or next to an area near East Jerusalem slated by Israel for Jewish settlement construction" ("Khan al-Amar"). In any case, Na'ama would not be assigned to an active combat role unless she asked to be.

4 | "The Jewish Semitone"

1. From the vantage point of spring 2022, with the full-scale Russian invasion of Ukraine underway, this ever-changing situation in the FSU is even more pronounced.

2. For a discussion of the history of the refuseniks, see Remennick's *Russian Jews on Three Continents*, page 39.

3. Due to the makeup of the Israeli Knesset, coalition governments are the norm, often placing political parties with differing views—secular, religious, right or left wing—in the same ruling government.

4. Judging from this unnamed prime minister's politics, he is definitely not modelled on Benjamin Netanyahu, who was prime minister during Bezmozgis's writing of the book and at the time of its publication.

5. Bezmozgis often uses the minyan as a symbol for Jewish community. The final story in *Natasha*, entitled "Minyan," ends with a landlord in a Jewish old age home's speech on the importance of the minyan to Jewish continuity: "My concern is ten Jewish men. If you want ten Jewish saints, good luck...I don't put a Jew who comes to synagogue in the street. Homosexuals, murderers, liars, and thieves—I take them all. Without them we would never have a minyan" (147).

6. The desire in reviewers to place less significance on Israel/Palestine content in new North American Jewish fiction is an interesting phenomenon, which is perhaps best witnessed in the majority of reviews of Jonathan Safran Foer's 2016 novel *Here I Am*. See my review of the book for an attempted corrective to this oversight (*The Rusty Toque*).

7. A recent novel by Jewish American author Joshua Cohen, 2021's *The Netanyahus*, is a satiric portrait of Benzion as a middle-aged academic, and his boisterous family, including a child-aged Benjamin.

8. According to Remennick, "the current composition of the Israeli Russian-speaking community is a virtual blueprint of the enlarged Jewish population of the FSU, with some 15–20 percent of educated and well-adjusted professionals at the top and the majority coming from all possible regions, occupations, and walks of life typical of late Soviet society" (*Russian Jews* 48).

9. Significantly, the nearly 400,000 Jews that immigrated to the United States and Canada have been the "main source of demographic growth of North American Jewry" in recent memory (Remennick, *Russian Jews* 5).

10. Remennick's book is not to be confused with the other *Russian Jews on Three Continents: Migration and Resettlement*, which is edited by Noah Lewin-Epstein, Yaacov Ro'i, and Paul Ritterbrand, and is an earlier collection of essays dealing with Jewish Soviet emigration. The use of both titles reveals the significance of the Soviet Jewish diasporas in North America, Israel, and Europe.

11. As Remennick explains in her article "Former Soviet Jews in Their New/Old Homeland": "A unique feature of the Israeli case of ethnic return migration is the significant contribution that this migration makes to the ongoing nation-building process in the context of insecure borders, contested territories, security threats, the demographic realities, and an unstable economy. Whereas in most European and Asian countries the nation-building process is over and the rationale for ethnic return migration is mainly ideological and humanitarian (compensation for historic grievances or asylum) or economic (labor shortages), in Israel economic grounds, while certainly present, are less salient than the nation-building cause, with the ensuing high stakes invested in the immigrants" (209).

12. According to Fred A. Lazin in his book *The Struggle for Soviet Jewry in American Politics: Israel Versus the American Jewish Establishment*, in the 1970s and 1980s, most Soviet Jews wanted to immigrate to America, a reality Israel found hard to accept, considering how they had initiated the Soviet Jewry movement in America; nonetheless, by 1979, over 85% of "the potential repatriates to Israel 'dropped out,' in Israel terms, and 'defected' to the West" (Remennick, *Russian Jews* 39). When Gorbachev came into power, and over a million Soviet Jews were allowed to emigrate, Lazin explains, "More than 90 percent wanted to

go to the United States; few preferred Israel. This embarrassed and incensed the Israeli government. In practical terms, Israel would receive few if any Soviet Jews. Therefore, Israel wanted to block the entry of Soviet Jews into the United States" (11). Lazin's book is an informative investigation of the tensions and relationship between the organized American Jewish community and the Israeli government. As Lazin puts it, analyzing "the response of American Jewish leaders to the plight of Soviet Jewry from the late 1960s to 1989 provides important information about the political behavior, influence and style of a well-established minority group in the United States" (4). Significantly, Lazin shows that one of the reasons Israel tried to convince the American Jewish institutions to help siphon the Soviet Jews to Israel was that they would be "essential for Israel's continued existence emphasizing that past absorption of many uneducated and unskilled immigrants from Arab lands gave Israel the right to receive the highly educated and skilled Jews of the Soviet Union" (2). With the previous chapter in mind, we can see the Israeli government's racism toward its own Jewish population, a population it had a large hand in bringing into the country.

13. Remennick cites Mark Tolts, who estimates that in 2004, "the number of Russian Jews who left Israel and did not return for at least one year stood at 58,400" (*Russian Jews* 157–158).

14. One thing the 2022 Russian invasion of Ukraine revealed is the existence of stable, tight-knit Jewish communities, who, nonetheless, had to flee from Russian aggression.

15. That Kotler is nearly a double of Sharansky leads to a tantalizing question: does Natan Sharansky exist in the fictional world of *The Betrayers*? The text itself supplies no answers, but one would think that it is impossible, seeing what similar roles they occupy in the Jewish world.

16. Sharansky's memoir, *Fear No Evil*, is a major source text for *The Betrayers*, and not just for the biographical details of Kotler's life. As just one example, a joke Sharansky reports hearing from one of his first cellmates while in prison—that the Soviet authorities dab iodine on the bullet hole after shooting prisoners in the head, in order to staunch the bleeding—appears verbatim in *The Betrayers*, though in a different context. This is also another example of the Soviet humour that suffuses the book.

17. According to Bezmozgis, it was while he was writing an obituary for Alexander Lerner, another famous refusenik who was also betrayed by Lipavsky, that he got the idea for *The Betrayers* ("A Conversation" 11). Bezmozgis writes: "I wanted to know why he had betrayed his comrades and I wondered what it might have meant to commit a betrayal for a seemingly indomitable regime that then ceased to exist. Companion to this was the question about Lipavsky's opposite, the

virtuous man who sacrifices everything for the sake of an ideal, and who later, quite inevitably, discovers that the ideal does not quite correspond to reality" (11).

18. This is an interesting recurring motif in the texts under study in this book: how spy work can have a life-changing effect on the person doing the spying. Tankilevich claims spying on Zionists turned him into a Zionist; Samir in Tsabari's "Borders" learned to empathize with Arabs while a spy; was Philip in *Operation Shylock*, perhaps, also swayed by what he saw as a spy in Athens?

19. The fact that Tankilevich did not admit to Svetlana that he was Jewish for the first ten years of their relationship speaks to the complicated ethnic matrix of the USSR.

20. As Levinas explains elsewhere, the project in *Totality and Infinity* was to "systematize these experiences [of encounters with the Other] by opposing them to a philosophical thought which reduces the Other…to the Same and the multiple to the totality, making of autonomy its supreme principle" (*Difficult Freedom: Essays on Judaism* 294).

21. In the lead-up to the publication of the French translation of *Parting Ways*, Bruno Chaouat critiqued Butler's reading/translating of Levinas's comments regarding Palestinians and the face, claiming that Butler was purposefully misquoting Levinas. (Some of Chaouat's other, Zionist-inflected critiques of *Parting Ways* are not made in good faith.) Butler wrote a defense of her reading, stating that she never claims Levinas actually *says* that the Palestinians are "faceless," but that his beliefs when it comes to Israeli's right to defend itself lead to the same conclusion. "When a population is destroyed by military power, or actively not defended by military power, that population becomes effectively 'faceless' under such conditions—or so this is my interpretive conclusion," she writes ("Levinas Trahi?" np). Butler also defends her reading of Levinas by asserting that the quotation marks she uses around the word "faceless" are not meant to denote a direct quote, but are, instead, a coinage of Butler's, which she points out is a common usage of quotation marks in academic English. I accept Butler's justifications for reading Levinas the way she does, and believe that the whole incident reveals the importance of clarity when it comes to nuanced, minority readings of famous figures, especially when translation is involved.

22. Another example the Boyarins give us of Jewish particularism that is benign in the diaspora but violent in a hegemonic state is the diasporic contempt for non-Jewish places of worship. This contempt, they write, "becomes darkly ominous when it is combined with temporal power and domination—that is, when Jews have power over places of worship belonging to others. It is this factor that has allowed the Israelis to turn the central Mosque of Beersheba into a museum of the Negev and to let the Muslim cemetery of that city to fall into ruins" ("Generation and the Ground" 712).

23. Dafna retorts by asking "But who cares about the country if it destroys our family?" (45).

24. It is possible, of course, to disagree with my reading of Kotler here, and to see Bezmozgis as satirizing Kotler's lofty moral code and sense of himself. Such is the nature of literary discourse. But, while I do believe that Kotler is meant to be seen as full of himself, in my reading of the novel and Bezmozgis's comments on Kotler and morality, I see no evidence that his actual morality is meant to be satirized. Bezmozgis has written humorous and satirical pictures before; it seems conspicuously missing from *The Betrayers's* portrayal of Kotler. From the opening epigraphs of the novel—the first, a quote from First Kings about Hada's desire to no longer live in Pharaoh's Egypt, the second, a quote from Mandate period Zionist underground leader David Raziel about the power of self-sacrifice in the "struggle for national liberation" (np)—to the final line of the novel—"*David, King of Israel, lives, lives and endures!*" (225)—if the novel is meant to satirize and critique Kotler, it has majorly missed the mark.

25. In Benzion, we see the detrimental affects of living in a highly militarized society, where young boys and girls live with the knowledge that they will be drafted into the army after high school and internalize the ethos that must go along with this. We see this in the juxtaposition of twelve-year-old Benzion's "shamefaced" explanation for playing a violent video game where you "shot at Chechens or the Taliban," that he was peer pressured by his friends, and his being an active soldier in the Israeli army, stationed near Hebron, where he was "no longer playing" (23). The theme of what it means to grow up with the ever-present army is often visited in Israeli literature and film, perhaps most notably in recent years in David Grossman's novel *To the End of the Land*. (For a look at how Grossman thematizes meat-eating, cruelty, and the occupation in this novel, see my article "'A Meat Locker in Hebron': Meat Eating, Occupation, and Cruelty in *To the End of the Land*.")

26. Further discussing this possibility as the grist for Jewish fiction, Bezmozgis writes that "this dilemma might provide a compelling and weighty source of material for literature, but, to be sure, one that is short-lived" (np). Not only do I disagree that this "dilemma" will be short-lived—seeing how it has been around since at least 1948 and will likely continue for the forseeable future—but I further disagree with Bezmozgis's implied idea that this short-livedness spells the end of Jewish literature.

27. Beinart's politics has moved significantly to the left since the publication of his book.

28. In his talk at UC Santa Cruz, Bezmozgis says the withdrawal would be "from the West Bank," but does not specify further ("An Afternoon with David Bezmozgis").

29. An excellent history of Kiryat Arba and the other Hebron settlers is found in Tamara Neuman's *Settling Hebron*, pages 50–69. As Neuman explains, "settling Hebron required incrementally producing a site on the ground in a Palestinian city that could then be apprehended as Jewish in order to make settler appeals to origins more plausible" (52).

30. Compare Bezmozgis's (nonexistent) treatment of Hebron with Jason Sherman's in his 1995 play *Reading Hebron*. The play is an incisive look at the situation in the beleaguered city. Focusing on the character of Nathan and his attempt to understand the 1994 Goldstein Massacre, the play is a kaleidoscope of voices, viewpoints, and narratives. Sherman employs the space of the play to maximum effect. The play climaxes in a surreal Passover Seder, where historical figures, including Noam Chomsky and Edward Said, as well as settlers and a thirteen-year-old Baruch Goldstein, speak. The play—an excellent example of diasporic heteroglossia—is chock full of quotes, allusions, and diatribes, including an essay the thirteen-year-old Baruch Goldstein wrote on why war is bad. Unlike in *The Betrayers*, the situation in Hebron is explored from all angles, and Nathan's doubt, paranoia, and driving desire to understand Israel/Palestine are powerfully and movingly showcased.

31. Einat Fishbain describes the effects of the Protocol thusly: "the Palestinian Authority would be granted control of 18 square kilometers and a population of 120,000 Palestinians (H1), while Israel controlled the remaining part of the city, which includes the Tomb of the Patriarchs, Shuhada Street and the Casbah (H2). At the time of the signing, 35,000 Palestinians lived in H2. Today only 22,000 remain, living alongside 750 settlers (100 families and yeshiva students)" (np).

32. For a succinct rundown of the hope and failure of the Oslo Accords, see Avi Shlaim, "The Iron Wall Revisited."

33. For more on the daily life of Palestinians living in Hebron, see "A City of Devastation: Hebron 20 Years After the Massacre" by Einat Fishbein, and "Hebron Still Under Siege 20 Years After Ibrahimi Mosque Massacre" by Ali Abunimah.

34. For more on Gaza, see Jean-Pierre Filiu's *Gaza: A History*, a fantastic historical account of Gaza from ancient antiquity until the present.

35. *White Sun of the Desert* is a fascinating example of Soviet cinema. The version I watched was uploaded to YouTube in 2017 and has over 2.5 million views, speaking at the very least to its enduring popularity. The film takes place immediately after a campaign in Soviet Central Asia during the Russian Civil War, and is a satire of the Hollywood Western. The protagonist, comrade Sukhov, is a typical every-man Soviet soldier hero, who gets involved at an old Tsarist outpost in a fight against a sadistic Arab warlord, accidentally freeing the warlord's harem of women in the process. Apparently, a ritual of Soviet astronauts was to watch the film before their missions into space (Menashe,

"Chapayev and Company" 20). As Louis Menashe puts it, *White Sun of the Desert* "is bathed in modernist irony; its tongue-in-cheek abandon exudes mockery, not only of Westerns and the Hollywood hero, but, between the lines, of official ideology itself" (20). It is interesting to note that, unlike *The Betrayers*, the film has sympathetic Arab characters.

36. As far as Tankilevich knows, the reason Podolsky returned from Israel is that he was too right wing for the country. "If it seemed odd that Podolsky, still ardent in his Zionism, when restrained from living in Judaea or Samaria, had opted for Simferopol over Jerusalem or Haifa, it was best to regard this as no more than a personal quirk" (66). Podolsky did not like that there were rules, a geopolitical situation, in Israel. He did not like that Israel/Palestine existed in a historical context. This raises an important characteristic of the current relationship between Israel and the Jewish diaspora: that Jewish Zionists can find Israel not ideologically rigid *enough*, and return to the diaspora—even a difficult one such as Crimea—in a kind of personal protest.

37. Treating the status of Palestine as up for debate is a recurring tactic of the CJN. In their special issue dedicated to the fiftieth anniversary of the 1967 War, for example, a long article on the word occupation states that some people prefer to use the terms "disputed" or "'administered' territories" (Csillag B2). Perhaps not surprisingly, there are no articles or reminiscences from Palestinians in the issue.

38. Plenty of Israeli novels discuss the crisis in Israel/Palestine with more nuance than Bezmozgis's diasporic perspective.

39. Coincidentally or not, the eponymous first story in Bezmozgis's fourth book, *Immigrant City*, and the book to come out immediately after *The Betrayers*, has Muslim characters. The story follows the first-person narrator—who, it would seem, is indistinguishable from Bezmozgis himself—as he and his young daughter visit a Somali apartment building to buy a car door. The interaction between the settled Soviet Jewish immigrant of the narrator and the newly arrived immigrants of the Muslim Somalis is a confrontation between two diasporic peoples. Bezmozgis also clearly satirizes the narrator's irrational fear of the Somalis. In the space of diaspora, Bezmozgis is able to imagine all of the world's refugees and immigrants as equals: "I thought of the Syrians, the Iraqis, the Afghans, the Eritreans, the Sudanese, as well as my father, my grandfather and all my persecuted forebears" (13). The political morality of "Immigrant City" is the polar opposite of *The Betrayers*, showing again how Bezmozgis is much more comfortable imagining diasporic spaces than ethnic nationalist ones.

40. Stalin ordered similar forceful transfers of a number of small Soviet ethnic groups as part of "Operation Deportation," deporting the Volga Germans, the Karachays, the Kalmyks, the Chechens, the Ingus, the Balkars, and the Tatars (Williams 331–332).

41. Williams's article on the Tatars is a great example of a historian working on a little-discussed subject. As Williams puts it, "Scholars of all disciplines have, in the Crimean Tatars, been given the unique opportunity to analyze the process whereby an ancient people with a long tradition of statehood in Eastern Europe rebuilt its culture, identity and political rights from the ground up after experiencing almost half a century of state-sponsored ethnocide designed to eradicate its culture" (324).

42. For a brief discussion of the history of Jewish autonomous zones in Crimea, see "Before Crimea was Russian, It Was a Potential Jewish Homeland," by Jeffrey Veidlinger.

43. The biting discussion of television continues: "This was what they had raised from the scraps of communism. This was what the struggle for freedom and democracy had delivered. Bread and circuses. Mostly circuses. From one grand deception to another was their lot. First the Soviet sham, then the capitalist. For the ordinary citizen, these were just two different varieties of poison. The current variety served in a nicer bottle" (97).

Conclusion

1. In a review of the anthology in The Washington Post, Matti Friedman, who is what Gabriel Sheffer would call a professional Zionist, excoriates the collection. Friedman opens his review by pretending that Chabon, Waldman, and Eggers (who is not one of the collection's editors) edited a collection of writers confronting Iraq. "I'm kidding!" he exclaims, "Reporting on Iraq is bothersome, and so is introspection." This is a move Zionists make constantly, blaming critics of Israel for not reporting on other world events. Later, he writes, "is there a reason they [Chabon and Waldamn] decided the world needs to know more about it and not say, Kandahar, Guantanamo, Congo or Baltimore?" Friedman writes that the authors are American and international, "with a few locals thrown in." Six of the writers are either Israeli or Palestinian, making their work 20% of the anthology, and Friedman does not return to their essays, spending the rest of his review lambasting the authors for various offenses—visiting for only a few days, not being "journalists," not writing about Syria, getting a year wrong, avoiding "Palestinian extremists and average Israelis, so it looks like all Palestinians are reasonable and all Israelis aren't"—which all boils down to not being able to understand the conflict.

Works Cited

Abuminah, Ali. *The Battle for Justice in Palestine*. Haymarket Books, 2014.

Abuminah, Ali. "Hebron Still Under Siege 20 Years After Ibrahimi Mosque Massacre." *The Electronic Intifada*, 26 Feb. 2014, electronicintifada.net/blogs/ali-abunimah/hebron-still-under-siege-20-years-after-ibrahimi-mosque-massacre.

Abuminah, Ali. *One Country: A Bold Proposal to End the Israeli-Palestinian Impasse*. Picador, 2007.

Adams, Lorraine. Review of *The Best Place on Earth*, by Ayelet Tsabari. *The New York Times*, 25 March 2016, www.nytimes.com/2016/03/27/books/review/the-best-place-on-earth-by-ayelet-tsabari.html?partner=IFTTT.

Aloni, Udi. *What Does a Jew Want? On Binationalism and Other Specters*. Columbia UP, 2011.

Alphandary, Idit. "Wrestling With the Angel and the Law, or the Critique of Identity: The Demjanjuk Trial, *Operation Shylock: A Confession*, and 'Angel Levine.'" *Philip Roth Studies*, vol. 4, no. 1, 2008, pp. 57–74. JSTOR, www.jstor.org/stable/10.5703/philrothstud.4.1.57.

Altshuler, Stuart. *From Exodus to Freed: A History of the Soviet Jewry Movement*. Rowman and Littlefield Publishers, 2005.

Amir, Shmuel. "Overseas Foreign Workers in Israel: Policy Aims and Labor Market Outcomes." *International Migration Review*, vol. 36, no. 1, 2002, pp. 41–57. JSTOR, www.jstor.org/stable/4149528.

Amit, Gish. *Ex-Libris: Chronicles of Theft, Preservation, and Appropriating at the Jewish National Library*. In Hebrew. Van leer Jerusalem Institute, 2015.

Arendt, Hannah. *Eichmann In Jerusalem*. Penguin Books, 2006.

Ariel, Ari. "A Reconsideration of Imam Yahya's Attitude Toward Forced
Conversion of Jewish Orphans in Yemen." *Shofar*, vol. 9, no. 1, 2010,
pp. 95–111. JSTOR, www.jstor.org/stable/10.5703/shofar.29.1.95.

Armstrong, Jeanette. "Land Speaking." *Introduction to Indigenous
Literary Criticism in Canada*, edited by Heather MacFarlane and
Armand Garnet Ruffo, Broadview P, 2016, pp. 146–159.

Avineri, Shlomo. "Zionism According to Theodor Herzl." *Haaretz*,
20 Dec. 2002, www.haaretz.com/life/books/1.4994304.

Bach, Ulrich E. "Seeking Emptiness: Theodor Herztka's Colonial Utopia
Freiland (1890)." *Utopian Studies*, vol. 22, no. 1, 2011, pp. 74–90.
JSTOR, www.jstor.org/stable/10.5325/utopianstudies.22.1.0074.

Baker, Peter, and Jodi Rudoren. "Jonathan Pollard, American Who Spied
for Israel, Released After 30 Years." *The New York Times*, 20 Nov.
2015, www.nytimes.com/2015/ 11/21/world/jonathan-pollard-
released.html.

Bakhtin, Mikhail. "Discourse In the Novel." *The Dialogic Imagination:
Four Essays by M.M. Bakhtin*, edited by Michael Holquist.
Translated by Caryl Emerson and Michael Holquist. Austin:
U of Texas P, 1982, pp. 259–422.

Balint, Benjamin. *Kafka's Last Trial: The Case of a Literary Legacy*.
W.W. Norton and Company, 2018.

Bartram, David V. "Foreign Workers in Israel: History and Theory."
International Migration Review, vol. 32, no. 2, 1998, pp. 303–325.
JSTOR, www.jstor.org/stable/2547185.

Bashi, Sari, and Kenneth Mann. *Disengaged Occupiers: The Legal Status
of Gaza*. Gisha: Legal Center for Freedom of Movement, 2007.

Bazyler, Michael J., and Julia Y. Scheppach. "The Strange and Curious
History of the Law Used to Prosecute Adolf Eichmann." *Loyola of
Los Angeles International and Comparative Law Review*, vol. 34, no.
3, 2012, pp. 417–461. Digital Commons, digitalcommons.1mu.edu/
ilr/vol34/iss3/7.

Beinart, Peter. *The Crisis of Zionism*. Picador, 2013.

Bernard-Donals, Michael. "Bakhtin and Social Change: Or, Why No One's
Bakhtin Is Politically Revolutionary (A History Play in Four Acts)."
The Centennial Review, vol. 39, no. 3, 1995, pp. 429–444. JSTOR,
www.jstor.org/stable/23739355.

Bernstein, Michael André. *Foregone Conclusions: Against Apocalyptic History*. U of California P, 1994.

Bezmozgis, David. "An Afternoon with David Bezmozgis." *YouTube*, uploaded by University of California Televion, 9 April 2018, www.youtube.com/watch?v=9gx5n4_Lep8.

Bezmozgis, David. *The Betrayers*. Back Bay Books, 2015.

Bezmozgis, David. "A Conversation with David Bezmozgis." In "Reading Group Guide," *The Betrayers*, pp. 9–17. Back Bay Books, 2015.

Bezmozgis, David. "The End of American Jewish Literature, Again." *Tablet*, 2014, www.tabletmag.com/sections/arts-letters/articles/bezmozgis-american-jewish-literature.

Bezmozgis, David. *The Free World*. HarperCollins, 2011.

Bezmozgis, David. *Immigrant City*. HarperCollins, 2019.

Bezmozgis, David. *Natasha and Other Stories*. Harper Perennial, 2005.

Bezmozgis, David. "The Novel in Real Time." In "Reading Group Guide," *The Betrayers*, Back Bay Books, 2015, pp. 3–8.

Bhabha, Homi. *The Location of Culture*, Routledge, 2004.

Biale, David. "The Case of Jonathan Pollard: Ten Years Later." *Tikkun*, May–June 1997, pp. 41+.

Blumenthal, Max. *The 51 Day War*. Bold Type Books, 2016.

Boyarin, Daniel, and Jonathan Boyarin. "Diaspora: Generation and the Ground of Jewish Identity." *Critical Inquiry*, vol. 19, no. 4, 1993, pp. 693–725. JSTOR, www.jstor.org/stable/1343903.

Boyarin, Daniel, and Jonathan Boyarin. "Diaspora: Generation and the Ground of Jewish Diaspora." *Theorizing Diaspora: A Reader*, edited by Jana Evans Braziel and Anita Manur, Blackwell, 2003, pp. 85–118.

Boyarin, Jonathan, and Daniel Boyarin. *The Powers of Diaspora: Two Essays on the Relevance of Jewish Culture*. U of Minnesota P, 2002.

Braziel, Jana Evans, and Anita Mannur. "Nation, Migration, Globalization: Points of Contention in Diaspora Studies." Introduction. *Theorizing Diaspora: A Reader*, edited by Jana Evans Braziel and Anita Manur, Blackwell, 2003, pp. 1–22.

Browning, Christopher R. "A Lesson for Netanyahu from A Real Holocaust Historian." *Foreign Policy*, 22 Oct. 2015, foreignpolicy.com/2015/10/22/a-lesson-for-netanyahu-from-a-real-holocaust-historian/.

Buber, Martin. "The Bi-National Approach to Zionism." *Towards Union in Palestine: Essays on Zionism and Jewish-Arab Cooperation*, edited by Martin Buber, Judah Leon Magnes, and Akibah Ernst Simon, Greenwood P, 1972.

Budick, Emily Miller. "Roth and Israel." *The Cambridge Companion to Philip Roth*, edited by Timothy Parish, Cambridge UP, 2007, pp. 68–81.

Butler, Judith. "Levinas Trahi? La Réponse de Judith Butler." *Le Monde*, 21 March 2013, www.lemonde.fr/idees/article/2013/03/21/levinas-trahi-la-reponse-de-judith-butler_5994702_3232.html.

Butler, Judith. *Parting Ways: Jewishness and the Critique of Zionism*. Columbia UP, 2012.

Butler, Judith. "Who Owns Kafka?" *London Review of Books*, 3 March 2011.

Chabon, Michael. *The Yiddish Policemen's Union*. Harper Perennial, 2008.

Chabon, Michael, and Ayelet Waldman, editors. *Kingdom of Olives of Ash: Writers Confront the Occupation*. HarperCollins, 2017.

Chaouat, Bruno. "Débat: Judith Butler ou Levinas trahi?" *Le Monde*, 13 Mars 2013, www.lemonde.fr/idees/article/2013/03/13/debat-judith-butler-ou-levinas-trahi_5994697_3232.html.

Chariandy, David. "Postcolonial Diasporas." *Postcolonial Text*, vol. 2, no. 1, 2006.

Childers, Erskine B. "The Other Exodus." *The Spectator*, 12 May 1961, pp. 8–11. *The Spectator Archive*, http://archive.spectator.co.uk/article/12th-may-1961/8/the-other-exodus.

Chowers, Eyal. "Time In Zionism: The Life and Afterlife of a Temporal Revolution." *Political Theory*, vol. 26, no. 5, 1998, pp. 652–685. JSTOR, www.jstor.org/stable/191767.

Choy, Catherina Ceniza. *Empire of Care: Nursing and Migration in Filipino American History*. Duke UP, 2003.

Clifford, James. *Routes: Travel and Translation in the Late Twentieth Century*. Harvard UP, 1997.

Cohen, Joshua. *Moving Kings*. Random House, 2017.

Cohen, Joshua. *The Netanyahus: An Account of a Minor and Ultimately Even Negligible Episode in the History of a Very Famous Family*. New York Review Books, 2021.

Cohen, Robin. *Global Diasporas: An Introduction*. Routledge, 2008.

Csillag, Ron. "The 'O' Word: The Many Sides of the 'Occupation.'"
 Canadian Jewish News 21. Sept. 2017, pp. B2+.

"Diaspora." *Oxford English Dictionary*, www-oed-com.proxy.library.
 carleton.ca/view/Entry/52085?redirectedFrom=diaspora&.
 Accessed 18 October 2022.

Dickstein, Morris. "Operation Shylock." *Tikkun*, May–June 1993, 41+.

Dobozy, Tamas. "The Holocaust as Fiction: Derrida's 'Demeure' and
 the Demjanjuk Trial in Philip Roth's *Operation Shylock.*" *Philip
 Roth Studies*, vol. 1, no. 1, 2005, pp. 37–52. JSTOR, www.jstor.org/
 stable/42922096.

Douglas, Lawrence. *The Right Wrong Man: John Demjanjuk and the Last
 Great Nazi War Crimes Trial.* Princeton UP, 2016.

Dubnov, Arie M. Review of *Ex Libris: Chronicles of Theft, Preservation, and
 Appropriating at the Jewish National Library. Judaica Librarianship*,
 vol. 19, 2016, pp. 93–102.

Dubnow, Simon. "Def. of Diaspora." *Encyclopaedia of the Social Sciences*,
 edited by Edwin R.A. Seligman, Macmillan, 1937, pp. 126–130.

Dufoix, Stéphane. *Diasporas.* Translated by William Rodarmor. U of
 California P, 2008.

Eliav-Feldon, Miriam. "'If You Will It, It Is No Fairy Tale': The First Jewish
 Utopias." *The Jewish Journal of Sociology*, vol. 25, no. 2, pp. 85–104.

"Elect." Def. 1, 3, 4. *The Oxford English Dictionary*, Oxford
 UP, 2022, oed-com.proxy.library.carleton.ca/view/
 Entry/60217?result=3&rskey=p9Wide&. Accessed 31 Oct. 2022.

Elon, Amos. *Herzl.* Reinhart and Winston, 1975.

Englander, Nathan. *For the Relief of Unbearable Urges.* Knopf, 1999.

Englander, Nathan. *What We Talk About When We Talk About Anne Frank:
 Stories.* Vintage, 2013.

Eraqi-Klorman, Bat-Zion. "The Forced Conversion of Jewish Orphans in
 Yemen." *International Journal of Middle East Studies*, vol. 33, no. 1,
 2001, pp. 23–47. JSTOR, www.jstor.org/stable/259478.

Exodus. Directed by Otto Preminger, United Artists, 1960.

Ezrahi, Sidra DeKoven, et al. "Operation Shylock." *Tikkun*, vol. 8, no.
 3, May–June 1993, p. 41+. *Academic OneFile*, go.galegroup.com/
 ps/i.do?p=AONE&sw=w&u=yorku_main&v=2.1&id=GALE%-
 7CA14413065&it=r&asid=e8f0b19ecb5ebb02a2a400debc70be96.
 Accessed 30 Nov. 2016.

Fezehai, Malin. "The Disappeared Children of Israel." *The New York Times*, 20 Feb. 2019, www.nytimes.com/2019/02/20/world/middleeast/israel-yemenite-children-affair.html.

Filiu, Jean-Pierre. *Gaza: A History*. Translated by John King. Oxford UP, 2014.

Fishbain, Einat. "A City of Devastation: Hebron 20 Years After the Massacre." *+972 Magazine*, 25 Feb. 2014.

Flipping Out. Directed by Yoav Shamir. National Film Board of Canada, 2007.

Foer, Jonathan Safran. *Here I Am*. Hamish Hamilton, 2016.

"Franz Kafka Literary Legal Battle Ends as Israel's High Court Rules in Favour of Library." *The Guardian*, 8 Aug. 2016, www.theguardian.com/books/2016/aug/08/franz-kafka-papers-israel-court-ruling.

Freud, Sigmund. *Moses and Monotheism*. Translated by Katherine Jones, Vintage Books, 1955.

Friedman, Matti. "Distant Cousins." *Jewish Review of Books*, Fall 2017, np. Accessed 22 Sept. 2017.

Friedman, Matti. "What Happens When Famous Novelists 'Confront the Occupation' in the West Bank." *The Washington Post*, 23 June 2017, np. Accessed 9 Sept. 2017.

Friess, Steve. "When 'Holocaust' Became 'The Holocaust.'" *The New Republic*, 17 May 2015.

Furman, Andrew. *Israel Through the Jewish-American Imagination: A Survey of Jewish-American Literature on Israel, 1928–1995*. State U of New York P, 1997.

Garfinkel, Jonathan. *The Trials of John Demjanjuk: A Holocaust Cabaret*. Playwrights Canada P, 2005.

Gavilan, Jodesz. "What You Need to Know About Overseas Filipino Workers." *Rappler*, 5 Dec. 2015, www.rappler.com/newsbreak/iq/114549-overseas-filipino-workers-facts-figures.

Geneva Convention Relative to the Protection of Civilian Persons in Time of War, Aug. 12, 1949. www.un.org/en/genocideprevention/documents/atrocity-crimes/Doc.33_GC-IV-EN.pdf.

Ginsburg, Aimee. "The Karma Kosher: Far from Their Drugged-Out Image, Goan Israelis are the New Entrepreneurs." *Outlook India*, 3 May 2010, www.outlookindia.com/magazine/story/the-karma-kosher/265168.

Gluzman, Michael. "The Zionist Body: Nationalism and Sexuality in

Herzl's *Altneuland*." *Brothers Keepers: New Perspectives on Jewish
Masculinity*, edited by Harry Brod and Rabbi Shawn Israel Zevit,
Men's Studies P, 2010, pp. 89–112.

Gold, Nora. *Fields of Exile*. Dundurn, 2014.

Goldstein, Yossi. "Eastern Jews vs. Western Jews: The Ahad Ha'am-
Herzl Dispute and Its Cultural and Social Implications." *Jewish
History*, vol. 24, no. 3/4, 2010, Special issue on Tradition
and Transformation in Eighteenth-Century Europe, Jewish
Integration in Comparative Perspective, pp. 355–377. JSTOR,
www.jstor/stable/40864858.

Gordon, Louis. "Three Voices or One? Philip Roth and Zionism." *A
Political Companion to Philip Roth*, edited by Claudia Franziska
Brühwiler and Lee Trepanier, UP Kentucky, 2017, pp. 119–134.

Gradus, Yehuda. "Is Eilat-Aqaba a Bi-National City? Can Economic
Opportunities Overcome the Barriers of Politics and Psychology?"
GeoJournal, vol. 54, no. 1, 2001, pp. 85–99. JSTOR, www.jstor.org/
stable/41147640.

Gries, Zeev. "Adding Insult to Injury: Zionist Cultural Colonialism.
In Response to Gish Amit's Eks Libris: Historyah Shel Gezel, Shimur
Ve-nikus Ba-Sifrayah Ha-le 'Umit Bi-Yerushalayim (Ex Libris:
Chronicles of Theft, Preservation, and Appropriating at the
Jewish National Library)." *Judaica Librarianship*, vol. 19, 2016.

Grossman, David. *To the End of the Land*. Translated by Jessica Cohen.
Alfred A. Knopf, 2010.

Grumberg, Karen. "Necessary Wounds and the Humiliation of *Galut* in
Roth's *The Counterlife* and *Operation Shylock*." *Philip Roth Studies*
vol. 5, no. 1, 2009, pp. 35–59. JSTOR, www.jstor.org/stable/10.5703/
philrothstud.5.1.35.

Halkin, Hillel. "What Ahad Ha'am Saw and Herzl Missed—
And Vice Versa." *Mosaic*, 5 Oct. 2016, mosaic-
magazine.com/essay/history-ideas/2016/10/
what-ahad-haam-saw-and-herzl-missed-and-vice-versa/.

Harkov, Lahav. "'Black Panther' is a Great Zionist Movie." *Tablet
Magazine*, 26 Feb. 2018, www.tabletmag.com/scroll/256186/
black-panther-is-a-great-zionist-movie.

Herzl, Theodor. *Altneuland*. Translated by Lotta Levensohn. Block
Publishing Company, 1987.

Herzl, Theodor. *The Jewish State.* Translated by Jacob M. Alkow. Dover
Publications, 1988.

Holocaust. Miniseries. Directed by Fred Schepisi. Titus Productions, 1978.

Holquist, Michael. "Introduction." *The Dialogic Imagination.* Edited by
Michael Holquist, U of Texas P, 1982, pp. xv–xxxiv.

Honig-Parnass, Tikva. *False Prophets of Peace: Liberal Zionism and the
Struggle for Palestine.* Haymarket, 2011.

Hutcheon, Linda. *The Politics of Postmodernism.* Routledge, 1989.

"Israel-Egypt Relations: The Yamit Evacuation (April 23, 1982)." *Jewish
Virtual Library: A Project of AICE,* www.jewishvirtuallibrary.org/
the-yamit-evacuation.

Israeli Knesset, Israel. "Nazis and Nazi Collaborators (Punishment) Law."
No. 64. 1 Aug. 1950. https://ihl-databases.icrc.org/applic/ihl/
ihl-nat.nsf/0/aacf823ae32ab469c12575ae0034c1fe/$FILE/Law%20
no.%2064.pdf.

Kafka, Franz. *The Trial.* Translated by Idris Parry. Penguin Books, 1994.

Kaplan, Amy. "Zionism as Anticolonialism: The Case of 'Exodus.'"
American Literary History, vol. 25, no. 4, 2013, pp. 870–895. JSTOR,
www.jstor.org/stable/43817606.

Kaplan, Brett Ashley. *Jewish Anxiety and the Novels of Philip Roth.*
Bloomsbury, 2015.

Kaye/Kantrowitz, Melanie. *The Colors of Jews: Racial Politics and Radical
Diasporism.* Indiana UP, 2007.

Khalidi, Muhammad Ali. "Utopian Zionism or Zionist Proselytism? A
Reading of Herzl's Altneuland." *Journal of Palestine Studies,* vol.
30, no. 4, 2001, pp. 55–67. JSTOR, www.jstor.org/stable/10.1525/
jps.2001.30.4.55.

Khalidi, Rashid. *The Hundred Years' War on Palestine: A History of Settler
Colonialism and Resistance, 1917–2017.* Metropolitan Books, 2020.

Khalidi, Rashid. *The Iron Cage: The Story of the Palestinian Struggle for
Statehood.* Beacon P, 2007.

"Khan al-Ahmar: Israel Court Approves Demolition of Bedouin
Village." *BBC News,* 5 Sept. 2018, www.bbc.com/news/
world-middle-east-45420915.

Kornberg, Jacques. "Introduction." *Altneuland,* Theodor Herzl,
translated by Lotta Levensohn. Block Publishing Company, 1987,
pp. v–xxxii.

Krauss, Nicole. *Forest Dark*. HarperLuxe, 2017.

Krauss, Nicole. *Great House*. W.W. Norton & Company, 2010.

Kreuter, Aaron. "Jewish Affect During the Second Intifada: Terror, Love, and Procreation in Ayelet Tsabari's 'Tikkun.'" *All The Feels/ Tous Les Sens: Affect and Writing in Canada / Affect et écriture au Canada*, edited by Marie Carrière, Ursula Mathis-Moser, and Kit Dobson, U of Alberta P, 2020, pp. 225–244.

Kreuter, Aaron. "'A Meat Locker in Hebron': Meat Eating, Occupation, and Cruelty in To the End of the Land." *Pivot: A Journal of Interdisciplinary Studies & Thought*, vol. 7, no. 1, 2019, pp. 33–53. *Open Journal Systems*, pivot.journals.yorku.ca/index.php/pivot/article/ view/40308.

Kreuter, Aaron. Review of *The Art of Leaving*, by Ayelet Tsabari. *Canadian Writers Abroad*, 22 Jan. 2019, https://canadianwritersabroad. com/2019/01/22/art-of-leaving/.

Kreuter, Aaron. Review of *Here I Am*. *The Rusty Toque*, Issue 13, 30 Nov. 2017, www.therustytoque.com/fiction-review-aaron-kreuter.html.

Lafontaine, Tamar. "Why Do Israelis Flock to India?" *Jerusalem Post*, 8 Dec. 2018, www.jpost.com/Jerusalem-Report/Mother-India-573686.

Landy, David. *Jewish Identity and Palestinian Rights: Diaspora Jewish Opposition to Israel*. NBN International, 2011.

Lavie, Smadar. *Wrapped in the Flag of Israel: Mizrahi Single Mothers and Bureaucratic Torture*. Berghahn Books, 2014.

Lazare, Daniel. "Operation Shylock." *Tikkun*, May–June 1993, 41+.

Lazin, Fred A. *The Struggle for Soviet Jewry in American Politics: Israel Versus the American Jewish Establishment*. Lexington Books, 2005.

Lehmann, Sophia. "Exodus and Homeland: The Representation of Israel in Saul Bellow's *To Jerusalem and Back* and Philip Roth's *Operation Shylock*." *Religion and Literature*, vol. 30, no. 3, 1998, pp. 77–96. JSTOR, www.jstor.org/stable/40059741.

Lerner, Michael. "The Jews and the 60s: Philip Roth Still Doesn't Get It." *Tikkun*, May–June 1997, pp. 13+.

Levinas, Emmanuel. *Difficult Freedom: Essays on Judaism*. Translated by Seán Hand. The Johns Hopkins UP. 1990.

Levinas, Emmanuel. *Ethics and Infinity: Conversations with Philippe Nemo.* Translated by Richard A. Cohen. Duquesne UP. 1985.

Levinas, Emmanuel. *Totality and Infinity: An Essay on Exteriority.* Translated by Alphonso Lingis. Duquesne UP. 2008.

Levy, André, and Alex Weingrod. "On Homelands and Diasporas: An Introduction." *Homelands and Diasporas: Holy Lands and Other Places,* Stanford UP, 2005, pp. 3–28.

Levy, Lital. *Poetic Trespass: Writing Between Hebrew and Arabic in Israel/ Palestine.* Princeton UP, 2014.

Lewin-Epstein, Noah, Yaacov Ro'i, and Paul Ritterbrand, editors. *Russian Jews on Three Continents: Migration and Resettlement.* Cummings Center Series, 1997.

Liebelt, Claudia. "On Gendered Journeys, Spiritual Transformations and Ethical Formations in Diaspora: Filipina Care Workers in Israel." *Feminist Review,* no. 97, 2011, pp. 74–91. JSTOR, www.jstor.org/stable/41288848.

Lozowick, Yaacov. "70 Years Later, These Holocaust Survivors' Names Are Still Tarnished." *Haaretz,* 28 May 2021, www.haaretz.com/israel-news/2021-05-28/ty-article/.premium/70-years-later-these-holocaust-survivors-names-are-still-tarnished/0000017f-dbcf-d3ff-a7ff-fbefd65f0000. Accessed 31 Oct. 2022.

Martineau, Joel. "Imagining Histories." Review of *The Betrayers,* by David Bezmozgis. *Canadian Literature,* no. 223, 2014, pp. 125–126.

Masalha, Nur. *The Bible and Zionism: Invented Traditions, Archaeology and Post-Colonialism in Israel-Palestine.* Zed Books, 2007.

Massad, Joseph. "Zionism's Internal Others: Israel and the Oriental Jews." *Journal of Palestine Studies,* vol. 25, no. 4, 1996, pp. 53–68. JSTOR, www.jstor.org/stable/2538006.

McLoughlin, Kate. "'Dispute Incarnate': Philip Roth's *Operation Shylock,* the Demjanjuk Trial, and Eyewitness Testimony." *Philip Roth Studies,* vol. 3, no. 2, 2007, pp. 115–130. JSTOR, www.jstor.org/stable/42922084.

Meir-Glitzenstein, Esther. "Operation Magic Carpet: Constructing the Myth of the Magical Immigration of Yemenite Jews to Israel." *Israel Studies,* vol. 16, no. 3, 2011, pp. 149–173. JSTOR, www.jstor.org/stable/10.2979/israelstudies.16.3.149.

Menashe, Louis. "Chapayev and Company: Films of the Russian Civil
    War." *Cinéaste*, vol. 30, no. 4, 2005, pp. 18–22. JSTOR, www.jstor.
    org/stable/41689902.

Merkin, Daphne. "Operation Shylock." *Tikkun*, May–June 1993, pp. 41+.

Morris, Benny. *Righteous Victims: A History of the Zionist-Arab Conflict,*
    1881–1999. Alfred A. Knopf, 1999.

Munayyer, Yousef. "Sorry, Black Panther is Not About Zionism."
    Forward, 28 Feb. 2018, forward.com/opinion/395519/
    sorry-black-panther-is-not-about-zionism/.

Nadel, Ira B. *Leon Uris: Life of a Best Seller.* U of Texas P, 2010.

Neuman, Tamara. *Settling Hebron: Jewish Fundamentalism in a Palestinian*
    City. U of Pennsylvania P, 2018.

Occupying Hebron: Soldiers' Testimonies from Hebron 2011 to 2017. Breaking
    the Silence, 2017, www.breakingthesilence.org.il/inside/english/
    campaigns/occupying-hebron/.

O'Donoghue, Gerard. "Philip Roth's Hebrew School." *Philip Roth*
    Studies, vol. 6, no. 2, 2010, pp. 153–166. JSTOR, www.jstor.org/
    stable/10.5703/philrothstud.6.2.153.

Omer-Man, Emily Schaeffer. "Separate and Unequal: Israel's Dual
    Criminal Justice System in the West Bank." *Palestine-Israel Journal*
    of Politics, Economics and Culture, vol. 21, no. 3, 2016, np, pij.org/
    articles/1682/separate-and-unequal-israels-dual-criminal-justice-
    system-in-the-west-bank.

Omer-Sherman, Ranen. *Diaspora and Zionism in Jewish American*
    Literature: Lazarus, Syrkin, Reznikoff, and Roth. UP of New England,
    2002.

"Operation Shylock." *Tikkun*, May–June 1993, pp. 41+.

Oria, Shelly. *New York 1, Tel Aviv 0.* FSG Originals, 2014.

Paller, Shalev. "Lifting Away the Weight of 3 Years: Why We Israelis
    Go to India After the Army." *The Times of Israel*, 29 June 2016,
    www.timesofisrael.com/lifting-away-the-weight-of-3-years-why-
    we-israelis-go-to-india-after-the-army/.

Pappé, Ilan. *The Rise and Fall of a Palestinian Dynasty: The Husaynis,*
    1700–1948. U of California P, 2011.

Pappé, Ilan. *Ten Myths About Israel.* Verso, 2017.

Parreñas, Rhacel Salazar. "Transgressing the Nation-State: The Partial
    Citizenship and 'Imagined (Global) Community' of Migrant

Filipina Domestic Workers." *Sign*, vol. 26, no. 4, 2001, pp. 1129–1154. JSTOR, www.jstor.org/stable/3175359.

Parrish, Timothy. "Imagining Jews in Philip Roth's *Operation Shylock*." *Contemporary Literature*, vol. 40, no. 4, 1999, pp. 575–602. JSTOR, www.jstor/org/stable/1208795.

Penslar, Derek. *Israel in History: The Jewish State in Comparative Perspective*. Routledge, 2007.

Pick, Alison. *Strangers with the Same Dream*. Knopf Canada, 2017.

Ravvin, Norman. "A Refusenik Returns." Review of *The Betrayers* by David Bezmozgis. *Literary Review of Canada*, January-February 2015, reviewcanada.ca/ magazine/2015/01/a-refusenik-returns/.

Reich, Tova. *The Jewish War*. Syracuse UP, 1997.

Remennick, Larissa. "Former Soviet Jews in Their New/Old Homeland." *Diasporic Homecomings: Ethnic Return Migration in Comparative Perspective*, edited by Takeyuki Tsuda, Stanford UP, 2009.

Remennick, Larissa. *Russian Jews on Three Continents*. Transaction Publishers, 2007.

Rich, Nathaniel. "Roth Agonistes." Review of *Why Write?: Collected Nonfiction 1960-2013* by Philip Roth. *The New York Review of Books*, 8 March 2018.

Roby, Bryan K. *The Mizrahi Era of Rebellion: Israel's Forgotten Civil Rights Struggle, 1948–1966*. Syracuse UP, 2015.

Rose, Jacqueline. *The Question of Zion*. Princeton UP, 2005.

Rosenfeld, Alvin H. "Promised Land(s): Zion, America, and American-Jewish Writers." *Jewish Social Studies*, vol. 3, no. 3, 1997, pp. 111–131. JSTOR, www.jstor.org/stable/4467506.

Roth, Philip. *American Pastoral*. Houghton Mifllin, 1997.

Roth, Philip. *The Counterlife*. Farrar, Straus and Giroux, 1986.

Roth, Philip. *Deception*. Simon and Schuster, 1990.

Roth, Philip. *The Facts: A Novelist's Autobiography*. Farrar, Straus, and Giroux, 1988.

Roth, Philip. *The Ghost Writer*. Vintage, 1979.

Roth, Philip. *Operation Shylock: A Confession*. Vintage International, 1994.

Roth, Philip. *Patrimony*. Simon and Schuster, 1991.

Roth, Philip. "Some New Jewish Stereotypes." *Reading Myself and Others*. Farrar, Straus and Giroux, 1975, pp. 137–148.

Roth, Philip. *Why Write? Collected Nonfiction 1960–2013*. The Library of
America, 2017.

Rothman-Zecher, Moriel. *Sadness is a White Bird*. Washington Square P,
2019.

Sacks, Rebecca. *City of a Thousand Gates*. Harper, 2021.

Safran, William. "Diasporas in Modern Societies: Myths of Homeland
and Return." *Diaspora: A Journal of Transnational Studies*, vol. 1,
no. 1, 1991, pp. 83–99. DOI: 10.1353/dsp.1991.004.

Sahwell, Aziz S. *Exodus: A Distortion of Truth*. Arab Information Center,
1960.

Said, Edward. "Freud and the Non-European." *The Selected Works of
Edward Said, 1966–2006*, edited by Moustafa Bayoumi and Andrew
Rubin, Vintage Books, 2019, pp. 494–517.

Said, Edward. *The Question of Palestine*. Vintage Books, 1992.

Salaita, Steven. *Israel's Dead Soul*. Temple UP, 2011.

Salt, Jeremy. "Fact and Fiction in the Middle East Novels of Leon Uris."
Journal of Palestine Studies, vol. 14, no. 3, Spring 1985, pp. 54–63.
JSTOR, www.jstor.org/stable/2536952.

Schechtman, Joseph B. "The Repatriation of Yemenite Jewry." *Jewish
Social Studies*, vol. 14, no. 3, 1952, pp. 209–224. JSTOR, www.jstor.
org/stable/4465079.

Schmemann, Serge. "Hebron Accord is Approved; Israel Army Yields
Main Base." *The New York Times*, 17 Jan. 1997, www.nytimes.
com/1997/01/17/world/hebron-accord-is-approved-israel-army-
yields-main-base.html.

Senderovich, Sasha. "Finally, a Russian Jewish Novel Breaks Out of
the Autobiographical Rut." Review of *The Betrayers* by David
Bezmozgis. *The New Republic*, 19 Sept. 2014, newrepublic.com/
article/119501/david-bezmozgiss-betrayers-review.

Shafir, Gershon. *Land, Labor, and the Origins of the Israeli-Palestinian
Conflict, 1882–1914*. Cambridge UP, 1989.

Sharansky, Natan. *Fear No Evil*. Translated by Stefani Hoffman. Random
House, 1988.

Shechner, Mark. *Up Society's Ass, Copper: Rereading Philip Roth*. U of
Wisconsin P, 2003.

Sheen, David. "Temple Movement Rabbi Proselytizes for Genocide."
Video. Electronic Intifada, 28 Sept. 2015, https://electronicintifada.
net/content/video-temple-movement-rabbi-proselytizes-
genocide/14870.

Sheffer, Gabriel Gabi. "Is the Jewish Diaspora Unique? Reflections on the
Diaspora's Current Situation." Israel Studies, vol. 10, no. 1, 2005,
pp. 1–35. JSTOR, www.jstor.org/stable/30245752.

Shenhav, Yehouda. The Arab Jews: A Postcolonial Reading of Nationalism,
Religion, and Ethnicity. Stanford UP, 2006.

Shenhav, Yehouda. Beyond the Two State Solution: A Jewish Political Essay.
Polity, 2012.

Sherman, Jason. Reading Hebron. Playwrights Canada Press, 1997.

Shlaim, Avi. "The Iron Wall Revisited." Journal of Palestine Studies, vol.
41, no. 2, 2012, pp. 80–98. JSTOR, www.jstor.org/stable/10.1525/
jps.2012.xli.2.80.

Shohat, Ella. Interview. Treyf podcast, 11 August 2017.

Shohat, Ella. "Introduction." On the Arab-Jew, Palestine, and Other
Displacements: Selected Writings of Ella Shohat. Pluto Press, 2017,
pp. 1–34.

Shohat, Ella. On the Arab-Jew, Palestine, and Other Displacements:
Selected Writings. Pluto Press, 2017.

Shohat, Ella. "Sephardim in Israel: Zionism from the Standpoint of
its Arab Jewish Victims." On the Arab-Jew, Palestine, and Other
Displacements: Selected Writings of Ella Shohat. Pluto Press, 2017,
pp. 37–76.

Shohat, Ella. "A Voyage to Toledo: Twenty-Five Years After the 'Jews of
the Orient and Palestinians' Meeting." On the Arab-Jew, Palestine,
and Other Displacements: Selected Writings of Ella Shohat. Pluto
Press, 2017, pp. 200–222.

Shostak, Debra. "The Diaspora Jew and the 'Instinct for Impersonation':
Philip Roth's Operation Shylock." Contemporary Literature, vol. 38,
no. 4, 1997, pp. 726–754. JSTOR, www.jstor.org/stable/1208935.

Silver, M.M. Our Exodus: Leon Uris and the Americanization of Israel's
Founding Story. Wayne State UP, 2010.

The Spy. Miniseries. Netflix, 2019.

Steiner, George. "Our Homeland, the Text." Salmagundi, no. 66, 1985,
pp. 4–25. JSTOR, www.jstor.org/stable/40547708.

Stewart, Desmond. "Herzl's Journeys in Palestine and Egypt." *Journal of Palestine Studies*, vol. 3, no. 3, 1974, pp. 18–38. JSTOR, www.jstor. org/stable/2535890.

Stolow, Jeremy. "Utopia and Geopolitics in Theodor Herzl's Altneuland." *Utopian Studies*, vol. 8, no. 1, 1997, pp. 55–76. JSTOR, www.jstor.org/ stable/20719606.

Thomas, Gordon. *Operation Exodus: From the Nazi Death Camps to the Promised Land: A Perilous Journey that Shaped Israel's Fate*. Thomas Dunne Books, 2010.

Thompson, Hunter S. *Fear and Loathing in Las Vegas: A Savage Journey to the Heart of the American Dream*. Vintage Books, 1998.

Thor: Ragnarok. Directed by Taika Waititi, Marvel, 2017.

Tsabari, Ayelet. "About Page." Ayelettsabari.com/about.

Tsabari, Ayelet. "After 20 Years in Canada, I Returned to Israel. But the Country I Returned To Is Not the Same Country I Left." *The Globe and Mail*, 5 April 2019, www.theglobeandmail.com/ opinion/ article-after-20-years-in-canada-i-returned-to-israel-but-the-country-i/.

Tsabari, Ayelet. *The Art of Leaving: A Memoir*. HarperCollins, 2019.

Tsabari, Ayelet. *The Best Place on Earth*. Random House, 2016.

Udovitch, Abraham L., and Lucette Valensi. *The Last Arab Jews: The Communities of Jerba, Tunisia*. Harwood Academic, 1984.

Uris, Leon. *Exodus*. Bantam Books, 1959.

Uris, Leon. *The Haj*. Random House, 1985.

Uris, Leon. *Trinity*. Avon, 2006.

Veidlinger, Jeffrey. "Before Crimea was Russian, It Was a Potential Jewish Homeland." *Tablet*, 4 March 2014, www.tabletmag.com/ jewish-news-and-politics/164673/crimea-as-jewish-homeland.

Verman, Alex. "Canadian Jewish News Loses Last Regular Left-leaning Columnist Over Word 'Occupation.'" *Canadaland*, 30 June 2017, www.canadalandshow.com/cjn-loses-mira-sucharov/.

Wagner, Mark S. *Jews and Islamic Law in Early 20th-Century Yemen*. Indiana UP, 2015.

Walkowitz, Rebecca. *Born Translated: The Contemporary Novel in an Age of World Literature*. Columbia UP, 2015.

Wanner, Adrian. *Out of Russia: Fiction of a New Translingual Diaspora*. Northwestern UP, 2011.

Weininger, Melissa. "Hebrew in English: The New Transnational Hebrew Literature." *Shofar*, vol. 33, no. 4, pp. 15–35. JSTOR, www.jstor.org/stable/10.5703/shofar.33.4.15.

Weissbrod, Rachel. "'Exodus' as a Zionist Melodrama." *Israel Studies*, vol. 4, no. 1, 1999, pp. 129–152. JSTOR, www.jstor.org/stable/30245731.

"What is BDS?" *Bdsmovement.net*. Accessed 4 Nov. 2022.

White Sun of the Desert. Directed by Vladimir Motly. Mosfilm, 1970.

Whitfield, Stephen J. "Israel as Reel: The Depiction of Israel in Mainstream American Films." *Envisioning Israel*, edited by Allon Gal, Wayne State UP, 1996, pp. 293–318.

Wild, John. "Introduction." *Totality and Infinity: An Essay on Exteriority*, by Emmanuel Levinas. Translated by Alphonso Lingis. Duquesne UP, 2008.

Williams, Brian Glyn. "The Hidden Ethnic Cleansing of Muslims in the Soviet Union: The Exile and Repatriation of the Crimean Tatars." *Journal of Contemporary History*, vol. 37, no. 3, 2002, pp. 323–347. JSTOR, www.jstor.org/stable/3180785.

Yaron, Lee. "Israel Set to Deport Dozens of Filipina Migrant Workers and Their Children." *Haaretz*, 18 Feb. 2019, www.haaretz.com/israel-news/.premium-israel-set-to-deport-dozens-of-filipa-migrant-workers-and-their-children-1.6941237.

The Yemenite, Mizrahi and Balkan Children Affair. Website. *Amram*, www.edut-amram.org.

Yeshurun, Helit. "'Exile Is So Strong Within Me, I May Bring It to The Land' A Landmark 1996 Interview with Mahmoud Darwish." *Journal of Palestine Studies*, vol. 42, no. 1, 2012, pp. 46–70. JSTOR, www.jstor.org/stable/10.1525/jps.2012.xlii.1.46.

Zilbersheid, Uri. "The Utopia of Theodor Herzl." *Israel Studies*, vol. 9, no. 3, Fall 2004, pp. 80–114. JSTOR, www.jstor.org/stable/30245640.

Žižek, Slavoj. *Welcome to the Desert of the Real! Five Essays on September 11 and Related Dates*. Verso, 2002.

Zureik, Elia. "Uris' Exodus from Reason." Review of *The Haj*, by Leon Uris. *Journal of Palestine Studies*, vol. 13, no. 4, Summer 1984, pp. 118–121. JSTOR, www.jstor.org/stable/2536995.

Index

current state of, 7

of Herzl's Austria, 102

Herzl's internalized, 113

L. Uris' acceptance of its tropes, 105

Muslim, 144–45

of Russians in *The Betrayers*, 235–36

view of in *Exodus* and *Altneuland*, 78, 93, 95

and Yemeni Jews, 152

anti-Zionism

and excision of last chapter of *Operation Shylock*, 74

and Geyer of *Altneuland*, 262n42

and G. Ziad of *Operation Shylock*, 34, 61

how it differs from post-Zionism, 243n4

increasing support for, 14, 240

and Pipik of *Operation Shylock*, 53

and P. Roth, 247n3

reading *Exodus* and *Altneuland* through lens of, 84–85, 115

reading *The Betrayers* through lens of, 190–91, 213–18, 230–31

views which define, 6–7, 243n5

Arab Jews

in *The Best Place on Earth*, 132–33, 136, 140–41, 148, 186–87

discussion on use of term, 263n7

in *Exodus*, 255n8

history of, 139, 141–43, 263n10

Israeli population numbers, 139

Israel's plan to import, 145–46

Operation Shylock view of, 54

racism toward in Israel, 146–48

relationship with Palestinians, 148–49, 150, 264n17

right wing politics of, 150, 265n18

and Samir in "Borders," 178–79, 180

seen as undifferentiated mass, 139–40, 142

Soviet Jews animus toward, 203

as theme of "Borders," 175, 178

and theory of Moses as, 183–86

in Tsabari's stories, 137–38, 148

used as spies by Israel, 179–80

and Zionist view of, 140–42

Arabs

in *Altneuland*, 58, 100

on conflict with Jews, 143, 264n13

erasure of from Palestine in Jewish time, 101

in *Exodus*, 58, 99–100, 106, 118, 119

fear of in Israel/Palestine, 181

history of Jewish, 143–45

as part of critical reception to *Exodus*, 106–07

view of in *Operation Shylock*, 51, 53–55. *See also* Palestinians

Ariel, Ari, 163, 267n36, 267n37

Armstrong, Jeanette, 22–23

The Art of Leaving (Tsabari), 134, 135, 168, 191, 262n4

autochthony, 3, 19, 21–23, 102, 107, 245n16

Avineri, Shlomo, 112–13, 114, 258n24, 259n29

Bach, Ulrich E., 86

backshadowing, 96–97, 256n11

Bakhtin, Mikhail, 28–30

Balint, Benjamin, 249n11

Bartram, David V., 162

BDS (Boycott, Divestment and Sanctions), 118, 260n36

Bedouins, 176, 269n47, 269n48

Begin, Benny, 221

Begin, Menachem, 47, 147

Beinart, Peter, 217, 273n27

Bellow, Saul, 105

Ben-Gurion, David, 146–47
Berlin, Irving, 52
Bernard-Donals, Michael, 30
Bernstein, Michael André, 78, 96, 98,
   128, 256n13
The Best Place on Earth (Tsabari)
   awards for, 135
   diaspora as theme of stories,
      132–33
   diasporic heteroglossia of, 25,
      132–33, 138, 149, 186, 238
   diasporic polycentric perspective
      in, 133, 238
   foreshadowing in, 265n26
   giving voice to Arab Jews, 132–33,
      136, 140–41, 148, 186–87
   and identity creation, 267n39
   and Israelis in India, 268n41,
      268n42
   Palestinian presence in stories of,
      149–50, 264n16
   role of gender in, 135–36
   and stories from Israel, 137
   themes of stories in, 132–33
   theories for improbable reunion in,
      208–10
   visible minorities in, 156
   Yemeni Jews in, 136
   Zionism in, 133, 150. See also
      "Borders"; "Invisible";
      "A Sign of Harmony"
The Betrayers (Bezmozgis)
   analysis of Zionism of Kotler and
      Benzion in, 213, 217–18, 223
   antisemitism in, 196–97, 235–36
   and author-as-god, 226, 230
   Crimea in, 191, 194, 196–97, 219,
      232–33, 235–36
   different views of living on the
      land in, 231–32

disavowal of diaspora in, 4, 218
example of Russian culture in
   Israel, 202
fuzzy geography of, 116
humour in, 199–200, 271n16
influence of Jewish Americans in,
   204
intended readership of, 228, 229
Israel and diaspora as structure of,
   2, 190, 199, 200
on Jewish collectivity in former
   Soviet Union, 189, 192–93, 195,
   197, 201, 204–08, 235–36
Kotler's forgivenss of Tankilevich,
   207–08
Kotler's story in, 193–96
Kotler-Tankilevich reunion, 197–98,
   206–07, 209–10
lack of diasporic heteroglossia in,
   190, 191, 193, 218, 227
and Levinas' theory of the face,
   210–11
Palestinian/Arab presence in, 189,
   194–95, 215, 226–27, 229–30
plot of, 192–93
and rise of nationalist right,
   216–17
and settlement withdrawal in,
   198–99, 215–16, 218–19, 222–23,
   225–26, 227, 229–30, 275n36
Soviet Jewish dissidence in,
   198–99
Tankilevich's story, 196–97
and Tatars' loss of land in, 232–33
univocalism of, 227–28, 230, 238
use of real-life analogs in, 205–06
use of Sharansky memoir in writing
   of, 271n16
and view of land through ethnic
   nationalism, 233–34

and Orphans' Decree, 164
of Palestinians, 251n22
possibilities of, 56–57, 249n14
potential value of, 2–3
recent Jewish authors being drawn
    toward, 240
and referent-origin, 13
scenes from fiction depicting, 1
significant question to be asked of,
    244n10
Soviet Jewish, 200–05, 270n8,
    270n11, 270n12
and Soviet Jewish literature, 192
as structure of *The Betrayers*, 2, 190,
    199, 200
temporality of, 86, 88
as theme of "A Sign of Harmony,"
    174–75
as theme of "Invisible," 161, 164–66
as theme of stories in *The Best Place
    on Earth*, 132–33
and tie of nomadism to, 269n47
as true mode of Jewish belonging,
    30–31
in Tsabari's stories, 137–38,
    186–87
two camps on theory of, 11–12
and use in Bible, 244n8
value of to future existance, 240–41
and Zionism, 250n16
Zionists who return to because of
    disappointment with Israel,
    275n36. *See also* Jewish
    diaspora; Soviet Jewish
    diaspora
diasporic heteroglossia
    Altneuland and *Exodus* as counter-
        examples of, 78–79
    and backshadowing/
        sideshadowing, 96–97

Bakhtin's theory of, 28–30
in *The Best Place on Earth*, 25, 132–33,
    138, 149, 186, 238
in "Borders," 181, 183
as challenge to Zionism, 3–4
defined, 3
and excision of last chapter of
    Operation Shylock, 65, 69–70,
    74–75
importance to the novel of, 31
lack of in *The Betrayers*, 190, 193,
    218, 227
and narration of history, 128
in *Operation Shylock*, 3, 24, 31–32,
    76, 238
Palestinian narrative as critical to,
    5
of recent North American Jewish
    novels, 239
role of challenging Jewish ethnic
    nationalism, 238
and theory of the face, 210
diasporic polycentric perspective, 25,
    133, 138, 164, 178
Dickstein, Morris, 56, 251n21
Dobozy, Tamas, 38–39, 50, 61
Dome of the Rock, 116
Douglas, Lawrence, 40–41, 248n10
dream time, 90
Druze, 123
Dubnov, Arie M., 155, 244n9,
    265n25
Dufoix, Stéphane, 13, 244n8

Eichmann, Adolf, 37, 42, 108
Eilat, 175–76, 177, 180
Eliav-Feldon, Miriam, 86
Ellis, Mark, 60
Enigster, Yehezkel, 41–42
Eraqi-Klorman, Bat-Zion, 163–64, 165

and destruction of Bedouin villages, 269n48

effect of militarism on, 161, 267n35, 267n40, 273n25

and ethics of Jewish justice, 45–46

Exodus' part in building up, 81–83, 90–92, 106, 127

foreign labour in, 158–59, 266n30, 267n34

Herzl and Uris' views of, 77

illegal alien raids, 162, 266n31

impact of Arab Jews migration on, 145–48

impact of Soviet Jews on, 200–04, 270n8, 270n11

importance of ethnic return migration to, 270n11

and Israelis in India, 267n40, 268n41

and Kafka trial, 249n11

liberal Zionist view of, 217

and military court in Ramallah, 43–45

and Nazis and Nazi Collaborators Law, 41–42

Palestinian view of in *Operation Shylock*, 59, 60–61

Philip's acceding to demands of in *Operation Shylock*, 66–75

Pipik's view of in *Operation Shylock*, 50–51

possibility of diasporism in future for, 56–57

possible nuclear destruction of, 52, 53

recent fiction challenging hegemony of, 240

as representative of all Jewish people, 42–43

role in creation of Hebron settlements, 223–24

and Soviet Jews preference for the US to, 203, 207n12

state of democracy in, 213, 217

and treatment of Yemeni Jews, 154–56

use of Arab Jews as spies by, 179–80. See also Israel–Palestine

Israeli Black Panthers, 147

Israeli/Palestinian conflict, 57, 63

Israel/Palestine

author's perspective on, 6–8

embracing binational existence of, 184, 185

E. Said's views on, 61–63, 184–85

face theory as way out of crisis in, 211

and fear of Arabs, 181

future of, 9–10

as highly stratified society, 141

and history of Arab Jews, 139, 141–42

how its fiction must include Palestinian narrative, 4–5

in "Invisible," 137

mistaken belief it's home of Jewish diaspora, 16

possiblity of changing course, 128–29

and Roth's fiction, 27–28

significance of in *The Betrayers*, 193, 198

in Tsabari's stories, 133, 137

use of Jewish time to link Jews to, 99–102. See also Israel, state of

Jabotinsky, Ze'ev, 147, 198

Jewish Americans, 203–04, 216–17, 270n12

influence on Bezmozgis of, 199

L. Uris' feelings about, 105

slippage of his persona with Philip
in *Operation Shylock*, 66, 72–73,
253n31, 253n32

Talmudic sensibility of, 254n37

and textual censorship, 73

view of Israel/Palestine in fiction,
27–28

views on Zionism, 28, 32, 36, 246n3.
See also *The Counterlife;*
*The Ghost Writer; Operation
Shylock; Portnoy's Complaint;
Reading Myself and Others*

Rothberg, Ro 'i, 120–21

Russian culture, 202

Russian Jews, 201–03, 204, 270n11,
270n12, 271n13. *See also* Soviet
Jewish diaspora

Russian Jews on Three Continents
(Remennick), 201–03, 204

Russian Zionists, 103

Safran, William, 11, 12–13, 245n11, 250n22

Sahwell, Aziz S., 106–07, 258n20

Said, Edward, 61–63, 184–85, 274n30

Salaita, Steven, 6, 7, 243n5

Salt, Jeremy, 99–100, 110, 124, 126,
257n14, 261n41

Saud, Ibn, 117

Schechtman, Joseph B., 152, 153–54, 162

Schwartz, Joseph, 154

self-determination, 10, 19

Senderovich, Sasha, 195, 199, 200, 212,
213

Sephardic Jews, 139, 140, 142, 143, 147,
149, 250n19

settler colonialism, 87, 121, 149,
178–79, 220, 224–25. *See also*
colonialism

Shafir, Gershon, 151

Sharansky, Natan, 191, 205, 271n15, 271n16

Sharon, Ariel, 224

Shechner, Mark, 34

Shenhav, Yehouda

on Arab Jews, 139, 179, 263n7

on conflict between Jews and
Arabs, 143, 264n13

on farhud, 144

and Hebron Protocol, 221

how his family fit in as Arab Jews,
148

on Israeli control of Gaza, 225

and Israel's colonialism towards
Arab Jews, 145

and Oslo Accords, 223

on peace process, 226

on population exchange theory, 149

and post-Westphalian sovereignty,
10

Shlaim, Avi, 225

Shoah

author's explanation for use of,
245n12

Boyarins' glossing over, 19

in *Exodus*, 90

horrors of connected to Arabs in
Exodus, 118

and Jews who failed to heed early
signs of, 256n13

as justification for mistreatment of
Palestinians, 227

Palestinian view of in *Operation
Shylock*, 59

unspeakability of, 38, 39, 50, *See also*
Holocaust

Shohat, Ella

and Arab Jews, 149, 185, 264n17

and diasporic polycentric
perspective, 133

societal pressures on during
publishing of *Exodus*, 102
use of conventions of westerns in
his writing, 87
use of Jewish time by, 99–102
view of Palestinians after *Exodus*,
126–27, 261n41
on writing westerns, 88. See also
Exodus; *The Haj*
utopianism
in *Altneuland*, 81, 84, 89–90,
255n3
and Arab Jews, 185
and development of New Society
in *Altneuland*, 92–94
in Herzl's work, 86–87

Wadi Salib Uprising, 150
Waititi, Taika, 258n22
Walesa, Lech, 52, 55
Walkowitz, Rebecca, 134
Wanner, Adrian, 192, 201
Warburg, Edward, 154
Wegner, Phillip E., 86
Weininger, Melissa, 134, 136, 141, 266n32
Weissbrod, Rachel, 87, 120
White Sun of the Desert (movie), 226,
274n35
Wild, John, 210
Williams, Brian Glyn, 233

Yahya, Imam, 163, 267n37
Yamit evacuation, 179, 268n45
Yaron, Lee, 159
Yemeni Children Affair, 154–55
Yemeni Jews
in *The Best Place on Earth*, 136
history of, 151, 265n21
Israel's mission to bring to Israel,
151–54

and Orphans' Decree, 162–64
and stolen babies, 150
as theme of "Invisible," 162, 163
treatment of in Israel, 154–56

Zee, Shabbatai, 105
Zilbersheid, Uri, 86–87, 103–04, 114,
259n29
Zionism
in *Altneuland*, 24–25, 79, 92–94,
98, 238
analysis of Kotler and Benzion's
version of in *The Betrayers*, 213,
217–18, 223
Arab Jew support for, 265n18
author's perspective on, 7
in Bakhtin's theory of language, 31
in *The Best Place on Earth*, 133, 150
in *The Betrayers*, 25–26, 189–90,
206–07, 212, 213, 227, 228,
235–36
and blaming critics for obsessing
over Israel, 276n1
Boyarins' view of, 18–20
and comparisons of Israel to
Wakanda, 109–10
corruption of by taking on diasporic
ideas, 17, 212–13, 272n22
in *The Counterlife*, 32–33
and criticism of *Altneuland*,
103–04
criticism of Israel, 275n36
current lagging support for, 9
D. Bezmozgis' liberal view of,
216–17, 273n26
demolishing of in Tsabari's fiction,
137–38
diasporic heteroglossia as challenge
to, 3–4
and diasporism, 14, 250n16

effect of Arab Jews on, 139–40

E. Said's criticism of, 61–62

and excision of final chapter of Operation Shylock, 74–75

in Exodus, 24–25, 79, 82–83, 91, 94–96, 238

Herzl and Uris' belief in, 102–03

and history of SS Exodus, 108–09

how Palestinians that believe in are portrayed, 110–11, 118, 123–25

impact of Exodus on, 117

importance of time to narratives of, 85–86

and ingathering narrative, 139, 141, 228

J. Butler's view of, 8

Jewish diasporic fiction's challenge of, 237–38

justification of colonization by, 254n2, 255n5

as mirror image of diasporism, 50–51

and Moses as Arab Jew theory, 186

and Nazi Collaborators Law, 41

Nietzschean and Marxist themes of, 255n4

in Operation Shylock, 52–53, 71–72

and Orientalism, 62, 101, 153, 154, 263n11

outside view of liberal Zionism, 217

possibility of its being reworked by diasporism, 56–57

and readers of Canadian Jewish News, 228–29

recent fiction challenging hegemony of, 240

and removal of Palestinians from Palestine, 114–15, 126

Roth's view of, 28, 32, 36, 246n3

Russian Jews view of, 103

and socialism, 264n14

and Soviet Jews rejection of, 204

and sundered history, 88–89

T. Herzl's role in developing, 103, 257n16, 257n18

this book's challenge of its narrative, 6

use of Jewish history to link Jews to Palestine, 101–02

view of Arab Jews, 140–42

view of Gaza pullout, 224

view of Hebron settlements, 223–24

view of Jew–Arab history, 143

view of Orphans' Decree, 163–64

view of transport of Yemeni Jews to Israel, 152

view that its principles would be positive for Palestinians, 111–12. See also anti–Zionism

Žižek, Slavoj, 9

National Literature in Multinational States

Edited by ALBERT BRAZ & PAUL D. MORRIS

Interrogates nationalism in the context of literary
production across several geo-cultural contexts.

All the Feels / Tous les sens

Affect and Writing in Canada /
Affect et écriture au Canada

Edited by MARIE CARRIÈRE, URSULA MATHIS-MOSER,
& KIT DOBSON

Essays in French or English use affect as a lens for reading
contemporary Canadian literatures.

Come My Children

HEKMAT AL-TAWEEL

Edited by GHADA AGEEL & BARBARA BILL

Foreword by ILAN PAPPE

Hekmat Al-Taweel's narrative sheds light on Muslim–
Christian relationships in Gaza and contradicts Western
stereotypes.